# REWRITING DIFFERENCE

SUNY series in Gender Theory

---

Tina Chanter, editor

# REWRITING DIFFERENCE

## Luce Irigaray and "the Greeks"

Edited by

Elena Tzelepis

and

Athena Athanasiou

SUNY PRESS

Cover art, Mira Schor, Postcard: August 29, 1976, front side, ink and media on rice paper, 6 3/4" x 5", 1976, courtesy of the artist.



Published by State University of New York Press, Albany



Printed in the United States of America



For information, contact State University of New York Press, Albany, NY
www.sunypress.edu

Production by Kelli W. LeRoux
Marketing by Michael Campochiaro

**Library of Congress Cataloging-in-Publication Data**

Rewriting difference : Luce Irigaray and "the Greeks"/edited by Elena Tzelepis and Athena Athanasiou.
p. cm. — (SUNY series in gender theory)
Includes bibliographical references and index.
ISBN 978-1-4384-3099-7 (hardcover: alk. paper)—
ISBN 978-1-4384-3100-0 (pbk.: alk. paper)
1. Irigaray, Luce.
2. Philosophy, Ancient.
3. Feminist theory. I. Tzelepis, Elena. II. Athanasiou, Athena.
B2430.I744R49 2010
194—dc22

2009033326

10 9 8 7 6 5 4 3 2 1

# Contents

# Acknowledgments

We wish to express our appreciation to the authors who entrusted their work to this volume. Special thanks go to Luce Irigaray for her vital contribution. We express our deepest gratitude to Jane Bunker, our editor at SUNY Press, and Tina Chanter, the editor of the Gender Theory series, for their generous incentive and enthusiastic support. We wish to thank the anonymous reviewers for SUNY Press for their helpful comments, which have improved significantly the final version of the manuscript. Elizabeth Weed helped us imagine this project and offered critical insight. Penelope Deutscher and Ewa Ziarek contributed greatly to the development of this volume. Dianne Chisholm has been an incisive reader of our introductory text. Our heartfelt thanks go to Judith Butler and Adriana Cavarero for their delicate reading of the manuscript. Elizabeth Grosz added to the book's thematic breadth with her invaluable suggestions. We are indebted to Mira Schor for kindly allowing us to use her artwork for the cover of the book. We would like to thank Lila Abu-Lughod, Claudia Baracchi, Drucilla Cornell, Vangelis Calotychos, Madeleine Dobie, Nicole Fermon, Stathis Gourgouris, Marianne Hirsch, Janet Jakobsen, Sylvère Lotringer, Rosalind Morris, Neni Panourgiá, Elizabeth Povinelli, Suzanne Saïd, Elizabeth Scharffenberger, Gayatri Chakravorty Spivak, Liana Theodoratou, Karen Van Dyck, and Gareth Williams, who helped in numerous important ways. Colleagues and administrative staff at the Hellenic Studies Program, the Classics Department, Maison Française, the Center for French and Francophone Studies, the Institute for Research on Women and Gender, the Institute for Comparative Literature and Society and the Department of Anthropology at Columbia University, and the Barnard Center for Research on Women have been supportive in various significant ways. Emma Kaufman has our appreciation for her impeccable assistance with the preparation of the manuscript during the initial stages. The Stanwood Cockey Lodge Foundation of Columbia University provided support for the final preparation of the manuscript. We are grateful for the assiduous efforts of Kelli Williams and Andrew Kenyon during the production process. Sherrow Pinder deserves a special note of fervent thanks for her gracious contribution and longstanding friendship.

Luce Irigaray's chapter, "The Return," was originally written for and presented at the conference "Luce Irigaray and 'the Greeks': Genealogies of Re-writing," which took place at Columbia University in New York in 2004, and which was the precursor to this volume. This piece thereafter appeared in *Luce Irigaray: Teaching*, edited by Luce Irigaray with Mary Green (Continuum, 2008), pp. 219–30.

# Foreword

Gayatri Chakravorty Spivak

It gives me great pleasure to open this important volume: *Rewriting Difference: Luce Irigaray and "the Greeks."* The importance of its thematic is in the quotation marks: "Greeks." This book is not committed to the disciplinary constraints of regional identity. The editors' invitation to me is an example of this. I am not a Hellenist, yet I have taught "Plato's Hystera" ever since I read it thirty years ago. Irigaray also, in spite of her immense learning, is not, strictly speaking, a Hellenist. I have shared with generations of students Irigaray's incredible attention to rhetoricity, beginning with *hysteron proteron*, a figure of speech in which the word or phrase that should properly come last is put first, thus inverting of the so-called natural or logical order. The importance of this cannot be exaggerated. It goes beyond feminism, bigger than psychoanalysis. It goes beyond the institutionalizing of psychoanalysis. Attention to this figure, dis-figuring it into an allegory of reading, even as its figurative task is attended to, takes on and transforms the insight of a big boy, Nietzsche, as he reads a great big boy: Plato. It was Friedrich Nietzsche who had assigned the philosopher the task of attending to "physiology and philology," a fleshy miming of the rhetorical. Here is Irigaray:

> Chained by the neck and thighs, they are fixed with their heads and genitals facing *front, opposite*—which, in Socrates' tale, is the direction toward the back of the cave. The cave is the representation of something always already there, of the original matrix/womb which these men cannot represent since they are held down by chains that prevent them from turning their heads or their genitals toward the daylight. They cannot turn toward what is more primary, toward the *proteron* which is in fact the *hystera*. . . . To the *hystera protera* that is apparently resorbed, blinded into the movement of *hysteron proteron*. For *hysteron*, defined as what is behind, is also the last, the hereafter, the ultimate. Proteron, defined as what is in front, is also the earlier, the previous. There is a fault in the *hysterien*

> which is maintained by the *proterein*. . . . Thus keeping up the illusion that the origin might become fully visible if only one could turn around. ("Plato's Hystera," *Speculum of the Other Woman,* 244)

I think also of another thing that I have said to generations of students. Another bond between Luce Irigaray and me. I have never been able to check this out with her. I am a bit in awe of her. I have been in her presence once at Cerisy-la-salle twenty years ago, but I have never actually conversed with her. Forewording this volume has allowed me, with trepidation, to testify to this connection that I have fostered without a countersignature. It concerns psychoanalysis—a "Greek" word established, like so many of our words, long after the ancient Greeks had disappeared. It is, let us say, a word resolutely in the Greek tradition, whatever cultural heritage has been claimed on its behalf.

Irigaray proved too strong for institutional and institutionalizing psychoanalysis. The testimony to that intolerance is inscribed in "The Misery of Psychoanalysis," which I first read in the '80s. If I understand right, here Irigaray laments the loss of the initial spirit of psychoanalysis—that its healing knowledge was acquired and changed in each new encounter. This is where I found a resonance, in the field specifically of subaltern education, I have spent half a lifetime learning to learn from what is diagnosed to be "from below." And I have understood that to be Luce Irigaray's insistence in that passionate piece. Yes, what is new about psychoanalysis is tapping the subject to restore social agency as far as possible. But we know how and what to tap, from what is diagnosed as "below"—the object of investigation, the patient of the cure. Psychoanalysis "knows" by learning to learn from below. Its knowledge is changeful, given over to the singular and the unverifiable. This is where I resonate.

I believed that Irigaray "read" Plato in this way, "learning" from him how to "cure" his singular predicament. I believed that was why so much of Plato's Greek was held in the French text, unfortunately Latinized in the English translation. The French gives a greater sense of this containment. The different sections, untitled in the French, give a sense of the repetitive healing-learning monotony of the analytic encounter. And through this con-versation, turning together, Irigaray seemed to me to turn the death of Socrates to the singularity of each birth. If only Plato had recognized that the way out was the door to birth. This was in stark contrast to the usual diagnostic flavor of so-called feminist psychoanalytic readings as well as to our attitude to the "below" in general.

"The Phenomenology of Eros," another Greek word, a Greek figure, claimed by that jewgreek, Emmanuel Lévinas. Irigaray congratulates him for bringing Eros into the house of philosophy, and then reprimands him for not understanding the pleasure of reproductive heteronormativity as follows:

> This autistic, egological, solitary love does not correspond to the shared outpouring, to the loss of boundaries which takes place for both lovers when they cross the boundary of the skin into the mucous membranes of the body, leaving the circle which encloses my solitude to meet in a shared space, a shared breath, abandoning the relatively dry and precise outlines of each body's solid exterior to enter a fluid universe where the perception of being two persons [de la dualité] becomes indistinct, and above all, acceding to another energy, neither that of the one nor that of the other, but an energy produced together and as a result of the irreducible difference of sex. Pleasure between the same sex does not result in that immediate ecstasy between the other and myself. It may be more or less intense, the quantitatively and qualitatively different, it does not produce in us that ecstasy which is our child, prior to any child [enfant avant tout enfant] a. In this relation, we are at least three, each of which is irreducible to any of the others: you, me and our work [oeuvre], and the ecstasy of ourself in us [de nous en nous] that transcendence of the flesh of one to that of the other become ourself in us [devenue nous en nous], a at any rate "in me" as a woman, prior to any child. (Irigaray's essay "Questions to Emmanuel Levinas: On the Divinity of Love" in *Re-reading Levinas*, ed. Robert Bernasconi and Simon Critchley, Indiana University Press, 1991, p. 111)

But childing is not where the ethical arises. It arises from in the difference between needing the child and making pleasure. Acknowledging that "the function of the other sex [is] an alterity irreducible to myself [that] eludes Lévinas," defines the ethical in the singular but generalizable fecundity of the caress, not a foreplay toward needing the child, but the marking of the difference between need and making.

This difference can lead to the passion for singularity as well as the toughness of generalizable politics, for it is in this difference that the justice of capital also arises. The texts where the fecundity of this difference is in play in Irigaray are not just *Speculum* (1974). *Ce sexe qui n'en est pas un* (1977), *L'Ethique de la différence sexuelle* (1984), but also *Amante marine* (1980), *Passions élémentaires* (1982), *Je, Tu, Nous* (1990).

When she writes *Democrazia cominca a due* (1994), she is too European, and she loses me. But I continue to believe that we exist in the same struggle, worrying if there can be a socialist ethics, as I have, since 1978. I open this volume, then, so that we can listen to that wise voice, again.

**Gayatri Chakravorty Spivak**

# Chapter 1

# Thinking Difference as Different Thinking in Luce Irigaray's Deconstructive Genealogies

Athena Athanasiou and Elena Tzelepis

> The new is not found in what is said, but in the event of its return.
>
> —Michel Foucault, "The Order of Discourse"

Ancient Greek logos, mythos, and tragedy have played a mobilizing role in Luce Irigaray's philosophical critique of Western metaphysics. Her persistent return and affective bond to Ancient Greek thought redraws the contours of the very field of intellectual kinship, a kinship whose multitude of forces remains in language and whose rearticulations are not fully to be anticipated or controlled. This volume is a reflection on how Luce Irigaray *reads* the classic discourse of metaphysics and how Luce Irigaray *is read* within and against this discourse. Such readings do not merely bear upon textual questions, but revisit some of the most complex and pressing epistemological aporias of the current historical moment, such as the workings of criticism, the question of ideology, the language of politics and the politics of language, the possibility of social and symbolic transformation, the multiple mediations between metropolitan and postcolonial contexts of theory and practice, the question of the other, and the function of the feminine—the feminine other—in Western metaphysics. Irigaray's ethics of the feminine other not only signals new ways to rethink self, relatedness, experience, subjectivity, and the body, but also creates a space for a fresh discussion of the politics of identity and the politics of difference. The essays in this collection attempt to employ Irigaray's strategies of rewriting the Ancient Greek intellectual traditions in ways fruitful and creative for a critical theory of the political, one that engages primarily with the question of the other.

In the context of Luce Irigaray's innovative rereadings of the Greek classical texts, transformative readings that are marked by her psychoanalytic feminism, the appellation "the Greeks"—stereotypically invoked to denote "Ancient Greek civilization"—is used critically. What are the theoretical, cultural, and political implications of the monologic emphasis on the Greek classical past? How can we trace its routes of rewriting and translatability into various contemporary identities? How does a de-authorization of the priority of "the classical" motivate new critical treatments of the canon of the "West"? Irigaray's rereadings of the "origins" of Western representation offer a critical frame in which to expose the founding violence involved in the production of the "origins" of "Western" intelligibility. "Origins" and the "West" must remain in quotation marks here, as Irigaray's textual practice of "romancing" the Greeks could be seen as being precisely about the very problem of quotation marks. As it designates the limits of referentiality and implies the catachresis of the proper name, the problem of quotation marks ultimately involves the question of what and who is rendered unintelligible in this male economy and imaginary of origination, what configurations of the feminine, racialized Others, and other unspeakable modes of humanness are produced as sites of constitutive impropriety and exclusion.

The book traces Luce Irigaray's rereading of "the Greeks" as history of metaphysics and as history of paternal nomination. In Irigaray's mode of deconstructive genealogy, going back to the Greeks is figured neither as an attempt to retrieve an originary question nor even as a restorative return to the question of origin. Irigaray's rereading does not seek to bring the disclosed aspects—the occlusions, the foreclosures, and the erasures—of the Greek text to the propriety of full presence and the mastery of interpretation. It is not a cognitive commentary but rather a performative engagement; one that, in bringing forth the internal production of difference and improper usage, works as an affirmation and reinvention of the dispersal.

Irigaray renders the archive of Western metaphysics available for a rereading. She reads ancient Greek grammatology to excavate, along its fissures, interstices, caesuras, lapses, resonances, and fault lines, what has remained repressed within its discourse of truth and identity, within the unifying force and violence of the logos, but also within its internal dynamics. Her reading and rewriting of Western histories of reading and writing engage with what Jacques Derrida invokes, in "The Double Session," as the undecidable duplicity of every text. Every text is inescapably double: while the one is open to the hermeneutics of reading and its technologies of transparent presence, truth, representation, and meaning, the second can be partly encountered through the tracing of fissures in the first. It is that second dimension—the always deferred quality of the text—that Irigaray seeks to capture. In theorizing how mimicry does not mechanically reproduce a prior referent, but rather exposes and constitutes the original as phantasmatic, Derrida significantly conveys the function of mimicry-imitating-nothing through the figure of a speculum reflecting no reality: "[I]n this speculum with no reality, in this mirror of a mirror, a difference or dyad does exist, since there are mimes and phantoms. But it is a difference without reference, or rather reference without a referent, without any first or last unit, a ghost that is the phantom of no flesh."[1] In Irigaray's reading and writing, the order of logos fails to achieve the phantasmatic ideal of authorial and authoritative unification. Spectralized/spectralizing and specularized/specularizing difference keeps the unifying drive of the logos from normative closure, completion, and commensuration; discourse never turns into a figure of plenitude and totality.

This is a philosophy that performatively resonates with the abject and fugitive other in Western discourse; a philosophy that affectively opens the possibility for the discourse of the displaced other at the limits of intelligibility. Irigaray's philosophy enacts the passage beyond phallic mimicry of the monologic propriety of logos to the possibility of an affective language in and through which to think difference without reducing it to the normative fantasy of oneness. The word *heteros* is inhabited by the Indoeuropean suffix -tero(s), echoing the monstrous liminality and indeterminate strangeness of *teras* (*teras*: both horrible and wonderful) that calls into question the closure of intelligibility. And it is the unintelligible other as female that may be grammatologically traced in the term *ys-teros*.[2]

Irigaray's writing performs the difference it puts in language. It performs the impossibility of such articulation of difference within the discursive system that has produced it as abject. The question of articulating difference in language is posed as a question of the very possibilities and impossibilities of intelligibility itself. Thus, this thinking of difference is committed, and gives rise, to a different thinking. Irigaray's challenge to the phallogocentric economy and its constitutive suppression of the feminine is particularly suggestive in that respect. Irigaray's non-phallic metaphor of the lips—neither singular nor plural—gestures toward what Tina Chanter calls an "ethics of eros," an ethical space where sexual difference is reclaimed and refigured beyond the Platonic economy of the same.[3]

Judith Butler is absolutely right to point out that, in deconstructing the form/matter distinction in Plato, Luce Irigaray's task is "to show that those binary oppositions are formulated through the exclusion of a field of disruptive possibilities."[4] Indeed, in what Butler provocatively calls "rude and provocative reading,"[5] Irigaray's tactically mimetic intervention exposes phallogocentrism as a proprietary economy of representation that produces the "feminine" as its improper, specular and spectral, constitutive outside: the necessary, albeit unspeakable and illegible, exclusion that enables this economy to proceed and operate in a legible fashion. The feminine is excluded and, at the same time, phantasmatically associated with materiality and corporeality, Irigaray argues. The feminine is erased and excluded as incoherent, excessive, and uncontainable "matter," a matter figured as receptivity. Reading the figurations, or dis-figurations, of the disavowed feminine through the *chora* (the receptacle, *hypodoche*) in Plato's *Timaeus*, in her well-known essay "Plato's Hystera," Irigaray resists the conflation of the *chora* and the maternal; she is, rather, interested in how the discursive articulation of this reduction performs a certain figuration of the feminine as perennial outside. The question whether and to what extent the sign of the feminine monopolizes the domain of exclusion in Irigaray's own discourse rightly attracts much of the authors' critical attention in this volume.[6]

As manifested in her textual strategy of mimesis, Irigaray is interested in the *chora* as a dimension of reading and writing. Reading the Greeks is not merely epiphenomenal but rather emblematically constitutive to Irigaray's overall project. In the scope of Irigaray's work, the encounter with "the Greeks" encompasses mimetic deconstructive readings of canonical texts but also appropriating Greek mythology especially in its aspect of female genealogies. The Greeks conventionally represent the idealized origin, the *arche* (in its dual sense, as both beginning and authority) of Western metaphysics. In her earlier writings, Irigaray inhabits this arche in order to deconstruct the logos—as both reason and discourse—of sexual in-difference, while in her later phase of her writing she uses the alternative beginnings figured by mythical female genealogies in order to articulate a re-figured sexual difference yet-to-come.

Irigaray's retrospective encounter with the Greeks stages a passage from logos to myth; it stages the interstice between them. Logos as reason and discourse which denotes authoritative beginning is displaced by mythology as logos of/for myth. The very idea of myth, as it signals the impulse of the West to retrieve and reclaim its own origin, is interrupted; mythology is appropriated as an inevitable, incessant, and indissociable recitation and invention, a mimetic poesis that brings forth a new articulation of myth, a new *mything*.[7] Irigaray recounts this interruption, or, to phrase it more accurately, she lets the myth recount its own interruptions and thus entail its own events. Here is how Jean-Luc Nancy puts it: "Thus, once myth is interrupted, writing recounts our history to us again. But it is no longer a narrative—neither grand nor small—but rather an offering: a history is offered to us. Which is to say that an event—and an advent—is proposed to us, without its unfolding being imposed upon us."[8]

In Irigaray's hands, myth is motivated, and proposed to us, as a route for refiguring sexual difference. In her later work, a more constructive and positive use of myths emerges in the context of her affirmative, re-creative articulation of female genealogies deriving from a pre-Hellenic matrix. From the authorial and authoritative logos of male philosophers Plato and Aristotle, Irigaray shifts to female figures emerging from the more polylogic horizon of mythology: Demeter and Persephone, Eurydice.

Luce Irigaray returns persistently to the founding discourses of Ancient Greek thought whose genealogical transmission through the ages has been too singularly generated through phallogocentric lines. She does so by deploying strategies of free-indirect citing, miming, specularizing, and displacing monologic classical Greek metaphysics with polylogic, pre-Hellenic genealogies. What is at stake in this movement of hers is not a nostalgic Odyssean return (although we know that even that homecoming was not entirely tranquil), but rather the infinite constitution of the unforeseeable, which rises upon an altering and disquieting interruption.

Irigaray's sustained commitment to strategies of deconstructing, demythifying, reconstructing, and remythifying seems to resonate with Nietzsche's perception of historicity, in *On the Genealogy of Morals*, as a sign-chain of ever new, random, contingent takeovers, adaptations, reinterpretations, and redirections to new ends. It also resonates with the way in which Nietzsche's eternal recurrence repeats perpetually the becoming of the arbitrary event. Ambivalently deriving from the Pythagoreans and the Stoics' cosmologies, the Nietzschean concept of perpetual recurrence refers to a circular repetition of time, one that is intimately related to self-overcoming and the overcoming of the will to truth. As in Nietzsche the self is an aggregate of actions and events, and there is no doer behind the deed, eternal return is a way to be actively open to the future through redeeming the past in the present. It is a way to affirm becoming. "There will be nothing new in it," Nietzsche writes, "and everything...in your life will have to return to you, all in the same succession and sequence."[9] As he expounds in *Thus Spoke Zarathustra*: "The will cannot will backwards; and that he cannot break time and time's covetousness, that is the will's loneliest melancholy."[10]

As Heidegger significantly considered, however, the notion of eternal return is by no means incompatible with the will to power. The question is: How to turn every "and thus it was" into "and thus I willed it," as the demon asks of Zarathustra? How to will the perpetual recurrence if human subjects are not afforded a full perception and control of temporal structures and occurrences? A theory of human time and subjectivity rather than a cosmology, then, eternal return can be understood as an iterative drive, wherein the momentariness of the moment is not negated—as in the Western metaphysics of eternity—but perpetually fulfilled. As Elizabeth Grosz has put it: "What eternal recurrence repeats is the random event that lives only by being willed again, by being actively chosen while passively bestowed."[11]

Irigaray's tarrying with the return as not simply a return to the "same" might prompt us to consider the act of returning as a performative one which wrestles with the limits and foreclosures of resignification. The movement of returning as open-ended responding, refiguring, and reauthoring is not an ascent into a plenitude of unencumbered and assertive difference. Rather, it is circumscribed and conditioned in part by what cannot be taken over and what cannot be refigured. We return, and we are returned, to the historicity of power relations no more than power arrangements return to us, containing the eruption of newness but also providing the devices of re-authorship and forming the condition of its possibility. It is this active recognition of what inevitably delimits all discursive practices and events that ultimately invigorates the eventness of our critical returning to the matrices of intelligibility. Such modality of return, both constrained and indeterminately contingent, would be more than an event in that it would eternally and inventively produce the question of the event: not an impetus to the future without a history of the present.

As a counterpoint to the joyous utopics of radical resignification within the discourse of power, Butler rethinks this Nietzschean notion of sign-chain of ever new possibilities of resignification (as well as its echoes in Foucault's commitment to genealogy) through the question of the power constraints on and in processes of resignification. We maintain that such rethinking is crucial in any attempt to capture the complex strategies of genealogy in which injurious discourses not merely mark but become the painful and enabling resources of every innovative, resignifying practice.[12]

Irigaray's return to "the Greeks," is not a nostalgic return to the ideality of the universal origin or to the original promised land of Hellenocentric antiquity, but an affirmatively critical (albeit not reduced to the normative positive/negative split) revisiting of this ideality; a revisiting not through an appropriative mastery, but rather through the means of a disruptive passage—proximity and distance, repetition and displacement—which conveys a certain affect of reciprocity. This return bears also connotations of the return of the gift and the return of the debt; furthermore, it might denote the specter of an unanticipated, terrifying reemergence. It is this multilayered return—repetition, recurrence, repayment, and rediscovery at once—in all its crucial performative exigencies of temporality and temporal/temporary productivity, that brings to the fore a certain unprogrammatic, noncategorical production of dissonance. This bringing forth evokes Michel Foucault's words, in "The Order of Discourse": "The new is not found in what is said, but in the event of its return."[13] This return is not a mere addition to a universal matrix, it is not a topographical movement to an inscriptional, enclosed space of discursive order; rather, it is an opening onto the boundless transformative possibilities erupting within the thought of the event. Let us recall Foucault again: "[T]he return to a text is not a historical supplement that would come to fix itself upon the primary discursivity and redouble it in the form of an ornament which, after all, is not essential. Rather, it is an effective and necessary means of transforming discursive practice."[14]

The essays collected here highlight the ways in which Irigarayan writing inhabits and challenges the fixed borders between such Platonic and Aristotelian distinctions as origin and copy, actuality and potentiality, sensible and intelligible. In this collection, Irigaray's engagement with the potential of forms and traces of iterability within the history of reading and writing is addressed as part of a deconstructive genealogy that runs from Homer, Sophocles, Plato and Aristotle to Hegel, Marx, Heidegger, Lacan, Foucault, Loraux, Derrida, Butler, Spillers, and Agamben. The book addresses these multilayered genealogies from a multitude of perspectives and disciplines. In their reading of Irigaray's engagements with "the Greeks," authors mobilize and engage the work of a diverse array of theories such as: contemporary feminisms, critical theory, comparative literature, postcolonial theory, psychoanalysis. Taken together, the essays follow the traces of Irigaray's own mode of reading: occasionally critical of Irigaray, but also, at the same time, critically responsive to the criticisms that have been leveled against her work. The guiding question that interlaces this volume is what kinds of refigurations of the theoretical and the political emerge from a gesture of reading Irigaray in an Irigarayan way, that is, in a way that "involves a far more controversial and riskier operation, a transvaluation rather than a repudiation" of the *master* discourse, as it was put by Naomi Schor, one of Irigaray's most adept readers?[15] Such reading, we believe, a reading that resists being reduced to idealization or dismissal, would necessarily entail politically and theoretically innovative ways to engage with both Irigaray and "the Greeks."

Discussing a certain illegibility that marks Irigaray's writing, Elizabeth Weed reads Irigaray's genre as a psychoanalytic-deconstructive critique that exposes the conditions of possibility of discourse and legibility; she does so by opening up the question of the relation between social and the psychic. Both in Irigaray's earlier phase marked by deconstructive readings of canonical texts of the Western tradition and in her second phase in which a different sexual difference is creatively articulated, the reader is called on to an *askesis* of deconstructive reading of Irigaray's critique. This encounter at the limits of intelligibility resonates with Irigaray's appropriation of the female genealogies occurring in Greek mythology, whereby myth performatively leads to theory through staging the psychic. The separation of Persephone and Demeter figures the darkness of monosexual culture whereas their reunion promises the possibility of an unthought mode of sexuation. It is this route from myth to theory that allows for the unprogrammatic to occur both in Irigaray's critique and in the reading that it calls on.

Inspired by Irigaray's "Kore: Young Virgin, Pupil of the Eye," Dorothea Olkowski confronts the complexity of the myth of Kore, a myth that implies the challenges of in/visibility and figures the position that understanding through seeing occupies in the metaphysics of presence. *Kore* is Demeter's daughter, the young girl who must be blinded and abducted by Hades so as to turn into the receptacle of his self-vision, so as to open onto en-visioning and understanding of an Other self; *kore* denotes also the "pupil," that part of the eye that gives vision and in which one must look in order to see oneself. The philosophical axiom that self-knowledge requires gazing into the kore of the eye, capturing the young girl, obscures the capacity of light to diffract. On the contrary, imagining Demeter-Kore as the creative story of diffracted light transmitting sensibly its energy to the world proposes a new image of philosophy.

Dianne Chisholm engages Kathy Acker and Luce Irigaray's leap beyond phallic mimicry of logos to the possibility of a primal, corporeal language of self-affection. Acker enacts Irigaray's call for a genealogy deriving from a pre-Hellenic matrix, an arche preceding the origins inaugurated by the Greeks. Her restaging of the myth of Orpheus and Eurydice, but also her restaging of Irigaray's deconstruction of Plato's cave allegory, find the "elsewhere" of sexual difference in the underworld that lies repressed beneath the Oedipal patriarchal civilization denoted by "Greece"; Eurydice's mythic descent in patriarchal reality's deathhouse tells the story of Acker's living and dying with breast cancer and her passage through the operations of obstetrical enlightenment.

Irigaray's ambivalent emphasis on the veil, and the veil as "Greek," is the focus of Anne-Emmanuelle Berger's contribution. In Irigaray's work, the analysis of veiling as a strategy of women's wrapping in the market of sexual exchange shifts gradually to an argument about a protective, maternal veil that would shield women against the expropriating gaze. Such shift implies Irigaray's complicated relation to deconstruction, as she progressively abandons the deconstructive approach adopted in her early work of critical mimicry, and comes to value the propriety of linguistic referentiality. In the context of Irigaray's recourse to Greek mythology and critical engagement with the conceptual borders of philosophical discourse, the distinction between the veil as material and the veil as metaphor proves untenable; a separation of (textile) matter from signification is impossible, as the concrete gesture of wrapping the body cannot be dissociated from abstracting the body. Thus, the veil as matter and trope becomes a point of entry into Irigaray's peculiar materialism, a materialism that is inscribed in her stance on sexual difference as well as her critique of Greek idealism as a process of dematerialization. Indeed, the veil-as-metaphor and the metaphor-as-veil allegorize Irigaray's ambivalent position vis-à-vis the metaphysical tradition (of veil weaving) she purports to critically mime.

Through an Irigarayan reading of relations among women under patriarchy, Gail Schwab traces the erasure of sexual difference in Aeschylus's *Oresteia* and Sophocles' *Antigone* and *Electra*. The severing of the intergenerational link between women is emblematized by the emphasis on the death of the father and the silencing of the originary matricide, which functions as the founding act for the establishment of the social order. As an antidote to the rupture of female genealogies, the mythological narrative of Demeter and Persephone points to a potential reclaiming of the lost utopia of creative relationships among and between women.

Mary Beth Mader sheds light on Irigaray's readings of Sophocles' *Antigone*, focusing on Antigone's reasoning for burying her brother against Creon's command and her enigmatic claim that she would not have broken the king's edict for a husband or child of hers. In an early account, Irigaray understands Antigone's violation as an allegiance to her maternal line, whereas in a later discussion Antigone figures the subsumption of female *genre* into male power and kinship order. Mader suggests that Antigone's favoring of Polynices is not a universalizable defense of a brother's irreplaceability or maternal filiation in general, but rather a struggle to restore her family's precariousness by releasing sexual difference from its genealogical bounds.

In our text, the figure of Antigone becomes the performative occasion for exploring the aporias of mourning. How does mourning turn from a proper language-in-the-feminine into a threatening performative catachresis expelled by and actively opposed to the very intelligibility of the political? Could Antigone represent the poetic horizon in which Luce Irigaray's *parler-femme* can be read in conjunction with catachresis of mourning-as-language-in-the-feminine? These questions resound in the questions that Irigaray herself poses with respect to Antigone's pathos: "Is mourning itself her *jouissance*?...Does she anticipate the decree of death formulated by those in power? Does she duplicate it? Has she given in? Or is she still in revolt?" (*Speculum*, 219). Drawing on Nicole Loraux's theorization of tragic mourning as central to the ways in which the polis imaginatively invents itself, we consider the ways in which the antipolitical inherent in laying claim to mourning rites for the other has the potential to hold intelligibility open to political rearticulation, and thus mobilize the affective force of the disruptive performative.

In Lynne Huffer's contribution, intertextual reading of Michel Foucault and Luce Irigaray—in their shared engagement with the Greeks—establishes the ground for reflecting on the moral implications of the queer-feminist dissonance, and for figuring the possibility of a queer feminism. The two philosophers' corresponding and contrasting readings of the Greeks—namely, Foucault's interest in politics of homosocial friendship and an economy of pleasures, and Irigaray's female genealogies and rewriting of the female body's morphology—articulate an ethics as a collective practice of freedom that retains the spirit of the Greek concept of *poiesis*.

Irigaray's notion of the impossible as the only possibility of a future becomes the focal site of reflection in Stathis Gourgouris's text. The possibility of "what does not yet exist" is read in conjunction with Aristotle's impossible requirement that rule can only be enacted from within the experience of being ruled. Irigaray offers the means with which to encounter the question of alterity without allowing heterology to disintegrate into heteronomy, without allowing the politics of the other to lapse into mere identity politics. Her epistemology of sexual difference enables a self-interrogation of alterity as a monistic, absolute One; by emphasizing that each other's alterity does not amount to mere opposition or arithmetic equation, Irigaray produces a mode of raising the question of autonomy as a continuously altering and altered question of the *praxis/poiesis* of self-alteration.

In her account of hospitality and sexual difference, Judith Still focuses on a close analysis of Homer's *Odyssey*. In this classical text, hospitality is performed as a male homosocial relation within which virtuous manhood is assessed. Women, however, are relegated to maidens to the master of the house, while female hosts—those who have a place of their own, such as nymphs and sirens—entrap their male guests. In her critique of the patriarchal mythology, Irigaray proposes another ethics of hospitality, where sexuate subjects are hosts in their own places, while, at the same time, forming a third place, in which the other is received by the self in all her/his strangeness.

Laine Harrington reads Irigaray's account of the Word, in which the Christian reiteration of the ancient Greek *logos* has formulated a religion where Man becomes God as Word. Criticizing the Platonic notion of dialectic upon which ancient Greek philosophy is founded, Irigaray shifts toward a rewriting of the dialectic of gender; evoking the return of the divine as love, this Irigarayan "other word" signals the crucial role that writing plays in articulating feminine subjectivity but also in opening up a space for two subjectivities.

In Claire Colebrook's text, Plato's allegory of the cave becomes the point of entry into the question of looking back at the ethic of life that permeates the history of metaphysics, and, more specifically, Aristotle's concept of *proper potentiality*. Whereas both Heidegger and Agamben seek to retrieve the concept of *aletheia* from the Greek text, Irigaray, by raising the question of sexual difference, reads the Greeks in order to challenge the normative image of life that governs Plato's allegory, in its dividing the sensible from the intelligible, and in its subjecting all difference to the rule of revelation. By criticizing the figuring of potentiality as that passive, feminized matter awaiting the proper form of masculine actuality, and by insisting on the positivity of what remains undisclosed, Irigaray opens the possibility of a life—and a reading—with no proper potential and no preceding origin. She therefore displaces the propriety of bringing all potential to full presence with the production of dissonance and the thought of the nonrelational.

Gayle Salamon reads Irigaray's reading of Aristotle, by focusing on the place of sexual difference. She asks whether Irigaray's notions of bodies, boundaries, and sexual difference might be deployed in nonheteronormative ways, in ways that do not necessitate the displacement of the sexually different or the differently sexed. If the Aristotelian model emphasizes the substitutability of one body for another, Irigaray suggests a bodily singularity that enables proximity: due to this unsubstitutability, two bodies might inhabit the same place without annihilating each other. The question that emerges from a critical reading of both Aristotle and Irigaray, however, is whether sexual difference is thinkable in other than dimorphic and *hylomorphic* terms, beyond the terms of a division fixed in place as a marked boundary between "male" and "female."

In order to address the crucial relevance of value theories to feminist theories of race and gender, Ewa Plonowska Ziarek intertwines Irigaray's engagement with Aristotle's notion of needs/desires (*chreia*) and Marx's notion of abstract labor with Hortense Spillers's reading of American "grammar" of slavery. The commodification of the black captive body as the bearer of "despiritualization" and non-value, which remains in the penumbra of Irigaray's rereading of the commodity form in the context of female embodiment, calls for a reinterpretation of the ways in which the essentialism/social construction binary occludes the traumas that commodification inflicts on racialized, sexed bodies. Read together, Irigaray's "sensible transcendental" and Spillers's spiritual monstrosity might imply an alternative model of social mediation beyond the opposition between the abstract and the sensible.

Tina Chanter unravels Irigaray's challenge to the phallogocentric discourse as an exploration of the possibility for a new symbolic that does not submit to Platonic monologism and its constitutive suppression of the feminine. The trope of fetishism, in particular the way in which Irigaray reads Marx who reads Aristotle in this context, provides a way of raising the question concerning the priority of sexual difference over racial classifications. The privilege Irigaray accords to sexual difference over other social differences dramatizes the formal problem of the Western thought—the ineluctable difficulty of thinking difference without reducing it to the fetishistic fantasy of the one.

Being concerned with the political and interpretative strategies through which "Ancient Greece" is conventionally evoked as the universal matrix of the modern imaginary, Eleni Varikas raises some questions regarding Irigaray's appropriation of Greek "tragedies and mythologies." She delineates the role that "tradition" plays in the philosopher's work: from a radical de-authorization promised by her earlier writings, to a re-authorization enacted in her later work, where tradition is summoned to articulate a universal and positive configuration of sexual difference. Drawing on Nicole Loraux's work as an antidote to German historicist classical studies, Varikas seeks treatments of tradition that unsettle the sexual two-ness of the body politic as well as its heteronormative and colonialist implications.

Does Irigaray's emphasis on sexual difference occlude other forms of alterity? Penelope Deutscher poses this question, while at the same time engaging with the conditionality of this very question. In revisiting the mode of critique that addresses the occlusions in Irigaray's work, she shifts to the more appropriate question whether Irigaray allows us to read her project from the perspective of its own conditionality. Turning to the conditionality of Irigaray's considerations of a corporeal hospitality between women and progeny, Deutscher claims that Iocasta, a figure occluded in Irigaray's engagement with Greek tragedy, has the potential to displace the figuring of the maternal in Irigaray's work as originally nonappropriative, and to incarnate the unpredictability that is integral to the maternal relationship.

Why does Western culture have to always *return* to the Greeks? Does this return imply an exile from the singularity and the reciprocity of the affective? In her own essay, Luce Irigaray takes on and re-signifies the theme of return, a theme that draws on the epic of Ulysses, in order to articulate a return to the interiority of the self through self-affection and reciprocity, beyond the metaphysics of appropriative mastery of the outside. This revisiting of the economy of home, belonging, and familiarity through affect resonates with a culture of being in relation with the other—the foreignness of the other as *heteros*.

Reaching one's own autonomous self-affection, however, requires the differentiation from the maternal. In Western culture, where the relation with the mother is both eclipsed and overemphasized, the repressed maternal element returns as an emphasis on genealogy at the expense of gender. So the Greek word *genos* has increasingly come to denote the vertical, hierarchical dimension of genealogy as biological reproduction, and less the horizontal dimension of gender and the relational affect of desire and love. Nevertheless, Irigaray warns against any resorting to feminization of genealogy as panacea: although the reassertion of the value of female genealogies can be usefully deployed as a tactical device challenging the idealized hegemony of masculine lineages, she argues, such gesture of reclaiming—especially in its biologized and naturalized configurations—is typically renormalized as a perilous adhesion that forecloses one's own subjective and autonomous becoming.

Thus, the cultivation of self-affection emerges in Irigaray's thought as a necessary condition for reaching a reciprocal relation with the other, a relation that does not reiterate the link with the mother and is not reduced to a dyadic pair of opposites. It is precisely this going beyond the pair of opposites active-passive that is portrayed in the Greek grammatical verbal form of the middle-passive or middle voice, which conveys a certain affect of reciprocity—to affect/to be affected—irreducible to the normative oppositional or hierarchical split of subjectivity between activity and passivity.

Indeed, Irigaray's mode of critique lies emphatically beyond the conventional binary pair exculpation versus repudiation, or endorsement versus dismissal, posited by the metaphysics of original authorship and reading. Perhaps, one could say, her critique is articulated in the middle voice: neither active nor passive, neither the one of subject nor that of object. We know, of course, from Derrida that the grammatical mode of the middle voice is associated with *différance*—differentiation/divisibility and deferral.[16] Irigaray's critique does not return the violence of discursive closure. It does not direct itself to the reflexes of denouncement and annulment. Hers is a critique that produces events, or, rather, the undecidable and indeterminate possibility of the event, in all its contingency and openness. It is ultimately a critical reading of past philosophies that lets the critical possibility of the present—or, critique as possibility of the present—take place.

## Notes

1. Jacques Derrida, "The Double Session," in *Dissemination*, trans. Barbara Johnson (Chicago: University of Chicago Press, 1981), 206.

2. In her own reading of "becoming-woman" in terms of Irigaray's "sensible transcendental," Rosi Braidotti enlists the monstrous feminine in mapping out a figuration of multiple becomings. In tracing the ways in which the feminine is posited as the Other in the techno-teratological social imaginary of the late postindustrial Western postmodernity, she unravels how the multiple patterns of feminized monstrous becoming overthrow humanistic axioms of representation. Rosi Braitdotti, *Metamorphoses: Towards a Materialistic Theory of Becoming* (Cambridge: Polity, 2002).

3. Tina Chanter, *Ethics of Eros: Irigaray's Re-writing of the Philosophers* (New York: Routledge, 1994).

4. Judith Butler, *Bodies that Matter: On the Discursive Limits of "Sex"* (New York: Routledge, 1993), 35.

5. Ibid., 36.

6. Inspired by Luce Irigaray's work, Adriana Cavarero has deployed a mimetic strategy of repossession in her own neo-materialist deconstructive reading

of Ancient Greek—mainly Plato, but also Homer and Parmenides—philosophical texts. Cavarero evokes and reappropriates central female figures in the phallogocentric imaginary, stealing them from their literary context and relocating them within the conceptual canvas of a feminine symbolic order. Adriana Cavarero, *In Spite of Plato: A Feminist Rewriting of Ancient Philosophy* (New York: Routledge, 1995).

7. Jean-Luc Nancy, "Myth Interrupted," in *The Inoperative Community*, ed. Peter Connor (Minneapolis: University of Minnesota Press, 1991).

8. Ibid., 69.

9. Friedrich Nietzsche, *The Gay Science*, trans. Walter Kaufmann (New York: Random House, 1974), Aphorism 341.

10. Friedrich Nietzsche, *The Portable Nietzsche*, trans. Walter Kaufmann (New York: Penguin Books, 1976), 251.

11. Elizabeth Grosz, "Becoming...An Introduction," in *Becomings: Explorations in Time, Memory, and Futures*, ed. Elizabeth Grosz (Ithaca and London: Cornell University Press, 1999), 5.

12. Butler, *Bodies that Matter*, 224.

13. Michel Foucault, *L'Ordre du discourse* (Paris: Éditions Gallimard, 1971), 28.

14. Michel Foucault, "What Is an Author?" in *Language, Counter-memory, Practice: Selected Essays and Interviews by Michel Foucault*, ed. Donald F. Bouchard (Ithaca: Cornell University Press, 1977), 135.

15. Naomi Schor, "This Essentialism Which Is not One," in *Engaging with Irigaray*, ed. Carolyn Burke, Naomi Schor, and Margaret Whitford (New York: Columbia University Press, 1994), 67.

16. Jacques Derrida, *Margins of Philosophy* (Chicago: University of Chicago Press, 1982), 9.

## Chapter 2

# The Question of Reading Irigaray

Elizabeth Weed

Irigaray is the most radical of feminist theorists and the most difficult to read. For signs of that difficulty, one need only look at the different kinds of reception her work has received over the last three decades. In 1974, at the time of the publication of *Speculum, de l'autre femme*, her doctoral dissertation in philosophy, Irigaray was a practicing analyst, a member of Lacan's École freudienne de Paris, and one of the EFP members who offered courses in psychoanalysis at the University of Paris at Vincennes. Several months after the publication of the book, she was suspended from her teaching at Vincennes. Accounts as to why she was given the cold shoulder by the Lacanian establishment indicate that some considered her book excessively philosophical and inappropriately political.[1]

A decade later when *Speculum* was translated into English, along with a collection of essays, *This Sex Which Is Not One*, the Anglo-American response was of a different sort. Toril Moi found the work to be insufficiently philosophical—that is to say insufficiently deconstructive—in its effort to go beyond the critique of woman as man's other to the formulation of a positive femininity.[2] For Jacqueline Rose, Irigaray's concern with the specificity of female drives displayed a failure of psychoanalytic rigor. We know from Lacan, Rose writes, that "there is no pre-discursive reality. And there is no feminine outside language. First, because the unconscious severs the subject from any unmediated relation to the body as such . . . and secondly because the 'feminine' is constituted as a division in language, a condition that produces the feminine as its negative term. If the woman is defined as other it is because the definition produces her as other, and not because she has another essence."[3] The Irigaray who is read as not knowing this truth—the scandalously incorrect Irigaray—came to be the nodal point of subsequent Anglo-American wars about essentialism. For readers less Lacanian than Rose, Irigaray's purported essentialism was seen more directly as a dangerous betrayal of a feminism whose very foundation was the dismantling of the notion of anatomy as destiny.

Thus was Irigaray's work caught between the French Lacanian objection that found her too political and too philosophical, and the Anglo-American feminist objection that found her not philosophical and political enough. Today, at a time when Irigaray's institutional marginalization has rendered her work nearly invisible in France, her most serious readers are Italian and Anglo-American feminists. Whereas the Italians receive her in the spirit of a vigorous female specificity reaching back to the Milan Women's Bookstore Collective, there are still some Anglo-American readers who find that specificity unsettling. For those readers, the old worries about essentialism take a new form, and this in response to Irigaray's later writings that theorize what she posits as a different sexual difference, a different coupling of male and female that gets beyond the current pathology of sexual indifference. This time, Irigaray's error is to be insufficiently historical and hence insufficiently political. Her theorizing of a new and unthought couple is seen to be, in a word, heteronormative, as well as universalist and racist.[4]

Not all of Irigaray's readers share these views, but even for them Irigaray remains difficult to read. It is this difficulty, this illegibility, that interests me. Irigaray's project is in itself a challenging one. She continues to argue that sexual difference has yet to be thought in Western culture and, much as Heidegger claimed the need to think the unexamined relationship between Being and beings, she urges us to seize this historical time of feminist awareness to grapple with the relationship between sexuate beings and an unthought sexual difference. In making this argument, Irigaray, like other French poststructuralist theorists who came of age during the 1960s and '70s, situates her project in the tradition of critique: that is, in a mode of reading that questions the conditions of possibility of thought, that examines the historical and symbolic determinants of the seemingly natural, and endeavors to expose conceptual and discursive blind spots.

Given these continuing critical interests, Irigaray cannot be said to be in style. The rise in the United States in recent decades of critical movements such as new historicism and cultural studies has been accompanied by the waning of poststructuralist critique. There are many ways to approach the question of changing theoretical styles and changing modes of legibility. My interest is not so much with the historical conditions of Irigaray's illegibility—how to understand these vastly different readings of her in different periods—than with more formal questions having to do with the genre of critique itself. What is it in Irigaray's writing over the decades that allows her to sustain—or not—the work of critique? My presumption is that the very practice of critique is difficult, that everything, from psychical to social formations, militates against it, and that it is always in some sense on the wane. Certainly there are political and epistemological conditions that favor the practice, but even under those conditions, as in the France of the era of poststructuralist theory, it is difficult. I suggest that almost from the moment that critique does its work—changing the way one sees a certain discursive field, whether in the sphere of philosophy or political economy or subjectivity—its critical force begins to decline. The new way of seeing becomes naturalized and the thrust of the critique is folded into the familiarity of the new.

French theorists of the poststructuralist era offer an interesting opportunity to examine this question in that they foreground the linguistic or discursive dimensions of critique in their very practice of reading. That is to say, theorists such as Derrida, or Lacan or Irigaray involve their readers in the very discursive resistances that their interventions seek to undo. This means that when reading their work, one needs to look as closely at how critique is mobilized as at the blind spots it exposes.

## "There is no such thing as Woman."

Irigaray's work involves the strongest possible form of critique, one that both disrupts the known and attempts to provoke the unthought. The theoretical stakes of the project are high. At issue is not just the call for sexual difference—a call that has been all too easy to dismiss as excessively feminist—but the very question of the relationship between the social and the psychic. Irigaray argues that sweeping political and economic change is crucial *but* that it cannot happen without a change in the symbolic. She refers here to the Lacanian term of the symbolic order, a complex register in which subjectivity is structured with relationship to language and cultural Law, entailing sexuation, in which the subject is positioned as masculine or feminine with relationship to radical alterity or to the field of the desire of the Other.[5]

Irigaray, like Lacan, takes the symbolic register to be an important corrective to those theories more comfortable with the ego and the workings of the imaginary alone. And Irigaray is completely in accord with Lacan's portrayal of the feminine within the existing symbolic order. Woman, that is to say, *la femme*, cannot be said to exist as such. The universality designated by the article *la* cannot be applied to woman because she in her lack guarantees the fantasy of the whole, the fullness of being that castration holds out as a promise in its very denial of that fullness. Woman is thus other to man and other to herself. Irigaray's objection is that we thereby a have a masculine universal posing as a human universal, a situation that has deleterious psychic and social effects: for women, for men, for social and political health. Where she most fully breaks with

Lacan is in her view that Lacanian psychoanalytic discourse is complicit in maintaining the symbolic order by not, as she says, examining its own historical determinants.

This is a critique that Irigaray first made thirty years ago and that she has continued to develop. Her more recent work brings her call for an unthought sexual difference to such issues as citizenship, the European Union, and ecology. But while she addresses herself to different audiences in different periods, Irigaray consistently maintains that social and political change will come only when there is a change in the symbolic, from which will emerge a different sexual difference. As recently as 2000, she writes that the horizon of thought must change before we have a culture in which the relationship between two different subjects, as opposed to the false universal male subject, comes about. "It won't just happen through social critiques and street riots," Irigaray says. "We need to go above and beyond: understanding that the human subject, woman or man, is not a mere social effect."[6]

As with all of Irigaray's arguments with Lacan, there is no simple dividing line between the two on the question of historical determination. It is not that Lacan has an ahistorical formulation of the symbolic. In Seminar XX, for example, he makes an offhand comment that the idea of a Marxist "world view" makes him laugh. A worldview would belong to the realm of philosophy, presupposing something that *is*, existing outside of discourse. "Marxism is something else," Lacan says, "something I will call gospel. It is the announcement that history is instating another dimension of discourse and opening up the possibility of completely subverting the function of discourse as such, and of philosophical discourse strictly speaking" (30). As early as Seminar II, Lacan discusses historical changes that have taken place in structural orders, offering as examples Socrates' inauguration of a new being-in-the-world, which Lacan calls subjectivity; the later advent of the concept of the ego; the discoveries of Freud, which he likens to the Copernican revolution. Commenting on how such changes are received, Lacan writes: "When something comes to light, something that we are forced to consider as new, when another structural order emerges, well, then, it creates its own perspective within the past, and we say—*This can never not have been there, this has existed from the beginning*?" (5)—a feeling, he adds, that commonsense experience seems to corroborate.[7]

It might be said that Irigaray bases her whole project on the argument that history is once again instating a new dimension of discourse, subverting the existing symbolic order and its structures of sexuation. Things have changed; the patriarchal social system no longer holds together in the West. It is time to apply critical pressure to discourses that serve to contain the status quo. Irigaray does this, through often brilliant deconstructive readings of canonical Western texts in her earlier writings; and in her later writing, through formulations of a different sexual difference in which much of the deconstructive work is concealed. It turns out that both these modes of critique are very hard to read, harder even than the notoriously difficult later texts of Lacan. When it comes to simple legibility—or decipherability—Irigaray's are, of course, the more accessible texts. Which is not to say that they are without formal difficulty. Her earlier works make rich use of sustained indetermination and ambiguity, of a sometimes startling mixture of theoretical precision and lyricism, of wit and irony and word play. However, what I am concerned with here is not simple legibility, but legibility as critique. Because of its radical reach, Irigaray's project demands the most rigorous of critiques—a critique that turns the screw one degree tighter than Lacan's. But can it be read? In order to suggest the problems involved, I will briefly compare the styles of Irigaray and Lacan and the very different ways readers are drawn into their texts.

## The Text of Jouissance

Lacan aims to rescue the psychoanalytic unconscious from the grips of any theory of the subject in thrall to the ego. Hence his expressed desire, particularly from the 1960s on, to thwart the tyranny of rational meaning. In the later writings, the relationships between sentences, even clauses within sentences, can make no sense, playing with adequation and with cause and effect so that things are never quite where one would expect them to be. The ellipses, language games, jokes, digressions, and bizarre transitions keep the reader unsettled and more often than not perplexed. The reader thus enters Lacan's text disoriented and remains disoriented, but without this estrangement from intelligibility as we know and imagine it, the text could not do its work. And it is, above all, *work* that Lacan wanted from his readers and from those who attended his seminars. As Bruce Fink comments, "Psychoanalysis, according to Lacan, is a *method of reading texts*, whether those texts be oral—the analysand's discourse—or written. And every text, whether doctrinal or therapeutic, is riddled with tensions and contradictions that must be read, reread, and pondered. Not necessarily *resolved*, but explored and worked on. Lacan even says that '[c]ommenting on a text is like doing an analysis."[8] Nonetheless, it can come as a surprise to the student of text—if not to the analysand—that the work Lacan aims to provoke must engage the *stupidity* of the reader. Early in Seminar XX, Lacan declares: "My sole presence—at least I dare believe—my sole presence in my discourse is my stupidity" (12). Lacan's discourse is, of course, the analytic, a discourse that does not try to flee stupidity because it knows that any effort to represent a whole and complete subject can only end in *bêtise*, or nonsense. Its job is to address the subject who is never whole, the subject who never knows everything he knows.[9]

Fink suggests that Lacan succeeds in evoking the analytic discourse in his published texts by a unique meeting of the written and the spoken. Something of the rich and reportedly charismatic and transferential speech of Lacan's seminars is rendered in the published texts, combined with the special kinds of difficulty the written text puts into relief: the bizarre look of written puns and other plays on words, the combination of conventional syntax with semantic incoherence, the lack of logical elaboration, demonstration, and examples. Added to these are Lacan's use of his mathemes and figures, which, he declares in Seminar XX, are the essence of writing. What Lacan achieves, Fink says, is something like the analysand's discourse: speech in its spoken address to the analyst, but a speech that is "based on or dances around a kind of writing": a kind of writing analogous to the inscription of psychic material in the subject's unconscious (69).

The great student of textual seduction, Roland Barthes, offers a perspective on how one might characterize the experience of a text so constructed. In *The Pleasure of the Text*, Barthes writes that the pleasure can take the form of a drift (*la dérive*): "*Drifting* occurs *whenever I do not respect the whole*, and whenever, by dint of seeming driven about by language's illusions, seductions, and intimidations, like a cork on the waves, I remain motionless, pivoting on the *intractable* jouissance that binds me to the text (to the world). Drifting occurs, whenever social language, the sociolect, *fails me*. . . . Thus another name for drifting would be: the Intractable—or perhaps even Stupidity."[10]

The stupidity of drifting would be something like analytic listening, and what would bind one to the analytic text would not be pleasure per se but a certain jouissance. For Barthes, as for Lacan, pleasure has to do with the law and with language whereas jouissance is, if not outside of both, at least not accessible to either. "[P]leasure can be expressed in words, jouissance cannot," Barthes writes (21). But jouissance *can* be expressed in writing, Lacan asserts near the end of Encore: "That which is written—what would that be in the end? The conditions of jouissance" (131). The writing Lacan refers to here is what he considers the essence of writing: mathematical formalization (or his adaptation of it), the formalization that alone approaches Lacan's notion of the real that cannot be expressed by language and symbolization. The penultimate session of Seminar XX closes with the following:

> Mathematization alone reaches a real—and it is in that respect that it is compatible with our discourse, analytic discourse—a real that has nothing to do with what traditional knowledge has served as a basis for, which is not what the latter believes it to be—namely, reality—but rather fantasy.
>
> The real, I will say, is the mystery of the speaking body, the mystery of the unconscious. (131)

## The Voyeuristic Text

If Lacan grapples with the various determined ways discourses close off the unconscious, Irigaray struggles against Lacan's continual shoring up of the symbolic, even as he continually exposes its fissures. Hers is, as I suggested, a second-degree critique. She is a Lacanian who aims to expose the blind spot of psychoanalysis. She similarly aims to turn the screw of critique on other master texts such as Freud's, Nietzsche's, Heidegger's, and Derrida's. Like Derrida, her writing closely engages other texts, though her way of inhabiting those texts is quite different. She is famous for her mimetic style, for taking on the words, the concepts, the tropes, of the texts she reads, from the Greeks to Descartes to Hegel and so on. Her mimeticism is theoretically crucial for her given her understanding of woman's relation to language, an understanding that comes from the Lacanian theory of sexuation, but also from her work in linguistics. Women are outside of language. They use it, of course, but what they use is man's language, a language forged by men, that reflects men, that is isomorphic with the male imaginary. "[W]hat claims to be universal," she writes, "is actually the equivalent of a male idiolect, of a male imaginary, of a sexed world—and not neuter. There is nothing surprising in this, unless one is a passionate defender of idealism. Men have always been the ones to speak and especially to write: in the sciences, in philosophy, in religion, and in politics."[11] Given the masculine nature of language, Irigaray mimes the male texts, inhabits them, and shows from within their language a powerful and defensive shoring up of an economy of the same that is closed to the possibility of a radically other mode of sexuation.

Irigaray's project is unapologetically impossible: to think a sexual difference that has been banished from Western thinking, at least since Socrates, and this through deconstructive mimetic readings that put forth words such as *woman*, *femininity*, *maternity*, the *couple*, the *divine*, that all look familiar but mean something new, is a difficult task. This is what Derrida calls paleonomy, "the occasional maintenance of an old name in order to launch a new concept," the strategy of someone who attempts to dismantle metaphysics from within.[12] With Irigaray, there is more than an occasional use of the new in the old; the practice is generalized and sustained from work to work so that there is scarcely anything that can be taken at face value. Instead of grappling with a text that displaces or short-circuits its meaning, Irigaray's reader is called on continually to read deconstructively and to keep the newly forged meanings in play. This task becomes even more challenging in many of the later published works where there is no explicit deconstructive engagement with another text and where the language can seem more or less straightforward. The harder it is, as in these later works, for the reader to maintain a deconstructive stance toward the text, the easier it is for the text to appear transparently referential. To maintain the integrity of the Irigarayan text, then, to hold it between the extreme poles of the impossibly difficult and the deceptively accessible, the reader is called on to practice a kind of askesis of reading, a rigorously disciplined stance something like a spiritual conditioning that opens out to the not yet fully thinkable.

But there is another problem for the reader: the question of textual intimacy. For those readers who manage to read Lacan's texts, the relationship between reader and the text of jouissance can only be characterized as intimate. With Irigaray's work, there is no such relationship between reader and text. It is blocked by the very mimetic technique crucial to its critical strategy. There *is* a site of intense intimacy in Irigaray's work, but that is located elsewhere, between the couple constituted by the feminist critical voice and the masculine text it inhabits. It is there that one finds the frisson of the writing, the energy that drives it. The reader may identify with the feminist voice or with the masculine text, but she is nonetheless called on to bear witness to the staged encounter. This is true even of a piece such as "When Our Lips Speak Together," where the feminist voice addresses itself to a woman—or to the woman in herself—in highly erotic terms.[13] Even there, or perhaps especially there, it is the power of the masculine foreclosure of sexual difference that calls forth the intensity of the lesbian imagery. How could it be otherwise? Irigaray does not speak of an existing femininity, of an existing relationship between women or between a woman and herself, but rather of something that might be brought forth, but only through this encounter with masculine language.

Irigaray is quite explicit about the erotized nature of her project. In the 1970s she claims that her only option is to have a fling—faire the noce—with the philosophers so as to find the blocked and contained feminine within their language and to return the masculine to itself (*This Sex*, 150). A decade or so later she adopts a modified and even more loving style:

> [E]very text is esoteric, not because it hides a secret but because it constitutes the secret, that which has yet to be revealed is never exhaustively revealable. The only response one can make to the question of the meaning of a text is: read, perceive, experience. . . . *Who are you*? is probably the most relevant question to ask of a text, as long as one isn't requesting a kind of identity card or an autobiographical anecdote. The answer would be: *how about you*? Can we find some common ground? Talk? Love? Create something together? What is there around us and between us that allows this?[14]

Irigaray's styles of desirous engagement span a range of modes of address and intensity, from *Marine Lover*, an amorous dialogue with Nietzsche, to "The Envelope: A Reading of Spinoza."[15] The reader is positioned differently in these texts but in all, the main event remains the crucial encounter of the masculine text and the drive of the foreclosed feminine. Even in writings that seem expository—such as Irigaray's linguistic studies, or essays and lectures of the 1990s to the present that deal with questions such as human rights, citizenship, ecology—even in those works where there is no staged meeting of the couple, the traces of that encounter are always there; they underwrite all theorizing and account for the startling formulations that can appear suddenly in the middle of what seems like conventional discourse. If this scene of the couple underlies all of Irigaray's writing, what can the reader be but a third party to the twosome? This third party position is something like what Barthes calls the "second-degree reader" of criticism. Citing Barthes:

> How can we read criticism? Only one way: since I am here a second-degree reader, I must shift my position: instead of agreeing to be the confidant of the critical pleasure—a sure way to miss it—I can make myself its voyeur: I observe clandestinely the pleasure of others. (17)

Of course, Irigaray's readings are not classical criticism in the sense of a commentary with a clear boundary between text and reader; her fling with the philosophers puts an end to all such boundaries. What Irigaray does is to expose the erotic dimensions of the commentary and turn them to her deconstructive ends. And the reader, like Barthes's second-degree reader of criticism, takes her pleasure, from a distance, as a voyeur.

The question remains as to whether Irigaray's critique can be read. Can such a project function as critique when the reader has both too much and too little footing in the text? too much if she reads the deconstructive words—woman, the couple, mother, divine—as if they were old words; too little footing if her position as voyeur leaves her cold?

## To Be Two

To compound the difficulty, there is the intimate theoretical entanglement entailed in Irigaray's writing.[16] Her intense and ongoing entanglement with Lacan's Seminar XX is a good example. It is as if Irigaray aims to so fully inhabit Lacan's text that its shoring will no longer hold. I will try, to the extent possible, to give some small indication of what this theoretical intimacy involves. By Seminar XX, indeed since Seminar XI, Lacan has turned away from desire to the drive in order to grasp the intractability of some symptoms. Whereas desire finds its cause in the object a—the term that Lacan uses to figure the unsymbolizable residue of the part-object (the breast, the feces, the voice, the gaze)—the drive circles around and around the unsymbolized—or real—object a, deriving its force precisely from its resistance to symbolization. In Seminar XX, called "Encore," Lacan returns to the woman question and, with that, to a knot of questions having to do with knowledge and sexuality, knowledge and jouissance, and most importantly with the relationship between the symbolic and the real.

It is there, in *Encore*, that he posits a feminine jouissance that differs from phallic jouissance.[17] According to Lacan, phallic jouissance always leaves something to be desired, as it were. Because of the promise of wholeness that castration holds out, the masculine subject holds on to a belief in another jouissance. As Suzanne Bernard puts it, "One could say that while man is wholly subject 'to,' and hence 'in,' the symbolic, he is 'in it with exception,' that is, he 'takes exception' to it in some way. As a result, the fantasy of the subject not subjected to the Law—the fantasy of no limit—determines masculine structure in an essential way."[18]

As speaking subjects, women, cannot *not* take part in phallic jouissance, but they do not share in the masculine fantasy, nor in the masculine anxiety. Through castration, the fundamental fantasy of the male subject entails his entering the field of the Other through the lost object, that object always to be sought. Bernard describes the male subject's dilemma:

> Within masculine structure, the drive remains haunted by the image of phallic presence, despite the fact that the masculine subject's place in the symbolic is fixed by its *exclusion*. Hence, one consequence of the masculine subject's attempts to realize the object of desire (to make it exist) is the (paradoxical) risk of dissolving the order in which *he* exists. As a result, he must remain at a certain distance from the object of his desire in order to maintain his sexual position, This is what Lacan refers to as the risk of annihilation the masculine subject takes in approaching the object. (180)

Within feminine structure, on the other hand, the feminine subject *knows* there is lack in the Other, and this different fundamental fantasy allows her a jouissance beyond the phallic.

This difference between phallic jouissance and the Other jouissance turns out to be crucial to the relationship between the real and the symbolic, or in other words, to the way the real functions in male and female sexuation. For the male subject, the Other is constituted through the loss of the real, and the field of the Other is structured by this loss. The female subject, who does not take on the fantasy of the paternal exception to castration, and hence, the fantasy of full presence, has a different relationship to the Other. She is not in the Law, but she is in the Law differently, not haunted by promised plenitude, nor threatened by the dangerous annihilation it represents, not traumatized, in other words, by the lack in the Other.

In *Encore*, Lacan reminds us that the sexual relation, far from being a fusion of the two in the one, partakes of the very death of the wholeness of being. He figures this death by the trope of meiosis, that process of cell division that reduces the number of chromosomes in reproductive cells so as to produce the gametes capable of fertilization. Already in Seminar XI he had used meiosis to figure the lack in being that haunts the male subject's relationship to the Other. The lack in the field of the Other, he says, in turn, takes up an earlier loss, "the blow of individual death," as he puts it, which the subject suffers at the time of sexed reproduction.[19] As against this death, Lacan wants us to think of the libido as a pure life instinct, pure, simple, indestructible life. Quoting Lacan, "[This] is precisely what is subtracted from the living being by virtue of the fact that it is subject to the cycle of sexed reproduction. And it is of this that all the forms of the *object a* that can be enumerated are the representatives, the equivalents. The *objects a* are merely its representatives, its figures. The breast—as equivocal, as an element characteristic of the mammiferous organization, the placenta for example—certainly represents that part of himself that the individual loses at birth, and which may serve to symbolize the most profound lost object. I could make the same kind of reference to all the other objects" (198).

If the male subject suffers from lack in being, the female has a different relationship to the real, one of "not not being," as Bernard says. And this relationship has something to do with what Lacan calls "lalangue" or the m(O)ther tongue, to which the female subject has a different access. Quoting Lacan: "The unconscious evinces knowledge that, for the most part, escapes the speaking being. That being provides the occasion to realize just how far the effects of *lalangue* can go, in that it presents all sorts of affects that remain enigmatic" (139). It is this lalangue and not language that the unconscious speaks. And it is this lalangue, the (m)Other tongue—en-corps—that is heard in the Other jouissance.

One reason Irigaray's work tracks Lacan's so closely is because he continues to strain against his own categories and because those strains in his theorizing help to open up hers. In *Encore*, Lacan puts into relief, as never before, the pathos of the phallic sexual economy. Irigaray's frustration is that he stops there. For in the end, what becomes of those crucial formulations other than a mysterious suggestion, perhaps, of something different? From Irigaray's perspective, "Encore" might be seen as "yet again." All the figural straining required to produce the Other jouissance, all the double negatives, might be taken as signs, here more than ever, that the discourse can barely express what it needs to express. An analytic discourse that sets out to read a culture that fetishizes the mother's body, must itself speak fetishistically. One might say that one is left with a sleight of hand: now you see it, now you don't.

It is here that Irigaray takes on a rhetorical impatience, here that she argues that Lacan should listen harder to what he hears from women. And it is here that she finds psychoanalysis complicit in furthering the very formations it reads so well. Her aim is to suggest that the subject's entrance into symbolization need not be structured forever within the pathos of male sexuation. She argues that psychoanalysis itself, in exposing this formation, leads us to see how women, but also men, might become subjects in a less pathological manner, were there shifts in the symbolic. To say that the unconscious knows no history is not to say that the unconscious is ahistorical.

The force of Irigaray's argument lies in her reading of the lost object and all its attendant effects as symptomatic of the child's inability to symbolize its relationship to the mother's body. Much is made, she says, of the ambivalence Oedipus feels toward his father, but isn't this an ambivalence projected retroactively upon the primitive relation to the mother's body? "Now, it is true," she writes, "that, in so far as it takes account of the drives, analysis does have things to tell us about the mother's breast, about the milk she offers, about the feces she takes away . . . and even about her gaze and voice. But analysis shows too little interest in these things. Furthermore, isn't it true that all this wrestling [*corps-à-corps*] with the mother, which has difficulties of its own, is part of a postoedipal phantasy projected backward onto the Oedipus phase? When the mother is cut up in stages, when each part of her body has to be cathected and then decathected if the child is to grow, she has already been torn to pieces by the hatred of Oedipus" (*Sexes*, 13).

Commenting on the importance of the Law, of language, the name of the father, she goes on: "The social order, our culture, psychoanalysis itself, are all insistent that the mother must remain silent, outlawed. The father forbids any *corps-à-corps* with the mother. I am tempted to add: if only this were really true! We would be more at peace with our bodies if it were, and men need peace to feed their libido as well as their life and culture. For the ban does not prevent a certain number of failures of compliance, a certain blindness" (14–15). The law of the father doesn't fully work, Irigaray says. If men were to effect real separation from the mother, their desire wouldn't depend on cutting her body into pieces; they wouldn't be threatened by the devouring vagina; they wouldn't need to find their mothers in their wives; they wouldn't need the woman as a guarantee that their body exists.

Irigaray has a strong rhetorical response to Lacan's trope of meiosis and to the placenta's role with regard to it. For Lacan, the placenta is a trope for the subject's—that is, the male subject's—lost object. But seen from the perspective of female jouissance, it can also be read, as Bernard suggests, as the loss of a certain strange relation to the Other, a relationship of not one, figured by the placenta's role in joining fetus and mother. For her part, Irigaray takes the trope out of the double negative. Let us read the placenta as it is, she suggests. The placenta is not a simple conduit of exchanges between two organisms, but a virtually independent organ that mediates a space between the tissues of the mother and the fetus and, at the same time, regulates exchanges between the two for the benefit of both, which includes moderating the mother's metabolism and secreting maternal hormones needed for gestation. Irigaray refers to biologist and theorist Hélène Rouch, who reflects on the common imaginary notion of the fusion of mother and child and the subsequent expulsion of the child from an undifferentiated paradise. Might this not have to do, Rouch asks, with the total dependence of the child at birth, which produces a fantasy of fusion and a cultural blindness to the relationship of mother and child as always already separated?[20]

Taking up the figure of the placenta, Irigaray is able to offer a different imaginary: were there a way for the child to symbolize its relations to the mother's body, and were that relationship imagined as always already separate and at the same time life sustaining, the whole fantasy of fusion, triangulation, law, loss, and refusal of loss would be interrupted. The double articulation of castration—into language, into sexuation—would be realized differently. Of course, this different imaginary would be the effect of a different symbolic order in which what is now figured as castration would be the work of what Irigaray calls negativity, the negativity of the absolute radical alterity of male subject and female subject, with a female subject who would be fully sexed in that her sexuality would be symbolizable. The interval between subjects would be productive of desire.

It is impossible here for me to do justice to Irigaray's full theorization of a different sexual difference. But I can point to the obvious challenges it faces. How to evoke a change in the symbolic when one's thematization is necessarily so dependent on the imaginary? Any elaboration of a different figural relation of mother and child, for example, can quickly read like idealist and voluntarist talk that makes the promise of a different social order seem dependent on our all being willing to embrace the truth of the placenta. It is to avoid such readings that serious critics of Irigaray never let her text stray far from the one she inhabits—in this discussion, the text of *Encore.* All critique is, of course, dependent on the text it reads in that it is the disruption of the closure of one text by the critical work of the other. But in Irigaray's case, we are dealing with a particular kind of dependency that mirrors the very relationship of femininity and masculinity within the existing symbolic order. To theorize a femininity that is not the other of the masculine, the symptom of the masculine, is a tricky business. Irigaray more than anyone appreciates its trickiness and sees her work not as a utopian description of a future but as an intervention—a performative intervention—meant to stimulate change in the form of disruptive formulations, without knowing in advance what the outcome might be.

But in the reality of reading, doesn't everything work against Irigaray's project? A comparison with Lacan is illuminating. His texts are enigmatic because so much, in the sense of ordinary meaning, is withheld. So much of the work of reading lies in the power of ellipsis to thwart the expected. The result is that even the most reductive readings of Lacan have to perform contortions in order to reproduce the banality of the already known. In contrast, Irigaray's later texts, with their talk of placentas and couples and maternal genealogies, seem to inhabit the very register of the known. If the reader of Lacan feels called on to produce intelligibility out of the impossibly difficult, Irigaray's reader feels impelled to restore the impossible to her intelligibility.

## The Forgotten Mystery

Because I am loathe to give up on the feminist hope Irigaray's project holds out, I turn briefly to an aspect of her writing that allows us to see the potential power of her performative interventions in a different way. I turn to her engagement with Greek mythology and to a 1989 lecture entitled "The Forgotten Mystery of Female Ancestry."[21] There, Irigaray revisits the story of Persephone. She begins with a genealogy that figures the originary coupling of Chaos and Gaia or earth. In the Olympian version, Gaia does not couple with but springs out of Chaos. In Irigaray's accounting, it is Eros who compels the sexually undifferentiated Chaos and Gaia to couple, and it is through the offspring of that couple that sexual difference emerges. Down the road genealogically we come to the couple Demeter and Zeus and their daughter Persephone. In Irigaray's telling, Persephone is not just snatched by Hades and taken underground, to the grief and despair of Demeter, she is, rather, given in marriage to Hades by her father, Zeus, who does this as a way of consolidating the power that will make him God of the gods. For Zeus comes from the line of Gaea, a child of the female pole, whereas Hades is a descendant of Chaos. In Irigaray's reading, "Zeus wishes to become God of gods despite the infernal male powers that wanted to annihilate him as an individual more differentiated than Chaos. He wants to overturn the divine male omnipotence of the initial Chaos" (103). So Zeus gives Persephone to Hades, who abducts and rapes her anyway. Zeus does this without consulting his wife or daughter but, of course, Demeter finds ways to express her displeasure, such as rendering the earth barren. When mother and daughter are eventually reunited, Persephone recounts to her mother everything that has happened to her, telling her story from beginning to end. "In a way," Irigaray says, "she goes back in time, as must any woman today who is trying to find the traces of her estrangement from her mother. This is what the psychoanalytic process should do: find the thread of her entry into the Underworld, and, if possible, her way out" (107).

The underworld Irigaray evokes is the hell of monosexual subjectivity and the ruin of sexual love, where the girl is estranged from her own virginity, deprived of all but the freedom to "seduce in accordance with male instincts." She "becomes a sort of puppet or movable object, reduced to being subjected to basic drives with passive goals." Irigaray goes on: "She thinks she needs to be 'screwed' by a man, she suffers from a basic oral need (partially an inverted projection stemming from male desire), Freud writes learnedly, without considering that this need might be symptomatic of woman's submission to male instincts. According to Freud, this need is a sort of relic of the initial chaos that male desire opened up in the earth's womb" (108). Concluding a pointed analysis of the bottomless hunger that psychoanalysis finds in women, Irigaray says: "None of this could happen if she had not been separated from her mother, from the earth, from her gods and her order. This is the original sin that makes woman a seductress against a backdrop of nothingness. But why abduct her from her mother? Why destroy female ancestries? To establish an order man needed, but which is not yet an order of respect for and fertility of sexual difference" (109).

What do I the reader make of this collapse of time so it is as if the separation of Persephone and Demeter happens in *my* time, with its deleterious effects on *my* desire? I suggest there is a way in which this very particular staging of the registers of the psychic present is at work in all of Irigaray's writing, which is another way of suggesting that her mythical interventions might be seen as allegorical of her work in general.

To clarify, consider Shoshana Felman's reading of mythology and psychoanalysis in her book, *Jacques Lacan and the Adventures of Insight*.[22] There Felman reminds us of Freud's words on mythology and the instincts: "The theory of instincts is so to say our mythology," Freud writes. "Instincts are mythical entities, magnificent in their indefiniteness. In our work we cannot for a moment disregard them, yet we are never sure we are seeing them clearly" (151). And Lacan, following Freud, comments that "in the final analysis we can talk adequately about the libido only in a mythic manner" (144). What this means, Felman says, is that "insofar as it is mediated by a myth [such as the Oedipal myth], the Freudian theory is not a literal translation or reflection of reality, but its *symptom*, its metaphorical account. The myth is not pure fantasy, however, but has narrative symbolic logic that accounts for a real mode of functioning, a real structure of relations" (151).

What is crucial in Felman's discussion is her observation that this symptomatic or metaphorical rendering is not just a static gloss, an embellished narrative version of a serious scientific theory of the way things work. *The myth is the route to theory and not the other way around*, and the way that movement works is analogous to the analytic dialogue. There, in the analytic dialogue, what is involved is not an informative act (through statements or meanings), but a performative one. "[T]he analytic interpretation in itself is a performative (not cognitive) interpretation in that it has a fundamental structuring, transforming function. At stake is not the accuracy of a particular reading but a relationship between the structuring address of the myth and the structuring reception" (121). And this is the relationship between reality and the psychoanalytic myth: "[T]he myth comes to grips with something in reality that it does not fully comprehend but to which it gives an answer, a symbolic reply. . . . [I]n much the same way as . . . the analytic interpretation, within the situation of the dialogue, acts not by virtue of its accuracy but by virtue of its resonance (received in terms of the listener's structure), works, that is, by virtue of its openness to a linguistic passage through the Other, so does the psychoanalytic myth, in *resonating in the Other*, produce a *truthful structure*. The psychoanalytic myth derives its theoretical effectiveness not from its truth value, but from its truth encounter with the other, from its capacity for *passing through the other*; from its openness, that is, to an *expropriating passage* of one insight through another, of one story through another" (151–52).

Looking at Irigaray's mode of critique from this perspective, there might be more to be said about the voyeuristic text. Perhaps there is a double structure of address in these texts, two scenes staged and not just the scene of the feminist critical voice and masculine text. The second scene would be that of Persephone telling her story to Demeter. The reader of that scene might find the space of critique, and, along the way, a route out of Hades.

## Notes

1. Luce Irigaray, *Speculum: Of the Other Woman*, trans. Gillian C. Gill (Ithaca: Cornell University Press, 1985). See Eugénie Lemoine-Lucciono's (then Eugénie Luccioni) review of *Speculum* in Esprit 444 (March 1975).

2. Luce Irigaray, *This Sex Which Is Not One*, trans. Catherine Porter with Carolyn Burke (Ithaca: Cornell University Press, 1985); Toril Moi, *Sexual/Textual Politics: Feminist Literary Theory* (London: Methuen, 1985).

3. Jacqueline Rose, Introduction to *Feminine Sexuality: Jacques Lacan and the école freudienne*, ed. Juliet Mitchell and Jacqueline Rose, trans. Jacqueline Rose (New York: W. W. Norton, 1982), 55–56.

4. For an interesting discussion of such concerns, see Penelope Deutscher, *A Politics of Impossible Difference: The Later Work of Luce Irigaray* (Ithaca: Cornell University Press, 2002).

5. See *Encore: The Seminar of Jacques Lacan, Book XX: On Feminine Sexuality, The Limits of Love and Knowledge, 1972–1973*, ed. Jacques-Alain Miller, trans. with notes by Bruce Fink (New York: W. W. Norton, 1999), 72–73.

6. Luce Irigaray and Sylvère Lotringer, eds., *Why Different? A Culture of Two Subjects. Interviews with Luce Irigaray*, trans. Camille Collins (New York: Semiotext(e), 2000), 11.

7. *The Seminar of Jacques Lacan, Book II: The Ego in Freud's Theory and in the Technique of Psychoanalysis, 1954–55*, ed. Jacques-Alain Miller, trans. Sylvana Tomaselli with notes by John Forrester (New York: W. W. Norton, 1988), 5.

8. Bruce Fink, *Lacan to the Letter: Reading* Ecrits *Closely* (Minneapolis: University of Minnesota Press, 2004), 42–43.

9. For a meditation on stupidity, see Avital Ronell, *Stupidity* (Urbana: University of Illinois Press, 2003).

10. Roland Barthes, *The Pleasure of the Text*, trans. Richard Miller (New York: Hill and Wang, 1975), 18–19.

11. Luce Irigaray, *To Speak Is Never Neutral*, trans. Gail Schwab (New York: Routledge, 2002), 250.

12. Jacques Derrida, *Positions*, trans. and annotated by Alan Bass (Chicago: University of Chicago Press, 1981), 71.

13. In *This Sex Which Is Not One*, 205–18.

14. Luce Irigaray, *Sexes and Genealogies*, trans. Gillian C. Gill (New York: Columbia University Press, 1993), 178.

15. Luce Irigaray, *Marine Lover of Friedrich Nietzsche*, trans. Gillian C. Gill (New York, Columbia University Press, 1991); "To the Envelope: a Reading of Spinoza," in *An Ethics of Sexual Difference*, trans. Carolyn Burke and Gillian C. Gill (Ithaca: Cornell University Press, 1993), 83–94.

16. *To Be Two* is the title of a book by Irigaray first published in Italian (*Essere Due*) in 1994. *To Be Two*, trans. Monique M Rhodes and Marco F. Cocito-Monoc (New York: Routledge, 2001).

17. For those not familiar with Lacan's use of the term, *jouissance* is "enjoyment," more in the sense of sufferance than of pleasure and one that the subject doesn't let go of, dependent for his or her very being on the satisfaction it brings.

18. Suzanne Bernard, "Tongues of Angels: Feminine Structure and Other Jouissance," in *Reading Seminar XX: Lacan's Major Work on Love, Knowledge, and Feminine Sexuality*, ed. Suzanne Bernard and Bruce Fink (Albany: State University of New York Press, 2002), 171–85.

19. *The Seminar of Jacques Lacan, Book XI: The Four Fundamental Concepts of Psychoanalysis*, ed. Jacques-Alain Miller, trans. Alan Sherman (New York: W. W. Norton, 1988), 205.

20. See Luce Irigaray, *je, tu, nous: Toward a Culture of Difference*, trans. Alison Martin (New York: Routledge, 1993), 37–44.

21. Luce Irigaray, *In Thinking the Difference: For a Peaceful Revolution*, trans. Karin Montin (New York: Routledge, 1994), 89–112.

22. Shoshana Felman, *Jacques Lacan and the Adventure of Insight: Psychoanalysis in Contemporary Culture* (Cambridge: Harvard University Press, 1987).

Chapter 3

# Kore

## Philosophy, Sensibility, and the Diffraction of Light

Dorothea Olkowski

### The Field of Flowers

"It was a place where dogs would lose their quarry's trail, so violent was the scent of the flowers. A stream cut deep through the grass of a meadow that rose at the edge to fall sheer in a rocky ravine into the very navel of Sicily. And here, near Henna, Kore was carried off."[1] It was a place that would attract a young girl, virgin daughter of two gods, beloved child of Demeter, born of a violent coupling with brother-father Zeus whose nostalgia for the radiant light out of which all life emerged found perverse expression and whose acts, although they were the acts of a god, could never approach the everything of she/he who had been the "first-born" of the world, the first appearance emanating from light.[2] Some claim the girl picked poppies, identifying her with their soporific qualities, their red color promising resurrection after death. Others, perhaps more attuned to the continuous usurpations of the male Gods who, of necessity, fixed upon Kore's eye, these others who may also have been more attentive to the sensibility, the mind, of a young girl, daughter of the goddess of three worlds—the heavens, the earth, and the caves beneath—these others assert that the girl, Kore, was looking at a narcissus, or perhaps it was a lotus, a lily, or a rose. For them, "the psyche as flower, as lotus, lily, and rose, the virgin as flower in Eleusis, symbolizes the highest psychic and spiritual developments. . . the birth of the self in the Golden Flower.[3] In any case, the accounts of the Greek poet say it was a narcissus, so overwhelming, so seductive, "a thing of awe. . . from its root grew a hundred blooms and it smelled most sweetly, so that all wide heaven above and the whole earth and the sea's salt swell laughed for joy."[4] Obviously, a flower begging to be picked.

If "Kore was looking at a narcissus. She was *looking at the act of looking*."[5] She is said to be looking at the flower of the youth, Narcissus, who, it was prophesied, would live to a ripe old age only if he never came to know himself. But this did not happen. Spurning all others, Narcissus was condemned to fall in love but denied the possibility of consummation. Seeing his own image in a spring "clear as silver," undisturbed by animal or plant, the already heartless, self-absorbed boy saw himself and came to know himself. Unlike the double-sexed goddess-god, Phanes-Eros—who men say is the offspring, the luminous male principle, the divine son of Persephone-Kore—unlike Phanes-Eros, Narcissus is unable to copulate with himself. Moreover, in seeing and knowing himself, Narcissus does not gain understanding. Self-love merely enhances his pridefulness. Overly proud, overwhelmed by self-love, overcome by grief; he plunges a dagger into his own breast. Little wonder that narcissus came to be used in the ancient wreaths of Demeter and Persephone, also called Kore.[6] For if to look at and to pick narcissus is to look at and to pick the act of looking, it is to see it and through seeing, to understand. So Demeter-Kore may well be the expression of seeing and seeing as understanding. But for Persephone-Kore, for this girl, understanding was, at the beginning, denied. Wandering alone on a sunny morning amid clusters of blossoms; Kore stops to look. Precisely at the moment when she reaches out to pluck the flower, precisely at the edge of her own look at the act of looking, at the edge of understanding through seeing, the earth opens and she is taken away by an unseen power to a dark, invisible place. Is this not the fate of many young girls? In the full light of the sun, at the very instant when they begin to look at the act of looking, on the verge of seeing and of coming to understand through sight, are they not also swept away by some unseeable power, a power that sees itself in them but which they cannot see? And unlike Persephone-Kore, most do not return.

Why does Hades come from the underworld with his golden chariot and four black horses? He sees and understands nothing of the world above but is made imperceptible by the gift of the Cyclops, the helmet that conceals him.[7] Is Hades the descendent of the serpent Ophion, created with the wind by the "Goddess of All Things," the naked Eurynome? Eurynome, wide-wandering goddess, the visible moon, diffuse light. Eurynome, exalted dove, the first and only, the universal goddess who arose from yawning Chaos, danced with the wind, and gave rise to all things. Eurynome, the dove, tumbles above the waves and is fertilized by the wind. Out of the union of dancer and wind is hatched the Universal Egg, from which all things emerge, a cosmos set in motion by the Goddess and forever transforming itself, its seven planetary powers now ruled over by the Titanesses whose interests the Titans serve and safeguard. But Ophion soon exasperates the goddess, claiming to be himself the author of the self-created universe, until she, incredulous, "bruised his head with her heel, kicked out his teeth, and banished him to the dark caves below the earth"[8]

And now it is Hades who claims supremacy in the dark caves below the earth; the other world, an invisible world defined as isolated, separated, and silent.[9] In the myths reported by men, this new Ophion returns to the earth, but not to see and not to understand through sight. On earth, once again, a snake wraps itself around a goddess. Hades returns to the self-created and visible world where formerly only deities ruled the seven days of the sacred planetary week: the Sun to illuminate; the Moon for enchantment; Mars giving growth; Mercury giving wisdom; Jupiter giving law; Venus granting love; Saturn granting peace.[10] There are no dark powers, no isolated, separated, silent, deathly powers among the *conceptions* of the goddess, Eurynome. The snake wanders in the caves beneath the earth; it is nothing more than wind whistling through cracks and crevices. Banished, defanged, not a god, for gods give, they do not take anything away. But men, Hesiod, Ovid, ensure the return of the once powerless, defanged creature in a much more despotic and dangerous form. They make him a sightless God who seeks a vision of himself. Perhaps then, we should note that for them, Eurynome, Goddess of All Things, has vanished from the cosmos she brought forth; she is the first goddess to disappear, but will not be the last.[11] For these men, poets and philosophers, Darkness is first and from Darkness springs even yawning Chaos. And from Chaos springs, not illumination, enchantment, growth, wisdom, law, and love, but Doom, Old Age, Death, Murder, Sleep, Discord, Misery, Vexation, Nemesis, and later, Terror, Anger, Strife, Vengeance, Intemperance, Altercation, Oblivion, Fear, Pride, and Battle. What little can Sleep or Joy, Friendship or Pity do to ameliorate the force of the dark planetary powers now unleashed?[12] And for them, for the philosophers, Nature is now the "God of All Things," *he* who does not bring forth but who *separates*, who *separates* earth from heaven, water from earth, the upper realms from the lower, unraveling all elements. And this unraveling is called "setting in due order," but it is an endless task in a cosmos set in motion by the Goddess of All Things, a cosmos ceaselessly transforming itself through the powers of illumination, enchantment, growth, wisdom, law, love, and peace.[13]

Perhaps then, given the arrival among men of the idea of setting the cosmos in due order, we should anticipate and acknowledge the importance that comes to be placed on the eternal model of the cosmos, that which always is and has no becoming, from which the world order is created in a *symphony of proportion* according to which what fire is to air, air is to water, and what air is to water, water is to earth. It is a structure that arises from a symphony of self-love ("he who framed the universe. . . wanted everything to become as much like himself as possible") and it produces a symphony of proportions consisting of Originals and their imitations. As such, Different is to Same as men are to Gods, and female to male (female being the inferior nature, the poor imitation, the formerly male soul that fails to live a good life).[14] Given all this, it is not surprising that Hades emerges from his separated and silent realm, from the realm of the invisible, into the field of flowers, into the visible, to abduct the daughter of Demeter, daughter of the "triple goddess of the cornfield," whose priestesses initiate the young and newly wed into "the secrets of the couch," but who takes no husband herself, who remains independent of all dark powers.[15] Perhaps we should not be surprised that the separated and silent world, the invisible world asserts itself, asserts what have been called its "rights" over the visible world, meaning over the visible body of a young girl about to reach out and pluck the act of looking, about to take this open flower, this opening to understanding for herself. Where do these rights of the invisible over the visible arise? What justifies such rights? Are they also the effect of the symphony of proportion?

We have been told, "I'm sure you've noticed that when a man looks into an eye his face appears in it, like in a mirror. We call this the 'pupil' (kore), for it's a sort of miniature of the man who's looking."[16] If an eye is to see itself, it must look into a mirror or an eye. Moreover, the best part of the eye is said to be the part with which it sees, and this is likened to the best part of the soul, said to be the part that knows. The best part of the eye and the best part of the soul are said to resemble the divinity, perhaps because the pupil is thought to be that part of the eye that gives vision and the intellectual soul is that part of the soul that gives understanding. In spite of a general injunction against the senses, which disturb the proportions to near breaking point, sight is acknowledged to be a great benefit to humankind. "None of our present statements about the universe could ever have been made if we had never seen any stars, sun or heaven."[17] Our capacity to see Nature is the gift of vision. And from the human ability to observe day and night, months and years, equinoxes and solstices, has come the invention of number, the idea of time, as well as numerous inquiries into the nature of the universe. And from these pursuits have arisen philosophy! Thus from vision—understanding, and not the reverse. But the philosopher is rather blind to this relation. He reasons that vision is the effect of particles shot out of the eyes, the *pure fire* that flows through the middle part of the eye, that part that is close textured, smooth, dense, so that pure fire and only pure fire passes through. From the contemporary perspective, "it is difficult to imagine now why Plato did not try to settle the matter with a few simple experiments."[18] But his conception of vision was inextricably linked to the mixing of fires, like coalescing with like, the pure fire from the eyes coalescing with daylight, mixing and forming a *homogeneous* body, a medium that is able to transmit the motions of whatever comes into contact with it. The homogeneous body transmits motions from objects that contact it or that it comes into contact with; it transmits these motions through the eye straight into the soul! Fire meets fire, and *kore*, the young girl about to pick a flower, must be blinded, lest vision lead to understanding. She must be abducted so as to become the pure, virgin opening onto knowledge of an Other self. Eyefire and dayfire mix, homogenize, and convey directly whatever they come into contact with to the invisible soul, the only thing said to properly possesses understanding, by which is meant, self-knowledge.[19]

And the soul? The soul is conceived of as a dark box, part of a *camera obscura* consisting of a pinhole opening through which passes one single ray of light; a single ray cuts through the *kore*, the tiny pupil, and is projected onto a screen for *direct* viewing. To see clearly, the soul must be completely dark, dark as the unlit and invisible place from which the God, Hades, emerges; it is the dark place into which the pinhole opening of the eye projects inverted images of the objects outside.[20] This is what the philosopher calls understanding, but it is little more than a view of the self, a view of the tiny image of oneself in the eye of the other, the very image of what is called self-knowledge. Precautions are put in place to ensure that nothing will enter the soul that should not enter—no diffuse or scattered light, scattered like flowers in a field. The *camera obscura* operates in accordance with the principles of the dark soul, the soul that knows what the eye perceives, but what the eye perceives is oneself. Contemporary perception theory agrees with the ancients that the mind does not record an exact image of the world but in fact creates its own picture.[21] Nevertheless, it can be argued that perceptions are neither arbitrary nor illusory; that they are unaffected by knowledge of ourselves or knowledge of the world. Our so-called direct perception of the world must be mediated by the senses but as veridical, our perceptions do correspond to things in the world when those things are considered objectively, meaning, independently of viewing conditions, meaning, something obtainable through some form of measurement.[22] But *is* vision direct perception, as has been claimed? Geometrical optics tells us that light does travel in straight lines, but the "law of refraction" operates due to the requirement that the speed of light can be constant only in a perfect vacuum. Strictly speaking, if a ray of light passes from something such as a glass of water (a dense medium) into air (a less dense medium), the ray of light will refract or bend. Light does travel more slowly in a denser medium and mediums do vary, they are not, as the philosopher hypothesized, homogeneous. Bending, refraction is inevitable and is the basis of image formation by all lenses including those of the eye.[23]

## Shadows and Light

The Goddess Eurynome, dancing in the wind across the sky, sets the sun in place to illuminate the daytime sky and the moon to illuminate the nighttime sky. Eurynome is both the Goddess of All Things from whom all things emerge and the transformative, dynamic element, the creative element, setting the cosmos in motion and impelling it toward change.[24] In the cosmos set in motion by the Goddess, it is the luminous moon and moonlight that form the background against which the sun and the cosmos stand out, light being the fruit or flower of the night. Ancient cultures calculated time from light of the stars and the planets, especially the moon. From this point of view, the light-bearing goddess of the night was identified with the moon and the moon was identified with life.[25] Such was the basis of the great mysteries of Eleusis, a celebration of the phases of the luminous moon, the joyful birth of the new moon, following the dark-moon, when the light of the heavens, the flourishing girl, Kore, is abducted by the death-sun.[26] Darkness corresponds, then, to the disappearance of the moon, its luminous, reflective rays and death, the darkening of the moon, *comes from the sun*. The winter solstice celebrates not only the return of Kore to Demeter from the caves of Hades, but also rebirth, Kore giving birth to the moon, the full moon, and the transformation of the girl Kore, herself becoming a moon goddess.[27]

A daring proposition? Dare we propose that the true transformation, the return of Kore to Demeter and to the moonlit earth is her transformation from girl to goddess, from sunlight to moonlight, an "immortal and divine principle, the beautific light. . . [so that with] Demeter, she becomes the goddess of the three worlds": the heavens, the earth and the caves beneath?[28] This conceptualization, speculative and, at its inception, untestable, is grounded in the idea of transformation. There is a transformation of material or natural elements, a quantitative and qualitative transformation in which something new is achieved, something that, like the moon, illuminates the heavens with its reflective light and by means of this reflective illumination, transforms all, not once, but again and again. Its limits are found, perhaps, in the ancient idea of the cosmos as finite and bounded, having actual edges beyond which. . . nothing, nothing to sustain an object's structure. In such a cosmos transformations are limited, possibly little more than repetitions or maximally a finite number of variations. Still, is there any reason to believe that the universe created by the Goddess is not at least *unbounded*, a sphere that is finite in area but delimited by no boundaries?[29] Nevertheless, what matters for the moment is the transformational aspect of this conception, for which it may prove to be of the greatest importance that, whether it is called *cosmos* or world-order, there is no severance of the connection between the concept and the reflective moon, the luminous aspect of the night.[30] The philosophers too began with a concept. What the Goddess has consigned to the dark caves below the earth diffusely lit by the reflective rays of the moon, they raised up to the highest heights. What had been lowest will be highest; what had been little more than the sound of the wind whipping through the caves below; what had no being and so no gift-giving, planetary power; the invisible realm of Ophion and Hades, the dark realm of the death-sun, this will be the model for a cosmos made in the image of being. No longer a cosmos undergoing transformation of its natural elements, but *mimesis*, a world made, guarded, and limited by a nameless *demiourgos*, now little more than a maker, a craftsman.[31] The philosophers therefore begin with the eternal *a priori*, with *sheer being*, *"that which always is* and has no becoming."[32] No becoming, no *genesis*, meaning no dawn, no dawning, no engendering, no generation, inception, opening, no origin. If it is only visible and perceptible, the cosmos lacks sheer being. If it has come to be, it is grasped not by understanding but only by opinion. But the cosmos has a cause. It is not simply set in motion out of its own material and natural elements. It has a maker, a father who makes it from fire and earth bonded together by water and air according to rules of proportion which are applied to these materials. Such rules belong to the a priori realm of what is stable, fixed, and transparent to understanding, in the hope that what is ruled over will have the same fixed and stable character. Nonetheless, there is something disturbing, something wide-wandering in these heavens (*ouranos*), for we are told that the god "took over all that was visible—not at rest but in discordant and disorderly motion—and brought it from a state of disorder to one of order.. . . [H]e made it a single visible living thing, which contains within itself all the living things. . . *one* universe."[33] For the Goddess, who is Goddess of All, the "All" is first, the sun arising from the night sky that is the totality of all things. For the philosophers, the discordant particulars precede the whole, and although the universe resembles a Living Thing, of which all other living things are parts, disorderly elements and unrest somehow crept into the maker's world, from where it is not clear. What is clear is that the maker orders them.[34]

This brings about a paradox. The begotten universe lacks eternity; it is a shrine for the gods, a copy of an everlasting Living Thing, but not eternal. The maker must nevertheless master the media. He makes a *moving image of eternity*, moving according to number, but as unified, eternal. He makes "time," using the planetary powers, but not to bestow the gifts of illumination, enchantment, growth, wisdom, law, love, and peace. When the philosopher's god kindles a light in one of the heavenly bodies that moves in a circular motion, it shines over the cosmos for the purpose of setting limits and standing guard over the numbers of time. The Sun serves as the measure of the slowness and quickness of all the other bodies;

its circle providing the measure of a day and night; its cycle the measure of a year. And beneath the stars the maker made men to whom were shown the laws of this cosmos and to whom were given sense perception, as well as love mixed with pleasure and pain, fear and spiritedness. Those who fail to master these emotions are reborn as women or wild animals.[35] And the wandering Goddess of All Things, stripped of her lunar reflection, is the wet-nurse, made invisible, dragged down to the dark and invisible realm of the death-sun, the intelligible realm where she can, at best, provide a necessary, a priori fixed space with no characteristics of its own, *chora*. An indeterminate space for whatever comes to be, for those things that resemble and imitate self-knowledge, that which remains forever unmoved by persuasion, that which keeps its own form unchangingly.[36]

And strange to say, for "men" (made from leftover fire, earth, water, and air, impure but not discarded)—whose purpose in this eternity remains a mystery, since the maker wanted everything to be as much like himself as possible—for men, some adjustments are needed. There is the necessity of visibility, the eye being a condition of the possibility of inquiries into the nature of the universe. The eye that sees by the light of the sun remains subject, in this account, to something else, something other than vision and the principles that govern sight. "The god invented sight and gave it to us so that we might observe the orbits of intelligence in the universe and apply them to the revolutions of our own understanding."[37] Crafted by "Intellect" the eye allows us to stabilize our own understanding through the symphony of proportions through *mimesis*. Thus, the human being may imitate the unstraying revolutions of the god—but only by seeing them first. And yet, self-knowledge seems to require something else. Not a view of Nature, but a view of the self, perhaps a view of the soul? For this it is helpful to look into the kore, the pupil of the eye, to capture the young girl, in order to come to know oneself. The question remains, for self-knowledge, why look into the kore of the eye; why not simply gaze into a mirror which after all would give one a much clearer image of oneself rather than a tiny doll-like image, an image reminiscent of a young girl? Perhaps the fascination with gazing into the eye of an other is due to the suggestion that to know itself a soul must look into another soul. Looking at the pupil allows another eye to see itself. Kore is both "girl" and "pupil," that part of the eye in which one must look in order to see oneself; to see oneself in the eye of the girl who does not yet see and understand makes it possible to know oneself. To look into the kore is to look into that Kore who reaches out to pluck the flower. She exists "on the brink of meeting a gaze in which she would have seen herself. She was stretching out her hand to pluck that gaze."[38] Hades asks brother Zeus for a living woman. Zeus, the god who does not set the cosmos in motion, who can only reproduce what he has devoured—the skies, sea and earth along with the Titanesses and Titans—this god devours the cosmos, then spits it out, an act of mimicry, not of creation. Henceforth, "the world from end to end is organized as *mimesis*; resemblance is the law."[39] This same god whose own power is nothing but *mimesis* is eager to acknowledge the reality of a second world, a separate and silent world of resemblance. He is ready to embrace the dark realm of an invisible mind, to let the power of shadows and darkness invade and overtake the world of the enchanting moon goddess, the Goddess of All who danced with the wind.

## The Visible and the Invisible

"The earth splits open and Kore is plucked so to be taken away by Hades." Did Kore's eye meet Hades'? Did her eye meet the eye of Ophion risen up from the world that until that moment had been invisible to her and who remains invisible under the vaunted helmet? Or, does the invisible Ophion, the god Hades, not see himself in the eye of Kore? Is this not his only reality? Far from recognizing herself in that invisible eye, is it not Hades who needs and seeks recognition, who can only find himself in the pupil, in the kore of Kore, daughter of the triple-Goddess? "But Hades wanted Kore as his bride, wanted to have a living person sitting on the throne beside him. . . in the kingdom of shades, there is at least one body, and the body of a flourishing young girl at that."[40] The necessity of this move may prove to be multiple. If Hades sees himself in Kore's eye and Kore sees nothing but his shadow, then indeed, vision is the prey. The beautiful visible world, the world granted by the powers of illumination, enchantment, growth, wisdom, law, love, and peace is invaded by the invisible world. Someone and something are taken from the visible to the invisible. The "girl," young and flourishing is abducted from the beautiful, visible world transforming itself through its material and natural elements and she is dragged down to the shadow world. "The eye pounced from the shadows to capture a girl and shut her away in the underworld palace of the mind."[41] Is the invisible realm, the realm of shadows, the realm of Hades, of death, one with the unchanging mind? How can this be? Are not the sun and sun light thought to be the very image of the Ideas or forms and the intelligible world? And if death and the unchanging mind are one, then what of the so-called divine Ideas? What of philosophy itself? Is it possible that the love of "Sophia," the goddess "Wisdom," has been transformed into a love of death? Sophia is also the flower. And what if it is the flower, Sophia, that Kore reaches out to pluck? What then? "Vessel of transformation, blossom, the unity of Demeter reunited with Kore, Isis, Ceres, the moon goddesses, whose luminous aspect overcomes. . . nocturnal darkness, are all expressions of this Sophia, the highest feminine wisdom."[42]

It has been asserted that "the Olympians developed a new fascination for Death."[43] Is not the reality that men, the philosophers and poets who told the stories about the Olympians, these men developed a new fascination for Death, a fascination not present in the earliest stories of the creation, the stories of the Goddess of All Things? Perhaps the fascination with death is related to the philosophers' and poets' fascination with the world of shadows. "The everlasting correctness of things seen, perceived rightly, has banished not only the darkness of night but also the fires of noon. The *episteme* begins it surveying, measuring, and calculating on the basis of *shadows* projected by/upon surfaces, screens, and supports."[44] The living, flourishing girl, ready to embrace vision and understanding, to affirm visibility and the beautiful world transformed in and through its material and natural elements and tended by the goddess Demeter, this girl is swept away by a shadow to the world of shadows, a world where nothing happens, where nothing changes. What would Kore have seen of Hades made invisible by his helmet? Only his shadow. So it has been noted that the divine Ideas or forms, absolutely invisible themselves, are able to be detected only by the light that they stop, that outlines them, the light they block or cut off.[45] Certainly it is true that the strange prisoners in the cave, when forced up the rough, steep path into the sunlight would be pained and irritated, able at first to see shadows and nothing more. Only at night would a former prisoner be able to see and so to study the stars and the moon and only after a long time would "his" eyes adjust to the light so as to be able to see and to study the sun.

But perhaps we misunderstand this tale when we forget the warning of the philosopher that "the visible realm should be likened to the *prison dwelling*, and the light of the fire inside it to the power of the sun. . . . [T] he upward journey and the study of things above [are] as the upward journey of the soul to the intelligible realm."[46] The visible realm—all visibility—is on this account a prison. The invisible realm in which one's eyes are blinded is the intelligible realm. If a person were to turn from the study of what is divine to the human realm, their sight would indeed be *dim*. The visible, human world, the beautiful, self-created cosmos of the goddess would be difficult for them to see insofar as they would be unaccustomed to using their eyes at all! Vicious, clever people are said to have keen vision. Their sight is not inferior at all insofar as they are able to sharply distinguish all that they survey. How much more keen must be the vision of these individuals who live in the realm of that which is *coming to be*, what is *becoming*, as opposed to those who see nothing because they look only at *true things*, which is to say, they do not look with their eyes at all, but only with the intellect. For such an individual, the return to the cave is the only possibility of seeing at all; their eyes function at all only in the deepest shadow. Indeed, there in the cave, they see vastly better than the people who dwell there.

Poor vision as well as insufficient, strained views wreak havoc throughout the cosmos.[47] When Zeus drives his winged chariot looking after and putting in due order the heavens, the gods follow him to a place beyond the visible heavens, a high ridge whose circular motion carries them round and round. It is a strange place, without color, shape, or solidity, where Justice, Self-Control, Knowledge, are each invisible to the eye yet are visible to intelligence.[48] Souls that cannot move themselves fast enough and with enough self-control, fail to "glimpse" these truths. Not only that but they trample and strike one another, their wings breaking, their plumage shredding in a heavenly image of carnage and destruction. So they fall, fall, fall to earth where they are burdened by earthly bodies, hence mortality, finally loosing the wings of angels to foulness and ugliness. They are the victims of a weak memory and of senses "so murky that only a few people are able to make out, with difficulty, the original [Idea] of the likeness they encounter here."[49] Initially it seems that only "if it does not see *anything* true" does a soul fall to earth "burdened by forgetfulness and wrongdoing," and yet, "a soul that has seen the most will be planted in the seed of a man who will become a lover of wisdom."[50] Thus in spite of having seen some truth, glimpsing some Reality, some additional souls are still condemned to earthly existence. How then does this account of souls—both those crippled and opinionated and those close to things divine—how does this accord with the claim that *every* soul is immortal, for what is *psyche* if not something self-moved that never ceases to move and so is immortal? As a source of motion for itself and other moving things, immortal soul must not be able to be destroyed, otherwise it would never start up again. Absent immortality, the cosmos itself would collapse, never to be reborn.[51] Absent immortality, no souls would ever glimpse "Reality." Perhaps this is why some souls are looked after by philosophers who are not, strictly speaking, mortal but who are in some sense divine and immortal and grow wings. Those philosophers stand outside human concerns and draw close to the divine. They are said to practice philosophy without guile, they look after the boys—philosophically—perhaps it is only these souls, the philosophers and the boys they look after, who will ever return to the realms where Justice, Self-Control, and Knowledge reign. The rest, it appears are condemned, punished in places beneath the earth.[52]

So it has been argued that strictly speaking, non-philosophers, those who are truly mortals do not, indeed cannot, *look* upon the invisible Good since such "beings" have their ideal inscription only in the *psyche*. A young girl, daughter of the triple-Goddess, who wanders through fields of flowers is thought to be too close to the light, which is too close to the senses. Her *guileless virginity*, her *flourishing body* are not left undisturbed; she is not to be allowed to come to understanding through vision in the flourishing cosmos of the Goddess. Little wonder that Hades looks into the pupil of Kore to see the soul, for he would make her the soul, the psyche, the receptacle of his self-knowledge. Little wonder too that the image of the sun, useful in pointing to the power of Truth, nevertheless "must fall once more below the horizon. [Its] rays of light, *flashing*, burning, glaring, must cease to harry the Truth—*aletheia*—unchanging in the guileless virginity of the *logos*."[53] But is this so? The philosophers make claims. They say the maker looked at an appropriate form for each thing made, that these things once made exist in time, that time is a moving image of eternity. They articulate a hierarchy of imitations, reflections that *chill the light*, shielding us from the capacities of light to diffract and to vary our perceptions. May we not question their claims? May we not, like Kore, return from the dark, invisible realm to the daylight of sight and diffused reflections, from vision to understanding (*Sophia*)? Or are we to be confined to the direct passage from the visible to the invisible, from the so-called prison of vision to the self-knowing realm of the intelligible, a passage that may be nothing less than the passage from life to death?

Unable even to risk looking into a mirror, Ophion-Hades, the snake, gazes directly into the eye of Kore seeking to see and to know himself. Her retinas focus the light, keeping it from dispersing. Looking directly into the darkest part of her virgin eye, he sees and he seeks. . . and what he seeks there is the reflection of his own soul. Looking into the virgin pupil, seeing himself, "the lover takes pleasure in seeing [gazing at] his beloved" which would be, himself.[54] Still, the philosophers' claim that "people with bad eyesight often see things before those whose eyesight is keener."[55] The eyes of any philosopher who turns from the study of divine forms in the invisible, intelligible realm to human life, "his" eyes are filled with darkness, his eyesight dimmed.[56] Moreover, the craftsman and his followers operate, always, within the "*matrix of appropriation*."[57] The god "makes" the being, the form of each thing: heaven, earth, Hades. But even the work of the god, is an imitation, every "being," Sun, Moon, and Stars, a moving *image* of eternity. The apprentice philosopher, less skilled in *mimesis*, uses a mirror to imitate each thing that the god makes. But, better not to look at what is made, better to have bad eyesight or no eyesight at all. Better to seek and to see one's soul only, in the virgin eye of the Kore.

Unlike the wide-wandering goddess, Eurynome, whose constant motion and diffuse light illuminates all things, the philosopher's god is " the result of systems of mirrors that ensure a steady illumination, admittedly, but one without heat or brilliance. . . . [A]nd the presence, the essence of forms (usually translated under the name of Ideas) will be determined only by the light they have stopped, trapped, and that outlines them. The force of ideas, and their hold on memory, will be a function of the intensity of light that they are able to block or cut off."[58]

## What Is Philosophy?

Let us see and understand then, two images of philosophy. There is the powerful and dark image that lurks nearby, one whose shadow is cast over the cosmos to this very day. It is the image of the snake made god. It is the image of the continuum, the perfection of the undifferentiated, the one, the image of him who wanted everything to be as much like himself as possible.[59] Thus, it has been argued that for the apprentice philosopher, for the "man" in the cave, only death will lead to something more, to something beyond the realm of shadows, of blocked light and direct vision. Is the philosopher the messenger of death since "were it not for the words of the philosophy teacher who talks to you about immortality, who would be preoccupied with such an issue?"[60] Conception, rather than the transformation of the light that enters the eye into energy that is transmitted to the brain, conception instead finds its proper meaning as the re-birth into truth, a truth situated in an eternity beyond appearances, in the *One* that is always, as a wise philosopher among us has noted, mirrored at least twice, once by the god himself and once more by the philosopher or "his" apprentice.[61] Let us dare to question this image of philosophy, let us use the reflected light of the moon and let us conceive of a second image of philosophy, not an imitation but a transformation of the material and natural elements, an image more difficult to obtain. So much has been lost, so much appropriated.

The pre-Hellenic Pelasgian account of creation survives only in the most fragmented manner, but the standard interpretation of even these fragments overlooks the wide-wandering goddess Eurynome and seeks to establish the patrimony of Ophion. His banishment by the Goddess does not prevent the resurrection of his myth. Let us recall again, that the hierarchy of mirroring chills the reflected light of the moon and shields us from its capacity to vary our perception of forms. No wonder, in the tales of men, Kore is abducted. How else to fill life with shadows? "What happened in Eleusis was the separation and reunion of the dual goddess Demeter-Kore (*Deó*), she who sometimes appears as two barely differentiated figures."[62] Kore, the reflected light of Demeter, Demeter who is the life-giving light, the photon whose energy is transmitted in diffracted light rays. Demeter-Kore is the story of the reflected, refracted, and diffracted energy of that light, wandering in the world, transmitting its energy. In this cosmos, Kore returns from darkness to her origins, light and energy are conserved. Thus, even for the gods, Kore is a thing of wonder. She is divine evidence of the conservation of energy. The dark gods claim that the girl, after eating nothing for the entire period of her abduction, suddenly, forgetfully, outwitted or worse, full of secret desire, eats the seeds of the pomegranate. They claim that the fecundating light within her is the divine child—Phanes-Eros—who will force himself upon her. Let us resist the reduction of radiant light to psyche, that is, to a dark soul that sees nothing but itself in the emptiness of the eye of the Other. Let us be skeptical of the reports of the derisive "gardener" of Hades who jubilantly proclaims the downfall of the young girl, who hoots that she has eaten the seeds of the pomegranate. What, after all, is a gardener doing in the dark caves of the snake where no flowers bloom and no moonlight gives life? Let us also then be skeptical of the scholarly claims of the new gardeners of the dark, those who argue that Demeter-Kore is the psychological manifestation of the feminine psychology. And let us be equally skeptical of the philosopher, for whom Demeter-Kore is the origin of the philosophical receptacle of all becoming, the wet nurse of the cosmos. Let us instead propose, imagine, theorize that the Goddess, that Demeter-Kore are themselves concepts, concepts that constitute a first philosophy, a description of the nature of reality and of its creative and transformational structure. Let us not forget that energy is not lost, only transformed, constantly transformed. And let us then propose this new image of philosophy.

## Notes

This chapter first appeared in Dorothea Olkowski, *The Universal (In the Realm of the Sensible)* (Edinburgh and Columbia University Presses, 2007), 229–46.

1. Roberto Calasso, *The Marriage of Cadmus and Harmony*, trans. Tim Parks (New York: Alfred A. Knopf, 1993), 209.

2. Ibid., 203.

3. Erich Neumann, *The Great Mother, Analysis of an Archetype*, trans. Ralph Manheim (Princeton: Princeton University Press, 1974), 319, 262.

4. The claim that the flower is a narcissus is made in the Homeric "Hymn to Demeter," in *Hesiod, the Homeric Hymns and Homerica,* trans. Hugh G. Evelyn-White (London and Cambridge, MA: Loeb Classical Library, 1920), 289. Cited in Neumann, *The Great Mother,* 308.

5. Robert Graves reports that Ovid claims Kore was picking poppies based on several goddess images found in Crete and Mycenae. Robert Graves, *The Greek Myths: 1* (New York: Penguin, 1980), 24.15.

6. Ibid., 287–88.

7. Ibid., 31e. Graves relates Kore's abduction to the male usurpation of female agricultural mysteries (24.3).

8. Ibid., 1.a b, c, d; 1.1 In this archaic religion, paternity was nonexistent, fatherhood being attributed to various accidents, and snakes were associated with the underworld.

9. Calasso, *The Marriage of Cadmus and Harmony*, 208. Calasso does not make this connection between Ophion and Hades. But see Graves, *The Greek*

*Myths: 1*, 2b and Homer, *Iliad*, xvi, 261. Hades' claim on Zeus is that "Zeus senses the time had come for a new ring to be added to the knot of snakes (208)."

10. Graves, *The Greek Myths: 1*, 1.d, 1.3. The planetary powers of the goddess Eurynome appear to correspond to the deities of Babylonian and Palestinian astrology.

11. "The Orphics say that black winged Night, a goddess of whom even Zeus stands in awe. . . the triple-goddess ruled the universe until her scepter passed to Uranus. . . with the advent of patriarchialism." Graves, *The Greek Myths: 1*, 2.a, 2.2.

12. Hesiod, *Theogony*, 211–32.

13. Graves, *The Greek Myths: 1*, 4.a, 4.b, 4.c; 4.1, 4.2. Graves cites Hesiod, *Theogony*, 211–32 and Ovid, *Metamorphosis*, i–ii.

14. Plato, *Timaeus*, trans. Donald J. Zeyl, in *Plato, Complete Works*, ed. John M. Cooper (Indianapolis: Hackett, 1997), 29d-e. Also, 32b,c; 37a; 42a,b,c. Plato requires two middle terms for solid objects (e.g., a cube which is represented mathematically as 2 to the power of 3), so air and water together are the middle terms for fire and earth.

15. Graves, *The Greek Myths: 1*, 24. Demeter was the general name of a tripartite goddess: Core, Persephone, Hecate (green corn, ripe corn, harvested corn) (24.1).

16. Plato, *Alcibiades*, trans. D. S. Hutchinson, in *Plato, Complete Works*, 133a.

17. Plato, *Timaeus*, 47a. Philosophy is the supreme good eyesight offers.

18. Richard L. Gregory, *Eye and Brain, The Psychology of Seeing* (Princeton: Princeton University Press, 1990), 23.

19. Plato, *Timaeus*, 45b,c, d, e; 46d,e. Vision and all sensations are auxiliary causes of all things because they do not possess reason or understanding.

20. Irvin Rock, "The Intelligence of Perception," in *Perception* (New York: Scientific American Library, 1984), 15–16. The eye, however, is not analogous to a camera obscura.

21. Rock, *Perception*, 16, 3.

22. Ibid., 4. Rock also notes how different our perceptions are from what appears on the retina, thus the extent to which there is no direct perception.

23. Gregory, *Eye and Brain*, 25–26. Newton, Hugens, Foucault (the physicist) all contributed to these realizations.

24. Neumann, *The Great Mother*, 56–57; 25–33. See my, *Gilles Deleuze and the Ruin of Representation*, (Berkeley: University of California Press, 1999), especially chapter 7, "The Ruin of Representation."

25. Neumann, *The Great Mother*, 56–57, 314–15.

26. Ibid., 315.

27. Ibid., 319, 320. Often called a divine son, the moon nonetheless is a "mere variant" of the goddess's own self.

28. Ibid., 319.

29. For a clear explanation of the difference between finite and infinite, bounded and unbounded, see Rudy Rucker, *The Fourth Dimension, A Guided Tour of the Higher Universes* (Boston: Houghton Mifflin, 1984), 91–93.

30. I am moving away from the limitations of the psychological analysis of an archetype. See Neumann, *The Great Mother*, 55–58.

31. Ibid., 58. Neumann cites Bachoffen as the source of the thesis that what comes last will be looked upon as first and original, a hypothesis found in Aristotle. Bachoffen, Johann Jakob, *Das Mutterrecht*, *Gessamelte Werke*, Vol. I (Basel: 1948), 412 and Aristotle, *Parts of Animals*, trans. A. I. Peck (London and Cambridge, MA: Loeb Classical Library, 1937), 2.1.

32. Plato, *Timaeus*, 27d-28. The Greek word for "coming-to-be" used in the text is *genesis*. See Neumann, *The Great Mother*, 55.

33. Plato, *Timaeus*, 30 a, b, c, d, 31a. Neumann claims that with this, the moon principle was devalued and made into the soul, the highest material development that contrasts with the pure spirituality of the male. Neumann, *The Great Mother*, 57.

34. Plato, *Timaeus*, 30a-32b.

35. Ibid., 42an, b, c.

36. Ibid., 51e, 52a, b, c.

37. Ibid., 47b-c. There is "kinship" between the undisturbed orbits of the planets and our own disturbed orbits of understanding. Not quite *mimesis.*

38. Calasso, *The Marriage of Cadmus and Harmony*, 209.

39. Luce Irigaray, "Kore: Young Virgin, Pupil of the Eye," in *Speculum of the Other Woman*, trans. Gillian C. Gill (Ithaca: Cornell University Press, 1985), 150. Originally published as *Speculum de l'autre femme* (Paris: Les Editions de Minuit, 1974).

40. Calasso, *The Marriage of Cadmus and Harmony*, 211.

41. Ibid., 210. The richness of Calasso's text allows the reader to draw contradictory conclusions.

42. Neumann, *The Great Mother,* 325–326. Sophia has been completely lost to us.

43. Calasso, *The Marriage of Cadmus and Harmony*, 214. Calasso seems to forget that "revisions" of myths are the creation of poets and philosophers, not of the gods themselves.

44. Irigaray, "Kore," 148.

45. Ibid.

46. Plato, *Republic,* trans. G. M. A. Grube, revised C. D. C. Reeve, in *Plato, Complete Works,* 516a, 517b.

47. Ibid., 519a, 520b.

48. Plato, *Phaedrus*, trans. Alexander Nehamas and Paul Woodruff, in *Plato, Complete Works*, 246e.

49. Ibid., 250.

50. Ibid., 248 d. If this is not a discrepancy or mistranslation, then we have to take it seriously. Emphasis added.

51. Bruno Snell, *The Discovery of the Mind, The Greek Origins of European Thought*, trans. T. G. Rosenmeyer (New York: Harper and Row, 1960), 8–10. Plato, *Phaedrus*, 245e; 248 b, c, d.

52. Plato, *Phaedrus*, 248- 249a. Women, it appears, are entirely absent from the list of souls who may eventually glimpse truth.

53. Irigaray, "Kore," 148.

54. Aristotle, *Nicomachean Ethics,* trans. A. I. Peck (London and Cambridge, MA: Loeb Classical Library, 1937), 8.1157a3–14. Cited in David Halperin, "Why is Diotima a Woman?" 131, 113–51.

55 Plato, *Republic*, 595c-596a.

56. Ibid., 516e-517e. Such beings are unwilling to involve themselves in human affairs.

57. Irigaray, "Kore," 151. See Plato, *Republic*, 596c-597b.

58. Irigaray, "Kore," 148. Irigaray continues, "light is too corruptible, too shifting and inconstant to form the basis of the relationship to the self and to the All."

59. Calasso, *The Marriage of Cadmus and Harmony*, 207. Plato, *Timaeus*, 29e.

60. Luce Irigaray, "Plato's *Hystera*," in *Speculum of the Other Woman*, 354.

61. Ibid., 355.

62. Calasso, *The Marriage of Cadmus and Harmony*, 210. The previous sentence is a restatement of Irigaray, "Kore," 149.

Chapter 4

# In the Underworld with Irigaray

## Kathy Acker's *Eurydice*

Dianne Chisholm

> Is it possible that the girl can find her actual body, and so what gender might be, in language?. . . I am Alice who ran into a book to find herself. I have found only reiterations, the mimesis of patriarchy, or my inability to be.
>
> —Kathy Acker, "Seeing Gender"

In 1995 in an essay titled "Seeing Gender," feminist avant-gardist Kathy Acker proposes to encounter *"languages of the body"* "other than mimesis" where she can "find herself."[1] Her proposal loosely reiterates Luce Irigaray's contention that discourses of sexual difference reproduce phallogocentricism by deploying a mimesis of masculine self-representation, and that for a woman to present herself in language as subject of her own perception (and not merely as an imitation of what masculinist convention conceives her to be) she must *disrupt* and *exceed* this mimesis. Irigaray cues Acker to find (a) language capable of making palpable her sense of her sex and to displace the discursive privileging of specular conceptions—phallic speculations—of the body wherein the female sex is reductively regarded as castrated. Acker, moreover, cites Judith Butler on Irigaray on Plato on sexual difference to doubly underscore the matter of the body that Platonic idealism problematically views as "mere" immanence. Citing these interventions from the perspective of Alice, Acker looks beyond the looking-glass of philosophy's *self-reflecting subject* to the *other of the other* (gender/matter) "who" serves as mirror. Again, she mimes Irigaray, who in "Le miroir, de l'autre côté," views the world from Alice's fictive vantage. And Acker's Alice doesn't stop at philosophical reiteration. She proceeds to cite "an example" of language that finds her sex at the site of orgasm.

Acker claims to have understood "before I had ever read Plato, Irigaray, Butler, that, as a girl, I was outside the world. I wasn't. I had no name.

For me, language was being. There was no entry for me into language."[2] Plato, Irigaray, and Butler prompt her to see how this world of girlhood intuition is an already represented, man-made linguistic order wherein she partakes only as an alien. Now that theory helps her to acknowledge the mimetic limits of her universe, she can explain her flight from self-expression: "I was unspeakable so I ran into the languages of others."[3] Up to the moment of this theory-instigated revelation, she writes herself into a "realism" that exposes and sabotages the *othering* devices of literary discourse. Until then, most of her fiction deploys obscene and violent unravelings of the girl-killing, Oedipal family narrative romance that Culture reproduces over the ages. *Hannibal Lecter, My Father* (1991), a prose collection, and *My Mother: Demonology, A Novel* (1993) stand out as bold and shocking experiments in anti-Oedipal deconstruction.

"Seeing Gender" marks a turning point when Acker, no longer satisfied with deconstructive mimicry, looks for language "other than mimesis." Her new aim in writing is not to *fabricate* a feminine language (or *écriture feminine*) nor to visualize the female body in language: "I have become interested in languages which I cannot *make up*, which I cannot *create* or even *create in*: I have become interested in languages which I can only come upon (as I disappear), a pirate upon buried treasure. The dreamer, the dreaming, the dream."[4] Having repeatedly and thoroughly pirated language, she would now plunder the treasure that lies inarticulate at the heart of linguistic (mis)representation. Looking for a language that is most proximal to, or that most approximates, the body's "manifest-text" of experience, she experiments with writing-to-orgasm (that is, writing while masturbating) where she encounters language "that moves through me."[5] Here language comes to her, becomes her, as a dream-like production that speaks itself, for itself, in its own medium, as its own oracle, an auto-production perversely akin to the automatic writing of surrealism and the Beats.

Shifting from parodic deconstruction to orgasmic production, Acker moves beyond what Irigaray calls "the initial phase" of language work that women must undertake to recover their other body. This move does not exit the realm of language or mimesis but enacts what Irigaray calls "the hypothesis of a reversal—within the phallic order."

There is, in an initial phase, perhaps only one "path," the one historically assigned to the feminine: that of *mimicry*. One must assume the feminine role deliberately. Which means already to convert a form of subordination into an affirmation, and thus to begin to thwart it. . . . To play with mimesis is thus, for a woman, to try to recover the place of her exploitation by discourse, without allowing herself to be simply reduced to it. It means to resubmit herself—inasmuch as she is on the side of the "perceptible," of "matter"—to "ideas," in particular to ideas about herself, that are elaborated in/by a masculine logic, but so as to make "visible," by an effect of playful repetition, what was supposed to remain invisible: the cover-up of a possible operation of the feminine in language.[6]

Acker initiates an advanced phase of finding resources of language that disrupt, exceed, and *precede* phallic mimesis. For Irigaray, women's writing has a genealogy that to lay bare we must "excavate deeper into the earth, to where the cultural vestiges lie concealed, and to rediscover there a more archaic arche behind that beginning represented by Greece, and the concept of origin which Greece set in place."[7] Acker cites this pre-Hellenic matrix directly in a leap beyond discursive mimicry to a language of prior possibility. A preliminary attempt to access a more primal, archaic and corporeal, dimension of language, "Seeing Gender" performs, or at least gestures toward, what Irigaray identifies in Plato as a *first mimesis*:

> In Plato, there are two *mimeses*. To simplify: there is *mimesis* as production, which would lie more in the realm of music, and there is the *mimesis* that would already be caught up in a process of *imitation, specularization, adequation,* and *reproduction.* It is the second form that is privileged throughout the history of philosophy and whose effects/symptoms, such as latency, suffering, paralysis of desire, are encountered in hysteria. The first form seems always to have been repressed, if only because it was constituted as an enclave within a "dominant" discourse. Yet it is doubtless in the direction of, and on the basis of, that first *mimesis*, that the possibility of a woman's writing may come about.[8]

Acker's orgasmic citation is expressly not mimetic in the *second* sense of mimesis that philosophy takes the prerogative to deploy since Plato. Instead, it invokes a repressed and forgotten "'first' stake in mimesis" which Irigaray interprets to be "that of re-producing (from) nature."[9] "Re-semblance cannot do without red blood," she explains. "Mother-nature-matter must go on forever nourishing speculation. But this re-source is also rejected as the waste product of reflection, cast outside as what resists it: as madness."[10] Acker cites a language that minding her orgasm produces in the process of having an orgasm. As proximal to her perception of her sex as she can come, she writes/masturbates/sees without deferring to received conceptions of her sex: her citation of perception "re-produces from nature" and avoids reproducing the prevailing (phallic) conception of nature.

Acker concurs with Irigaray that for women to come into their own in language, they must *do more with* language than mime phallogocentric discourse, however parodically. To rediscover material of its own, woman's writing must be *mimetically re-sourceful.* It must, as Irigaray says, "cross back through the mirror that subtends all speculation" and find the "elsewhere of 'matter,'" and above all the "'elsewhere' of feminine pleasure."[11] If what patriarchal discourse "sees" in its conceptual regard of sexual difference is centered on the phallus to the exclusion of female difference, then nothing could be more disturbing and ex-centric to that conception than "seeing" that other body revealing and reveling in its own otherness. Irigaray calls for a transgression that writes woman's ecstasy into expression where it has otherwise been inhibited, repressed, and misrecognized in the service of phallic jouissance:

> Feminine pleasure has to remain inarticulate in language, in its own language, if it is not to threaten the underpinnings of logical operations. And so what is most strictly forbidden to women today is that they should attempt to express their own pleasure. . . . *Feminine pleasure* can be found only at the price of *crossing back through the mirror that subtends all speculation*. . . . A playful crossing, and an unsettling one, which would allow woman to rediscover the place of her "self-affection." Of her "god," we might say.[12]

To clarify: instead of a language other than mimesis, Acker's orgasmic passage presents what Irigaray invokes as that other "first mimesis." She performs what Irigaray proposes, crossing the mirror she has been holding *as yet* to discourse *to* the site of pleasure where language comes to her. Language is Acker's expressive medium but it does not mediate her orgasm in the Name of the Father. An onanistic production, her orgasmic passage mimes a self-affection that is irreducible and inappropriate to His desire. Her/e sensation finds expression in language that foregoes sentential logic and the copula of predication—the *logos* of the Subject—and that "lie[s] more in the realm of music." She cites her pleasure with tactile arousal ("so intense it can hardly be handled"), citing its acoustic rhythms and oneiric (animistic) images. A performative utterance of efficacious affect, this passage exemplifies what Irigaray postulates as feminine *style*: "tactile," "fluid," replete with motifs of "'self-touching,' of 'proximity.'"[13]

"Seeing Gender" exemplifies "that first mimesis" to which Irigaray alludes. So I argue as prelude to my discussion of a later, more exemplary production. "Eurydice in the Underworld" is literally, and literarily, a play with *both mimeses.* Part drama, part diary, and part epistolary fiction, Acker's "Eurydice" is a postmodernist play with *second* mimesis that re-produces simultaneously (1) the myth of Orpheus and Eurydice, (2) Irigaray's deconstruction of the dramaturgy at work in Plato's cave allegory, and (3) Acker's report of her cancer treatment in "The Gift of Disease."[14] In this manifold production of reproductions, Acker's mimesis is excessive and disruptive. And more. In its play with myth, it finds the "elsewhere" of Eurydice/woman, on the other side of the cave, in the underworld that lies repressed beneath "Greece" (patriarchal civilization/Oedipus) or the "enclave" of that first mimesis.

In "Plato's *Hystera*," the last section of *Speculum of the Other Woman*, Irigaray uses a critical mimesis to expose the phallogocentric rhetoric of Plato's idealism. Focusing on the trope of the *hystera* (uterus/cave) of Plato's allegory, she recites and reveals discursive passages where matter/mother/nature figure as mere mirror to observations that, in a tricky dialectical maneuver, lose sight of their material origins altogether. "Eurydice in the Underworld" reenacts Irigaray's deconstructive display. It puts a face (prosopopeia) to the feminine "who" Plato defaces in speculations that interpellate matter/mater/nature as unbecoming ground to Man's transcendent form, and it locates Eurydice where she can see herself coming in and out of perception and existence. Shades of Alice, Acker's Eurydice withdraws into the recesses of the underworld beyond the screen that subtends the Platonic mirror, re-turning our vision to the obscurely lit side of the cave. In so doing, she stages a reversal in the history of enlightenment, finding resources of knowledge in myth in place of Platonic science. She re-instates that *first* mimesis of an embodied perception of the world over that *second* mimesis of an idealized conception (of an embodied perception) of the world *that overlooks (sublimates) its materiality.*

Acker's Eurydice wears the tragic mask of today's woman who faces an ordeal with breast cancer. In Acker's recasting, the operating theater of modern Western medicine is a late and deadly reproduction of the *hystera*/speculum of Plato's founding allegory of philosophy, which is arguably already a gynocidal reproduction of the Orphic myth. If, in the speculative language of philosophy, Plato restages Orpheus's passage to and from the underworld where Orpheus deflects Eurydice/woman to the chthonic shades before ascending to the light of the upper world, Acker reverses this philosophical stage and subverts Plato's sublimation of the myth. She re-restages the passage to the underworld, reverses the orientation of transcendence and transubstantiation, and resurrects the chthonic subtext of Plato's cave allegory into an "overworld" of flesh, blood, and dream.

Given naturally to ecstasy, sensation, and dream, Acker's Eurydice resides in "the overworld." Only after being "poisoned" by diagnostic and therapeutic surgery, does she "sink" into "the underworld"/"hell" of disease. We see Eurydice's passage from Eurydice's perspective, reflecting Acker's ordeal with conventional medicine. Orpheus descends with Eurydice. She addresses him as "OR" (personifying his ambivalence); he addresses her as "YOU" (her second person to his primary narcissism). Dialogue parodies Socratic dialogue in that, in place of a master subject who feigns ignorance to promote knowledge, we see an institutional authority who feigns knowledge to deploy ignorance. Displaced is Socrates, wisdom's midwife who solicits ideas already pregnant in the mind of his pupil. Focus is on "YOU," second person and second sex. YOU receives information from her oncologist and his "gynaecological colleage" who, under question, concede they "don't know."[15] Orpheus enters the scene in epistemic "shambles." He loves sex with Eurydice despite the removal of her breasts that makes her seem boyish. He accompanies her "monologue," chanting doubtfully, "Eurydice. Is she nothing/Or is she your mirror? I don't know anymore."[16] He follows her to the point of no return—to death where she resolves to turn as her only escape from metaphysical disease. Repelled by YOU's "U-turn," as he calls it, he hovers ambivalently between worlds, and hysterically between sexes, where he hopes to love again.

Acker's Eurydice "escapes" hell by becoming "dead" to its operations of truth. She retreats into the the grave to unearth deadened layers of repressed memory and perception. She thus balks every tradition of Eurydice, from classical myth to classical opera to Maurice Blanchot. How, then, does Acker's restaging of Irigaray's restaging of Plato's restaging of the Orphic myth draw that first mimesis to the fore?

## Plato's Hystera/Eurydice's "Overworld"

"Plato's *Hystera*" reveals what Irigaray calls the "stage-set up" of Plato's complex speculation on the origin and illumination of Truth in that passage of *The Republic* known as the cave allegory. Irigaray recites the staging of speculation and amplifies its "scenography" ("the architectonics of its theatre, its framing in space-time, its geometric organization, its props, its actors, their respective positions, their dialogues, indeed their tragic relations, without overlooking the *mirror*, most often hidden, that allows the logos, the subject, to reduplicate itself, to reflect itself by itself").[17] She exposes the mimetic device whereby Plato sees a paternal heaven of self-generating Forms, not mother earth, to be source of all conception, including those shady percepts that appear to emanate from the mythic underworld, as well as shimmering sense-impressions of the natural world. Laying bare the hysteria of Plato's theatre, Irigaray shows how the *hystera* acts as a speculum that paranoically screens what it would illumine with projections of phallic narcissism. It is this phantasmatic space of obstetrical enlightenment that sets the stage for the primal scene of patriarchal mimesis. Irigaray reviews the scene stage by stage in architectonic detail I will not rehearse here. Suffice it to say that Acker pirates the mimetic parody of "Plato's *Hystera*" and recasts mater/matter/nature as center stage of Eurydice's passage of revelation.

"Eurydice in the Underworld" recasts Eurydice into a space of *three* worlds: "the overworld," "the underworld," and "the dead world." Parodying in contradiction Plato's teleological stage-set, which casts the natural (sensual) world between the mythical (maternal/chthonic) underworld and the paternal (Ideal, solar) heaven, Acker sets the overworld of dream and sensuality above the dead world of patriarchal reality and the underworld that is the creepy core of the dead world. Eurydice's underworld is the "operating room" of the dead world's mimetic machinations. Eurydice passes from the overworld to the underworld and to death's obscure depths, where, "dead" to the reality(-claims) and torturous prognostications of patriarchy, she digs up wasted potential for reimagining the maligned and malignant body of Western thought.

The Irigarayan genius of Acker's "Eurydice" is its recasting of "Plato's *Hystera*" as the scene of obstetrical enlightenment where the meta/physicians of Western medicine perform radical surgery on the diseased female body. As we know from Dr. Susan Love, foremost authority on breast cancer, standard treatment is to "slash, burn, and poison."[18] According to Love, the body and not just the cancer (which is also the body) is targeted for warfare, and the breast is the site for the eradication of delinquent mat(t)er. Love's body is poignantly represented in "The Gift of Disease" where Acker outlines her oncological reduction to "dead" or "diseased, meat."[19] In "Eurydice in the Underworld" Acker returns to the scene of her double mastectomy in the guise of the specularized woman of Greek myth and gravely reiterates the patriarchal thinking to which she is subjected. "Eurydice's monologue" starts to tell the story of Acker's diagnosis and treatment (reciting "The Gift of Disease"), but is interrupted by Orpheus's song of love's descent "into the unknown." There follows the scene of Eurydice's passage through hospital "hallways" to the O.R. Foregrounding the space of that passage, Acker performs a topographic mime that reverses the specular trappings of "Plato's *Hystera*."

Eurydice descends into the underworld from the overworld to where she escapes *after* surgery. The scene opens in the overworld two days after her meeting with the doctor where she is told her prognosis and schedule of chemotherapy. She sits on a "red bed" with stuffed animals, her hair aflame "since she's mad."[20] "Huge windows surround the head of [her] bed" in a "room [that] overlooks the world. Through the glass, there are hills." Looking "through the glass," Eurydice sees that "earth and air contain the same light: light coming out from them rather than to them," thus verifying the cliché "everything bathed in light."[21] A device of *hysteron proteron* casts the space of recovery as prior to the space of surgery, reversing Plato's casting of the paternal solar world as prior to and above the maternal chthonic world. The recovery room is "perched" above the world though it is exceedingly womb-like or natal with its red bed and stuffed animals. Plato's *hystera* is below the world where the lighting is very bad, especially for prisoners of the cave who can see only the shadows of idols cast by the artificial light of fire and are thrice removed from the true light of the upper world. Eurydice's womb/room opens to the natural light of earth and air, just as it is lit on the interior by her "flaming hair."

Eurydice's recovery is nourished by "childishness, dreams, insanity" or precisely those realms of life that Plato's cave prisoner must renounce (as regressive) if he is to arrive at enlightenment.[22] "A spitting image of Hades,"[23] Orpheus joins Eurydice in this world and, defying the (clinical) reality principle, they begin to fuck. If breast cancer treatment is one of woman's most alienating passages through patriarchy's speculum, Acker's antidote is to get back in touch with her body. Fucking is especially potent since it nourishes her senses and lifts her elsewhere, to love, where she "loves *being*"[24] and where she is delivered from the prognostic death sentence and anaesthesia of institutional logic. But surgery exhausts her resources. As Orpheus "lifts himself over her body," Eurydice "sinks into sleep" and into the scene of oblivion that awaits her in the underworld.[25]

Acker recasts Eurydice's descent into the underworld as the scene of her transport to the O.R. This in turn casts another light on Plato's scenography. Acker's womb/room of recovery is radically other than the operating room of patriarchal mimesis. *They are "worlds" apart.* Here, the metaphysical conceit with which Plato occludes sight of the mat(t)er and asserts paternal superiority, originality, and luminosity is dramatically subverted. Eurydice enters the underworld's operating room and senses, with painful acuity, her subjection to various machinations of "enlightenment." Transported by wheelchair, she is intimidated by the "highly polished" and "grandiose" walls of the first hallway. As the scene "progresses" to a "far wider hallway devoid of warmth," she withdraws under the "baby blue wheelchair blanket." All is illumined with piercing intensity. "Above, glaring lights dominate reality. Yet such over-the-top lighting does not lessen the spectrality of the scene. It is haunted by "moving figures in pale, that is, puke-green, who may or may not be human"[26] and who wield instruments of torture. Surgical technicians and anaesthetists, these figures prepare Eurydice for her operation. Like the obstetric "necromancers" of "Plato's *Hystera,*" they "uphold the process of mimesis" but do not see "the effects of their own sorcery."[27]

Though medical technology is more advanced than the dissembling smoke and mirrors of Plato's magicians, it is also more brutal: "the premed" makes her brains nauseous, the anaesthesia threatens to make her vomit and choke to death, and cardio-cables threaten to electrocute her. As un-womb-like as could be, the O.R. is "a room designed to suck up human life." A horror-parody of Mother Nature, it strikes Eurydice as a puppeteer's execution chamber: "splashes of pale green can be seen and cords hanging from the walls" and "all of the machines possess a great number of cords."[28] Orpheus is barred entry to the O.R. since the operations of obstetrical enlightenment are reserved for women. We see him "wandering around the grounds of the hospital," looking for Eurydice who is now lost to this world.

As the scene draws to an end, we see that medical theatrics have had little effect on Eurydice's worldview. At their most potent, they force her to "escape reality by being dead."[29] Such course of action runs wildly counter to the teleological rebirth or "renaissance of truth" undertaken by Plato's prisoner in his ascent from the cave. But as Irigaray muses, "the second birth, secondary origin, renaissance or reminiscence of truth will never, simply, defer the *hysterical tropism.* The discourse of reason, solar and paternal metaphor, will never oust the fantasy structure of the cave completely."[30] Eurydice sinks even deeper into the grave where the fantasy of medicine/metaphysics deposits her. She finds herself "in the middle of dirt" in a subversive, subterranean fantasy of female immanence and other waste-products of enlightenment. Dead, she stages her return in writing, though she refuses to rely on the "dead letter" of communicative discourse. Instead, she draws on the matrix of body, memory, and language that envelops her cryptically in dream.

## Writing Matters

The "Diary written by Eurydice when she's dead" is subversive in the sense Irigaray intended for woman's writing. It inscribes "*disruptive excess*" from the "feminine side" that "puts the torch to fetish words, proper terms, well-constructed forms" and it de-sublimates woman's embodied sense of herself.[31] Being dead, Eurydice breaks out of the "deathhouse" that "rules had placed [her] in" in life. "The fuck with rules,"[32] she writes and, indeed, her writing fucks with the reality principle and narrative logic. On the other side of the grave, she is optimally poised to revisit the deathhouse and dig up the dirt on its nefarious executions.

Eurydice reappears in scenes written in her diary. Diary writing is intimate writing, the obverse of philosophy's overseeing, metadiscourse. What she excavates there is a perverse archeology of knowledge. For *there* is a scene of writing that supplies the debris and detritus of memory that has been repressed and sublimated according to reality's rules. The scene of Eurydice's diary writing is the crypt of (her) memory. *What* gets written there is the cryptic material of remembering without observing the rules. Eurydice writes what matters to her and other girls who have been executed in reality's deathhouse. Her writing re-members the shattered body of girlhood memory and entails the dream work of sur-realism. Though intimate, her diary is not personal. Wearing the mask of classical myth, memory descends underground to reveal the re-sources of subculture. Girlhood memory, not the Library of official, grown-up Culture, comprises the dirt of memorial substance. When Eurydice remembers the deathhouse, she mimes the regressive speech of the girl. Or, she mimes a girl's memory of female subculture that official culture recuperates in language reserved for patriarchal significance.

The diary records girlhood memory-fantasies of deathhouses. These memory-fantasies revisit the scene of the cave/underworld as structured by Eurydice's (not her meta/physician's) phantasmatic vision. Two deathhouses stand out: "the courtroom" and "the school." In the scene of "the courtroom of the dead" Eurydice sees herself "in the back of the courtroom" from the "entrance of all that lies upstairs." From her vantage, she witnesses "a case that is being heard" of another girl who previews her own case. If she sees copies of herself everywhere, she, herself, escapes trial as she is judged to have "become insane."[33] Exploiting the asylum of insanity, she entertains a mad dream of another mad girl on trial. Maria Tsvetaeva appears as Eurydice's re-semblance, that is, not as rehabilitative nationalism sees her but as her unruly *girl* self: "forever wild-cropped hair, boy's look, blew smoke in parent's face, fucked around, not yet seventeen." With a girlish delight in the obscene, Eurydice invokes the bloody and tearful, excremental excess of Tsvetaeva's "yucky story" that ends with her suicide in prison. The courtroom transmogrifies into the "red room" of girlhood memory where Tsvetaeva's passionate life is thrown into relief.

In "the school of the dead," Eurydice enters a scene of disciplinary order that quickly degenerates into a scene of murder which she obscurely remembers having committed. Fearing "the authorities," she escapes "out toward the sea"[34] from where she can see the entire necropolis of deathhouses. She draws a "picture of the underworld" that retraces her route on a horizontal plane over her vertical line of descent. The picture reveals space around, beside, between the courtroom and the school: interstices in institutional space that she can safely navigate. "What was there was hidden, but not to me. Through passageways that were unable to be remembered. . . . To where I'd be safe."[35] With this other map of the world she orients herself as if "reality was emotional" and as if she can "perceive solely by feeling."[36]

In the final scene, the schoolhouse becomes a theater and disciplinary sex gives way to carnival and sexual anarchy. Eurydice fucks a troupe member with joyful abandon, and proclaims: "We are gods." The curtain of the theater's red room draws back to reveal the overworld. "Trees. . . bend rather than reach up toward the sky, down to the ground, where there's a rose above the earth."[37] Instead of arising from the cave into Truth's transcendent light, Eurydice beholds the rose of earthly dawn and sensual revelation. Plato's theatrical tropism is entirely reversed.

"Eurydice in the Underworld" carries through the Irigarayan project that Acker began with "Seeing Gender" in 1995. If that project aims to rediscover the first stakes of mimesis, namely to reproduce from nature in resemblance to red-blooded matter, then the stakes are higher for Acker who in 1997 is living and dying with cancer. Eurydice is Acker's *semblable* whose mythic passage Acker advances from specular violence to visceral insight. En route from life to death and back again, she sees the mortifying girl-killing institutions of "real living." But from the grave vantage of seeing herself dead to this reality, she looks again on mortality, with all the senses of a feeling and bleeding creature, of matter/mater born. "Eurydice in the Underworld" re-turns reality and re-produces mortal sense with obscene and touching re-cognition.

## Notes

A different version of this chapter was published under the title "Kathy Acker's Grave Songs and Visceral Insights," in *Parallax: Journal of Metadiscursive Theory and Cultural Practices* 11, no. 3 (2003): 40–54.

1. Kathy Acker, "Seeing Gender" (1995), in *Bodies of Work: Essays* (New York: Serpent's Tail, 1997), 166.

2. Ibid., 161.

3. Ibid.

4. Ibid., 166.

5. Ibid., 167.

6. Luce Irigaray, *This Sex Which Is Not One*, trans. Gillian C. Gill (Ithaca: Cornell University Press, 1985 ), 76.

7. Luce Irigaray, *Speculum of the Other Woman,* trans. Gillian C. Gill (Ithaca: Cornell University Press, 1985), 64. Irigaray refers to Freud's finding of the pre-Oedipal phase in girls "as a *surprise*, like the *discovery* in another field [but is it really another?] of the *Minoan-Myceanaean civilization behind the civilization of Greece*."

8. Irigaray, *This Sex Which Is Not One*, 131.

9. "As guardians of 'nature,' are not women the ones who maintain, thus who make possible, the resource of mimesis for men? For the logos?" (*This Sex Which Is Not One*, 77).

10. Ibid.

11. Ibid., 76.

12. Ibid., 77.

13. Ibid., 79.

14. "The Gift of Disease" (1996) was published online: http://acker.thehub.com.au/gift.html. "Eurydice in the Underworld" was published in book form, along with "Requiem" and excerpts from previous publications under the title *Eurydice in the Underworld* (London: Arcadia, 1997). "The Gift of Disease,"

"Eurydice in the Underworld," and "Requiem" are Acker's consecutive "treatments" of disease in writing; they correspond to different phases of her metastatic malignancy and of her search for alternative therapies.

15. Acker, "Eurydice in the Underworld," 6.

16. Ibid., 9.

17. Irigaray, *This Sex Which Is Not One*, 75.

18. "We have always talked about breast cancer in militaristic words—the 'war on cancer,''she lost her battle with cancer.' This comes from approaching cancer as if it were a foreign invader attacking a woman's body, and our job is to kill every last cancer cell. Surgery, radiation therapy, and chemotherapy (slash, burn, and poison) are very crude treatments, attempts to blast away cancer cells while hoping we don't kill too many healthy cells in the process. But, in reality, cancer cells aren't foreign invaders; they're our own cells" (Susan M. Love, *Dr. Susan Love's Breast Book*, 3rd ed. [Cambridge, MA: Perseus, 2000], xviii).

19. "I realized that if I remained in the hands of conventional medicine, I would soon be dead, rather than diseased, meat. For conventional medicine was reducing me, quickly, to a body that was only material, to a body without hope and so, without will. To a puppet, who separated by fear from her imagination and vision, would do whatever she was told" ("The Gift of Disease," 3 <http:// acker. the).

20. Acker, "Eurydice in the Underworld," 1.

21. Ibid.

22. Irigaray, *Speculum of the Other Woman*, 273.

23 Acker, "Eurydice in the Underworld," 2.

24. Ibid., 25; my emphasis.

25. Ibid., 4.

26. Ibid., 10–11.

27. Irigaray, *Speculum of the Other Woman*, 251, 263.

28. Acker, "Eurydice in the Underworld," 13.

29. Ibid., 12.

30. Irigaray, *Speculum of the Other Woman*, 274.

31. Irigaray, *This Sex Which Is Not One*, 78–79.

32 Acker, "Eurydice in the Underworld," 24.

33. Ibid., 19.

34. Ibid., 21.

35. Ibid., 22.

36. Ibid., 21.

37. Ibid., 22.

# Chapter 5

# Textiles that Matter

## Irigaray and Veils

Anne-Emmanuelle Berger

### "Luce Irigaray is obsessed with veils."

Going beyond the psychoanalytic account of feminine masquerade in "The Blind Spot of an Old Dream of Symmetry," Irigaray analyzes veiling as a strategy designed to facilitate women's participation as commodities in a market economy of sexual exchange: "*To sell herself*," she writes, "*woman has to veil* as best as she can how priceless she is in the sexual economy" (my emphasis).[1] The veil does not only hide the hole in the woman's middle, it sells her off. How so? "By wrapping her up." And Irigaray goes on: "By abstracting 'products,' by making them universal and interchangeable without recognizing their differences" (BS, 115). Here, the veiling gesture is not so much conceived as a cover-up of woman's threatening sexual "difference" (her lack), than as a way of masking differences between women, rendering them invisible in order to make them look identical, hence ready for both infinite substitutability and commercial circulation. The "wrapping" of human subjects turns them into "products." The "veil" in this sense is shown to be that which makes women into generic objects of consumption.

In *An Ethics of Sexual difference*, Irigaray offers yet a different view of the veil: she wonders how a woman can appropriate for herself the place that she is, culturally, for others. The place that she is in the first place, is the home, and the first home in the cultural unconscious is the womb. Irigaray describes the womb as a protective envelope, a kind of inner skin that the patriarchal order has appropriated for men's use, leaving the homemaker paradoxically homeless, hence also motherless. "The maternal-feminine remains the place separated from 'its' own place, deprived of its place. She is or ceaselessly becomes the place of the other," writes Irigaray.[2]

The drama of woman's expropriation plays itself out on the cultural theater of her exploited nudity, be it for pornographic or artistic ends. Deprived of her envelope or rather of the use of it, woman is as if naked. This is why she actually exhibits herself as such and why she appears as such in the cultural imaginary. Irigaray reads woman's perverse undressing as a symptomatic staging of her symbolic destitution as well as a sign of her enforced complicity with a phallocentric order that imposes its spectacularizing gaze on her. In this context, and contrary to the argument she puts forward in "The Blind Spot," Irigaray does not describe the practice of veiling or rather of "enveloping" oneself as a means for woman to compensate for the wound of castration and to sell herself off by propping herself up. Rather, she reads veiling as an effort women make to shelter themselves from the expropriating gaze, and to recreate, if not redeem, a protective place for themselves, that is, ultimately, the mother('s) place.[3] Note that the veil undergoes a gender change in *An Ethics*, thanks to the preferred use of the word *envelope*. Such a lexical change makes the veil differ linguistically—thus also, one might argue, symbolically—from the wrap women weave under the ironic gaze of Freud, Lacan, and Marx. For the word *envelope* is feminine in Irigaray's mother tongue, hence better suited to the purpose of making up for a woman's skin. Here then, against her analysis of the function of "wrapping" in *Speculum*, Irigaray is making an argument in favor of a certain kind of veil. A maternal veil, gendered feminine, the "envelope" would shield women against violent exposure and self-effacement.

In "Plato's *Hystera*," the other major piece of *Speculum*, Irigaray describes the cave, this obscured base (and basement) of Platonic idealism, in the following manner:

> An enclosure, veil-wrapping of the originary blind incarceration, which has been turned over to become the circus and backdrop of representation. . . . Limiting the view but ensuring the reproduction by *reflection* of what is claimed to take place behind.[4]

The "enclosure" or "*enceinte*" in French recalls "la femme enceinte" (the pregnant woman). According to Irigaray, the cave of Plato's *Republic* figures the material and maternal enclosure of life. Countering Plato's metaphysics with a strange mythophysics, Irigaray reads men's attempt to peep outside the cave by turning their back to it in order to get a glance at the shining truth, as an allegory of the willful masculine repression of maternal origins. In her view, the dark envelope of the cave is not so much pierced through by men's gaze in their effort to look outward and upward, as it is stretched inside out like a veil, to be used as the very screen that will allow for the spectacle of origin to be replayed, and for speculation on origin to arise as if from above, from the sky of ideas, for man's exclusive enlightenment. Covering up the original cover amounts to covering the original and actual process of all production, including the production of ideas. In three words that Irigaray likes to repeat from book to book, the "hystera" is and always has been: "*violée, volée, voilée*," a linguistic chain of unfortunate events felicitously translated by Gilian McGill as: "Rape, Rob, Robe."[5]

In "Belief Itself," written on the occasion of the first big international conference on Derrida at Cerizy, Irigaray states in a footnote that "the intent of [her] text" is "to raise a veil from the scene of belief and the scene of truth." "The woman's revelation," she goes on to say, "may seem violent and sacrilegious to some people, both male and female. But without that revelation which reaches beyond the canonic enclosure of revelation, fidelity in history and confidence in certain of its figures become beliefs, dogmas, rites that are in part sacrificial and repressive."[6] Now, as one knows, the word *revelation* literally means "the lifting of a veil" (*velum* in Latin). As Irigaray herself obliquely points out, the original and canonical use of the term is a theological one. "Revelatio" is a late Latin neologism first found in Christian writings to designate the divine knowledge bestowed on chosen humans by God. Such a sentence, with its preaching overtones and its sweeping pronouncements, is prudently hidden in the folds of a footnote; but it will become a stamp of Irigaray's later work, when she boldly decides to lift the veil on her own womanly ability (and right) to reveal new ways to love to the world.

For the time being, what Irigaray reveals in "Belief Itself" is indeed the presence and action of a hitherto unnoticed veil. Commenting on the famous scene of the Fort-Da game analyzed by Freud, she draws the reader's attention away from the reel whose manipulation by little Ernst had captivated the semi-blind eyes and minds of a string of great male thinkers from Freud up to Derrida, and directs it toward the small semi-transparent veil that, according to her, surrounds the little boy's crib. Now, she assumes, as she says in a footnote added in the English version of her essay, that the bed mentioned in Freud's account is a crib, and that the "veil" ("*verhangten Bettschens*") is white and semi-transparent. Yes, look, she sees it almost clearly, just lift your mental eyelids. I quote:

> The curtain or veil that covered the bed or the crib was white or very light in color, and probably was not fully opaque. . . . The child throws something over there, beyond but not behind a wall or behind a curtain that concealed, hid her [the mother], hid him definitively. (BI, 30)

Through the lens of the little white veil, Irigaray rewrites the Fort-Da scene and turns it into an allegory of the genesis of a masculine (thus specular) sexual economy, whereby the veil that "stands between [mother and son]" (34) allows the latter not so much to overcome the mother's absence as to keep her at a distance, neither present nor absent, behind the veil, as if she was an image of herself, already a ghost, blurring by her spectral presence the limits between "reality and unreality, truth and untruth" (32).

The veil performs yet one more important function in this revelatory scene, which, you may remember, is meant to take place at Cerisy, in the very presence of Derrida. The revealing veil held out by Irigaray manages to hide Derrida completely from view, at least from her view, with an efficiency that outmatches the veiling of his mother by little Ernst. There is, strikingly, hardly any mention of Derrida's argument in this piece, which presumably takes as its point of departure Derrida's reading of Freud's reading of little Ernst's play, and whose stated goal is to say something about Derrida's work. Certainly, the veil or sail (*sail* and *veil* are the same word in French, albeit gendered differently) used by Irigaray to signal and play out her intellectual relation to Derrida at that moment, is not white. One can in turn read this piece as an allegory of her complicated relation to Derrida and deconstruction. It becomes more and more apparent as one reads on in Irigaray, that the deconstructive approach adopted in part in her early work is progressively abandoned. Yet, Irigaray's texts have strangely retained certain elements of the language of deconstruction, as mere props, it seems; a way, perhaps, of dressing up on some occasions, when she goes to town.

Spurred on nonetheless by Derrida, *Marine Lover* takes on Nietzsche's statements on the seduction of women in a long section entitled, as one might expect, "Veiled lips," and goes on to rewrite Nietzsche's *Birth of Tragedy* and *Twilight of the Idols* from a different sexual or gendered point of view in a section called "When the Gods Are Born."[7] *Marine Lover* may be Irigaray's most thoroughly "Greek" text. "Veiled Lips" reads as a kind of "Greek" rewriting of "The Blind Spot." Irigaray repeats her argument about the construction of femininity as screen, but this time she aims at Zeus rather than at Freud. Zeus has authored, indeed borne, Athena. And Athena, in Irigaray's view, is the veiled woman par excellence, that is to say, man's perfect cover-up: her gender masks the operation of the veil as male: See what she writes on page 101: "Athena: horror concealed, wound masked, the difference in values covered over. Pretense of the God of gods—standing in the long white robe that veils even the feet." Or on page 102: "Without any doubt, virile, if she lets fall her tunic. Armed: femininity. Playing with every disguise. . . . Adorned, femininity—the father's thought appearing over female authority." And again, on page 103: "Pallas—the white veil over her body, the affected candor, the shroud over the woman, the mortal trappings."

Already in "Plato's *Hystera*" and in *An Ethics of Sexual Difference* but more insistently in *Marine Lover*, Irigaray emphasizes the paradoxical results of a certain politics of veiling. In places and cultures where the veil is conceived as both a tool and a figure for separation, a hymen, a border—the very border of sexual difference construed and enforced as a (violent) opposition—such policing of sexual difference provokes violations and desperate crossings. The fate of Persephone exemplifies in "Veiled Lips" the violence ensuing from the use and notion of the veil as hymen. Irigaray pictures Ceres's daughter as "veiled without within":

> Carried off, far away, away from herself, ruined, Persephone becomes the ice being. Truth of any production that has been cut off from the natural world. Henceforth enslaved to a mirage technique that separates her from herself. Veiled without within. (ML, 114)

The veil falls as a kind of iron curtain upon her, divides her from within, torn as she is between her husband and her mother. Her "marriage" (or "hymen" in French) with Hades is nothing less than the carrying out of a robbing and a rape. The traditional heterosexual line she is forced to follow cuts her away from her mother; the course of her destiny fits perfectly the Freudian account of the path toward womanhood; but, just as Freud also observed in his talk on "Femininity," the separation from the mother is never successfully achieved. Persephone returns to her mother, at the latter's call. This return, though, is clandestine; she can only undertake it in hiding, at great risks: "veiled" as she is now; from then on, her story is one of dangerous and traumatic crossings—or attempted crossings—of thresholds, the very thresholds or borders that constitute sexual difference and sexuality in general as an oppositional and defensive structure, whose primary aim, the myth suggests, is to keep the mother out: outside the husband's household, outside the daughter's heart.

Irigaray's recourse to Greek mythology, here, as well as in the following section ("When the Gods Are Born") repeats Nietzsche's gesture in *The Birth of Tragedy.* Because it deals with origins and does not cover over the violence at work in any world ordering (kill rape rob), mythology is recalled against philosophy, that is, Socratic philosophy, in an attempt to uncover what this philosophy, Athenian or Athena-like philosophy, has obscured and expelled from its sight.

"When the Gods Are Born" retraces the course of Western patriarchal civilization in three mythical steps (the rise of Dionysos, the triumph of Apollo, and the advent of Christ). Here, the veil Irigaray sees operating casts its net over the entire earth, if not the whole cosmos. The phallic erection of Dionysos is described as a "mask" which "freezes" the virile member and turns it into a fetishistic prop, imposing its cold stiffness upon the archaic wetness of the nursing earth. Against Nietzsche's, Irigaray's Dionysos already heralds the reign of appearance, the new veiling order subsequently established by Apollo:

> The gaze . . . weaves a dream garment that carries the whole far away from its earthly blossoming. All is shrouded in an appearance that gives it a more striking and glorious aspect. Beauty shines in the face. Is laid over the face, like the mask of desire. (ML, 141)

The cult of the phallus, cause of desire according to Lacan and "mask of desire" according to Irigaray, precedes and announces the triumph of patriarchy, which Irigaray clearly interprets as the triumph of Greek idealism in Western thought: With Apollo, a certain idea of the idea (eidos) comes to occupy center stage, as a beautiful if not the most beautiful sight: "Does not Apollo's splendor already prefigure the splendor of the idea?" (148).

Irigaray shares Nietzsche's distrust of "Apollinism," but once again, and contrary to Nietzsche, she casts the triumph of Apollo in the context of patriarchy's attempt to cover up sexual difference. Apollo is not only contrasted with Dionysos; he is opposed to Artemis, his twin sister, whose skin he symbolically robs in order to "robe" himself in it.[8]

Now, it is easy to understand why Greece appears in *Marine Lover* and elsewhere as the exemplary and original site of patriarchy's cover-up. On the Western side of the world, the discourse on sexuality, its vocabulary and conceptual apparatus, are Greek. Greek philosophy, from Plato onward, also provides, as Irigaray states in "The Blind Spot," a concept of origin, which she reads as masking (other) stories of origins, the stories Greek myths tell on the theatre of literature and the altars of religion. Finally, Greek mythology, and mythical thinking in general, encompass a range of phenomena and experiences that speak to Irigaray's taste for cosmogonies, if not totalizing worldviews.

It is less easy, however, to understand her emphasis on the veil, and on the veil as "Greek," since there is no compelling evidence that it is a prominent cultural or theological motif in Ancient Greece. True, Athena is the patron of weavers, spinners, and embroiderers. And there are famous figures of female weavers, such as Arachnea or Penelope. Goddesses and mortals alike wear pleated garments, when they are not pictured naked. The goddess Hera wears a white veil on the top of her head to seduce Zeus; And Aphrodite's scarf, worn across the body, endows whoever wears it with powers of sexual attraction. But there are many words in ancient Greek to designate these pieces of cloth and none seems to have acquired as dominant a position and as extended a meaning as the veil has in modern French or English. *Keredemnon,* from *kara* (head) and *deo* (to tie), or perhaps *kalyptra,* from *kalypto* (to hide) might be used to designate Hera's head ornament. *Peribolaion* designates the veil or drapes one throws around oneself or around an object. *Katapetasma* can name a piece of cloth that is used as "cover," but it comes from a verb that means "to unfold" rather than to hide. The gesture of covering one's face, so important in Ancient Greek culture, and so often mentioned from Homer to Plato, indicates a feeling of shame; but even though one speaks of "*se voiler la face*" (to veil one's face) in French, no "veil" is necessarily implied by the verb *kalypto* traditionally used in this case.[9] Finally, the transparent veils surrounding the goddesses' bodies, which are such an important feature of early modern Western painting, seem to belong to a late (hence Christian) representation of the Greek world, perhaps prompted by Christianity's semi-disavowal of pre-Christian nakedness, or by its close association of the veil with the presence of the divine. Nothing like a veil or curtain seems to mark the sacred place of God(s) and shield it from reach and view in "Greece," as it does in Abrahamic religions.

You may ask: But what about the philosophical notion of "Aletheia," so central to Athenian philosophy as well as to its legacy and commentary up to the present in continental philosophy? "Alethia," the deconcealment or bringing forth of/as truth is indeed traditionally translated in French by the word *dévoilement* (unveiling). But the trope of the veil and of veil lifting is absent from the Greek word, even if "Aletheia" involves a bringing into view, a rendering visible.

On the other hand, the word *veil* in its modern form was first used in old French (and in old English) to designate the nuns' head cover. And, as I recalled earlier, the notion and language of "revelation" first appeared in Church Latin before it made its way in Romance languages. The bestowing of higher knowledge as a form of veil lifting is a function of the Judeo-Christian thinking about the place and manifestation of the divine: always behind a veil or curtain. There is no doubt that the lexicon of the veil, both in its denotative and connotative dimensions, comes from and belongs to the area of Christian theology. The translation of "Aletheia" by "*dévoilement*" only testifies further to the Christian character of the reception of Greek philosophy in the Western world. And yet, for Irigaray, the advent of Christ calls into question the specular disembodiment of humanity, which the presence of a veil, whatever form it takes, signals and effects.[10] Christianity would halt or at least complicate the ascent of Greek idealism by "mixing up" the maternal envelope of living beings, which Mary embodies in giving birth to Christ, with the veil of appearance through which truth shines from the sky of ideas. This may explain why the veiling topos is conspicuously absent from Irigaray's speculations on Christianity and why, on the other hand, whenever she gets arrested by a veil, it brings about Greek references.

In spite of Irigaray's heavy recourse to Greek mythology (or because of it), the veil cannot, as I suggested, be completely understood or trusted as a cultural artifact. How does it function in her text then? And in what capacities?

One might be tempted to draw distinctions between "proper" uses or realistic mentions of the veil on the one hand, and tropological uses of the word, on the other. The veil-as-ornament or as wrap Irigaray analyzes in "The Blind Spot," and the bed-curtain of little Ernst might fall in the first category; the Platonic allegory of the cave conceived as a cover-up operation, and the characterization of Apollo's language as "veiled speech" in "When the Gods Are Born" (ML, 148–49) in the second. Veils proper, one might say, are material objects; the veil as metaphor is by definition immaterial. But these distinctions may prove unstable. Even as a piece of cloth, the veil matters beyond its materiality. Cultural systems are semiotic systems. Any veil, as soon as it is worn or waved, is a sign of something other than itself. Irigaray's own analysis of the function of women's "wrapping" in a Western context, testifies to the impossibility to separate (textile) matter from signification. "Wrapping" the body may be a very concrete gesture, but it works, as she says, to abstract the body.[11] Add to that the already tropological nature of Irigaray's discourse in "The Blind Spot," where concrete ornaments, jewels, glitter, and all kinds of beauty enhancers are described metaphorically as "veils" and "wrapping" in a metonymic designation of the veil's cultural operation, and our tentative distinctions threaten to fall apart.

At stake is indeed Irigaray's peculiar brand of materialism, as Judith Butler rightly pointed out,[12] a materialism that informs—or derives from—her critique of Greek idealism and which bears upon her view of language and symbolic operations in general, as well as [upon] her view of the world and her stance on sexual difference.

Let's look again at her critical reading of Plato's cave allegory to try and see how her choice of the veil as metaphor affects the materialist thesis she develops, and conversely. The veil trope operates at many levels. The cave as matter hence mother is veiled by the idealist gesture; this veiling is both the condition and limit of vision in the phallocentric order of metaphysics. And the whole allegory of the cave is seen as a cover-up. But the metaphor of the veil is not any kind of metaphor. In "Plato's *Hystera*" it is not so much a tactile figure as an optical metaphor—if a blinding one—which, as such, Derrida reminds us in "White Mythology: Metaphor in the Text of Philosophy," "belongs to the metaphysical heliotropism that has always considered truth and reason as strokes of light and lack of insight as blindness."[13] Indeed, the metaphorical recourse to a generic veil is an old catachrestic device used to make one's way unnoticed from figural speech to philosophical pronouncements in a Neoplatonic Christian language. Philosophy traditionally enlists the veil to create or illustrate important metaphysical oppositions such as the opposition between the visible and the invisible, the hidden and the revealed, appearance and being, etc. One could argue that the tropological use of the veil undermines the distinctions between image and idea, concrete and abstract, and ultimately fiction and truth, that are supposed to establish and secure the rhetorical and conceptual borders of philosophical discourse. Perhaps it is precisely this denied appeal of the figural—and the seduction of a figure always conjures up the specter of femininity—that attracts Irigaray to such veils, while it repels her at the same time.

Whatever the case, the veil metaphor inscribes Irigaray's argument in the metaphysical tradition she purports to fight, making it difficult, once again, to distinguish her stance from the one she "mimics" critically, or her own design from traditional thinkers' veil weaving. The veil she sees operating in "Plato's *Hystera*" masks the truth of the matter. As in the metaphysical tradition she denounces, it is on the side of delusion, fiction, blindness, and exteriority, as opposed to truth and insight, reality, and interiority. The oppositions between truth and fiction, physis and techne, presentation and dissimulation, which rely on the workings of a veil, are ultimately upheld. The difference—and it is of course an important difference but not a radical one—lies in the fact that the truth of the matter doesn't rest with or hang in the idea. The truth of the matter for Irigaray is matter itself. Through a reversal, which is one of her methodological signatures as she herself claims in *I Love to You*,[14] Irigaray invents or promotes a kind of platonic materialism. The deceptive thinness of a material veil doesn't hinder the sight of ideational truth. On the contrary, the idea of the veil—and as veil—produces the disembodied truth of idealist philosophy: it masks the truth of the body, the body of/as truth, which Irigaray proceeds to uncover.

Now, what is the veil of ideas or the idea as veil, if not a metaphoric construction? Irigaray's materialism, while ensconced in a Platonic framework, leads her to indict not so much (or not as much) veils proper, material veils (garment or textile), as indeed the veil as metaphor, and, furthermore, as metaphor of metaphor, because she understands both the idealist project and the metaphoric process as agents of dematerialization. Greek idealism is described as a process of dematerialization through a series of displacements and substitutions. The sky is substituted for earth as the ground of truth, the light of the sun replaces the obscurity of the cave as the original site of thought, and ultimately idea itself substitutes for matter itself. This double move of idealism (dematerialization and—as well as through—substitution) resembles very closely Hegel's definition of the metaphoric process, a process he conceives as one of replacement of a material meaning or referent (the veil as fabric) with a spiritual one (the veil as immaterial agent of an intellectual blinding).[15] Metaphoricity, understood as the conversion of matter into idea, or more precisely into a quasi-idea, a veiled idea, would fully partake in the idealist project and belong to metaphysics. One of the reasons, then, why the veil as metaphor is so prominent in Irigaray's work, may be that it is not only a metaphor, and not only a metaphor of metaphor, but a metaphor of the metaphor-as-veil, since all metaphors, from a certain philosophical perspective (and here idealism and materialism converge), hide the truth of the matter. This might help explain Irigaray's double dealings with metaphors in general and the metaphor of the veil in particular, which she both uses profusely and condemns at the same time.

Now, as we saw, Irigaray tries to counter the veil of metaphysics with another kind of "veil," a material envelope that would delineate boundaries without closing borders, and that would neither veil the truth nor be subjected to cover-ups, whether philosophical or cultural. As early as *Speculum* and throughout a number of subsequent works, the "envelope" designates body layers or folds (the skin, the placenta, or the lips, for instance) that are neither closed nor opened, neither hidden nor revealed, neither external nor internal, etc. These types and sites of body folds would defeat the conceptual tearing apart that produces the oppositions commanding metaphysics, including the opposition between the spiritual and the material that informs a certain notion of metaphor and of the production of meaning in general. The problem is that the "envelope" is not the skin itself or the placenta itself. The word *envelope* is as much a metaphor for certain body folds or spatial configurations as the veil is a metaphor for what covers them. As a metaphor, the "envelope" risks "veiling" its object, unless its use gives rise to another notion of metaphor. And it is not clear that it does. Not only is Irigaray's materialism as metaphoric (and perhaps unavoidably so), hence ideational, as the idealism she comes up against, but it becomes very difficult to maintain the quasi-ontological distinction put forward by her between (patriarchy's) "veils" and (maternal) "envelopes." For the "veil" has the ability to copy the "envelope" and trap everything in its mimetic game, and, rhetorically speaking, the "envelope" is a "veil."

Because of its centrality and its status as a metatrope (that is, as a metaphor for the metaphor as veil), the "veil" commands a huge analogical network. One metaphor-as-veil resembles another metaphor-as-veil, which resembles and relies on any kind of veil, proper or figurative. As a result, when it comes to bed curtains, shining armor, shields of all kinds, white robes, jewels, "gleaming skin,"[16] or even the "body armor of individuation" (ML, 148), the "veils of beauty," and the dressing up of the world through poetry (ML, 149), Irigaray doesn't seem to be deterred by idiomatic singularity or by what one could call the specific cultural syntaxes of the veil's appearances. Dionysos's "mask" becomes an equivalent of Athena's "toga," which is an equivalent of Apollo's "speech," which becomes an equivalent of women's "wrappings," etc. Whether textile or not, all are "veils," because all have the same subtext. They are all metaphors of sorts, that is, hostage signifiers carried away from their original site of reference, just as Persephone is taken away from her mother, to become covert agents of the phallus, this fake erected penis, this immaterial master signifier, which, for those very reasons, Lacan reminds us jokingly in "The Signification of the Phallus," only operates when veiled, or as veil.[17] It may be, finally, because the phallus or *phallos*, this great old prop of the Dionysian processions, which Lacan, and Irigaray even more so, treat as the prototype of all masks, is originally "Greek," that the "veil," for all its Christian underpinnings, gets associated predominantly with "Greece" in her work.

The privilege granted to the "veil," then, is a metaphorical effect of the privilege of the phallus. The latter does not only order signification, again according to Lacan, but unifies it, gathers it around itself, thus preventing the dissemination of meaning that could occur when metaphors are carrying language away without end or center. The binding of figures within a system of generalized analogy in Irigaray's work illustrates the operation of the phallus as the master of symbolic sameness.

Now, as we have seen, the phallocentric veil Irigaray is busy shaking in her early work extends its folds and orders the masquerade way beyond the stage where the comedy of sexual and familial relations is infinitely replayed. Persephone's abduction, her tearing apart from her mother and subsequent veiling as she goes underground, affects and shapes nature's cycles. In her reading of the births of Dionysos and Apollo, Irigaray also insists on the cosmic repercussions of their promotion of a veiling order. The phallophoria staged by the veil(s) encompasses everything, and conditions the perception of all phenomena. The paradox of this move beyond the confines of psychoanalytic inquiry, is that the phallus is granted even more centrality than in Lacan's symbolic ordering of human relations.

Certainly, Irigaray wants to free signification and metaphoric play from the ghostly grip of the phallus. And even though the subordination of metaphor to analogy through the metatropic game of the "veil" in her own text may be said to exemplify the constricting and domesticating power of the master idea of the phallus, the overflow of metaphors in her text points toward another possibility. However bound, metaphors always risk carrying language away not only from the original meaning of the word or expression used as a trope but from its intended metaphorical meaning or destination, Derrida reminds us again in "White Mythology." And perhaps metaphors have a special charm for Irigaray because, for all their complicity with metaphysics, they nonetheless retain a trace or a memory—they are indeed a memorial—of the materiality from which they allegedly abstract themselves: they might be, in short, specters (only specters but enduring specters) of the mother's body. Critics have commented on Irigaray's metaphoric style and she too has asserted her desire to blur rhetorical and disciplinary borders. In *Le Corps-à-corps avec la mère*, she dismisses the opposition or even the distinction between fiction and theory, or, one might say, between fabric and optic.[18] One more step, then, and Irigaray might find herself on the side of literature. And yet, she doesn't take that step. She actually ends up going the other way, as we will see shortly.[19]

"When the Gods Are Born" is not only a phallo-Theogony, it is an account of the birth of logocentrism. Apollo, the god of beautiful appearances, is also, Irigaray insists, the god of speech, that is, of speech as essentially deceiving, pretending, lying, saying one thing in order to hide another, enchanting with the soothing lyre while it is really making war: of speech as veil.[20] Irigaray describes Apollo's ascent in and through language, his endowment with the gift of poetical speech, as a process of both confiscation and assumption of the Word, which rises to prominence as it becomes a conveyor of the law of the Father. Because the Word reigns and its reign is based on a lie in the phallocentric symbolic order, because it says something in order to shut out something else, all statements are double-edged. The veiling order of the phallus condemns the locutors—including Irigaray until she exits from that order—to ambiguity.

Just as metaphors are said to carry meaning away from its original site, so does the ambiguity produced by veiled speech lead meaning astray. This is, as we know, a traditional argument, and one that Irigaray is close to making in "When the Gods Are Born." Not that she wants meaning to rest assured within phallocentric confines. Quite the contrary. She faults the order of the "phallus" for creating ambiguity in the process of covering up the matter it purports to control.

What are we to make, then, of this conflation of poetry and phallogocentrism, of this indictment of poetry *as* phallogocentrism?

Both "Veiled Lips" and "When the Gods Are Born" are full of derogatory remarks about artistic practice and artful language. The close relation established between painting and poetry and their condemnation on similar grounds suggests that Irigaray conceives of the art of words as a mimetic art: *ut pictura poesis*. Art, and the optics (or speculum) of plastic arts in particular, contribute to faking woman; painting, at least in a certain tradition, is a covering up, a violence done to the truth of female "physiology"[21] under the pretense of paying reverence to it. As an art of concealment, it is at the service of death. As for the art of words, the trickery of beautiful speech practiced by Apollo also participates, as we have seen, in the establishment of the veiling order of the phallus.

The target of Irigaray's remarks may not be art in general but indeed Western classical art, with its Greek motifs, its insistent display of woman's nudity, enhanced by veils and curtains of all kinds, its invention of perspective, which fakes depth and dangerously mimics the volume of bodies, and, above all, its reliance on a Platonico-Aristotelian notion of mimesis. And it may be that the notion of poetry as beautiful speech, as deceiving as a golden veil thrown over a woman's body, is not so much a reflection of Irigaray's stance on the issue than a critical appraisal, along Nietzschean lines, of the Western, Apollonian, aesthetics of representation. The problem is that neither here nor elsewhere does Irigaray dwell on works of art or literary works that might either confirm or complicate her views on the matter.

Irigaray seems to be dreaming at times of an Adamic (or "Adam-and-Evic") state of language, without guise or disguise, where words would signify unequivocally and gendered truths would be uttered clearly, without shame, play, or trickery, by the subjects of discourse. Again, from a certain materialist perspective, metaphoric speech is complicit with metaphysics. Meaning becomes equivocal when it ceases to be bound to its matter or material in a straightforward way. In as much as she subscribes to this argument, Irigaray joins a cohort of thinkers who have expressed great distrust of literature in the name of materialism, often recalling, in their pronouncements, Platonic and Christian views on literature's intellectual and moral faults. Perhaps this is why she hardly ever engages literary works as such.

When Irigaray operates what she calls a "self-reversal" rather than a "simple" reversal of philosophical systems in *I Love to You*, when she attempts to see and show herself, a woman, not as the prop or screen she is for men, but as a gendered subject, agent of her own viewing, finally revealed and repaired, she does away with "veils" and the seductions of speech all at once. *I Love to You* is a didactic text, as are many of Irigaray's later works, which aims to teach the "way of love," to borrow the title of one of her last books. Its style is markedly different from that of *Speculum*, *Marine Lover*, or *An Ethics*. It is simpler, barer, "depleated," one might say, stripped of ambiguities. Indeed, she spends a number of pages explaining what the title of her first book *Speculum. Of the Other Woman* really meant, denying any playful ambiguity of style and intention, and trying to indicate what a proper translation might be. Her lengthy comment of the phrase she coins, "I love to you," obeys the same imperative of linguistic clarification. She makes a similar gesture toward her intellectual models, or frames of reference. She doesn't engage in the kind of "critical mimicry" of the Western intellectual canon typical of her earlier works, a comedy of veils whose ambiguous status and rhetorical oddities have puzzled her readers and provoked contradictory assessments of her work and intentions. Far from "criticizing" Hegel as she did Plato, Freud, or even Nietzsche, she puts him to use and assesses his legacy favorably. True, Irigaray's Hegel is not de Beauvoir's Hegel; she sets aside the theoretician of the sovereign Subject, dear to existentialism, who strives to conquer otherness outside and inside himself. From him, she borrows a notion of negativity which she puts to work in interesting ways, while fully acknowledging her debt toward him: a grateful father's daughter after all.

But, you might say, what about her frequent recourse to myth, at least in the first half of her work? Isn't myth close to literature in some ways? Doesn't "mythos" mean both "speech that matters" and "fable," ignoring the distinction between truth and fiction, or proper and figural meaning, just as literature does? And aren't the mythical figures she relies on in her philosophical musings found first and foremost in literary works, Homer's epics or Euripides' plays for instance? Even though Irigaray doesn't reflect explicitly on the theoretical significance or methodological status of her recourse to myths, it is clear that the latter are endowed for her with a power to reveal, which seems at times to extend beyond the realms and range of explanation to which modern epistemology confine them. For Freud, what (Greek) myths reveal are the unconscious structures of sexual relations. This understanding of myth, of the function of myth and its epistemological value came into being, as we know, with the rise of modern human and social sciences. Whether myth is thought to uncover the underlying structures of social relations, of sexual relations, or of both in a given culture, it has become an important tool and locus of the modern epistemology of mankind. And yet, what are myths if not allegories? What are they made of, if not stories? Not only do they rise from an impulse to tell stories, to transpose the world—to "mythologize"—that has to be accounted for, but they seem to suggest (and certainly their place in modern epistemology confirms that view) that only through allegorical processes can one have access to a form of "truth," at least to what Freud called the other scene, the scene of the unconscious, which might otherwise remain hidden.

Perhaps Irigaray would argue that allegorical speech is different from metaphorical substitution and its abstracting, "veiling" effect. Allegory, in this sense, wouldn't hinder, veil, or cover up the path that leads to the other world, the inner and underworld of social and sexual relations Irigaray aims to uncover on her way to the other woman (and the other man). If anything, when the curtain is drawn on the other scene, myth and the literary impulse that stems from it or brings it forth might grant us and her, if not the clearest, at least the closest view of the scenes where such stuff as we are made of is weaved, "beyond the canonical enclosure(s) of revelation."

## Notes

1. Luce Irigaray, "The Blind Spot of an Old Dream of Symmetry," in *Speculum Of the Other Woman*, trans. Gillian C. Gill (Ithaca: Cornell University Press, 1985), 115. Subsequent page references are cited in the text as BS.

2. Luce Irigaray, *An Ethics of Sexual Difference*, trans. Carolyn Burke and Gillian C. Gill (Ithaca: Cornell University Press, 1993), 10.

3. Irigaray already takes a similar stance in another section of *Speculum* entitled "Volume Fluidity" (see p. 228).

4. *Speculum of the Other Woman*, 254.

5. The "robe" as garment and the act of "robbing" are indeed etymologically related. For Gill's translation, see *Marine Lover of Friedrich Nietzsche*, trans. Gillian C. Gill (New York: Columbia University Press, 1991), 103. Subsequent page references are cited in the text as ML.

6. Luce Irigaray, "Belief Itself," in *Sexes and Genealogies*, trans. Gillian C. Gill (New York: Columbia University Press, 1993), 27 note 4. Subsequent page references are cited in the text as BI.

7. See Friedrich Nietzsche, *The Birth of Tragedy*, trans. Douglas Smith (Oxford/New York: Oxford University Press, 2000) and *Twilight of the Idols, or, How to Philosophize with a Hammer*, trans. Duncan Large (Oxford/New York: Oxford University Press, 1998).

8. Irigaray describes Apollo as "floating between two skins" (ML, 152). And she adds, more explicitly: "In this excess of appearances that he borrows from women, in those endlessly multiplied veils, a body in the process of abstraction is shown and hidden" (155).

9. I want to thank Pietro Pucci and Laurent Dubreuil for their comments on the Greek "veiling" lexicon.

10. "Isn't it possible," she asks in the last section of "When the Gods Are Born," "that in [Christ], two skins have been mixed up? The skin called veil of appearance that imperceptibly covers over the Truth, and the skin that marks the boundaries of a living being?" (ML, 185).

11. As we have seen earlier, Irigaray characterizes the "wrapping" process whereby differences between women are erased in favor of so called universal and uniform "products," as one of "abstraction" (see BS, 115). The connection between veiling, commodifying, and abstracting is made even more explicit in another piece, "Women on the Market," where Irigaray talks of the "phantom like reality" of the marketed women. See *This Sex Which is Not One*, trans. Catherine Porter with Carolyn Burke (Ithaca: Cornell University Press, 1985), 170–91, 175.

12. See *Bodies That Matter: On the Discursive Limits of "Sex"* (New York: Routledge, 1993).

13. See Jacques Derrida, "White Mythology: Metaphor in the Text of Philosophy," in *Margins of Philosophy*, trans. Alan Bass (Chicago: University of Chicago Press, 1982), 307–30.

14. Luce Irigaray, *I Love to You: Sketch for a Felicity within History*, trans. Alison Martin (New York: Routledge, 1996).

15. Metaphors, says Hegel in his *Lectures on Fine Art*, "arise from the fact that a word which originally signifies only something sensuous is carried over in the spiritual sphere." See *Aesthetics: Lectures on Fine Art*, trans. T. M. Knox (Oxford: Clarendon Press, 1975), Volume I, 404. For a full discussion of metaphor as a process of abstraction and spiritualization, see Part II, chapter III, B.

16. See *Speculum*, "Volume Fluidity," 228.

17. See Jacques Lacan, "The Signification of the Phallus," in *Ecrits* (A selection), trans. Alan Sheridan (New York/London: W. W. Norton, 1977), 288.

18. See Luce Irigaray, *Le Corps à corps avec la mère* (Montréal: Editions de la pleine lune, 1981).

19. I didn't know when I first wrote this piece that Irigaray had recently published a diary of poems, akin to a medieval "book of hours" with Hölderlinian and Rilkean overtones. Having now read it, I do not think, however, that it invalidates the present argument.

20. The "veiling" or "enrobing" of the word started of course with a "robbing": Apollo has stolen his oracular power from ancient women deities, deprived them of their power to speak the truth and to do so forcefully.

21. "In art, that perspective will again have simulated her, painted her, contrived her to suit an optics that is not—perhaps?—that of her 'physiology'. Which makes her— perhaps?—still absent from it" (ML, 114).

Chapter 6

# Mothers, Sisters, and Daughters

## Luce Irigaray and the Female Genealogical Line in the Stories of the Greeks

Gail M. Schwab

### Parricide and/or Matricide

The question of the relationship of contemporary Western culture to our Greek heritage has always been a central one in Luce Irigaray's work. Following in the footsteps of her much pondered and much beloved, as well as much criticized, forefathers—Hegel, Nietzsche, and Heidegger—Irigaray looks back to Greek mythology, tragedy, and philosophy as a model and a source of inspiration, and asks: Where did we go wrong? For Irigaray, as well as for Heidegger, if we do not succeed in finding answers to this question, we are doomed to perpetuate the intellectual and technological errors that threaten Western civilization today.[1] When Irigaray asks the question of what she calls our "dereliction" in contemporary culture, however, she asks it differently from her male philosophical predecessors. For her, the answer is tied to the problem of the effacement of sexual difference under patriarchy, and to the disappearance of the female genealogical line, and of a lost utopia of loving, fruitful relationships among and between women. Using as principal intertexts Irigaray's "Body against Body: In Relation to the Mother" and "The Female Gender," from *Sexes and Genealogies* (Irigaray1993, 7–21, 105–23 [1987, 19–33, 119–38]), and "When the Gods are Born," from *Marine Lover* (Irigaray 1991, 121–90 [1980,129–204]), this chapter will examine this effacement and this disappearance through an Irigarayan reading of both sororal relations and mother-daughter relations in Aeschylus's *Oresteia*, Sophocles' *Antigone* and *Electra*, and in the myth of Demeter and her daughter Kore-Persephone, making some reference to Sophocles' *Oedipus the King*, *Oedipus at Colonos*, and Euripides' *Electra*.

Aeschylus's *Oresteia* is frequently read as the representation of, as well as the literary and religious justification for, a crucial transition or transformation—the establishment of the civic and juridical order of the polis, the triumph of the political authority of the Greek city-state over an older, more agrarian society and its chthonic, as opposed to Olympian, gods and goddesses, a society that existed prior to the rupture of the female genealogical line, one that was less rigidly patriarchal, more egalitarian from the point of view of gender. Thus, the murder of Clytemnestra by Orestes, the focus and principle incident of the *Oresteia*, can be read as the representation of the founding act of patriarchy—the sacrifice of the mother in favor of the father and his name and genealogical line. Feminist philosopher Joanna Hodge, in an article entitled "Irigaray Reading Heidegger,"[2] applies the Heideggerian term *originary*, and it very usefully illuminates this foundational sacrifice, as well as the whole problem of origins—here, the origin and continuing existence of the patriarchal social order.[3] Traditional academic anthropology, philosophy, and psychoanalysis have established the originary of Western culture through a male-centered reading of the Oedipus myth, or of its retelling in the derivative Freudian tale of the primal horde in *Totem and Taboo*.[4] This originary is supposedly a parricide, the murder of the father by the son or sons, result of oedipal rivalry, the desire to possess the mother and/or all of the father's women. These narratives are actually, according to Irigaray, screens, or coverings over the real originary of our culture—the sacrifice of the mother, a sacrifice that has been taking place since the dawn of patriarchy, in our own births and lives (Irigaray 1993, 11 [1987, 23]), a sacrifice that results in the severing of the genealogical link between women—the separation of daughter(s) from mother(s)—and in the appropriation of the daughters' virginity by the father(s) and brothers, and its sale in order to consolidate bonds with other men—that institution that we call exogamy.

In the first two plays of the *Oresteia*, the *Agamemnon* and the *Libation Bearers*, the matricide is presented with a good deal of ambiguity. Clytemnestra *is* guilty of murder; she deceitfully plotted with her lover Aegisthos, and lured Agamemnon and his new slave mistress Cassandra to their deaths. However, as Irigaray is careful to emphasize in "Body against Body," where she reads the *Oresteia* (Irigaray 1993, 11–12 [1987, 24]), Agamemnon had murdered Iphigenia, Clytemnestra's daughter and his own. He sacrificed his young virgin daughter upon the altar of Artemis, in order to appease the offended goddess who had been holding the Greek fleet immobilized at Aulis, preventing their departure for Troy. The murder of Iphigenia by her father is the symbolic rupture for all time of the mother-daughter link, for the sake of the consolidation of relations among/between men, specifically here for the sake of the brother-to-brother link between Menelaus and Agamemnon, and undoubtedly for the sake of the "male bonding" of the entire Greek army; Clytemnestra is convinced that, at least in the case of the father of her children, parricide/regicide was a perfectly justifiable act of justice and revenge[5] (see Aeschylus, *Agamemnon*, lines 1521–29, in *Oresteia*, trans. Richmond Lattimore [Chicago: University of Chicago Press, 1953]).

## Electra, Antigone, and Their Siblings

The mother-daughter bond that was severed at the death of Iphigenia is a link that will never be reformed, as is demonstrated by the violence and conflict characterizing Clytemnestra's exclusively adversarial relationship with Electra, observable both in Aeschylus's *Libation Bearers* and in Euripides' *Electra*, but rendered glaringly obvious in Sophocles' *Electra* (See Sophocles, *Electra*, in *The Complete Greek Tragedies*, vol. 2, ed. David Grene and Richmond Lattimore, trans. David Grene [Chicago: University of Chicago Press, 1960]). The latter play could in itself be an illustration of the mimetic conflict that results between women when the female genealogical line is severed. Nothing strikes the reader of Sophocles' *Electra* so forcefully as the resemblance between Clytemnestra and her daughter, two damaged women, each accusing the other of being a "shameless creature," bringing only disgrace upon her family, each capable principally of doing the other harm.[6] Even though Electra is sister to Iphigenia, the memory of Iphigenia's death does nothing to mitigate her anger at her mother over the death of her father; in fact, she defends Agamemnon against Clytemnestra's condemnation (lines 558–584), and she treats her living sister, Chrysothemis, with contempt, rejecting her completely when she refuses to join in Electra's absurd plot to kill Aegisthos (lines 1027–1035). Female kin relations seem to have little importance here.

Electra is as obsessed with the idea, or ideal, of the absent male members of her family, as she is with her hatred of her mother. It is interesting to note that, as the story is presented by all three tragedians, Electra can never really have known either Orestes or Agamemnon. Agamemnon left when she was a child to lead the Greeks to Troy, and was speedily dispatched by Clytemnestra and Aegisthos as soon as he came back; Electra herself had sent Orestes away from Argos when he was a baby, to protect him, the legitimate royal heir, from the usurper. Neither Agamemnon nor Orestes can ever have been more to Electra than stories she was told, or told herself. Those stories have become her identity in a way, and she sees herself as one who willingly accepts wretched poverty and abuse at the hands of her mother's lover, sacrificing her own life in order to remain a model of filial and sororal love and piety, while awaiting the return of the brother who will avenge the father. Forced to abandon that dream when

Orestes is falsely reported dead in the chariot race, Sophocles' Electra tries to, in effect, become Orestes, and take his place as avenger (see lines 974–985). In an article entitled "The Politics of Pathos: Electra and Antigone in the Polis," Molly Ierulli shows how Sophocles' Electra fantasizes herself as "Electra the Hero," and envisions herself celebrated in all of Greece for having taken on the male role of tyrannicide, murderer of Aegisthos—a role that Orestes will eventually step into.[7] Aeschylus also emphasizes the close identification between the two siblings; he underscores Electra's physical likeness to her brother. Early on in the *Libation Bearers*, Electra is able to assert that Orestes has finally returned when she finds a lock of hair on Agamemnon's tomb, a lock of hair so like her own that it could belong only to Orestes. She also measures her foot against a footprint left at the tomb, the perfect match confirming the hope conceived at the sight of the lock of hair. Alienated from the female members of her family, living or dead, Electra is totally identified with her brother.

Although Electra has become in popular culture the symbol of daughterly devotion to the father for whom she mourns obsessively, it should be pointed out that she is also living an intense passion for her brother Orestes. This is particularly striking in Euripides, who fleshed out what was already subtly present in both Aeschylus and Sophocles. When Euripides' Electra and Orestes first meet, Orestes is incognito, as he is in Aeschylus and Sophocles, but Euripides plays up an underlying sexuality, and hints at rape. Orestes and his companions are armed, and Electra is alone and frightened: "Go from me! Wouldst thou lay/Hand on a body that is not for thee?" (See Euripides, *Electra*, 356–57, in *Fifteen Greek Plays*, ed. Lane Cooper, trans. Gilbert Murray [New York: Oxford University Press, 1967]). When the siblings are finally brought to recognize each other, they embrace ecstatically and passionately. "And fearest thou still to throw/Thine arms around him thou lovest?" (369).

In some ways the Euripides version of Electra's story is as much about marriage, sex, and reproduction as it is about the matricide. Electra, still a virgin although married to a peasant living outside of Argos who respects her royal name and person and refuses to exercise his conjugal rights, lures her mother to her house with the news that she has given birth to a son. Clytemnestra arrives in state, very much in her regal Aeschylean character, expecting to find Electra's husband, or Electra's son, but enters the house to find her own son Orestes taking their place. After the matricide, Euripides typically wraps things up with a *deus ex machina*; Castor and Polydeuces appear, and punish both Orestes and Electra with exile, closely identifying brother and sister: "Thy hand was as thy brother's hand,/Thy doom shall be as his. One stain,/From dim forefathers on the twain/Lighting, hath sapped your hearts as sand" (395). Electra is then betrothed to her brother's friend and alter-ego Pylades, a man in many ways indistinguishable from Orestes himself.

Traditionally, of course, the great sororal heroine[8] of Greek tragedy is Antigone, and her relation to her brother Polynices can be read as parallel to that between Electra and Orestes. In the most controversial and undoubtedly the most often quoted and discussed passage in the play, Antigone explains that she would never have done what she did—defy authority and the law and face death—for a husband or a child, both husbands and children being "replaceable." She would only have gone ahead and risked execution for her brother, irreplaceable once Oedipus and Jocasta were both dead (Sophocles, *Antigone*, ed. William Arrowsmith, trans. Richard Emil Braun [New York and London: Oxford University Press, 1973], lines 1057–1066). In an article entitled "Woman's Third Face," a psychoanalytic analysis of the *Antigone*, and indeed of the entire Labdacid cycle,[9] that is decidedly different from Freud's, Patricia Johnson emphasizes the incestuous overtones of the relationship between Antigone and Polynices.[10] In *Antigone's Claim*, Judith Butler takes a position similar to Johnson's on this issue.[11] In the family of Oedipus, where what Oudemans and Lardinois label excessive "fission and fusion" in family relations is the norm,[12] brother-sister incest, although traditionally not emphasized, or even mentioned, seems no more implausible than mother-son incest. In any case, it is not necessary to insist on a literal *passage à l'acte* in order to assert that the brother-sister relation here is undeniably the primary one.

In a fascinating chapter of her book entitled "Promiscuous Obedience," Judith Butler very carefully analyzes the fractured kinship lines in the *Antigone*, and emphasizes that Antigone and her sister Ismene "have quite literally taken the place of their brothers, acquiring masculine gender along the way," since, as Oedipus bitterly points out to Polynices, his daughters "'are [the] men, not [the] women,'"[13] of the family. So as sister to Polynices and Eteocles, and also to Oedipus; as his son, hence brother; as his daughter and his caretaker, hence as his wife and/or his mother; Antigone seems to fulfill all the family roles here—or almost all. In the literary and philosophical traditions, Antigone is the revered ideal of sisterhood; nevertheless, she is actually sisterly only to brothers, and dead ones at that. She is certainly not much of a sister to Ismene. In this once again she forms a close parallel with Electra, who takes little account of the death of one sister, and treats the living one contemptuously. Antigone behaves toward Ismene in exactly the same way as Electra toward Chrysothemis, telling her how she will "hate" her if she insists on keeping secret Antigone's role in the burial of Polynices, and brutally dismissing her support when Creon accuses them both of having done the deed together. As Johnson points out, counter to "Antigone's own logic in her final scene, sisters too are irreplaceable . . . her treatment of Ismene is incomprehensible and inconsistent."[14]

Looking back to a prior chapter of Antigone's story, *Oedipus at Colonus*, we should remind ourselves that Antigone, who guided Oedipus all through his years of wandering exile, had always belonged to the father. She is the daughter of her father far more than that of her mother. Indeed, throughout the whole story of the Labdacids as depicted by Sophocles, Jocasta does not play a principle, active role. In *Oedipus the King*, her calming words and her advice are never heeded by Oedipus, who is driven exclusively by his own passion. Once she comes to the realization of who Oedipus really is, knowledge that transforms her own identity as well, she has only to die and make way for Oedipus's self-blinding, leaving Ismene and Antigone to live their lives in the company of men. In "Body Against Body: In Relation to the Mother" (Irigaray 1993, 13–15 [1987, 25–27]), Irigaray criticizes the male bias in the literary, philosophical, and psychoanalytic traditions that has resulted in an exclusive focus on the murder of Laios, and in neglect of Jocasta's death—another reenactment of the originary matricide. Tradition generally holds Oedipus to account for his father's demise, minimizing any responsibility that might be assigned to the gods, or to Laios himself, or to Jocasta, all of whose actions were instrumental in bringing about that fatal meeting at the crossroads, and has not even asked itself the question of Oedipus's role in the death of his mother.[15] While it is true that Jocasta took her own life, and that she—and Laios and the gods—certainly had a role to play in the events that culminated in her suicide, Oedipus, who insisted on pushing his investigation to the limit, deaf to Jocasta's advice, or even eventually to her pleas, had more than just a little to do with her death. It is Johnson who, in her non-Freudian psychoanalytic interpretation, questions whether Oedipus, when he charges off to find her hanged in her room, may not even have intended to kill Jocasta himself.[16]

For a representation of a vibrant and loving mother-daughter link, Irigaray turns away from the tragedians and back to the earlier narratives of mythology, to the story of Demeter and Kore-Persephone. She has written about this myth several times, but perhaps her fullest development of the theme can be found in "The Forgotten Mystery of Female Ancestry" (Irigaray 1994, 89–112 [1989, 101–23]). The myth of Demeter and her daughter Persephone shows some of the same structural elements that play an important role in the stories of Antigone and of Clytemnestra and her children, and like those stories it illustrates the father's role in the rupture of the female genealogical line. Like Antigone and, as we shall see, the Erinnyes of the *Oresteia*, Persephone is sent below, walled off from life and the light, to become the bride of death. Like Clytemnestra, Demeter cannot forgive the father for taking her daughter from her. Like Iphigenia, Persephone is, according to Irigaray, a virgin daughter used by the father—here Zeus—in a power move, to make a deal with another man. "The episode of Kore-Persephone's abduction involves a power struggle between Zeus and Hades, two brothers. . . . This transaction takes place without the consent of either his daughter or her mother" (Irigaray 1994, 102–103 [1989, 114–15]). Zeus and Hades are forced to give in, and release Persephone for half the time, because Demeter, angered and aggrieved by her loss, withholds her bounty, and the earth becomes sterile, threatening to eliminate mortals, and thus all worship of the gods. What distinguishes the Demeter-Persephone myth from the stories of Antigone and Clytemnestra is the still powerful bond between women, between mother and daughter. The link between mother and daughter is shown here to be absolutely indispensable to the survival of the earth, the human race, and the gods. This is particularly interesting in that it is not the horizontal heterosexual relation that is crucial for the flowering of the fruits of the earth—that is, traditional reproduction, procreation—but rather the vertical homosexual relation between women. When the link between mother and daughter—the intergenerational link between women—is lost, life does not flourish. The story of Demeter and Persephone even shows that it is threatened with extinction. And it is quite clear that Irigaray is convinced that is the situation in which we find ourselves in Western culture today.[17]

## Apollo, Athena, and Justice

In the *Oresteia*, there is actually more than one matricide. Along with Clytemnestra, figuratively murdered, in the sense that they are deprived of power and authority, and physically removed from the community, are the female group of the Erinnyes, functioning in the *Eumenides*, the final play of the trilogy, as the chorus. These ancient chthonic goddesses whose traditional role was the protection of the family, had the authority to administer justice against those who did it harm or injury. It is they who pursue Orestes, threatening madness and death, after he murders his mother. Since they were guardians of the family, why was it that they did not pursue Clytemnestra, or Aegisthos, Agamemnon's cousin, for murdering Agamemnon, or Agamemnon after the death of Iphigenia? Why do they seem to have singled out Orestes when the entire house of Atreus was generally prone to kin murder? The Erinnyes are actually the guardians of an archaic kinship structure, the old clan system of the pre-political age, in which descent was matrilinear, and children belonged to the clan of their mothers. Thus, when Agamemnon sacrificed Iphigenia, he killed a member of Clytemnestra's clan, but not his own, and therefore did not come under the authority of the Erinnyes. Agamemnon was no relation to Clytemnestra, and his murder by his wife is of no concern to them either. It is only Orestes in this story who kills within his own clan.[18]

Orestes had waited many years before returning to Argos to avenge his father, and might perhaps never have done so, had Apollo not insisted. "It was I who made you strike your mother down" (Aeschylus, *Eumenides*, line 84, in *Oresteia*), he states unequivocally at Orestes' trial. In order to goad the reluctant Orestes into action, Apollo had threatened ostracism from the community, including exclusion from the community of worship (Aeschylus, *Libation Bearers*, lines 291–296, in *Oresteia*), as well as physical tortures (lines 279–282). When the deed is done, Apollo offers Orestes refuge in his temple at Delphi, in order to shield him against the Erinnyes' violence. The age, deformity, ugliness, and disagreeable odor of these old women disgust Apollo who drives them out, calling them "flock of goats," and specifically accusing them of sadistic sexual cruelty against young men:

> This house is no right place for such as you to cling
> upon; but where, by judgment given, heads are lopped
> and eyes gouged out, throats cut, and by the spoil of sex
> the glory of young boys is defeated, where mutilation
> lives, and stoning, and the long moan of tortured men
> spiked underneath the spine and stuck on pales.
> (*Eumenides*, lines 185–190)

In this passage, and indeed, in the whole of the *Eumenides*, Aeschylus seeks to demonstrate that the ancient custom of *talion* was brutal, uncivilized, and inhuman, and that the time had come to legislate for the future of Greece. It is not my point to argue that the *talion*, as practiced by the Erinnyes, could have been worthy of the new order of the polis, where all would be subject to the established rule of law. My point rather is that Apollo's—and Aeschylus's—sleight of hand glosses over the non-gendered nature of the *talion*. It was not only the province of the Erinnyes, but rather the universal custom of archaic Greek culture. Aeschylus, through Apollo, manages to identify the "lopping off of heads," the "gouging out of eyes," "the cutting of throats," and mutilation, stoning, and impaling with the female Erinnyes. Brutality and violence, in a strange reversal, become that which was traditionally perpetrated by women, not only against guilty, but also against innocent young men, who then, through identification with Apollo, become the ones who seek to enlighten and civilize, throwing off the old ways. The push to civilize is here equated with the need to control a dangerously violent female power, as opposed to the need simply to forego violence and vengeance.

On his own, however, Apollo has not the power to defeat the Erinnyes; he is forced to enlist the help of his sister Athena, who arranges for Orestes to be tried in front of the Athenian Areopagus. When the male jurors, unable to reach a verdict, render a tie vote, it is Athena who breaks the tie by casting the deciding vote in favor of Orestes. Although a "goddess," Athena is not a woman, as Irigaray has so clearly understood (Irigaray 1993, 12–13 [1987, 25]); not conceived in a womb, nor born of woman, she is, as Irigaray writes, a "divinity conceived in the head of the God of gods. . . . A phantasy of the father of the gods" (Irigaray 1991, 94–95 [1980, 101–102]). Matricide and justice for its victim are not of concern to her; as the father-identified embodiment of the Athenian polis, she wants to persuade the Erinnyes, deeply offended by the outcome of the trial, and continuing to threaten both Orestes and the city (see *Eumenides*, lines 778–787), to cooperate in Orestes' exculpation, and agree to bring no avenging curse upon Athens. Athena proposes a deal: the Erinnyes are to "live with [her] and share pride of worship" (line 833); although they will no longer be empowered to execute violent justice against those who rupture the female genealogical line, they will retain a certain honorary status in family rituals. "You are goddesses . . . /. . . Here/is a big land, and from it you shall win first fruits/in offerings for children and the marriage rite" (lines 824–836). "No household shall be prosperous without your will" (line 895).

In *Marine Lover*, in Irigaray's version of the taming of the Erinnyes, Athena is not even named. Irigaray calls her simply "femininity"—that is, in this case, woman emptied of any identity of her own, and tricked out, decked out, made up, to correspond to the male ideal of woman. "A murder has occurred—femininity appeases the anger, calls for the blood to be forgotten, lulls vengeance to sleep with sweet words, promises homage, honor. . . . Femininity doubles the burial of the mother when she buries the chorus. So that Zeus may triumph" (Irigaray 1991, 96 [1980, 103]). The Erinnyes acquiesce. Newly dubbed the Eumenides by Athena, they change into kindly protectresses of the polis, and agree to go underground, hide themselves and their disgracefully primitive nature from view, and do no more harm to anyone, but rather call down blessings upon the city (*Eumenides*, lines 937–948). And it seems that Athena did keep the promise she made the Erinnyes, for in *Oedipus at Colonus* we see the citizens of Athens, including Theseus himself, honor the sanctuary of the Eumenides at Colonus. It remains nonetheless true that it was the Erinnyes' sacrifice of their freedom, and their power, and their place in the outside world, that bound the Athenians—male Athenians, that is—together as a people. Female power and authority were thus co-opted by the neuter goddess, for the benefit of a social order whose foundation the Erinnyes, down in their crypt, will quite literally underpin, but of which they will not be part. "Civil war/. . . shall/not thunder in our city./Let love be their common will;/Let them hate with single heart" (lines 976–987). Conflict among citizens must be transformed into external aggression; Athenians must "hate with single heart," and it is the scapegoating and expulsion of the Erinnyes that will permit them to do so.[19] From the beginning to the end of the *Oresteia*, Aeschylus demonstrates the "originary" and foundational nature of the matricide. There would be no polis without it.

Athena's bribe to the Erinnyes can in many ways be read as patriarchy's perennial bribe to all women. They agree to behave themselves, to stop complaining, to repress their true nature, and so be rewarded with male homage, as they are stripped of their power. Down in their crypt—that is to say, with their identity carefully repressed—they will be allowed to help the men establish the social order, and render civilization glorious. Irigaray also makes it clear, despite Aeschylus, that she believes that the Erinnyes cannot have gone quietly, even though they did go. Their protests, silenced in the civic optimism of the climax of Aeschylus's trilogy, are echoed in the hysteria of hundreds of generations of women, all walled up and silenced in femininity. Athena

> needed all her powers of persuasion to conquer the savage behavior of a nature that still resists. . . . The snarlings, shrieks, grumbles, howls, the hurtful reproaches—addressed to the gods, no less—the thirst for blood. . . . The oaths, squabbles, exclamations, questionings . . . the laments, the groans, the curses . . . the songs, the hymns, the delirious noise. . . . And the dances, the races, the leaps . . . the movement. . . . All at once and together. Until the final silence. The chorus mastered, repressed into a subterranean crypt. (Irigaray 1991, 96–97 [1980,103])

Electra was threatened with the same fate if she did not learn to stay indoors and keep quiet—that is, to behave like a proper woman; Aegisthos was going to have her buried alive (see Sophocles, *Electra*, lines 329–331, 378–385). Antigone, of course, does suffer that fate, but is "compensated" eventually by the homage of the citizens of Thebes, just as the Erinnyes are compensated by that of the citizens of Athens. And Antigone also "enjoys" the worship of centuries of male philosophers and literati, for whom she is the ideal woman, young and innocent, charming and seductive, and most of all, fanatically loyal to the male members of her family.[20]

## Conclusion

In conclusion, I would like to take up once again the story of Antigone and to think about her in relation to Irigaray. I will not attempt to unravel all the tangled threads of their relationship. Others have pointed out its ups and downs,[21] and Luisa Muraro has even traced it out to a logical and consistent conclusion.[22] Instead, I would like to look closely at a long analysis that appears in "The Female Gender," a 1985 essay published in English in 1993 in *Sexes and Genealogies.* I recognize, not only that "The Female Gender"[23] has been examined by Irigaray readers before, but also that, when it comes to Irigaray and her readings of Antigone, this choice is in some ways arbitrary and undoubtedly limiting. I have nonetheless selected "The Female Gender," in part because it illuminates the play in some interesting ways, in part because Irigaray seems to be carefully marking her position off from Hegel's, and it is useful to emphasize this point, and in part because she also seems to be challenging, at least implicitly, certain other generally received ideas—the incest taboo as the foundation of culture, for example.

In "The Female Gender" Irigaray makes it clear that Antigone cannot be the defender of Hegel's female realm of divine law, tradition, the family, and morality, but rather that she is already a figure caught in the ethics of patriarchal law. Very much within the sphere of the polis, the Antigone of "The Female Gender" is actually a woman who is doing her duty within the state in order to "affirm" it.

> Antigone. . . already bears the stamp of the male universe. Antigone is no longer a woman protecting the light, the hearth fire, its gods, its life. . . . Already Antigone is working in the service of the god of men. . . . It is no longer a case of her fulfilling her role as a member of the *female gender.* Antigone already serves the state in that she tries to wipe away the blood shed by the state. . . . Thus the female has already ceased to serve her own gender, her dialectic. . . . Antigone is already the desexualized representative of the *other of the same.* . . Antigone is no longer fulfilling her own task, her *affirmative* relationship to ethics, she no longer serves *her* gods. The female gender, in its singularity, has been lost. . . . Antigone is no longer a *goddess.* (Irigaray 1993,110–11 [1987,125])

The verb tenses—"has already ceased," "has been lost"—indicating an action or a state that started in the past—that is, before Antigone—and is still going on in the present—that is, the present of the events in Thebes leading up to Antigone's death—point up what Irigaray considers to be Antigone's position as a woman who has lost a tradition that should still have been hers, and who is acting now under another tradition not really her own. The temporal adverbs and adverbials reinforce this impression. There are five "already's" in twelve lines, and there are five "no longer's." It is worth mentioning here that the English has eliminated some of the "already's" in Irigaray's original passage. There are actually eight "*déjà,*" some of them figuring as part of "*ne . . . déjà plus*"—literally, "already not any more," or "already not any longer"—in what amounts to twenty-seven lines in the original text.

This is not careless writing. One thing Irigaray would seem to be doing here is refuting the "*toujours déjà*," the "always already" of deconstructionist philosophy and structural anthropology. She is giving us to understand that women were not "always already" "working in the service of the god of men," etc. Irigaray is being very clear; civilization *is* now patriarchal, but that does not mean that it has "*always already*" been patriarchal. The coming of patriarchal law is *not* that "always already" taken step from nature into culture. It does not stand outside history, but was a historical evolution, or a revolution—probably both. So one of the things that Irigaray is calling into question here is the Levi-Straussian narrative of the origin of culture through the incest taboo, or, as he names it, the law of exogamy that requires the exchange of women and the establishment of bonds among men.[24] As we know, Irigaray rewrites this narrative a bit. What Levi-Strauss calls exogamy, she calls "the theft and violation of the daughter's virginity and the use of her virginity for commerce between men, including religious commerce. . . . Patriarchy has constructed its heaven and hell on this original sin" (Irigaray 1994, 111–12 [1989,123]). The insistence on the words *already* and *no longer* is there to remind us that although our own social order may have "always already" functioned as patriarchy, another, very different social order, reflected in Greek myth and tragedy, as well as in countless artifacts, predated it. Irigaray is insisting that there was a time—a time Western civilization has chosen to forget, has tried very hard to forget, despite the mythological evidence—when culture itself used to be different, when the female "served her own gender, her dialectic," when she fulfilled "her own relationship to ethics" and served "*her* gods."

It may seem that Demeter and Persephone are closer to that moment than Clytemnestra, Electra, or Antigone; certainly their story points to a love that is still strong, that refuses to be cut off in favor of establishing relations with men and among men. It is a love that continues to blossom—at least for half the year. Nevertheless, Irigaray also insists that Demeter, in her grief over her loss of her daughter "never turns to her own mother. . . . Like Kore-Persephone, like Iphigenia, like Antigone, like Mary and like Eve, these women *no longer* [25] have a mother in whom to confide. The female genealogy[26] is *already* interrupted" (Irigaray, 1994, 106 [1989, 117]; my emphasis). In other words, the story of Demeter and her daughter reveals that the intergenerational link between women has "already" been damaged. Must we then wonder if we are back in the province of "always already?" The strength of Irigaray's reading of the Greek myths would seem to point the other way. Nevertheless, since there would seem to be "no longer" any access to the pre-patriarchal female genealogies, except through interpretation of stories and artifacts that have all "already" been corrupted in the (re)writing of history, there is no choice but to project the lost utopia of relations between and among women into the future, and to (re)create it ourselves.

## Works by Luce Irigaray

*Marine Lover of Friedrich Nietzsche*, trans. Gillian Gill. New York: Columbia University Press, 1991; originally published as *Amante Marine De Friedrich Nietzsche*. Paris: Minuit, 1980.

*Sexes and Genealogies*, trans. Gillian Gill. New York: Columbia University Press, 1993; originally published as *Sexes et parentés*. Paris: Minuit, 1987.

*Thinking the Difference: For a Peaceful Revolution*, trans. Karen Montin. New York: Routledge, 1994; originally published as *Le Temps de la différence: Pour une révolution pacifique*. Paris: Librairie Générale Française, 1989.

## Notes

1. See in particular the opening paragraphs of "A Chance for Life," in *Sexes and Genealogies*, 183–206 [197–222]).

2. Joanna Hodge, "Irigaray Reading Heidegger," in *Engaging with Irigaray*, ed. Carolyn Burke, Naomi Schor, Margaret Whitford (New York: Columbia University Press, 1994), 191–209; see 191–95 in particular.

3. Ibid., 192.

4. Sigmund Freud, *Totem and Taboo: Some Points of Agreement between the Mental Lives of Savages and Neurotics*, trans. James Strachey (New York: Norton, 1952).

5. In his *Electra*, Sophocles' Clytemnestra uses the same language of justice as Aeschylus's (see Sophocles, *Electra*, 527–34).

6. Sophocles' Electra repeatedly condemns her mother's sex life (see, for example, lines 585–593). Clytemnestra reciprocates, condemning her daughter's behavior, and declaring it unbecoming a woman (see lines 612–625).

7. Molly Ierulli, "The Politics of Pathos: Electra and Antigone in the Polis," *South Atlantic Quarterly* 98, no. 3 (Summer 1999): 477–500 (see 491–95 in particular).

8. See George Steiner, *Antigones* (New York and Oxford: Oxford University Press, 1984), 12–14.

9. See Patricia Johnson, "Woman's Third Face: A Psycho-Social Reconsideration of Sophocles' *Antigone*," *Arethusa* 30, no. 3 (Fall 1997): 375 and *passim.*, for a psychoanalytic analysis of Antigone and her relationships with Haemon and with Polynices.

10. Regarding Antigone's relationship to Haemon, supposedly her betrothed, see Sophocles, *Antigone*, lines 1025–1048.

11. Judith Butler, *Antigone's Claim: Kinship between Life and Death* (New York: Columbia University Press, 2000), 15–19, and *passim*.

12. See the structural analysis of the Labdacid cycle, in Th. C. W. Oudemans and A. P. M. H. Lardinois, *Tragic Ambiguity: Anthropology, Philosophy, and Sophocles'* Antigone (Leiden: E.J. Brill, 1987), 22 and *passim*.

13. Butler, 62.

14. Johnson, 391.

15. See also Hodge, 192. See Sophocles, *Oedipus the King*, ed. William Arrowsmith, trans. Stephen Berg, Diskin Clay (New York: Oxford University Press, 1978).

16. Patricia Johnson insists upon the importance of the death of Jocasta, and on the fact that it has generally been ignored not only by Freud, but by almost all commentators—except Irigaray, who is not mentioned by Johnson (see Johnson, 380–81).

17. See "A Chance for Life." See also Luisa Muraro, "Female Genealogies," in *Engaging with Irigaray*, 317–33, in particular 317–19.

18. Apollo asks the Erinnyes, "What if it be the woman and she kills her man?" The chorus answers, "Such murder would not be the shedding of kindred blood" (*Eumenides*, lines 210–221). They reiterate later on during the trial scene, "The man she killed was not of blood congenital" (605).

19. For an analysis of the social function of scapegoating, see René Girard, *Violence and the Sacred*, trans. Patrick Gregory (Baltimore: Johns Hopkins University Press, 1977).

20. Antigone rejects her uncle, Creon, her mother's brother. One might be tempted to read this as another form of rejection of the mother's genealogical line.

21. I would note in particular Carol Jacobs, "Dusting Antigone," *MLN* 3, no. 5 (December 1996): 890–917.

22. See Muraro for a reading of this issue that is different from the one presented here.

23. See Jacobs, for example.

24. See Claude Levi-Strauss, *The Elementary Structures of Kinship*, trans. James Harle Bell, John Richard von Sturmer, Rodney Needham (Boston: Beacon Press, 1969).

25. I have changed the translation slightly here. The French is "*ces femmes n'ont plus de mère*," and the wording I have used, in addition to making my point, is a more literal rendering.

26. I have used the term *genealogy* in preference to "line of descent."

# Chapter 7

# Antigone and the Ethics of Kinship

Mary Beth Mader

Sophocles' *Antigone* has elicited many superlatives. Hölderlin considered the play to be the most difficult, the most enigmatic and the most essentially Greek of plays. This chapter treats a matter of enigma in the play, one that is crucial to understanding the central stakes of the drama. Its main purpose is to propose a novel account of this enigma in order to permit a discussion of two of Luce Irigaray's readings of the play. This discussion aims to shed light on Irigaray's two readings by considering them in relation to the proposed solution to the enigma. In broad terms, the chief thematic focus throughout is the question of the relation of ethics to kinship, and to *genre* or sexed kind.

One passage in particular has prompted the view that the play is extremely enigmatic; it is a passage that has been read with astonishment by many commentators and taken to demand explanation. This is Antigone's defense speech at lines 905–914. Here, she famously provides what appear to her to be reasons for her burying her brother Polynices against the explicit command of her king and uncle, Creon. Her claim is she would not have deliberately violated Creon's command, would not have intentionally broken his law or edict, had this edict barred her from burying a child or husband of hers. She says that if her husband or child had died "there might have been another." But since both her mother and father are dead, she reasons, "no brother could ever spring to light again."[1] Reasoning of this sort has a precedent in a tale found in Herodotus's *Histories*, and Aristotle cites it in *Rhetoric* as an example of giving an explanation for something that one's auditors may at first find incredible.[2] To Aristotle, then, Antigone's defense speech appears to have been "rhetorically satisfactory," as Bernard Knox says.[3] However, such a reception is rare among commentators.

## Dramatic Implausibility

Indeed, commentators including Goethe and Lacan have considered this supposed reasoning a scandal and something closer to nonreasoning, something nearly inhuman. Goethe hoped that the passage would one day be shown to be interpolated.[4] Therese Ahern Augst[5] writes that Antigone's valuing this particular brother uniquely means that she "approaches the limit of what is commonly understood to be human nature." Others, such as Bernard Knox, find Antigone's thinking both distressing and contradictory. Knox argues that in this speech Antigone abandons the justification she has put forth throughout the course of the play, namely, that of the priority of blood relations, especially over state commands or the laws of mortals or men.[6] He alleges that

> her assertion that she would not have done for her children what she has done for Polynices is a spectacular betrayal of that fanatical loyalty to blood relationship which she urged on Ismene and defended against Creon, for there is no closer relationship imaginable that that between the mother and the children of her own body.[7]

It is, he argues, a "strange piece of reasoning" that Antigone marshals to justify the "disturbing statement" that she would not have committed her lawbreaking deed for a husband or child of hers. Knox sees that the defense involves the irreplaceability of Polynices. But his reading does not see that questions that are the motor of the dramatic course and tragic problems of the play itself, and the answers, which he takes for granted, are precisely what are either unanswered or in play in the dramatic action of the work.

## Attempted Solutions: "But You're in Love with Impossibility"

Knox interprets Antigone's true motive as betraying a general principle of devotion to blood relations. He holds that though she begins by defending herself in universal terms, with such claims as "Hades longs for the same rites for all,"[8] she ultimately demonstrates that this is not the genuine motive for her prioritizing of her brother over a hypothetical husband or child in the defense speech. He finds that in the end,

> the driving force behind her action, the private, irrational imperative which was at the root of her championship of the rights of family and the death against the demands of the

> state . . . is her fanatical devotion to one particular family, her own, the doomed, incestuous, accursed house of Oedipus and especially to its most unfortunate member, the brother whose corpse lay exposed to the birds and dogs.[9]

How does this relate to her championing of the divine law, for Knox? He argues that this "purely personal" motive of devotion to her own family is the "determinant" for her allegiance to the divine law. He identifies Antigone as an instance of a Sophoclean hero whose determined actions and unyielding character are those of "human beings who refuse to recognize the limits imposed on the individual will by men and gods, and go to death or triumph, magnificently defiant to the last."[10]

Others have regarded the passage as turning on a question of love, as either a rejection of the erotic, as in Martha Nussbaum's assessment, or as the incoherence of extreme passion, as in Elizabeth Wyckoff's account. Nussbaum writes:

> The best explanation for this coldly determined priority-ordering of duties is that Antigone is not animated by personal love at all, but by a stern determination to have a fixed set of ordered requirements that will dictate her actions without engendering conflict; her refusal of the erotic . . . is then sufficient to explain her choice of the brother.[11]

And Wyckoff offers the view that Antigone is "clinging to her irrational profundity of feeling for her lost and irreplaceable brother, devising legalistic arguments for her intellectual justification."[12]

These, then, are a few of the many reasons for which readers of the play have found this passage confounding and several of the ways that they have sought to account for its oddness. Before a sketch of this chapter's understanding of the enigma of the passage, a brief presentation of Irigaray's readings of the play follows.

## Irigaray: "The Tragedy of the Difference of the Sexes"

Luce Irigaray treats Sophocles' *Antigone* often in her works and teaching and offers at least two different readings of Antigone's plight and significance. The earlier discussion in *Speculum: Of the Other Woman* reads the play through Hegel's well-known account of the play. In Hegel's account, the conflict between Antigone and Creon is essentially one between the human law of the *polis* and the divine law of the family. In rough outline, for Hegel, this human law is the province of men while honoring the divine law is the special duty of women. Antigone's favor for her brother stems from, and is an instance of, the uniqueness of the brother-sister relation in general. This relation is distinguished from both parent-child relations and husband-wife relations by being untroubled by erotic desire and untainted by ontological dependence, since neither is a cause of the other's existence.[13] The details of Hegel's complex account and of Irigaray's rich and imaginative critique of it are not the focus of this essay, though, and others have done more justice to their merits than I can. I especially cannot laud Hegel's account of the play since he falls prey to the same interpretive error that most commentators do. I want, rather, to present Irigaray's readings and eventually to point to some moments in Irigaray's critique that relate to my own suggested understanding of the play and the enigmatic passage at issue.

In the reading she offers in *Speculum*, Irigaray understands Antigone's violation as a form of allegiance to her maternal line. It is an allegiance to those issued from the "same womb,"[14] but Irigaray specifies that it is also based on Antigone's identification with her mother. Antigone will sacrifice her life, and future marriage and children, to this devotion to her mother and to her mother's desire. Here, Irigaray implies that the source of Antigone's suffering is her incestuous origin.[15] But identifying with her mother is identifying with a confounding variable: mother Jocasta is both mother and wife to her own son, Oedipus. Irigaray writes:

> Whatever her current arguments with the laws of the city may be, another law already drew her along to where she was going: identification with her mother. *But how are mother and wife to be distinguished?* This is the deadly paradigm of a mother who is both wife and mother to her husband. Thus the sister will strangle herself in order to save at least the mother's son.[16]

Irigaray also implies that Antigone's favoring of Polynices may be a way to rediscover her relation to her mother and, further, that saving her mother's son is saving "her brother, *the desire of her mother.*"[17] This last suggestion is radically but appropriately ambiguous. Irigaray is addressing Antigone's sacrifice for Polynices, but the brother of Antigone who is clearly "the desire of her mother" is her husband, Oedipus. And it is this relation, between Jocasta and Oedipus, to which Irigaray is evidently referring in the passage on Antigone's difficult identification with her mother.

In any case, on this account Antigone pays with her life for her mission to honor the maternal genealogy she shares with her fallen brother Polynices. Moreover, this attempt is done in the face of the male ruler's effort to establish a state founded on arbitrary power that issues commands in the name of the welfare of the citizenry as a whole. So, Irigaray, argues, Sophocles' drama showcases a gradual historical transition from a matriarchal to a patriarchal social order.[18] But it displays with particular clarity the mixed and uncertain passage from one to the other, a point at which the undecidability of the value of each relative to the other is evident. But the endpoint of the play requires the sacrifice of female genealogies, bloodlines marked by *genre* (sexed kind), a matriarchal order, and Antigone's struggling "autonomy."[19]

Later, in *Sexes and Genealogies*, another account is developed. Here, the emphasis is on the subsumption of gender into kinship, where kinship means a denial of sexual difference and a culture suicidally devoted to a monosexual male order. This can be seen as an extension of the earlier account. But a new view of Antigone emerges, as well. Here, both the crime she attempts to purge and her allegiance have changed. It is now her brothers' crimes of mutual fratricide, specifically as instances of destructive power seeking that belongs to the laws and sphere of men, that she aims to rectify.[20] And she is no longer the defiant defender of her maternal bloodline, recognition of which Creon forbids. Rather, she operates already in the service of the *polis* itself, appeasing the gods of the dead for crimes committed against their divine law by the two brothers who killed each other on the path to political power. So, Irigaray charges Antigone with having already given up her allegiance to her own *genre* (sexed kind), her own gods, her own task, and with having already been "taken in by the passage out of divine law, out of the law of nature, of life, into male human law."[21] In her very violation of Creon's decree, then, Antigone "already serves the state."[22]

But Irigaray identifies a further motive for this deed, proposing that Antigone is trying to eliminate a prior "stain," namely, that of "belonging to the female race, of having a maternal filiation."[23] Antigone's sacrifice, on this view, is her capitulation, a tacit admission that the legacy of belonging to the female sexed kind demands penance. Antigone goes along with a male destruction of the female sexed kind's relation with itself.[24] This prohibited relation would be a robustly self-developed relation of the female sexed kind with itself. An important feature of it, and one that is easy to overlook, is that despite Irigaray's emphasis on female genealogy, the specific identity of the female sexed kind is precisely not simply or solely a matter of kin relations or the creation of new living beings. Irigaray argues that after female genealogies are collapsed into male ones, *genre* or sexed kind is "subservient to kinship."[25] That is, what it is to be of the female sexed kind has been reduced to occupying a position in an unjustly indifferent and asymmetrical genealogical system.

In fact, she contends that the accounts of human sexuality that employ a model of incest are excellent examples of the complicity of modern accounts of sexual relations with the male monosexual order that cannot discern, or permit, two distinct sexed kinds in culture, subjectivity or sexuality. The specific blindness of Oedipal incest is its primary blindness to sexual difference. Oedipus's first fault is not registering or knowing the presence of a sexed other. The fault in this incest is not that a limit of blood relation has been breached, it is the prior fault that the patriarchal order has either eliminated or barred the culture and cultivation of an other sexed kind. Irigaray claims that this other, which has no present, effective, cultural instantiation, could serve as the paramount limit for the formation and integration of human existence. Were it to be developed, its ubiquity and its allegedly unique location at the sensitive and transformational junction of "nature" and "culture," would amount to the overcoming of many current forms of destruction. Kinship is the forgetting of gender in the substitution of man for the species. Irigaray means by this that the female sexed kind has been denied a nongenealogical identity, as well as that it has been denied a genealogical identity that is not bowed to the purposes of an emphatically male genealogy. In other words, relations between women who are not currently considered to be genealogically related have no cultural standing or representation. This is in addition to the fact that in the genealogical systems that she considers women appear with only a punctual rather than a linear scope; each mother is the beginning and terminus of her "line."

## Another Answer: "[Doom.] It Extends to All the Kin."

Although commentators are correct to stress the irreplaceability of Antigone's brother Polynices, it is an error to consider her reasoning to concern Polynices as *a* brother, that is, as *any* brother of *any* sister. In other words, many readers, like Hegel, extend the argument to apply to all brothers and sisters. This is an error for at least one crucial reason, and it is an error that almost all commentators on the play commit. Within the dramatic logic of the play, Antigone's family form itself is both singular and monstrous. In other words, most commentators have not taken seriously the very dramatic core that gives the play its tragic element: the horror that *is* the family and the very figures in the play, and especially the fact that the play treats this family as distinctly aberrational. To act as if Antigone, in her defense speech, could be providing a universalizable or generally recommendable rationale for her action, then, is to ignore the exceptional nature of her family form, and for any kinship relations within it. (Perhaps Sophocles' contemporaries did not make this error, and thus perhaps did not experience the same baffled incredulity at her attempted explanation as have subsequent commentators.) When Antigone argues for the irreplaceability of Polynices, then, she should not automatically be taken to be arguing for the irreplaceability to a sister (or even to a sibling), of a brother (or even a sibling). This should not be done because her family form is singularly aberrant according to the play itself: the incestuous nature of her family *is* the source of her suffering, as the play makes clear repeatedly.

Many readers tend to miss the profundity and meaning of Antigone's "family affection" for her brother. They also tend to ignore the importance of what she might wish not to do. Further, the question of Antigone as agent, what she can do or effect and what she cannot or will not do or effect is one of the play's great issues. This issue takes urgent shape in the questions: (1) in particular, what exactly is a brother?, and more generally (2) how are family or kin relations created and maintained? *Antigone* is about the establishment, erosion, or reestablishment of a certain type of kin relation and a family constellation that preserves it.

Antigone is not honoring her brother because he is her brother, she is making a man be her brother by her treatment of him. Most importantly, she is establishing (or attempting to establish) her brother as *only* her brother by symbolically refusing a family precedent, namely that of *generating one's own sibling*. Antigone's devotion to her brother must be understood against the backdrop of her family story. Jocasta is both her mother and her grandmother. Oedipus is both her father and her brother; she is both his sister and his daughter. Further, taking into account Antigone's relation to Polynices by way of her relations with other family members, Polynices could also be said to be Antigone's uncle or her nephew. By way of Oedipus as Antigone's brother, Polynices is the son of Antigone's brother, which makes him her nephew. But by way of Oedipus as Antigone's father, Polynices is Antigone's uncle, since Polynices is her father's brother. So, she is sister, aunt, and niece to Polynices.

In order to understand Antigone's tragic efforts, consider two categories of kin relations:

1. Relations that one cannot generate oneself. Of these, one cannot "get another" because one cannot get one *tout court*. According to the vocabulary of the normative form of kinship order from which the Oedipal family has departed, this category includes: father and mother.[26]
2. Relations that one can generate oneself or help to generate oneself. Of these, one can "get another" in the sense that one plays a causal role in their coming to be. According to that same vocabulary of the normative form of kinship order from which the Oedipal family has departed, this category includes: child, husband, and wife.

We can understand the question *haunting* Antigone as: Is "brother" of the first or the second sort of relation; is "brother" in category 1 or 2? For when productive of a child Oedipal incest amounts to putting the sibling relation or the brother relation in category 2. That is, Antigone *could* "get another" brother, were she to follow in her father's footsteps and generate a brother by him. Against the background of Oedipal incest placing the sibling relation in category 2, we can read Antigone's violative deed as a passionate attempt to restore the sibling relation to category 1. Her burial of her brother is the making of a brother as something that "cannot" be made by oneself; it is an attempt to make a "can not" of an "ought not," to impart to a social or moral necessity the strength of an ontological necessity. A chief point of the play is that we may not assume that this is given, but that brothers are *made* as brothers-who-are-not-also-uncles by a refusal of the Oedipal type of incest. In a sense then, if this refusal is a making, Antigone's insistence on performing the burial rites for her brother as brother consecrates not just a dead beloved sibling but a certain precarious version of siblinghood or brotherhood itself, and attempts to bring a lost generational order back to the family. It is precisely the precarious status of this generational order that is the source of the deep distress and anguish that fuels Antigone's determined course and the dramatic line of the play.

Given the uniqueness of her family genealogy, then, Antigone cannot be said to be fighting for parental, paternal, or maternal filiation or right per se. Her action, her violation of Creon's prohibition on burying her dead brother, is essentially both a necessary and an impossible attempt at restoration of her family's skewed genealogy. It is necessary because she must affirm the priority of the genealogically given, of those who were made and made siblings, by others, in this case Polynices. Note that she did perform "with my hands" burial rites for her dead brother Eteocles, as well.[27] In some translations, it is also clear that Antigone has already so honored her parents as well as Eteocles: "All three of you have known my hand in death."[28]

So, given Antigone's family heritage, what can she do to try to restore or create a generational order that is not horrifying? In my view, she is adamantly affirming—with rites that are supposed to be for family members, and hence, especially mark them *as such*—family relations created not by her but by other family members. She is desperately trying to ratify these relations—not instituted or created by her—as, precisely, beyond her creation. This is the tragic paradox of having to *make* someone be a brother—and only a brother—through stressing that a brother is precisely what one ought not, though one can, make. Notice also that Antigone stresses that Polynices is her brother (rather than her nephew, or uncle) precisely by stressing that Oedipus is their father (rather than their brother). She is trying to disambiguate the dual status of brother-father in the case of Oedipus and the multiple status of brother-nephew-uncle in the case of Polynices, and of herself as sister-daughter relative to Oedipus and sister-niece-aunt relative to Polynices. She is trying to insist upon one of these positions—father for Oedipus and brother for Polynices—in an essentially restorative effort, that is, an effort to reestablish a family tree with less horrifying articulations.

The obvious objection to these speculations is that, as Antigone herself says, her parents are both dead, at this point in the tale. But perhaps we need to recall that Antigone interprets her suffering and that of her siblings as stemming from her father's wrongs.[29] And from this recollection, it is plausible that Antigone would be extremely vigilant about her family's criminal status and about her own potential for offense against the gods of the dead. If her father's offense is "getting another brother" in part through his own agency, then Antigone could understandably be concerned to efface that offense and bar its possible recurrence throughout the course of her life, even prior to her father's death. Hence, the elevation of the brother as "that which I cannot get for myself." Granted, here she implies that the only reason she cannot get one is because both of her parents are dead. The obvious interpretation of this is that *they* (that is, both Oedipus and Jocasta) are required to get her another brother and, being dead, cannot do so. Her insistence on her parents being the unique source of a brother is obviously significant in her task to efface the family crime. And it makes sense that she would be publicly proclaiming her realization of this unique source, in the form of an action known by the city as a whole, the burial of Polynices. But we can also easily imagine a knowing audience noting with bitter humor, perhaps, that of course, if Antigone's father *alone* had been alive, she could have followed in his own footsteps and procured for herself a brother by her parent.

Perhaps, then, Antigone endures a feared identification with her father. It is Oedipus's crime, after all, that predominates in the tale as a whole, obviously, and this crime is essentially that of not recognizing both mother and father. For not recognizing his mother, though, he has created his children and their suffering. But Jocasta's crime is different; it is the crime of not recognizing her child, her son. So, by symbolically recognizing Polynices as her brother, as not only irreplaceable in general but as uncreatable by *her*, Antigone can affirm that her parents' generative power is irreplaceable, thus symbolically "avoiding" Oedipus's crime, since he supplanted his father in the couple that was his parents.

## Conclusion

How do Irigaray's readings of *Antigone* correspond to the proposed understanding of the enigmatic passage and the play? First, it seems that her two accounts are incompatible: the early account, in which Antigone seeks to honor and retrieve a threatened and obscured maternal filiation, does not square with the later account of Antigone as a servant of male political power animated by guilt about the taint of that same maternal filiation.

Her earlier account, with its emphasis upon Antigone's attempted sanctification of the origin in a "same womb" conforms to part of the suggested reading this chapter has advanced. For it has claimed that Antigone is particularly disturbed by her own understanding of her confused genealogy, and especially by her relation with the hyperrelated Oedipus. It is clear that the entire tragic incestual crime, that is, that according to the play such a thing is incestual and criminal, depends in fact on the importance of maternal filiation. For if the blood tie went primarily through the father (as it clearly is legally determined to do at the end of Aeschylus's *Oresteia*), Antigone's and Oedipus's relations would not be problematically mixed, or would not be maximally so mixed. If paternal filiation were the rule, here, then Antigone and Oedipus, having different fathers, would not be both siblings *and* in a relation of descent—for they simply would not be siblings. So, the incestuous nature of Oedipus's procreation depends on the social logic in which parentage is importantly carried by maternity. In this family, the mother legates criminality with her very issue or at least with the children of her second husband.

In Irigaray's later reading, she argues that a robust cultivated form of *genre* (sexed kind) should replace incest as a concrete and universal limit to human action and should be the foundation for an ethics. This is partly because for Irigaray incest, in particular Oedipal incest relative to Jocasta, represents a moment of women's multiplication into indistinction: mother and wife are indistinguishable in the figure of Jocasta, in relation to one and the same person, Oedipus. So, within the logic of this tale, womankind is stripped of its occasion to be both (1) generationally singular and distinct, on the one hand, and (2) allied amongst itself, though not by marriage. The alliance of women as women requires as a prerequisite this generational spacing, as well as clarity and distinctness, though it does not imply a rigidly defended and predatory self-identity as women.

Since Irigaray sees clearly the confusion about the distinction of mother and wife in the tale, it is conceivable that she might accept the suggestions of this chapter about Antigone's aim to un-double her overwritten kin, even those kin who are dead. Even though in her later reading Irigaray may seek and not find an unquestionable allegiance of Antigone with her mother, there is an important reason for why she may still be able to find it, but to find it elsewhere. How can anyone in this family free or honor the next—or the previous—generation when its generations are barely or tenuously individuated? If the reading sketched here has any plausibility, it indicates that fragile, confected kin relations can be approached by indirection as well as by targeted directness. If "doom extends to all the kin" precisely *as* the kin, if the helplessness of human beings in such netted bonds as families joins them by their choice and not, then Antigone's election of her brother Polynices as the point at which to pluck at the generational tangle is likewise the choice to release her mother from the genealogical ground.

## Notes

Acknowledgments: Many thanks to Kelly Oliver, Kyoo Lee, Tina Chanter, Alan Kim, Elena Tzelepis, and Athena Athanasiou.

1. *Sophocles: The Three Theban Plays*, trans. R. Fagles, Introduction by Bernard Knox (New York: Penguin Books, 1984), 105, lines 995–1005. Abbreviated as "Fagles." The relevant passage is: "Never, I tell you/if I had been the mother of children/or if my husband died, exposed and rotting—/I'd never have taken this ordeal upon myself,/never defied our people's will. What law,/you ask, do I satisfy with what I say?/A husband dead, there might have been another. A child by another too, if I had lost the first./But mother and father both lost in the hall of Death,/no brother could ever spring to light again./For this law alone I held you first in honor."

2. Aristotle, *The Rhetoric and Poetics of Aristotle*, trans. W. Rhys Roberts (New York: The Modern Library, 1984), 209. (Book III, chapter 16, l.1417a 25–35: "Where any detail may appear incredible, then add the cause of it; of this Sophocles provides an example in *Antigone*, where Antigone says she had cared more for her brother than for husband or children, since if the latter perished they might be replaced, 'But since my father and mother in their graves/Lie dead, no brother can be born to me.'"

3. Fagles, 47.

4. Ibid., 46–47.

5. Therese Ahearn Augst, "Difference Becomes Antigone: Hölderlin and the Ethics of Translation," *seminar* 38, no. 2 (May 2002): 101.

6. Fagles, 45.

7. Ibid., 45–46.

8. Ibid., 85.

9. Ibid., 49.

10. Ibid., 51.

11. Martha Nussbaum, *The Fragility of Goodness* (Cambridge: Cambridge University Press, 1986), 440, n.44.

12. See Tina Chanter, *Ethics of Eros: Irigaray's Rewriting of the Philosophers* (New York: Routledge, 1995), 290, n. 39.

13. Hegel apparently did not notice that precisely this criterion is false for the family he has chosen to treat; Oedipus is certainly a cause of the existence of his siblings, who are also his children.

14. Sophocles, *The Complete Greek Tragedies: Sophocles I: Antigone*, ed. David Grene and Richmond Lattimore (New York: Washington Square Press, 1967), 180, l. 511: "When was it shame/to serve the children of my mother's womb?" abbreviated as *GL*.

15. Luce Irigaray, *Speculum. De l'autre femme* (Paris: Minuit, 1974), 271 and *Speculum of the Other Woman*, trans. Gillian Gill (Ithaca: Cornell University Press, 1985), 218. The text titles are here abbreviated *Speculum* (F) for the French original and *Speculum* (E) for the English language translation.

16. *Speculum* (E), 219, translation adapted; *Speculum* (F), 272.

17. *Speculum* (E), 219; *Speculum* (F), 272.

18. I cannot endorse this view as a matter of actual human history, though I am not well placed to evaluate its merit.

19. *Speculum* (F), 274–75; *Speculum* (E), 220. See also the chorus' description of Antigone as "a law to yourself" (Fagles, 102, l. 821). The Greek word here is *autonomos.*

20. Luce Irigaray, *Sexes and Genealogies*, trans. Gillian C. Gill (New York: Columbia University Press, 1993), 110. Luce Irigaray, *Sexes et Parentés* (Paris: Editions de Minuit, 1987). Abbreviated as *SP* (F) for the French original, *SP* (E) for the English translation.

21. *SP* (E), 111.

22. Ibid.

23. Ibid.

24. Ibid., 120: "The greatest fault committed by the race of men was to deprive one gender of its ethical consciousness and of its effectiveness as a gender."

25. Ibid., 4.

26 Plainly, I leave aside the issue of children selecting parents through adoption and analogous means, as well as the question of the status of full- or half-siblings.

27. *GL*, 194, l. 900–902.

28. Ibid., 194, l. 900.

29. Antigone's first words include these: "dear sister, dear Ismene,/how many griefs our father Oedipus handed down!" (Fagles, 59, l. 2). Another rendering of the line is: "You would think that we had already suffered enough/For the curse on Oedipus" (Sophocles, *The Oedipus Cycle*, trans. Dudley Fitts and Robert Fitzgerald [New York: Harcourt Brace Jovanovich, 1977]).

# Chapter 8

# Mourning (as) Woman

## Event, Catachresis, and "That Other Face of Discourse"

Athena Athanasiou and Elena Tzelepis

> At school, we studied *Antigone*. Antigone's mask fell and her desire was revealed to me only in her lament. It puzzled me that it was so radically at odds with her "rebellious" act.
>
> —Jina Politi[1]

In this chapter, we wish to inquire into the catachrestic or improper appropriation of mourning as the other of politics or another politics that denotes the inscriptional site of women's propriety and women's erasure at once. We point to Antigone's work of mourning in order to invoke the aporicity inherent in the mimetic deployment of what Luce Irigaray terms "speaking (as) woman" (*parler-femme*): an opening toward the (future of the) radically irreducible other that has been left out and resists dialectical closure by the Same—the mark of a responsible responsiveness to the singular figure of the dead other. We ask: How else can the radical singularity of the dead other (i.e., Antigone's br/other) be not incorporated into the selfsameness of the performing and commemorating "I" than through an unresolvably misfired, unfulfilled, eccentric—in short, catachrestic—act of mourning? This would be an act of mourning that, instead of idealizing an essential otherness and thus putting the other in her proper place, makes room for the other; for what remains other to proper intelligibility; and for the eventness of what remains to take place. Let us trace then what is done to the authoritative conventions of the stereotypical "female mourning" by feminine alterity: the one relegated to the encrypted or buried other, the foreign inside the house, and, above all, the inner enemy of the polis.

What is at stake here is a consideration of the politics of performative appropriation itself, the possibilities (for subversion) and also the perils (of renormalization) it entails. Our question is this: What would it take to radicalize the political so as to reinvent it beyond the horizon of the intelligible itself? Instead of providing answers, we propose to consider the ways in which the antipolitical inherent in laying claim to mourning rites for the ungrievable other has the potential to hold intelligibility open to political rearticulation, and thus exemplify the affective force of the disruptive performative—of what Judith Butler calls "the political promise of the performative…one that offers an unanticipated political future for deconstructive thinking."[2] Making a promise, however, understood as a performative, is unpredictably tied to the capacity for misfire; its (political) future is never ensured. As a performative, it is, still and always, the place of suspense: at once the reinscribing of the historicity of the norm and a holding open of the possibility of the event.

How might Antigone, as figure of mourning and figure of politics, dramatize the promise of performing disruptively beyond the automatism of retroactive irony—in other words, the promise of displacing rather than reinstating? If we take mourning as a sign (of the proper place) of the feminine as other, but also as a sign of incorporating the other, let us consider how this figure of inappropriate mourning would raise the problem of the performative as a giving of the possibility of embodying the other, and as an exposing of the foreclosures and abjections upon which the delimitations of the political are constituted. If irony and mourning are stereotypically cast in opposing terms in the context of idealist interpretations, then the intertwining of these modalities in the figure of Antigone might indicate the limits of the logic of the performative but also the potential of performing differently. Given that Irigaray suggested that laughter is "the first form of liberation from a secular oppression,"[3] and that she located the very force of laughter in the possibility of undermining the seriousness of meaning—whereby "seriousness" signals to the univocity of truth that has expelled "woman" from the order of discourse—then how would Antigone's ironic mourning *and* mournful irony further complicate Irigaray's account of irony but also her perception of the political?

The figure of Antigone, which has held a peculiar attraction for philosophers, retains an emblematic position in the work of Luce Irigaray as well: not only in her theorization of power but also her own biographical encounters with academic power, specifically in the context of her suspension from teaching at the Department of Psychoanalysis of the University of Vincennes in the fall of 1974. In her response to the question "What do you propose to do in your teaching?" which the department addressed to her, Irigaray defined the stakes of her teaching by invoking the figure of Antigone. She would be interested, she replied, in asking how, by confronting the discourse that lays down the law, Antigone "makes manifest… that other 'face' of discourse that causes a crisis when it appears in broad daylight."[4] Irigaray condensed her theory in a question: "Why, then, has the verdict of the King and the City-State, of Knowledge and discursivity—but also of her brothers and her sisters—always been to condemn her to death in order to assure his/its/their power?"[5] We are interested here, however, not so much in what Irigaray *says* about Antigone (which can be traced in a sequence of Irigaray's various engagements with Antigone over the years) but rather how Antigone is *played out* in her work.

In repudiating Creon's proclamation and in claiming the rite/right to mourn Polynices (indeed, in her unwavering commitment to the symbolic ritual of sprinkling dust on his corpse abandoned outside the wall of Thebes), Antigone emerges as figure for exposing the peculiar overlay between the performative and the political. Without underestimating the differences, we can see how the ghost of Antigone persists in a host of contemporary gendered embodiments of mourning. In the aftermath of armed conflict and ensuing unmourned individual and collective losses, women assume the social role of carrying out the work of mourning and healing. The figure of Antigone persists in political forms that performatively appropriate "female mourning," a sign imbued with heterosexist and ethnocentric connotations. From the Argentinean Mothers of the Plaza de Mayo and the Greek-Cypriot wives and mothers of the disappeared, to women's testimonies before South Africa's post-apartheid Truth and Reconciliation Commission concerning their efforts to recover the bodily remains of their sons, but also to artistic configurations such as Diamanda Galas's performances of mourning incantation for those dead from AIDS, mourning is encoded as always already gendered; in Irigaray's words, "femininity consists essentially in laying the dead man back in the womb of the earth, and giving him eternal life."[6] What is more, mourning is always already premised upon kinship normativity; in Irigaray's terms again, "the purpose that moves blood relatives to action is the care of the *bloodless*."[7]

The specter of mourning woman is also evoked, however indirectly and ambiguously, by the international feminist and antimilitaristic movement *Women in Black*. In their politics, a certain displacement of the discursive historicity that governs the sign of "female mourning" can be traced. They speak the sexually and nationally marked language of mourning, but they do so catachrestically: in tending to the death of others instead of their "brothers," *Women in Black* transgress the blood codes—patriotic loyalty, kinship affinity—of intelligible mourning, which forbids the care of the other. Through their unthinkable mourning for the dead other, *Women in Black* give body to the political promise, the not yet, of the performative. Like Antigone, they are necessarily implicated in and, at the same time, move away from the propriety of mourning, whereby "mourning" is the name of or for that which is generally ascribed, entrusted, or abandoned, to the feminine.[8]

In her resilient claim to tend the exposed dead body of her brother who has been declared a traitor and thus denied the honor of a proper burial, Antigone confronts the exclusions of legitimate mourning and unsettles the assumptions of political normativity upon which mourning is historically founded. In spite of Creon's prohibition, she affirms her philia of incestuous and matrilinear kinship and bears witness to the absolute corporeality of her mother's son turned into an internal enemy. Polynices is the *echthros* (and not *polemios*, the external enemy), a kin (being of the same blood to Creon) who has transformed into an enemy to the polis; an enemy reduced to mere body, bare death. Antigone, on the other side, is a mourner who figures and tests the split in polis, not, however, in the Hegelian sense of a split between universality and particularity resolving into the master category of dialectical idealism (*Aufhebung*), but rather in the sense of what Nicole Loraux calls the "bond of division," that is, in the sense of opening up the question of belonging and nonbelonging to the polis. In her political deed of burying her "brother"—singular, irreproducible, irreplaceable, and above all an enemy of the state—Antigone not only refuses to enact her feminine role as guardian of the realm of the home, but rather, she displaces the political boundaries and the proper limits of the polis.

In light of such aporias that inform the "politics of mourning," in its modality of mourning otherwise, or of otherwise than mourning, we might ask whether there is a subversion beyond the appropriation—property and propriety—of alterity; whether there can be a reenactment that lies beyond the dialectic of appropriation and its implications of order, literalness, and ownership; or whether there can be a transgressive reinscription that is not recuperable by the dominant order; or to what extent a sign is caught within and thus limited by the historical horizon of its discursive systematicity (however discontinuous, fissured, and thus nontotalizable) within which it attains meaning and from which it takes its locutionary force; to what extent the performative is bound and determined by the burden of its sedimented histories and regulatory conventions. Put another way: How can a performative be necessarily implicated in the paleonymy of propriation, appropriation, reappropriation, misappropriation, or expropriation that authorizes it, and at the same time be capable of exposing and exceeding its prescribed limits? And, finally, would this be the right question, or one that, in an attempt to guard responsive openness to the political futures of alterity against the dialectical (fore)closures of appropriation, ineluctably succumbs to the idealistic infinity of a transcendent "outside," a utopian or even messianic ethics of the "beyond"? The question raised by the catachreses of mourning we discuss here is if/how the arrival of the event, the arrival of the other, can be fully and effectively received (rather than captured) through the performativity of mourning. But how is the potentiality of the event linked to the actuality of praxis, here? In other words: Where is Antigone speaking from when she responds to the arrival of the event through opening to the law of the other? Is she speaking as a woman, in the place of a woman, or in the name of a woman?[9]

For Irigaray, woman has no proper name.[10] "Woman" is a catachresis, a misname, or a name without a literal referent; a catachresis that captures and interrupts the stakes of private property as well as of appropriation by discourse: "Woman exists only as an occasion for mediation, transaction, transition, transference, between man and his fellow man, indeed between man and himself."[11] "Woman" emerges as the always already catachrestic name of leaving open the possibility of a different language—an *other* writing, an *other* meaning; a language that challenges the discursive order that renders women necessarily aphasic. Women cannot become "speaking subjects" just by complying with the phallogocentric discursive order; neither by means of defining "woman," nor by means of appropriating the feminine to the dominant discourse, but rather by means of repeating/questioning the conditions in which the feminine has been rendered inarticulate in discourse. As an exploration of the possible connections between female desire and female language, Irigaray's speaking (as) woman summons a place for the "other" as feminine. Speaking (as) woman is simultaneously singular and plural; it would involve proximity instead of privileging "oneness." As such, speaking (as) woman appeals to a novelty that can and ought to confound the sociosexual rules of univocal phallic discourse. This syntax, in which there would no longer be either subject or object, would no longer be organized around proper names and proper meanings. It would exceed the discursive order that grants women no language other than that of the hysteric, and it would so by precluding any logic of appropriation.[12] In this horizon of catachrestic engagement with (that other face of the) discourse, the notion of the event would encompass a certain inextricability of positivity and negativity, as well as activity and passivity. It would also entail going beyond, and against, the ontological division between *dynamis* (potency, potentiality, power) and *energeia* (actuality, acting, actively existing). The experience of the event does not emerge from a pure newness, but rather from a constant—actual and untimely—disruption of the discursive order.

The urgency of Antigone's affirmative claim is marked by a suspension between preserving the sanctity of her br/other's dead body and allowing its spectral arrival, or return, to happen. Is, however, the actual connectivity with the event always already revolutionary? Does not Antigone's desire to bury her brother also imply a necessary disallowing the other to be other? Is not such summoning of the specter at once an expelling of the specter? Antigone's untimely act of burying Polynices' traitorous corpse becomes the occasion on which, by deploying the feminized work of mourning, she transgresses the gendered mandates of kinship-polis antinomy, she (en)genders the boundaries of the polis, and compels others—the chorus, Creon, and the messengers—to regard her as "manly." In reiterating the conditions of her subordination, however, Antigone could also, tragically, mobilize an eventual return of/to a regressive configuration of the very law of familial conformity and moral normality. Could then the tragic figure of Antigone as a "manned" woman before the law represent the poetic horizon in which Irigaray's *parler-femme* can be read in conjunction with catachresis of mourning-as-language-in-the-feminine? How does the sign of mourning turn from a pious and proper language-in-the-feminine into a threatening performative catachresis expelled by and actively opposed to the very intelligibility of the political?[13] To explore this question, let us turn to the tragic act of mourning bearing in mind that mourning, as central to tragedy, plays a crucial role in the ways the polis discursively and imaginatively invents itself.[14]

The Athenian polis is the biopolitical site in which women, along with slaves and foreigners, constitute the irreducible limit of humanity: the marked and dreaded Other who is banished from the political domain as mere body, and, at the same time, represents the abjected ground on which the body politic claims to be constituted. Women, more than anyone else, come to exist only and exclusively through the fleshly prerequisite of biological life; men, on the other hand, are invested with the aura of the incorporeal logos—the emblematic characteristic of the human at large. In the discursive regime of the ancient polis, where the political is emphatically defined as the sexually neutral domain of disembodied reason and essential logos, the female body—or, perhaps more accurately, the female as mere body—is considered to be essentially unpolitical: ascribed to the less-than-human sphere of simple and mere life; as such, it is expelled from the polis, buried outside its boundaries. Affective impulses and the unruly exigencies of the body and the soul lie resolutely within the female space as the "natural" domain of human life. Indeed, what must be subdued and expelled from the paradigmatic universality of the political sphere is the female in its dreadful association with passion (*πάθος*)—in the dual sense of the Greek word: as wound and affect.

"Passion in the city-state? *Páthos* affecting the citizens? Danger."[15] As Loraux argues, unforgettable grief (*álaston pénthos*) and unappeasable memory wrath (*mênis*) are two of the worst enemies of politics in the context of the ancient Greek polis. Politically coerced amnesia comes as an antidote to these antipolitical forces; this officially administered forgetting is *amnesty*, an enforced eradication of grief and memory. "If it were not for Achilles," Loraux remarks, "whose *menis* is in all Greek memories, I would readily say that we have here a female model of memory, which the cities try to confine within the anti- (or ante-) political sphere. And, in fact, wrath in mourning, the principle of which is eternal repetition, willingly expresses itself with an *aei*, and the fascination of this tireless 'always' threatens to set it up as a powerful rival to the political *aei* that establishes the memory of institutions."[16]

In her reading of Greek tragedy, Loraux emphasizes the importance of the vocal register—the phonē—and the antipolitical at the expense of the logos and the political. Loraux reads tragedy, as opposed to the orthodoxy of civic discourse, as a song of mourning lament (thrēnos). Mourning lamentation—especially the excessive mourning of women wailing, this paradigmatic other to civic orthodoxy—is strictly banished from the public scene by civic legislation, as the memory of the dead is restricted to the sanctioned Athenian speech form of the official funeral oration (epitaphios logos), which eulogized the true andres, autochthonous Athenian male citizens and soldiers, as opposed to women, barbarians, and immigrants who constituted the rest of humanity, the others, merely anthropoi. Mourning is a women's task, but also one that is forced to remain outside of the political and ethical walls of the polis, one that is ideally either limited to the stage or sequestered inside the boundaries of the home. The mourning voice is fraught with dangers, as Loraux reminds us pointing to emblematic moments of expelling the thrēnos: from Plato who flatly declares that even the names that imply lamentation have to be banished from the city-state because they cause a shudder in those who hear them[17] to Jean-Paul Sartre who, writing his 1964 adaptation of Euripides' *Trojan Women* at the time of the U.S. escalation of the Vietnam War, considered mourning irrelevant and censored it in order to emphasize the message of struggle and illuminate the political dimension of the play. It is by virtue of its antipolitical implication that women's mourning voice, when it becomes public, exceeds civic order and threatens its conventions of intelligibility. What Loraux calls "antipolitical" (and not a-political, which would misleadingly convey a notion of exteriority and neutrality) designates the political act that is actively opposed to the very intelligibility of the political, in her words, "the other of politics, but also another politics, no longer based on consensus and living together, but on what I call the 'bond of division.'"[18]

But what is the political positioning that Antigone's passionate "antipolitics" sets in motion? Butler rightly points out that Antigone has been read by Hegel, Lacan, and Irigaray as a figure who articulates a pre-political opposition to politics, the constitutive outside of the polis. Irigaray comes to critically reinscribe Hegel's reading, who claims in *The Phenomenology of Spirit* that Antigone—as well as "womankind in general," to which Hegel shifts in a rhetorical act of abstracting Antigone as femininity—is "the eternal irony of the community."[19] In Hegel womanhood constitutes "an internal enemy," an idiosyncratic aberration of human universality (a *daimon*, as the chorus calls her). Antigone, although not explicitly named in Hegel's passage, is clearly there, embodying the "mere particularity" that forms the common ground, the *topos*, of the political, while lying outside of it, as the one who cannot be named properly. Improper public mourning for the *external* enemy is proscribed by the sovereign; this unthinkability is compelled into a fatal crisis by a "woman," the perennial *internal* enemy. As a representative of the ties of the "hearth and blood"—the domain of the home, the body, and funeral rites—Antigone is, and must remain, outside the terms of the polis, but she is, as it were, an essential outside without which the intelligibility of the polis could not be.

In *Speculum*, Irigaray, who remains ambiguously within a certain Hegelian legacy of Antigone's interpretation, takes Antigone to be the representative principle of feminine defiance of authoritarianism: "Her example is always worth reflecting upon," she writes, "as a historical figure and as an identity and identification for many girls and women living today. For this reflection, we must abstract Antigone from the seductive, reductive discourses and listen to what she has to say about government of the polis, its order and its laws."[20] By contrast, Butler argues for the impossibility of representation marked by the figure of Antigone. Putting into question Irigaray's gesture of "abstracting" Antigone as an emblematic figure for feminist politics, Butler asks: "But can Antigone herself be made into a representative for a certain kind of feminist politics, if Antigone's own representative function is itself in crisis?...Indeed, it is not that, as a fiction, the mimetic or representative character of Antigone is already put in question but that, as a figure for politics, she points somewhere else, not to politics as a question of representation but to that political possibility that emerges when the limits to representation and representability are exposed."[21]

As a figure for politics that points to the very exposure of the limits of representability, Antigone enacts, first and foremost, the problem of the "figure," of "standing for," of "representing," and thus the problem of "where one speaks from." As a figure of the unfigurable, she not only cuts across the limits of intelligibility but she also exemplifies a form of political agency that is fraught with the performative antinomies of reiteration, event, irony, and catachresis. If Antigone is the eternal irony of the community this is so because, Hegel notwithstanding, she "neither buries nor fails to bury, neither leaves her brother above nor below, neither universalizes nor fails to universalize the male, because what she performs is not intelligible to those around her and, perhaps, not even to herself."[22] She violates law (the sovereign's rule, "written nomos," Creon's *kērygma* in the name of law ("unwritten laws," *nomima* [customary law]);[23] she stands neither for nor against the law.[24] She is *in* the polis—and, at the same time, *without* the polis (*autonomos*)[25]—in acting on behalf of a certain enactment of kinship, on behalf of a certain modality of desire, and, ultimately, on behalf of a certain relation between the two. She represents not the ideality of kinship but rather the displacement of kinship, and thus fulfilling the promise given by the very polyphonous etymology of her own (unuttered) name, a catachrestic name embodying both an opposition of lineage to the polis and an opposition to lineage, and also, both in opposition of and in compensation of genos.[26] Despite Hegel's didactic attempt to showcase Antigone as a transhistorical emblem of idealized kinship and family ethics, Antigone has never remained in her place; true to the etymology of her name, she has already departed from the norms of kinship, long before she left the family to risk her life in the polis by acting on behalf of her beloved dead brother: she has already been "against generation," as she has been the daughter of an incestuous bond, but also as she has renounced motherhood.

Antigone's usurpation of the sovereign's manhood leads her outside of the realm of life, to her "living death" in a "deep-dug home." Power, the condition of her own agency and alteration, puts her finally in her place; at the same time, power does not remain intact by Antigone's act of appropriation. Through her passionate claim, indeed a feminine desire attached to death, Antigone herself has transformed into an enemy to the city—an ill-adjusted foreign body. As a result of her transgressive passion, Antigone is condemned to be walled in alive; she must be entombed, sealed alive inside a cave, thus not only uncannily mirroring her dead brother's unburied body that rots by the Theban walls, but also exemplifying her own ambivalent position of exclusionary inclusion vis-à-vis the polis: once again, she figures the limits of intelligibility. Sophocles reserves for Antigone a feminine, unheroic, bloodless act of suicide, as Loraux remarks. She hangs herself in the tomb, while Creon's son Haemon kills himself by sword, out of love for Antigone.[27] Haemon's mother Eurydice commits suicide and Polynices is finally buried by the repentant Creon.

Antigone's mournful iterability (difference in repetition) of the fraught relation between kinship normativity and political agency figures as a genre of mourning-as-catachresis emerging when performative misappropriation seeks to go beyond symptomatic duplication of the intelligible and its dialectical machinery. The question now becomes: Is Antigone's crypt the only possible topos for stepping out of the provinces of the "proper" and for animating, in Irigaray's terms, "that other 'face' of discourse which provokes a crisis when it appears in broad daylight"?[28] Can we speak "outside" the vicious circle of a static dialectics according to which each pole of the binary opposition implicates the other in a perpetual logic of transposability? Is performative misappropriation inescapably failed and fatal? But here we need to ask, What is the effect and affect of the critical recitation of the feminine as at once the discursive impropriety of metaphysics and the nonthematizable necessary condition for its own propriety? Irigaray herself poses similar questions with respect to Antigone's pathos: "Is mourning itself her *jouissance*?...Does she anticipate the decree of death formulated by those in power? Does she duplicate it? Has she given in? Or is she still in revolt?"[29] Or, to put it yet differently, is she a rebel or a hysteric?[30] Antigone's crypt alerts us to the ambivalences and exigencies organizing the figure of the expelled feminine. The boundary between underground subversive work and enforced entombment in the fatal feminine of the masculine imaginary becomes crucially permeable; as does the boundary between banishment to a living death and the ultimate agency of taking one's own life. The question of how the movement beyond the "social death" of conventional constraints avoids merely rearticulating the norm within which it remains entombed cannot be answered by any teleological or programmatic certainty.

The idealized normativity within which the subject is entombed is inextricably tied to the subject's melancholic incorporation and performative enactment of unacknowledged, unmournable, and unperformable losses. According to the narrative that Freud provides in his 1917 essay, "Mourning and Melancholia," melancholia is described as a process by which the lost other becomes internalized, preserved, encrypted within the self. Refusing her loss, the melancholic takes the lost object into herself ("introjects" it) and preserves it mimetically as an identification. Writes Freud: "The ego wishes to incorporate this object into itself, and the method by which it would do so, in this oral or cannibalistic stage, is by devouring it."[31] Indeed, the politics of mourning, in its peculiar relation to gender performativity, risks becoming afflicted with the very predicaments it seeks to address. Antigone's desire is necessarily implicated in the norm that subjects her and, at the same time, moves away from the propriety of mourning-as-language-in-the-feminine. Not only is mourning made up through the gender propriety of femininity, but also gender intelligibility itself is performatively acquired through ungrieved loss, most significantly, through the repudiation of homosexual attachments. Rather than being merely a site of suffering, however, this process is also a means of disruptive event and potential revolt against the "melancholy of the public sphere," that is, against the demarcation of the intelligibly human polis according to gender, sexual, and familial norms.[32]

The question then is not only how to go beyond the encrypted feminine of the masculine imaginary, beyond the immanence of Antigone's crypt, but also how this movement beyond the enclosure and foreclosure of the feminine does not end up being absorbed by the metaphysics of representation and the heteronormative binary logic of sexual difference. The point is not for women to relinquish their claims to polis, but rather that the polis be radically refigured, most importantly so in its naturalized link to what Hegel called the natural domain—that is, the "unpolitical" practices of affect, desire, mourning, and love; the point is to challenge the idealized heteronormative assumptions and the depoliticized family injunctions upon which the polis is premised. In that respect, what Loraux calls "antipolitical" would evoke "the other of politics, but also another politics," that is actively opposed to the regulative ideal of what is to count as a family according to the normative order of the polis. As Loraux has shown, grieving heroines "use lamentation for their own purposes and on their own behalf."[33] Indeed, Antigone resorts to an act of mourning in order to convey her defiance against the sovereignty of the law. She inhabits the gendered discursive mode of "speaking (as) woman" in a way that tests the limits of the polis and its democratic promise.

In our reading of Irigaray's speaking (as) woman through Antigone's mourning-as-catachresis and Loraux's "antipolitical," the call for the other of politics is an interminably aporetic call for another politics—for a deconstructive redefinement of the contours of the political in ways that are responsive to the exclusions and abjections that constitute it as such. Keeping in mind this resolutely political understanding of the antipolitical, let us conclude: What is at stake in the relationship between the feminine and the antipolitical is neither a "pathological" refusal nor a "normal" acceptance to grieve, as a conventional sharp division between mourning and melancholia would require; it is rather a responsive engagement with the political foreclosure of grief—a sustained openness to histories of political loss involved in the constitution of normative limits between *anthropos* and the *polis*. What may emerge from this openness is not only the melancholia of the ungrievable, but also an occasion for eventually undoing the melancholic properness of gender intelligibility through the political promise of the performative.

To render "woman" and "mourning" open to unprefigurable future significations is to always allow for a performative excess of social temporality that resists capture by the authoritative forces of signification. To deploy catachrestic female mourning as a certain undoing, a performative displacement, a spasm, or a "scandal of the speaking body"[34] will thus mean engaging in aporetic relations between language and the body, between power and act, norm and desire, as well as between the performative and the political, in order to articulate an untenable promise; it entails, instead of making oneself symptomatic, rather allowing one's politics the risks of the aporetic. It encompasses burying the very proprieties of our strategies and proper names, including the proprieties of the Woman that was. Beyond the name, the misname, the catachresis of "woman." Beyond the matrix, or the "proper," of "sexual difference."

## Notes

1. Jina Politi, "Antigone's Letter," *Gramma: Journal of Theory and Criticism* 14 (2006): 131–40.

2. Judith Butler, *Excitable Speech: A Politics of the Performative* (New York: Routledge, 1997), 161.

3. Luce Irigaray, *This Sex Which Is Not One*, trans. Catherine Porter and Carolyn Burke (Ithaca: Cornell University Press, 1985), 163.

4. Ibid., 167.

5. Ibid., 167–68.

6. Luce Irigaray, *Speculum of the Other Woman*, trans. Gillian Gill (Ithaca: Cornell University Press, 1985), 225.

7. Ibid., 214.

8. On the catachrestic mourning-as-language-in-the-feminine performed by *Women in Black*, see Athena Athanasiou, "Reflections on the Politics of Mourning: Feminist Ethics and Politics in the Age of Empire," *Historein: A review of the past and other stories* 5 (2006): 40–57.

9. Such questions echo Shoshana Felman's famous provocative question about Irigaray: "If, as Luce Irigaray suggests, the woman's silence or the repression of her capacity to speak, are constitutive of philosophy and of theoretical discourse as such, from what theoretical locus is Luce Irigaray herself speaking in order to develop her own theoretical discourse about women?" Is she speaking *as* a woman, or *in the place of* the (silent) woman, *for* the woman, *in the name of* the woman? See Shoshana Felman, "Women and Madness: The Critical Phallacy," *Diacritics* (Winter 1975): 2–10.

10. Irigaray, *This Sex*, 26.

11. Irigaray, *Speculum*, 193.

12. Irigaray, *This Sex*, 134.

13. Judith Butler, *Antigone's Claim: Kinship between Life and Death* (New York: Columbia University Press, 2000), 78. In her reading of Antigone's legacy, Butler refers to catachresis as a "shadowy form of signification [that] takes its toll on a life by depriving it of its sense of ontological certainty and durability within a publicly constituted political sphere." If the socially instituted foreclosure of recognizable humanness expels language out of its referential conventions and compels it into the suspensions of catachresis, then what emerges is not only the melancholia of the foreclosure, but also an occasion for undoing the properness of intelligibility through catachreses to come (in all their promising as well as fatal possibilities).

14. Nicole Loraux, *The Invention of Athens: The Funeral Oration in the Classical City*, trans. Alan Sheridan (Cambridge: Harvard University Press, 1992).

15. Nicole Loraux, *Mothers in Mourning* (Ithaca: Cornell University Press, 1998), 9.

16 Ibid., 98.

17. Plato, *Republic*, III, 387 b-c, 398 d-e. "Excessive female mourning" was outlawed in the Athenian city-state around the sixth century BCE. The banning (attributed to Solon), however, does not amount to disappearance. As Loraux has shown, lamentation finds its way—it is "cited"—into the genre of tragic

performance (*The Invention of Athens*, 328). See also, Olga Taxidou, *Tragedy, Modernity, and Mourning* (Edinburgh: Edinburgh University Press, 2004). Taxidou views Athenian tragedy as a structure of performance permeated by the tensions of the male homosocial democratic politico-discursive domain.

18. Nicole Loraux, *The Mourning Voice: An Essay on Greek Tragedy* trans. Elizabeth Trapnell Rawlings, foreword by Pietro Pucci (Ithaca: Cornell University Press, 2002), 23.

19. G. W. F Hegel, *The Phenomenology of Spirit,* trans. A. V. Miller (London: Oxford University Press, 1977), #475, 288.

20. Irigaray, *Speculum*, 70.

21. Butler, *Antigone's Claim*, 2. See also Yannis Stavrakakis, "The Lure of Antigone: Aporias of an Ethics of the Political," *Umbr(a): A Journal of the Unconscious* (2003): 117–29. In critically discussing Slavoj Žižek's idealization of Antigone as a model of radical ethico-political action ("Passionate (Dis)attachments, or, Judith Butler as a Reader of Freud," in *The Ticklish Subject: The Absent Centre of Political Ontology* [London: Verso, 1999], 247–312), Stavrakakis shows that it is impossible to sustain a sharp distinction between the ethics of assuming lack—denoting negativity—and the politics of assuming the act—denoting positivity. We agree with Stavrakakis' understanding of the fidelity to the event-ness of an event in terms of an "infidel fidelity," one that encompasses "fidelity to the openness of the political space and to the awareness of the constitutive impossibility of a final suture of the social" (126).

22. Carol Jacobs, "Dusting Antigone," *MLN* 111, no. 5 (1996): 889–917.

23. Sophocles, *Antigone*, in *The Theban Plays,* trans. E. F. Watling (Harmondsworth: Penguin, 1947), line 1454.

24. See Costas Douzinas, "Law's Birth and Antigone's Death: On Ontological and Psychoanalytical Ethics," *Cardozo Law Review* 16, nos. 3–4 (1995): 1325–62. In treating the question of Antigone's encounter with the law through Heidegger and Lacan, Douzinas views Antigone as an ambivalent figure that puts into operation unexpected similarities between the ethics of ontology and the ethics of psychoanalysis. At the same time, Antigone's ethics, her excessive love for the suffering br/other in the midst of the law, becomes a site where the limits of both Heidegger's ontology and Lacan's psychoanalytical ethics can be valuably exposed.

25. Sophocles, *Antigone*, 1821.

26. Stathis Gourgouris, *Does Literature Think? Literature as Theory for an Antimythical Era* (Stanford: Stanford University Press, 2003), 133.

27. In Greek dramaturgy, confinement in a crypt is a typical threat for punishing women who did not behave properly. This symbolic repression of the female alterity in the controlled bounds of (the male fantasy of) femininity functions like a foundation for the establishment of civilized social order. Aegisthos threatened he was going to have Electra buried alive if she did not learn to stay at home and behave like a proper woman (Sophocles, *Electra*, lines 329–331, 378–385); and the Erinyes, the group of archaic chthonic goddesses who pursue Orestes after he murders his mother, were stripped of their power and forced by Athena to go underground and hide themselves (Aeschylus, *Eumenides*, lines 937–948).

28. Irigaray, *This Sex*, 167.

29. Ibid., 219.

30. On the ways in which Irigaray's mimesis deploys hysterical resistance as a counterdiscursive strategy, see Dianne Chisholm, "Hysteria," in *Engaging with Irigaray*, ed. Carolyn Burke, Naomi Schor, and Margaret Whitford (New York: Columbia University Press, 1994). See also Elena Tzelepis, *Mimesis as Philosophical Critique: Eventuality and the Feminine*. Unpublished Ph.D. dissertation. New York: New School for Social Research, 2007. Indeed, the problem of transforming symptomatic-hysterical mimicry into performative subversive mimesis and revolutionary change is central not only to Irigaray's dissimulation of philosophy and psychoanalysis, but also to collective feminist action (including the one performed by *Women in Black*).

31. Sigmund Freud, "Mourning and Melancholia," *Collected Papers,* vol. 4, trans. Joan Riviere (New York: Basic Books, 1959), 160. In what is both a critique and an extension of Freud's theory of melancholia, Nicolas Abraham and Maria Torok speak of the "crypt" as an intimate recess, an inner closed non-place the subject constructs inside her psyche, in order to conceal there the precious corpses of desires, memories, and unspeakable secrets. Organized around the figure of the crypt as a live burial of the love object, this poetics of psychic entombment plays a crucial role in what Abraham and Torok call "disease of mourning," as endocryptic identification inhibits the work of mourning. Nicolas Abraham and Maria Torok, "L'objet perdu-moi: Notations sur l'identification endocryptique," in *L'écorce et le noyau* (Paris: Aubier-Montaigne, 1978), 295–317.

32. Butler, *Antigone's Claim*, 81.

33. Loraux, *The Mourning Voice*, 59.

34. Shoshana Felman, *The Scandal of the Speaking Body: Don Juan with J. L. Austin, or Seduction in Two Languages* (Stanford: Stanford University Press, 2002 [1980]).

Chapter 9

# Weird Greek Sex

## Rethinking Ethics in Irigaray and Foucault

Lynne Huffer

This chapter begins with a simple observation: despite the centrality of Luce Irigaray's work to contemporary thought about gender and sexuality, she remains virtually absent from queer theory.[1] This is somewhat surprising, at least at first glance, since Irigaray's attempt to rethink sexuality and the morphology of the body in the context of sex-gender inequality could be said to constitute a central concern not just of feminism, but of queer theory as well. But even a casual perusal of influential queer thinkers—Eve Kosofsky Sedgwick, Gayle Rubin, Michael Warner, Lauren Berlant, David Halperin, Leo Bersani—reveals Irigaray's glaring absence.[2]

This absence might reflect, at least in part, the well-documented tension between feminism and queer theory, and the fact that Irigaray has been definitively claimed by the feminist camp. But there are deeper philosophical reasons for queer theory's lack of attention to Irigaray than the simple fact of her feminist label, especially considering queer theory's origins in the feminist work of Rubin, Sedgwick, and Butler.[3] If queer theory developed, at least in part, as a self-critical, sexual alternative to feminist thinking about gender, Irigaray scarcely registers on the radar screen of that queer resistance to feminism.[4]

I argue that Irigaray's absence from queer theory can be illuminated by an analysis of the specific differences that separate Irigaray's thought from queer theory's philosophical grounding in the work of Foucault. Indeed, as Rosi Braidotti observed more than twenty years ago, there is a "profound 'dissonance'" between Irigaray and Foucault.[5] An examination of the precise nature of that dissonance can do much not only to explain queer theory's almost total disregard for Irigaray's work, but also to establish, in more constructive terms, some common theoretical ground for bridging the gap that separates feminists and queers. In other words, thinking Foucault and Irigaray together—and specifically, in their shared attention to the Greeks—is useful for the project of a queer feminism.

In light of that project, it is worth pointing out that the queer disinterest in Irigaray's work is not, in fact, symmetrically mirrored by any feminist dismissal of Foucault. To be sure, many feminists have criticized the gender bias and the gender blindness of Foucault's oeuvre, but some thinkers continue to find in Foucault a useful framework for understanding gender inequality as a particular kind of subjugating discursive formation. In other words, Foucault is very much on the feminist radar screen, while the inverse for Irigaray and queer theory is not the case. Obviously enough, like the queer-feminist divide, the division between Foucault and Irigaray is asymmetrical, repeating the falsely symmetrical, specular structure identified by Irigaray in *Speculum of the Other Woman*[6] as the exclusionary logic undergirding Western thought. In this sense, Irigaray herself becomes, in relation to queer theory, another version of the maternal feminine: queer theory's excluded other, its silent and invisible ground.

This chapter explores the asymmetrical dissonance between Irigaray and Foucault by examining how each of them, in reading the Greeks, contributes to the articulation of an ethics. I focus on ethics here for a number of reasons. First, ethical problems lie at the heart of the feminist-queer tension because of the historical relation between sexuality and morality. Symptomatically, in a recent articulation of a profound moral dissonance between feminism and queer theory, Janet Halley calls for a "break from feminism" to make way for "a different ethics"[7] that is explicitly queer. Indeed, the historical relation between sexual and moral questions is precisely the problem that pushed Foucault to turn from his study of nineteenth-century sexuality in the first volume of *The History of Sexuality* to the practices of the Greeks in the second volume, *The Use of Pleasure*.[8] As Foucault explained in an interview not long before his death: "I absolutely had intended to write historical studies on sexuality starting with the sixteenth century and to analyze the evolution of this knowledge up to the nineteenth century. And while I was doing this project, I noticed that it was not working out. An important problem remained: why had we made sexuality into a moral experience" ("Final," 10)?[9]

In a contemporary context, one of the forms this problem has taken is the theoretical and political dissonance between libidinous queer sex radicals and the prudish feminist guardians of a moral order. And while historically ethics has been claimed primarily for the morally virtuous feminist side, increasingly queer theorists have attempted to reclaim ethics without abandoning the antifoundationalist premises of the queer position. Both feminist and queer theorists have contributed to the contentious and oppositional nature of this struggle, where ethics becomes the prize to be won in a broader battle over the political meaning and value of each camp's challenge to an unjust social order.

The purpose of this chapter is to foreground the moral dimension of this queer-feminist dissonance through an examination of the constructive ethical projects of Irigaray and Foucault in their readings of the Greeks.[10] I begin by looking at Foucault's work in relation to queer theory, with a particular attention to his ethical claims in the last two volumes of *The History of Sexuality: The Use of Pleasure* and *The Care of the Self*.[11] Second, I examine how Irigaray's work on ethics can be brought into dialogue with some of the issues raised by Foucault. And third, I conclude by pointing to the ways in which the dissonance between Irigaray and Foucault can become productive for us in our attempts to enlarge our thinking about ethics, especially with regard to questions of gender and sexuality.

## Foucault, Ethics, and the Greeks

David Halperin—a well-known classicist, one of the leading voices of queer theory, and perhaps Foucault's most enthusiastic interpreter—nicely sums up the interest of the Greeks to queer theory when he says: "the ancient Greeks were quite weird, by our standards, when it came to sex."[12] Indeed, the sexual "weirdness" of the Greeks is essential to the point Halperin wants to drive home about sexuality generally: historically speaking, there is no norm when it comes to sex. This historical observation about sexual practices is key both to Halperin's and queer theory's ethical position with regard to sex: that normativity itself is to be resisted in favor of a "pluralistic sexual ethics" (Rubin, 15) that would celebrate the variety and sheer diversity of human sexuality.

Like Halperin, Foucault too was interested in the sexual "weirdness" of the Greeks, descriptions of which he gleans primarily from his readings of Plato, Aristotle, Demosthenes, Xenophon, and others. However, Foucault's detailed description of the sexual practices of elite Greek men is subsumed into a larger philosophical project centered on what he calls technologies of the self in relation to an ethics of freedom. Having exhaustively demonstrated, in *Discipline and Punish*[13] and the first volume of *The History of Sexuality*, the extent to which modernity has produced us as subjected subjects (*assujettis*), Foucault turns to the ancient Greek world to find a way out of this subjectivation (*assujettissement*). Thus, in volume two of *The History of Sexuality: The Use of Pleasure*, Foucault explores not only Greek sexual practices, but also modes of living and dietary regimes in order to show that it is possible to shape one's own subjectivity through the work one does on oneself. Indeed, this work led Foucault further and further away from his initial theme of sexuality. As Foucault put it a year before he died: "I must confess that I am much more interested in problems about techniques of the self and things like that rather than sex. . . sex is boring."[14]

In *Insult and the Making of the Gay Self*,[15] Didier Eribon conveniently delineates two vectors of this "aesthetics of existence" epitomized for Foucault by the Greek world: first, a "politics of friendship" and, second, an "economy of pleasures." The politics of friendship has to do with the way men lived among each other—what Foucault calls friendship as a way of life. The second vector, an economy of pleasures, derives from Foucault's attention to particular practices that Halperin describes as "weird," practices that predate the age of Christian confession and the subsequent psychoanalytic economy of sexuality and desire. Both aspects of Foucault's reading of the Greek world have been taken up by queer theory, either directly or indirectly. Foucault's question about men together—"What relations, through homosexuality, can be established, invented, multiplied, and modulated?"[16]—has been reconfigured, for example, in the work of Lauren Berlant and Michael Warner as the "counterintimacies"[17] of a "queer counterpublic" (560): new ways of being together in the project of world-making through cultural transgression and transformation.

The second line of thinking that Eribon identifies as an "economy of pleasures" is connected to the first, and has to do with establishing relations with others based not on the psychoanalytic conception of the subject of desire, but rather on a self who engages in strategic, regulated practices of pleasure. At the end of the first volume of *The History of Sexuality*, Foucault famously proclaims that "the rallying point for the counterattack against the deployment of sexuality ought not to be sex-desire, but bodies and pleasures" (157). In their interpretation of this evocation of a new economy of pleasures, some queer theorists have hailed Foucault as a prophet of corporeal and subjective freedom, the harbinger of a postsexual utopian future brought into being through strategic acts involving "strange parts of [our] bodies"[18]—updated versions of "weird Greek sex." Queer theorists thus use Foucault to put forward a vision of bodily pleasure freed from the normalizing constrictions of sexuality and desire. According to Halperin, for example, S/M, fisting, and other "new" sexual practices thereby contribute to the creation of "a gay praxis,"[19] or even, as Foucault puts it, a "way of life [that] can yield a culture and an ethics" ("Friendship," 138).

All of this constitutes what Foucault calls an ethics of freedom, a form of self-fashioning in relation to others. As many of Foucault's admirers have pointed out, this Foucauldian work on the self is hardly the narcissistic obsession of a dandy, but rather, in its emphasis on one's relation to others, is connected to the development of new forms of sociality. Further, Foucault's ethical project in the last two volumes of *The History of Sexuality* is crucially linked to what Braidotti identifies as "the central concern of Foucault's work": "the criticism of the despotic power exercised by the philosophical text and by the history of philosophy as a monolithic block of knowledge" (4). Significantly, this critical project is perhaps most coherently articulated by Foucault in the book that centers on the writings of philosophy's Greek fathers. In *The Use of Pleasure* Foucault writes: "There is always something ludicrous in philosophical discourse when it tries, from the outside, to dictate to others, to tell them where their truth is and how to find it" (9). Philosophical discourse, Foucault argues, "is entitled to explore what might be changed, in its own thought, through the practice of a knowledge that is foreign to it" (9). The source of that change and that practice is philosophy as "*askesis*—an exercise of oneself in the activity of thought" (9).

To be sure, although Foucault, like Irigaray, argues against the monolithic knowledge of philosophical tradition, his work has been severely criticized by feminists for its masculinist philosophical bias. Feminists have found fault with Foucault for failing to acknowledge the limitations of Greece as a historical model for thinking about ethics precisely because the ethical practices identified by Foucault apply only to elite Athenian men. As Amy Richlin puts it somewhat acerbically: "Not that women are the only glaring absence in Foucault's history; Foucault has reproduced for his readers an antiquity without Jews. . . without Africans, Egyptians, Semites, northern Europeans; without children, babies, poor people, slaves. All the 'Greeks' are Athenians and most of the 'Romans' are Greeks; in many ways these books are not salvageable."[20] Similarly, Jean Grimshaw argues that "Foucault's work on ethics is disappointing. . . . It seems trapped," she continues, "in a highly masculinist view of ethics as the concern of a male elite to stylize their own lives. It sees this stylized aestheticization of life as the only alternative to a morality based on adherence to a rigid or universal code."[21] And although more recent feminist readings of volumes two and three of *History of Sexuality* have been overwhelmingly positive,[22] many feminist theorists remain ambivalent about Foucault's value for ethical thinking.

## Irigaray, Ethics, and the Greeks

How, then, does this snapshot of Foucault, ethics, and the Greeks apply to Irigaray in the context of queer theory? As in Foucault, the role of the Greeks is important for Irigaray's conception of the ethical field. Irigaray draws extensively on Greek culture as a source of inspiration and object of critique, from her deconstruction of Platonic mimesis to her constructive uses of the stories of Antigone, Demeter, and Kore, or Orestes, Electra, and Clytemnestra. More specifically, as many of Irigaray's interpreters have demonstrated, the Greeks are an especially important source for Irigaray's ethical thinking because she uses myth as a vehicle for the reconstruction of an ethical field that would allow for true sexual difference. With regard to Irigaray, then, "weird Greek sex" refers to a capacious notion of sex-as-gender and gender-as-sex—"sex" in the French sense of *le sexe*, as in the name Irigaray gives to her famous book, *This Sex Which Is Not One*.[23]

To flesh out the importance of the Greeks for Irigaray's ethics, let me return to the rubric I borrowed from Didier Eribon to sketch out Foucault's ethics in relation to the Greek world, where his thinking about the Greeks was thematically divided into a politics of friendship and an economy of pleasures. Conveniently, both of these rubrics are relevant to Irigaray's thought as well.

First, in Irigaray's work the politics of friendship plays itself out as female genealogies, the practice of *affidamento*,[24] and the reinscription of the relationship between women as a rewriting of the relation between mother and daughter. The practice of *affidamento* was developed by Italian feminists involved with the Milan Women's Bookstore Collective and involves women's public and collective access to symbolization through their symbolic recognition of one another. Irigaray's use of the Greeks is central to this aspect of her work, as she draws on the *Oresteia*, the story of Antigone, and the myth of Demeter and Kore to rethink women's relations to each other. For example, as the Italian philosopher Luisa Muraro points out, "Irigaray perceives the violent beginnings of patriarchal society in the *Oresteia*."[25] For Irigaray, the *Oresteia* narrates the denial of the genealogical relation between women in the murder of Queen Clytemnestra by her son, Orestes, with the help of his sister, Electra—an Irigarayan spin on "weird Greek sex." In her reading of the myth in "The Bodily Encounter with the Mother,"[26] Irigaray focuses on this denial of the maternal relation at the founding of Western culture, a matricide that reinforces the impossibility of true difference and the ubiquitous repetition of a paternal Same already uncovered in her reading of Plato in *Speculum*. Further, methodologically Irigaray's shift to myth here is important in her move from the deconstructive approach of *Speculum* to the more constructive character of her later work. As Muraro points out, Irigaray is "less interested in critique [here] than in finding a positive use for myths" (320). So while Greek stories narrate the subjugation of women in an unjust social order, Irigaray also finds in those stories a mythical expression of history that is "more closely related to female, matrilineal traditions."[27]

The precise form taken by this constructive use of Greek myth is the Irigarayan articulation of female genealogy: "If we are not to be accomplices in the murder of the mother," Irigaray says in reference to the killing of Clytemnestra, "we also need to assert that there is a genealogy of women."[28] This female genealogy is best represented for Irigaray by another Greek myth, the story of Demeter-Kore, and further developed through her reading of Antigone in Sophocles' tragedy.[29]

The story of Antigone involves the conflict between human law and a higher law. After both her brothers are killed in a battle over the succession of power over Thebes, Creon, now ruler, refuses to bury Antigone's brother, Polynices, because he had attacked the city in order to claim his right to succession. Antigone, invoking her fidelity to a higher law than human law, violates Creon's order and buries her brother. As punishment, Antigone is herself buried alive in a cave, where she hangs herself. Irigaray argues that in order to avoid Antigone's fate, women must generate an ethical order of their own, and this order must have both vertical and horizontal dimensions.[30]

Irigaray's ethical thought ultimately moves beyond female genealogies to the assertion of an ethical order of men and women together; Muraro in particular shows how that shift in her thought can be read through her changing interpretations of Antigone's story. As Muraro points out, in her early readings of Antigone in *Speculum* and *Ethics of Sexual Difference*,[31] Irigaray does not consider Antigone to be a heroic model, but rather sees her as a figure for female imprisonment inside men's symbolic order. Trapped, like Demeter's daughter Kore, in what Philippa Berry calls a "'marriage[ ]' to death,"[32] Antigone is, as Margaret Whitford puts it, the "entombed woman, buried alive, not put to death by violence, but deprived of air and sustenance."[33] In Muraro's view, it is not until after her 1986 lecture, "The Universal as Mediation," that Irigaray's interpretation of Antigone changes dramatically.[34] Thus, by 1989 in *Thinking the Difference*, Irigaray celebrates Antigone's insistence on burying her brother as a defense of her community and an honoring of maternal genealogies. For Muraro, this moment in Irigaray's thought marks her as an explicitly political thinker, where Antigone becomes a figure of woman as political witness and agent of direct action.

This reading of myth in Irigaray's thought highlights her famous celebration of the female genealogical relation. Although Irigaray herself moves on in her later work to focus more explicitly on the relation of difference between the sexes, writers such as Muraro have remained faithful to Irigaray's earlier vision of women together. This moment in Irigaray's thought parallels the Foucauldian "politics of friendship," except in a feminine form. As Muraro puts it:

> I think we are witnesses and protagonists of a change that has to do with women's relation to the figure of the mother, and, consequently, with the meaning of sexual difference. Knowing how to love the mother is the basis of our liberation. . . . What we know, on a superficial level, as feminism, is the manifestation,

> I think, of a change in our civilization on a structural level—that level Braudel calls long-term history. I am not referring to the feminism of rights and equality, but to the movement that has led us to choose to stay among women, to choose to act in accordance with the judgment of our fellow women, to accept the authority of women, and to seek the nourishment of female thought for our minds. (331)

In the third section of this chapter I will return to the implications of this Irigarayan "politics of friendship" when I compare Irigaray with Foucault. But let me briefly move to the second theme evoked by Eribon in his reading of Foucault: the economy of pleasures. Foucault's famous interest in an economy of pleasures—evoked at the end of the first volume of *The History of Sexuality* and developed in his reading of Greek technologies of the self—could be translated in Irigaray's work as her rewriting of the morphology of the female body, epitomized by the famous figure of the lips from her essay, "When Our Lips Speak Together": "Two lips kissing two lips: openness is ours again. Our 'world.'"[35] Obviously this most celebrated of Irigarayan images is explicitly evoked and developed in the last essay of her 1977 book, *This Sex Which Is Not One.* But it is actually introduced earlier, in *Speculum* (1974), in the context of Irigaray's readings of Freud and Plato. Countering the transcendent shining light of truth to be reached through a phallic ascension toward the Forms, Irigaray posits in her reading of Plato's cave the possibility of another model: the lips. At the end of "Plato's *Hystera*," Irigaray invokes the image of the lips as the figure of another path of pleasure, the space of the past conditional (*aurait pu*)—a way out of Plato, philosophy, and thought as we know it. Unfortunately, Plato and the canonical philosophers who follow him close down the possibility of sexual difference and therefore a different pleasure—the unnameable space of the *hétérogène* whose denial is figured by Irigaray as the closing of the lips (452). As many of Irigaray's interpreters have shown, this nonphallic image of the lips figures an alternative to the Platonic economy of the same by inscribing what Tina Chanter calls an "ethics of eros" where true sexual difference is made manifest. But the lips figure that alternative as catachresis—the figure of rhetoric that names a metaphor or figural term for which there is no literal term. Many have argued that because Irigaray's "lips" refer both to the lips of the mouth and the genital lips, but also to neither, they are catachrestic. As an "impossible" catachresis, the lips inscribe what Jane Gallop calls a "poetics" or "*poiesis*"[36] of the feminine-maternal body of pleasure—what we might call the body of the other's other, the body of the one who, silent and invisible, both exceeds and grounds philosophical reason. So as catachresis, the lips mark an Aristotelian *poiesis* or making of the female body—yet another meaning of "weird Greek sex."

## How Can Irigaray and Foucault Speak Together?

This final section sketches out the parameters of an ethics that would allow Irigaray and Foucault to speak together, a bit like the lips—neither singular nor plural—in that space of contestation between feminists and queers. Although potentially generative of new modes of thinking, this contestation must insist on acknowledging the ongoing "dissonance" that continues to separate Irigaray from Foucault. For example, in comparing their politics of friendship, we can see that Foucault is only concerned with men together while Irigaray is, from the start, interested in theorizing the relations among women. Again, as always, that gendered difference between Foucault and Irigaray is not symmetrical. If Foucault is able simply to ignore women, Irigaray can hardly ignore the existence of men in a world still dominated—now more than ever—by men who uphold a masculinist order. This asymmetry so famously demonstrated in Beauvoir's introduction to *The Second Sex*[37]—where man occupies both the positive and the neutral, while woman occupies only the negative pole—accounts, in my view, for the fact that while Irigaray moves farther and farther in the direction of thinking about difference beyond the sameness not only of men but also of women together, in his ethical work Foucault becomes increasingly fixated on a homosocial sphere in which the other sex is nowhere to be found.

Irigaray, on the other hand, is most centrally concerned with sexual difference. Even in her most "separatist" work on female genealogies, Irigaray's primary concern is how to make space for difference, first as the excluded feminine forever absorbed as part of the Same, and later as the sexes together. As I argued earlier, Irigaray in her quasi-separatist moment—in the "Lips" essay, *Thinking the Difference*, *The Ethics of Sexual Difference*, "The One Doesn't Stir Without the Other,"[38] "The Bodily Encounter with the Mother"—the Irigaray of the genealogies project is, in a sense, the mirror of Foucault's masculine separatism. But precisely because that gendered mirroring is asymmetrical, Irigaray evolves to a different place, the place of thinking the sexes together.

These differences between Irigaray and Foucault can serve to give us further insight into the well-documented tension between feminism and queer theory. A primary point of tension between feminism and queer theory is the conception of sexuality, where feminism remains primarily concerned with the yoking of sexuality to gender as constraint—the ways in which our freedoms are limited or even violated by institutions, individual practices, and other social forces that produce relationships of dominance and subordination. One could think of the work of Catherine MacKinnon as the epitome of this direction in feminist thought. Queer theory, on the other hand, begins with the assumption of the shattering of those constraints and is, therefore, much more aligned with the ethics of freedom outlined by Foucault: to rethink the self as a technology or practice and thereby to "get free of oneself" (*Use*, 8). In this sense, one could say that these contrasting visions of gender, sexuality, and freedom go back to the Greeks—to a vision of elite Greek men who carry all the privileges of a dominant class, on the one hand and, on the other, a vision of the Greeks who were women and slaves, those whose freedoms are limited and whose choices are constrained. These are the Greeks Irigaray is interested in, those whose limited choices and freedoms are captured by myth and story: Antigone, Clytemnestra, Demeter and Kore. Indeed, Irigaray's interest in the Greeks is primarily made manifest through myths about the limits of freedom, the same freedom that is so deeply cherished by Foucault.

So where does this leave us? Again, as I stated earlier, the dissonance between these two visions can be productive: despite their differences, Foucault and Irigaray have much to offer each other. First, both have a similar conception of the meaning of ethics: not as system of norms, moral values, or set of rules, but as ethics as way of life. Second, both Foucault and Irigaray move in their thought from a place of critique to a constructive project, and both articulate that constructive project in terms of ethics. For Foucault, that project takes the form of the refashioning of the self. For Irigaray, that reconstruction takes the form of the relation between the sexes. However, for both Irigaray and Foucault, building something new does not mean that anything goes. Rather, both Foucault and Irigaray describe an ethical system where ultimately those who participate in it are neither completely constrained nor completely free. Indeed, this is an aspect of Foucault's thought that has been misread by some of his feminist critics. Both Foucault and Irigaray are trying to find a way out of subjectivation/*assujetissement*—more generally, in Foucault, from the *assujetissement* of the modern panopticon; more specifically, in the case of Irigaray, from the *assujetissement* of a gender system that denies the possibility of sexual difference. At the same time, both could be said to view subjectivity, or the mode of subjectivation/*mode d'assujetissement* (Foucault, *Usage*, 38) as a possibility for reconstruction as well. We are more than the institutions and social norms that "construct," limit, or violate us; we are also more than the pure negation that simply rebels against or ignores those norms. Subjugation, ultimately, is never absolute; but then again, neither is freedom.

So let me offer, provisionally, what I see as a potentially fruitful path toward thinking our way out of subjectivation and into freedom through the concept of *poiesis*. This is also a path that leads, like the lips, toward an opening that would allow Irigaray and Foucault to speak together. Gallop's Irigarayan Greek term, *poiesis*, is relevant for Foucault as well. In his consideration of Plutarch's *Lives* in one of his later courses at the Collège de France, Foucault highlights Plutarch's ethical *poiesis* as an act that transforms the *ethos*, an alteration in the mode of being or existence of an individual.[39] Thus, in *The Use of Pleasure*, Foucault's analysis of Greek "practical" texts for everyday conduct leads him to suggest that their function was "etho-poetic" (13), allowing individuals "to shape themselves as ethical subjects" (13). This confluence of Irigarayan *poiesis* with Foucauldian *ethopoiesis* is precisely the place where the two might speak to each other and, in so doing, open up possibilities for what Foucault calls "a different way of thinking" (*Use*, 11).

For Foucault, the *ethopoietic* reconstruction of the self through an aesthetics of existence requires, as James Faubion puts it, "not simply a repertoire of technologies but also an 'open territory,' a social terrain in which a considered freedom might actually be exercised."[40] Foucault did not take for granted the existence of that "open territory" for a tiny minority of elite Athenian men. Rather, for Foucault the ancient Greeks provide a space for thinking about freedom as a technology of the self that has been denied most human beings for most of human history. This does not mean that Foucault sees in the Greeks a social model to be emulated: as he put it in his final interview, he finds the Greeks to be neither exemplary nor admirable ("Final," 2). Rather, the historical example of ancient Greece provides Foucault with what Faubion calls "the tool kit of the ancient ethical economy" (95) in which the *poiesis* of the self can be read as a mode of living "that aims at bringing ethical practice into existence" (Faubion, 93). And that ethical practice, Foucault insists, can only be conceived as a relational one, which is why he insists in "Ethics of the Concern for Self as a Practice of Freedom" that "the freedom of the subject and its relationship to others . . . constitutes the very stuff [*matière*] of ethics."[41]

Irigaray, for her part, opens up that as yet unrealized territory of freedom by poetically reconstructing the stuff/*matière* of the female body as philosophical reason's silent and invisible ground. Beginning in 1977 with her "Lips" essay, Irigaray discovers that territory as a kind of revelation, the uncovering of that which has been covered over. She unveils in this essay an imaginary space that has yet to come into being—"How can I say it?" she incessantly asks—and then brings it into being by naming it as "lips." It is here, in this naming—in this *poietic* act—that Irigaray most dramatically interrupts the philosophical tradition by poetically constructing what the edifice of logic and reason cannot imagine. That poetic naming also constitutes an *ethopoiesis*, in the Foucauldian sense—the *poietic* construction of the self in relation to others that constitutes, again, the stuff or *matière* of both the body and of ethics. In that construction, Irigaray, like Foucault, retains the spirit of the Greek understanding of *poiesis*, as a making or producing involved in all forms of *technê*. Thus, Irigaray's elliptical phrase at the end of the "Lips" essay—"Our all will come"[42] (212)—can be reinterpreted as a proleptic, collective *ethopoietical* act of transformation.

Together, Foucault and Irigaray provide us with a different, modern tool kit for thinking about ethics in the context of long-standing debates between feminists and queers. To be sure, there is much work to be done with those tools toward the creation of a full-fledged ethical theory. This chapter makes a contribution to that process by pointing to ways for moving beyond the static positions of a socially constrained feminist moralism versus a fragmenting libidinal queer critique. But from both a feminist and queer perspective, *ethopoiesis* is potentially fruitful for an understanding of ethics as a collective, conscious practice of freedom whose horizons of possibility include political transformations that we cannot, in the present, fully imagine. What the future holds remains to be seen or, more accurately, *ethopoietically* created. And that is the work not just of theory, but of poetry and politics as well.

## Notes

1. General overviews of queer theory tend not to cite Irigaray at all. For examples, see Brett Beemyn and Mickey Eliason, *Queer Studies: A Lesbian, Gay, Bisexual, and Transgender Anthology* (New York: New York University Press, 1996) and Robert J. Corber and Stephen Valocchi, *Queer Studies: An Interdisciplinary Reader* (Malden, MA: Blackwell, 2003), two widely used anthologies in which not a single reference to Irigaray occurs. William B. Turner's *A Genealogy of Queer Theory* (Philadelphia: Temple University Press, 2000) similarly does not mention Irigaray, despite Turner's claim that "the originators of queer theory are all feminist scholars" (34). And in her *Critical Introduction to Queer Theory* (New York: New York University Press, 2003), Nikki Sullivan briefly mentions Irigaray, but only in the context of feminist thought or poststructuralism more generally, not as a specifically queer thinker.

2. The exception is Judith Butler, often cited as a source of queer theory, whose work on performativity in *Gender Trouble: Feminism and the Subversion of Identity* (New York: Routledge, 1990) and *Bodies that Matter: On the Discursive Limits of "Sex"* (New York: Routledge, 1993) is as much indebted to Irigarayan mimicry as it is to Austinian speech act theory. It is worth noting that Butler's relationship to queer theory is vexed at best (see "Against Proper Objects," in *Feminism Meets Queer Theory*, ed. Elizabeth Weed and Naomi Schor [Bloomington: Indiana University Press, 1997], 1–30), evidenced by her gradual move away from sex-gender work altogether in her later work.

3. See Gayle Rubin, "Thinking Sex" (1984), in *The Lesbian and Gay Studies Reader*, ed. Henry Abelove, Michèle Aina Barale, and David M. Halperin (New York: Routledge, 1993), 3–44; Eve Kosofsky Sedgwick, *Epistemology of the Closet* (Berkeley: University of California Press, 1990), and Butler, *Gender Trouble.*

4. The one exception I have found to this almost total queer silence about Irigaray is a footnote in Sedgwick's essay on Diderot's "The Nun," where Sedgwick criticizes Irigarayan "hommosexuality" for its transhistorical conflation of homosexuality with "the male homosocial bonds that largely structure patriarchal culture" (49). Sedgwick calls this "a potent polemical move," as well as "a dangerous and demagogic one" (49). See Eve Kosofsky Sedgwick, "Privilege of Unknowing: Diderot's *The Nun*" in *Tendencies* (Durham: Duke University Press, 1993), 23–51.

5. Rosi Braidotti, "The Ethics of Sexual Difference: The Case of Foucault and Irigaray," *Australian Feminist Studies* 3 (1986): 1–13.

6. Luce Irigaray, *Speculum of the Other Woman*, trans. Gillian C. Gill (Ithaca: Cornell University Press, 1985); originally published as *Speculum de l'autre femme* (Paris: Minuit, 1974).

7. Janet Halley, *Split Decisions: How and Why to Take a Break from Feminism* (Princeton: Princeton University Press, 2006), 60.

8. Michel Foucault, *The History of Sexuality. Volume 1: An Introduction*, trans. Robert Hurley (New York: Random House, 1978); originally published as *La Volonté de savoir: Histoire de la sexualité, Volume 1* (Paris: Gallimard, 1976); *The Use of Pleasure: The History of Sexuality. Volume 2*, trans. Robert Hurley (New York: Random House, 1985); originally published as *L'Usage du plaisir: Histoire de la sexualité, Volume 2* (Paris: Gallimard, 1984).

9. Michel Foucault, "Final Interview," *Raritan* 5, no. 1 (1985): 1–13.

10. Other than Braidotti's 1986 article, to my knowledge the only other sustained comparison of Irigaray and Foucault is Shannon Winnubst, "Exceeding Hegel and Lacan: Different Fields of Pleasure within Foucault and Irigaray," *Hypatia* 14, no. 1 (1999): 13–37. Although Winnubst's focus on Irigaray and Foucault through a reading of the Hegelian Concept differs from my own, her interest in thinking Irigaray and Foucault together resonates with my concerns in this essay. Also see a brief early review of Irigaray and Foucault in Françoise Colin, "Repenser l'éthique," *Cahiers du grif* 29 (1984–85): 97–99. Finally, in "Irigaray Reading Heidegger" (in *Engaging with Irigaray*, ed. Carolyn Burke, Naomi Schor, and Margaret Whitford [New York: Columbia University Press, 1994]), Joanna Hodge briefly aligns Irigaray with Foucault and Levinas as thinkers who respond to Heidegger in order to prioritize ethics over metaphysical thinking (196).

11. Michel Foucault, *The Care of the Self: The History of Sexuality, Volume 3*, trans. Robert Hurley (New York: Random House, 1985); originally published as *Le Souci de soi: Histoire de la sexualité, Volume 3* (Paris: Gallimard, 1984).

12. David M. Halperin, *How to Do the History of Homosexuality* (Chicago: University of Chicago Press, 2002), 2.

13. Michel Foucault, *Discipline and Punish: The Birth of the Prison*, trans. Alan Sheridan (New York: Vintage, 1979); originally published as *Surveiller et punir: Naissance de la prison* (Paris: Gallimard, 1975).

14. Michel Foucault, "On the Genealogy of Ethics: An Overview of Work in Progress," in *Ethics: Subjectivity and Truth*, ed. Paul Rabinow, trans. Robert Hurley et al. (New York: New Press, 1994), 253.

15. Didier Eribon, *Insult and the Making of the Gay Self* (Durham: Duke University Press, 2004); originally published as *Réflexions sur la question gay* (Paris: Fayard, 1999).

16. Michel Foucault, "Friendship as a Way of Life," trans. John Johnston, in *Ethics*, 136.

17. Lauren Berlant and Michael Warner, "Sex in Public," *Critical Inquiry* 24, no. 2 (1998): 562.

18. Bob Gallagher and Alexander Wilson, "Michel Foucault: An Interview: Sex, Power, and the Politics of Identity," *The Advocate* 400 (August 7, 1984): 29.

19. David M. Halperin, *Saint Foucault: Towards a Gay Hagiography* (New York: Oxford University Press, 1995), 93. In his subsequent book, *How to Do the History of Homosexuality* (2002), Halperin admits to having overstated his bodies and pleasures argument in *Saint Foucault.*

20. Amy Richlin, "Foucault's *History of Sexuality*: A Useful Theory for Women?" in *Rethinking Sexuality: Foucault and Classical Antiquity*, ed. Larmour, Miller, Platter (Princeton: Princeton University Press, 1998), 139.

21. Jean Grimshaw, "Practices of Freedom," in *Up Against Foucault: Explorations of Some Tensions between Foucault and Feminism*, ed. Caroline Ramazanoglu (London: Routledge, 1993), 70.

22. In *Feminism and the Final Foucault*, ed. Dianna Taylor and Karen Vintges (Urbana: University of Illinois Press, 2004), the contributors enlist the later Foucault for a feminist ethics of the self. See especially Jana Sawicki, "Foucault's Pleasure: Desexualizing Queer Politics" and Mariana Valverde, "Experience and Truth Telling in a Post-humanist World: A Foucauldian Contribution to Feminist Ethical Reflections" for essays of particular interest to queer feminism. None of the essays engage Irigaray in relation to Foucault.

23. Luce Irigaray, *This Sex Which Is Not One*, trans. Catherine Porter (Ithaca: Cornell University Press, 1985); originally published as *Ce sexe qui n'en est pas un* (Paris: Minuit, 1977).

24. *Affidamento*, or entrustment, refers to the practice developed by Italian feminists associated with the Milan Women's Bookstore Collective that involves women's public and collective access to symbolization through their symbolic recognition of one another.

25. Luisa Muraro, "Female Genealogies," in *Engaging with Irigaray*, 320.

26. Luce Irigaray, "The Bodily Encounter with the Mother," trans. David Macey, in *The Irigaray Reader*, ed Margaret Whitford (Oxford: Blackwell, 1991), 34–46; originally published as *Le Corps-à-corps avec la mère* (Montréal: Editions de la pleine lune, 1981).

27. Luce Irigaray, *Thinking the Difference: For a Peaceful Revolution*, trans. Karin Montin. (New York: Routledge, 1994), 101.

28. Luce Irigaray, *Sexes and Genealogies*, trans. Gillian C. Gill (New York: Columbia University Press, 1993), 19; originally published as *Sexes et parentés*

(Paris: Minuit, 1987). It is important to distinguish between Irigaray's and Foucault's uses of the term *genealogy* here. In Foucault, genealogies refer to historico-conceptual configurations of power-knowledge that are both discursive and nondiscursive; in Irigaray, genealogies refer to a more common understanding of intergenerational descendance, as reflected in the original French term, "*parenté*" (kinship), of her title *Sexes et parentés.*

29. On the numerous literary and philosophical treatments of Antigone see George Steiner, *Antigones: How the Antigone Legend Has Endured in Western Literature, Art, and Thought* (New Haven: Yale University Press, 1996). On Antigone in Irigaray see Judith Butler, *Antigone's Claim: Kinship Between Life and Death* (New York: Columbia University Press, 2002); Tina Chanter, *Ethics of Eros: Irigaray's Rewriting of the Philosophers* (New York: Routledge, 1995); Carol Jacobs, "Dusting Antigone," *MLN* 3, no. 5 (1996): 890–917; and Cecilia Sjoholm, *The Antigone Complex: Ethics and the Invention of Feminine Desire* (Palo Alto: Stanford University Press, 2004). For a queer critique of Butler's reading, see Lee Edelman, *No Future: Queer Theory and the Death Drive* (Durham: Duke University Press, 2004), 102–107.

30. By vertical Irigaray means mother-daughter (intergenerational) as well as a transcendental relation to the divine; by horizontal she means a kind of solidarity among women best represented as a relation between sisters.

31. Luce Irigaray, *An Ethics of Sexual Difference*, trans. Carolyn Burke and Gillian Gill (Ithaca: Cornell University Press, 1993).

32. Philippa Berry, "The Burning Glass: Paradoxes of Feminist Revelation in *Speculum*," in *Engaging With Irigaray*, 234.

33. Margaret Whitford, "Irigaray, Utopia, and the Death Drive," in *Engaging With Irigaray*, 391.

34. Although in "The Universal as Mediation" Irigaray does not discuss Antigone directly, Muraro sees this lecture as a turning point in Irigaray's thinking about ethics and female genealogies. See Luce Irigaray, "The Universal as Mediation," in *Sexes and Genealogies*, 125–49; originally published as "L'Universel comme médiation," in *Sexes et parentés*, 139–64.

35. Luce Irigaray, "When Our Lips Speak Together," in *This Sex Which Is Not One*, 210; originally published as "Quand nos lèvres se parlent," in *Ce sexe qui n'en est pas un*, 203–17.

36. Jane Gallop, *Thinking Through the Body* (New York: Columbia University Press, 1988), 94.

37. Simone de Beauvoir, *The Second Sex*, trans. H. M. Parshley (New York: Vintage, 1989); originally published as *Le Deuxième sexe* (Paris: Gallimard, 1949).

38. Luce Irigaray, "And the One Doesn't Stir Without the Other," trans. Hélène Vivienne Wenzel, *Signs: Journal of Women in Culture and Society* 7, no. 1 (1981): 60–67; orig. published as *Et l'une ne bouge pas sans l'autre* (Paris: Minuit, 1979).

39. See Michel Foucault, *The Hermeneutics of the Subject: Lectures at the Collège de France, 1981–1982*, trans. Graham Burchell (New York: Palgrave MacMillan, 2005); originally published as *L'Herméneutique du sujet: Cours au Collège de France, 1981–82*, ed. Frédéric Gros (Paris: Seuil/Gallimard, 2001).

40. James Faubion, "Toward an Anthropology of Ethics: Foucault and the Pedagogies of Autopoiesis," *Representations* 74 (2001): 88.

41. Michel Foucault, "The Ethics of the Concern for Self as a Practice of Freedom," trans. P. Aranov and D. McGrawth, in *Ethics*, 300.

42. The agrammatical construction of this phrase in the French original, "Le toute va venir" (212), reinforces the disruption of gender in this poetic act of transformation.

# Chapter 10

# Autonomy, Self-Alteration, Sexual Difference

Stathis Gourgouris

> Ταύτην γὰρ λέγομεν εἶναι τήν πολιτικήν ἀρχήν, ήν δεῖ τὸν άρχοντα άρχόμενον μαθεῖν [This we call political rule, when the ruler learns by being ruled].
>
> —Aristotle, *Politics*

> I am militating politically for the impossible, which doesn't mean I am a utopian. Rather what I want does not yet exist, as the only possibility of a future.
>
> —Luce Irigaray, *J'aime à toi* (1992)

The terrain suggested by a co-incident reading of the above two quotations—which at first glance appear to belong to entirely different signifying registers—prefigures accurately this chapter's orientation. Aristotle's well-known requirement that rule can only be enacted from within the experience (and understanding) of being ruled, is by contemporary standards—in a world where democratic politics exists precariously, if at all—an impossible demand. It is a gesture that points simultaneously to the nonexistence of democratic rule and to its possible pathway into existence in the future. This impossible demand is not a utopian proposition, if nothing else because the materials for its articulation exist in the here and now, despite the fact that their originary force (*arch*) is nowadays hardly taken into consideration.

Irigaray's statement attempts to clarify that the impossible and the utopian are hardly identical. This is not because the utopian may be in fact possible, but because desiring the impossible is an entirely real and actual way to commit oneself to what is possible in the future. Her emphasis on "what does not yet exist" does not entail investment in a predetermined or providential element that will come to be in the future—in other words, some sort of future nascent in the present. Rather, "what does not yet exist" is configured as a permanent condition of alterity within present existence, a kind of unknown variable in the equation of what may come to be possible in the future, which is an equation that obviously carries no mathematical consistency but remains always permeable to the ever unpredictable contingencies of human action. This condition, therefore, knows no time—it is, as X factor, *achronos*—but it is, nonetheless, in place across the entire range of history's temporalities, perhaps as an already inscribed heterotopia. It is a condition open to the indefinite possibility of something whose "nonexistence" as "the only possibility of a future" is a presently existing condition, insofar as without this X the equation (present or future) cannot be constituted.

Aristotle's impossible demand also points to these coordinates of achrony and heterotopia within existing conditions. We must not forget that *arch* means both origin and rule, much in the sense that, in the English language, we understand rule to pertain both to matters of governance and to matters of principle, indeed first principles, the essential rules of the game, of proposition, of order. The ruler, after all, is a primary figure (even in cases articulated as *primus inter pares*), the premier in a constitutive mechanism of ruling that presupposes in him the primary guardian of the set of rules he represents. In any archaic configuration of power, the *archon* commands authority not only over the domain of rules that govern a society. He also embodies the point of departure of whatever trajectory such rules are to have in their implementation, whether they are to be enforced in principle or not, safeguarded for future generations (of rulers and ruled), or dismantled in favor of another course of rule, another departure. Such is obviously the essence of the figure of the *patriarch*, which is why even when the primordial parricide takes place, according, let us say, to Freud's tales—when, in fact, the singular origin of principle and rule is to be multiplied and distributed (in Freud's analysis, institutionalized) in the hands of the many murderous sons—the patriarchical order is hardly abolished. On the contrary, in its multiplication, the authorial origin is consolidated.

But when Aristotle demands that the *archon* must also be *archomenos* something else entirely takes place. The singular notion of *arch* is deconstituted by a corresponding alterity. In order to know how to rule, one must know how to be ruled: this is the quintessential element of autonomy. Knowledge of being ruled does not mean mere experiential accounting from the standpoint of the (always) ruled. In a direct sense, it means knowing the other side of rule, enabling an affirmative investment in the object of rule from a subject position that is not consumed in the typical objectification suffered by those ruled. In this respect, it provides the sort of knowledge that relativizes a ruler's presumed monopoly over the authority to determine what rule means and, in effect, abolishes the presumed epistemic distinction between rulers and ruled.

This can be considered from two standpoints. On the one hand, the ruled authorize their own position as ruled; that is, they are not ruled in the simple sense of submitting to the authority of the ruler, an authority predicated on the assumption that the ruler is also the origin of rule. They are ruled by virtue of their own decision to be ruled, which is to say, they hold the reins of interrogation (and thus signification) over the terms of ruling—who rules, why, and how?—the very same mode of interrogation of the rule of law. This is why this notion has nothing to do with the paradox of "voluntary servitude" that Etienne de la Boetie so brilliantly exposed several centuries ago. The ruled who hold the reins of interrogation over the signifying framework of rule can never become servile by definition; they are motivated by a principle of self-limitation that safeguards their autonomy, their self-determination. By this logic, a ruler who has never known how to be ruled—a ruler who has not known the autonomy of being ruled—cannot possibly rule without abusing autonomy in favor of ruling in its name. Aristotle's injunction against such a ruler opens the way toward considering the project of autonomy as an interminable exercise of self-rule even in the political domain of being ruled.

On the other hand, Aristotle's configuration of *arch* also subverts the signification of ruler as primordial authority. If, concurrently to rule, *arch* signifies origin, the requisite knowledge of *archomenos* dismantles the ruler's singular occupation (*Besetzung*) of the origin of authority, introducing thus a difference at the origin, a foundational *différance*. If knowing how to be ruled is essential to ruling, no ruler can claim self-authorization, and *arch* can no longer constitute itself as a singular origin. Authority begins already cleft and differential, open to question at the point of its constitution, by virtue of the fact that both subject and object of power are *co-incidental* positions. Each other's alterity does not disintegrate to mere opposition, but rather remains involved in a mutual complicity that exposes the whole business of ruling as a veritably *an-archic* condition. I don't mean to suggest thereby that rule is abolished, nor does, in any case, a politics of anarchy mean lack of rule. I am merely pointing to the grammatical deconstruction of *arch* as a monadic origin of both power and meaning. As *archomenos*, a ruler can never claim to be the first and only. At the very most, he can acknowledge the position of *archon* as a transitory moment in the process of ruling, which is a process whose ultimate beginning is unknown and irrelevant and whose ultimate endpoint is incomprehensible as such—a process undertaken by society as a whole, provided society recognizes and enacts its autonomy.

For an *archon* to recognize the *archomenos* as a subject position means to recognize an alterity within, which, by rules of traditional logic, is an impossibility. What makes it possible—a process of *self-alteration*—is even more far-fetched, logically speaking. It signifies a condition by which alterity is internally produced, dissolving the very thing that enables it, the very thing whose existence derives meaning from being altered, *from othering itself.* I understand that such condition requires the contemplation of an impossible concept—at least, impossible within the conceptual framework that identifies alterity to be external, a framework, I might add, that is essential to any semantics (and, of course, politics) of identity. Such framework cannot but vehemently defend, by contradistinction, the bona fide existence of internality, even if, in a gesture of cognitive magnanimity, it accepts a fragmented, fissured, indeterminate, or even boundless internality. Internality thus conceived, however "open-ended" it claims to be, cannot enact self-alteration because alterity will always remain external to it, precisely so as to secure its meaning. No doubt, it must be said, this framework of an internally/externally conceived distinction of identity and difference gives meaning to the language I am using at this very moment. It is, inevitably, the framework that enables us to build communicative avenues by positing totalities and identities that we consider recognizable even if we might significantly disagree over their content. I understand that, in this framework, self-alteration is an impossible concept, but I have a hunch that it is nonetheless possible, that it *takes place*, in the only way anything can take place in the world—*in* history, *as* history. At the limit, the conceptual inquiry I am suggesting produces its groundwork in the world of human action, not in the universe of concepts and propositions.

Already, given the terms of this initial and cursory rumination, our trajectory is set up to pass through the conceptual straits of alterity with the enormous body of heterological discourses that shadow it. Be that as it may, the impetus is to attain, in a certain dialectical sense, an *altered relation to alterity*, with an aspiration ultimately to counteract the allure of transcendence that is foundational in the contemporary lexicon of the Other, to the extent of reproducing consistently a cognitive figure of transcendence that is itself untranscendable. At the same time, I am aware that this trajectory thereby plunges us into the chimerical waters of the Self, whose own conceptual lexicon has long been both the bane and the ridicule of the most intriguing tendencies in psychoanalytic and feminist theory. This is all the more complicated by the often irresistible association of discourses concerning the subject with discourses concerning the self, which makes conspicuously evident indeed how problematic—that is to say, how political—becomes any theory of subjectification insofar as it must involve a theory (or, in essence, a politics) of sublimation, whether acknowledged or not. In the last instance, we must restate the utterly obvious because it is so crucial: subject-formation is a political matter, as it signifies the inaugural negotiation with power—indeed, with the power of the other, or with power *as* other, but also, inevitably, with power as altering (*othering*) force. It is this latter aspect that problematizes the entire equation, raising, by its very constitution, the question of the political pure and simple: Where does the power of othering, of alteration, of transformation reside? Wherefrom does it emerge? What is its referential frame? Its location? Its standpoint of interlocution? And finally, what is its mode and terms of articulation?[1]

A reconsideration of Irigaray's work may be useful here, considering that, of all philosophers in recent decades—only Levinas shares her persistence, but his impetus couldn't be farther askew—she has placed "alterity" and "the other" at the core of her epistemological inquiries, thereby granting us, in especially incisive fashion, a novel armory with which to encounter the question of how can a politics of the other not disintegrate into heteronomous politics. My objection to decontextualized uses of "otherness" as an allegedly pure philosophical concept (in ethics, ontology, or even psychoanalysis) or simply as a formal rhetorical category (in aesthetics or politics) still holds.[2] The impetus on that occasion was to draw attention to how certain heterological discourses effaced any tangible indications of otherness by virtue of an avalanche-like process of ever increasing abstraction. At the height of identity politics during the so-called Culture Wars of the late '80s, the Other had already come to mean nothing, while at the same time signifying anything deemed marginal, minoritarian, oppositional, or disenfranchised. As a formal category, and essentially emptied of historical content even when ascribed to specific historical terms, otherness was suffering, I argued at the time, a *catachresis*. I meant the term literally, in the Greek sense, as *abuse*: a kind of ultimate counterutility which, in plain language, marks an essential uselessness. It might be worthwhile, however, to resurrect the rhetorical content of the term in the English language and consider additionally the "catachresis of otherness" to signify an improper transfer of the sense and attributes of the other, an inappropriateness that returns to haunt whoever claims the domain of the other as an alibi for abstracting meaning away from the real historical battlefield. In either case, my concern remains essentially the same: an abstracted, disembodied other lends itself seamlessly to authorizing an empty and total Other—an absolutist, indeed, totalitarian Other. That is, even the most articulate heterology becomes an authorization of heteronomy if it fails to configure "otherness" as a limit concept—i.e., a concept permeated by an undeconstructible *différance* at the same time that it unleashes conditions of *différance* on all other concepts it encounters.

Levinas certainly enjoys heterology as heteronomy, but Irigaray doesn't. At least, there remains a certain *an-archic* element in her thinking, even in the later work of heterosexual affirmation, which refuses to grant the other the markings of *arch* and *telos*.[3] The reason is the singular importance that the notion of sexual difference has held for her throughout the trajectory of her work, despite the obvious shifts in terminology and orientation this work has taken over the decades. Reading Irigaray without latching onto the issue of her various turns and periods—bracketing, that is, the otherwise important historical reading of an oeuvre that does indeed follow a circuitous and at times contradictory path—helps us recontextualize her insistence on sexual difference as a concept that acts like a hinge to the opening and closing of her various pathways: not simply a key concept, that is, whose content remains stable, uniquely comprehensible, and transferable across discourses, but an epistemological threshold whose crossing requires and also produces a continually altered (and altering) mode of raising and thinking about certain questions (even the same questions).

Irigaray alerts us to the fact that sexual difference can never be described in terms or signs of an equation, even a differential equation. Its mathematics, as it were, is incalculable. This is not simply because there is no equality between the different parts, between the sexes, but because the two contrasting elements of difference cannot possibly share a mutual means of measure. Even in the most complex differential equation one equals one. But the other, in this case, is not one—or more precisely, not merely one. She is at least double, or not merely double. She is multiple, though hardly multiplied as mere reproductions of the one. This enables her to be one, to register as singular presence, without ever occupying the position of the one. The other who is always more and less than one is always else than one. And this else cannot be signified even by the mathematical capacity to designate it as X, the unknown one, the variable one, the one that can have many (or any) values, the one who can have many faces or any face. This is because the many faces of X become possible—calculable—only within the terms of the equation, an equation which, in a peculiar self-authorizing way, X, through its unknown presence, makes possible and calculable. In terms of sexual difference, the other defies even setting the terms of the equation, perhaps because she knows (though who knows how she knows?) that any equation to which she grants her otherness will erase sexual difference.

In this respect, Irigaray's insistence on sexual difference transforms it from a concept to an epistemological condition that ultimately reaches beyond the strict referential framework of sexual relations. Incidentally, let us note that Irigaray increasingly opts to reconfigure the phrase as "sexed difference" (*la difference sexué*), which may be a bit awkward in English, but is nonetheless more precise: sexual difference has meaning insofar as it denotes the fact that difference itself is sexed, not as a matter of sexuality but as a matter of disjunction between the sexes and repression of this disjunction in favor of one sex over the other. Sexual difference therefore pertains to matters beyond sexual relations, strictly speaking, because its specific epistemology is already grounded in a *différance*, a kind of irreducible separation from the presence of a simple difference—let us say, a "natural" biological difference, or strictly speaking, the "formal" philosophical difference between Self and Other. This irreducible separation enables the risk to conceptualize otherness as an "internal" position, as an exteriority within. The tremendous complication of this positioning—always marked by *différance*, as *différance*—is an essential departure point for any meditation on self-alteration, conceptual, epistemological, or psychoanalytic.

For our purposes in this context, I would therefore suggest that Irigaray's insistence on an epistemology of sexual difference has consistently aimed—despite the different terms, concerns, or textual targets—at disrupting the classic philosophical adherence to the "universal," without which, in any case, no conceptual possibility of the Other would have arisen. Irigaray has always acted as a philosopher—in the Greek sense as much as against the Greek sense. (To be provocative, but also more precise: inasmuch as she acts against the Greek sense, she has always acted as a philosopher in the Greek sense.) One might argue that her epistemology of sexual difference enables a self-interrogation of alterity—an interrogation of alterity within alterity and by virtue of alterity—that alters in turn any possibility that the politics of the other might lend itself to simple politics of identity. In this sort of argument, one could, very productively, place Irigaray at the core of the Hegelian problematic of subjectification as subjugation, which prefigures (without understanding) how autonomy and self-alteration are *co-incidental* processes. But Irigaray might also be said to reconfigure this Hegelian frame as a mode of interrogating the universalist morality of traditional philosophy—this is at least what I understand her to be doing in the series of texts collected under the title *Sexes and Genealogies.*

She finds Hegelian *Sittlichkeit*, for example, to be haunted by an unacknowledged content of a fissured doubleness, the repression of which cannot be exorcised by a progressive dialectics of the spirit in history. According to her reading of Hegel, this doubleness arises from two instances: (1) the chasm opened between a primary social imaginary (the "law of the ancestors") and its contemporary manifestation (modernity's "emancipatory" ethical predicament after the French Revolution)—a symptom of not addressing genealogy in history as a problem, as Nietzsche would shortly thereafter; (2) the fissure the social imaginary opens in its configuration of nature as it passes into history, which silences the fact that both nature and this passage are undeconstructibly sexed. The two instances are obviously interwoven as a genealogical problem—the epistemic framework is not merely the juxtaposition of sexes and genealogies, but the fact that all genealogies in all societies are sexed. But the second instance, specifically, enables Irigaray to underscore Hegel's implicit (unacknowledged) *double nature* of the spirit. As it becomes (part of) history, a sublated (and in a very real sense always sublimated) nature exceeds itself but is hardly abolished as nature: "History is the soil in which a second nature, a double nature grows: cultural, spiritual nature, which goes beyond its natural potential."[4] That this soil cultivates a condition—let us say, in Hegelian terms, a civil society—that deliberately (by necessity) occludes this double nature corresponds, metaphorically at least, to the self-occultation of the universal as unmediated exteriority, as objective singularity, that cannot but ultimately assume, even in strict historico-political matters, a theological (indeed theocratic) content.

Against it, Irigaray proposes what she calls "the ethics of the couple," a differential entity that does not repress the doubleness of nature in history. This requires that "the ethics of the couple" be understood in light of the deconstructive mathematics of "the sex which is not one." I understand the legitimacy of various objections to the explicitly heterosexual content Irigaray grants to the notion of the couple, though obviously this heterosexual double is not a matter of sexuality but strictly of gender. In any case, such critique will gain further if it diverts its attention from the content of this figure and (re)considers the form. By insisting on the "ethics of the couple" Irigaray challenges the formal identitary monism of the ethical demand that permeates traditional philosophy, not only in terms of Kantian autonomy but Hegelian *Sittlichkeit* as well:[5] "The most powerful goal of interpretation is the analysis of discourse as sexualized [*sexué*] and not neuter. This can be demonstrated with linguistic and semiotic tools. To undertake this task is to complete that extra turn into self-consciousness that Hegel failed to make: reflexion upon discourse itself as a content that is the outcome of its forms, forms that are arbitrary" (SG, 138).

Going ahead to practice this sort of interpretation, Irigaray disputes the capacity of the Hegelian dialectic to account for sexual difference; in fact, she points to sexual difference as the limit point of Hegelian dialectics. She does so because she exempts the law of sex from contradiction, preferring instead to ascribe to it a sort of mimetic performativity: "Sex does not obey the law of contradiction. It bends and folds to accommodate that logic but it does not conform. Forced to follow that logic it is drawn into a mimetic game that moves faraway from life" (SG, 139). Irigaray enables herself to make this argument by taking Hegel literally, at his word, that social action is but an interminable (re)enaction of the spirit. In that respect, she is right to point out the alienation—literally, the despiritualization—that the lack of acknowledgment of sexual difference brings to human relations. Fair enough, but I cannot resist insisting that, whatever might be Hegel's absolutist aspirations regarding the various embodiments or even purity of the Spirit, the dialectical method itself is not even possible except as a performative process which is, moreover, not even simply characterized by mimesis but by bona fide impersonation: as a series of instances where one is, becomes, acts as an other—indeed, even as an other within oneself. Irigaray seems cautious here not to be understood in terms of a vulgar Hegelianism, whereby, as dialectics is contorted into confirmation of identity, ultimately "the one is reduced to the other" (139). This is not the occasion to delve into disputes over interpretations of Hegel, but this caution is unnecessary. Hegelian dialectics can be dissociated from the march of the Spirit, as an enormous and vastly varied precession of Hegelian dialectical practices that reject Hegelianism tout court (from Marx, to Adorno and Benjamin, to Žižek, Butler, or, I would argue, Irigaray herself), after all, testifies. Dialectics is a performative method whose content is therefore always provisional and occasional, (over)determined by whatever may be the historical or epistemic demands of the dialectical instance.

Be that as it may, what interests us here is not Irigaray's outright claim that "there is no dialectic between the sexes" but that Hegel fails (as does all traditional philosophy) because "he gives no thought to the living being as a sexed being" (SG, 139–40). To think the two assertions together, one might say, as Walter Benjamin did in his own way, that only a dialectics of the living really matters. Irigaray adds the obvious but deeply repressed qualification: life matters are irreducibly sexed. This is to say, in so many words, that the inability of philosophy to come to terms with sexual difference makes it unfit for matters of life. But Irigaray's grander point, and the one most crucial to our inquiry, is that the universality traditional philosophy produces is essentially anchored in monistic mathematics, capable (even if in relatively rare instances) of contemplating contradiction, yet even then reducing contradiction to singular units of time whereby the integrity of the opposed agents (subject-object, self-other, man-woman, history-nature, internal-external, etc.) ultimately remains total, separate, and closed. Against this, Irigaray argues that the universal is itself nothing more than a mediation: on the one hand, historically speaking, because humanity's yearning for its spiritual nature always comes up against the necessity for its worldliness, and on the other hand, because humanity's worldliness—whatever might be the flights of spirit or plunges into repression—is itself a constant reiteration of the problematic of sexual difference, a problematic that registers precisely in the enormous expenditure of significational energy to efface it.[6]

The gesture of depicting the universal as mediation also aims at destabilizing the equation by which the figure of Other lends itself to certain theological imaginaries—monotheistic ones, to be sure. Despite

Irigaray's own peculiar investment in a certain recuperation of religious significations (whether her romanticized evocations of early Christianity or her uninterrogated exoticism of Hinduist or Buddhist categories), she nonetheless succeeds in making alterity concrete at the same time that she makes sexual difference historical—in other words, the primary condition in humanity's production of meaning in the real world. In the same way that the epistemology of sexual difference exposes the universal as mediation, it configures alterity as a worldly condition, limited by its interruption of history while at the same time unlimited as psychic energy of human transformation. As threshold to history, sexual difference dismantles the fetishism of absolute, monological alterity—it detheologizes alterity. It is, of course, banal—if not plainly idiotic—to note here that monotheism is the theological symptom of a patriarchical imaginary. The self-congratulatory delusion one sees in various New Age discourses that like to refer to God as She makes for a stunning confirmation of their subjugation to this imaginary, no matter what might be their feminist pretensions. God cannot be a She in the same sense that a world conducted in terms of a female imaginary cannot possibly invent monotheism. A sex which is not one cannot imagine a god who is merely (and only) One. Worshipping the Absolute Other, the One (and only) Other, paralyzes the conduits of an open relation to the other. Monotheism channels an obsession with the power of the One—an obsession with submitting to a monopoly of power—into the worship of the absolute, transcendental Other. This devotion to the One who is the Other makes engagement with otherness literally impossible. It is an instance when subjectification by means of the power of subjection is, very simply, incapacitation, pure heteronomy.

This raises the most salient political question of all: Can a process of subject formation that takes place distinctly through a process of subjection conjured as pure subjugation produce an autonomous subject? To put it directly, can B or how can B an autonomous subject emerge out of a heteronomous order? Obviously, in risking the use of the term *autonomous subject*, I do not mean to suggest a self-enclosed, self-supposing, narcissistic subject, suspended in the ahistorical void of its own essence. Pure autonomy is itself a theological concept, even in Kant's glorious rationalist mind. It pertains to a self-referential, tautological meaning that the monotheistic mind—in fact, any monomythical mind, as the German philosopher Odo Marquard has so incisively put it—attributes to the one and only power of signification. In a philosophical language, the name "I am that I am" is the name for the total attributes of Being, including, of course, all the possible languages of Being, the plurality of which is abolished by the monistic source that enables them. Thus, such pure ("autonomous") ontology cannot be named, cannot be represented. By extension, it cannot enter history because it cannot "know" history—it cannot know anything other to what it knows absolutely, which is (and can only be) itself. Hence, it cannot change—not merely history, but anything at all, including itself. Not only does this Being not "know" alterity; it has no altering—and most significantly, no *self-altering*—powers. At its most extreme, it may be said to exist as absolute alterity for someone else, someone who believes his/her being to be determined by it, derived from it. In other words, this absolute and tautological equation of Being-in-itself has meaning only in a heteronomous universe of meanings, in a universe whose signification is guaranteed by the presence of an unreachable, unutterable, and unapproachable Other who precludes any alternative authorization.

In other words and to come back to the Aristotelian problematic posed at the outset, autonomy can exist only as project: an ever-presently restaged project whose primary condition or rule (*arch*) is the capacity for self-alteration. This means an *arch* that always begins anew, elsewhere, and as something else, an *arch* that re-authorizes itself as an other. That's why autonomy as self-alteration is not some fancy way of considering self-constitution, or *autopoiēsis.* In fact, as an ever-restaged and ever-interrupted *arch*, self-alteration renders all received paradigms of self-constitution unfeasible, unconstitutible claims. Thus, in terms of self-alteration, an autonomous subject can be considered a self-determining subject, but only if we keep in mind Aristotle's requirement of *archon* as *archomenos* in the instance of self-rule. In literal terms, by autonomous subject I am considering here a subject that makes the law—a poet of the law—whose most prized achievement is the limitless interrogation of the law in its full range: first of all, law's emergence, and then its referential framework and justification, its authorization and canonical execution, and most of all, its metatextual presumption of authority. To be the poet of the law is first and foremost to recognize the existence of the law not as transcendental dimension but as historical privilege. This is tantamount to thinking of the subject (whether of oneself or one's society) as a historical entity, whose ground is otherwise abyssal, whose *arch* is indeterminate, and whose *telos* is nothing more than the very process of worldly existence.

It is unclear what social-historical conditions are needed for subjectification to take this form. It is safe to say, however, that social autonomy is hardly a natural, human condition. It can only emerge as the *praxis/poiēsis* within a certain social imaginary, which is hardly to say that it is the mere expression or application of a certain social imaginary. On the contrary, in such an instance, the radical interrogation of the terms of one's existence would be itself the ground of *praxis/poiēsis*, in full cognizance of its otherwise ontological groundlessness. Autonomy is impossible without self-interrogation, indeed without limitless self-interrogation, in the sense that autonomy cannot be attained once and for all but must be, by definition, open to reinstitution (i.e., alteration), whose limits cannot be set outside the process of alteration. Contrary, then, to traditional notions of autonomous subjectivity which, one way or another, cannot avoid equating self-determination with the self-presupposition of both origin and end, my use of the term insists on an open figure in which the limits of both "subject" and "autonomy" remain indeterminate as such. The determination of limit that presumably distinguishes the domain of relation between subject and object, internal and external, individual and society, etc. is always a political determination.

To conclude, it would be essential to add that autonomy signifies a particular sublimation: a sublimation that confronts the definitional heteronomy "experienced" by the psyche when it encounters the social imaginary as the pleasure of/in the force of alteration itself. This sort of sublimation would enact a subject whose psychic reception of society's *Vorstellung* would consist in an experience of *poiēsis*: a performative experience of othering, which moreover signifies the non-self-referential poetic pleasure of altering one's world. In this respect, it seems apt to recall John Cage's often quoted phrase "Art is self alteration"—provided, however, that we don't take this to mean some sort of artistic redemption or self-actualization (in some New Age sense), but that self-alteration names the core process by which our worldly existence can be radically transformed, which is also, after all, the deepest significance of art: the radical transfiguration of form. To this end, self-alteration cannot be conceptualized or articulated if the self remains a notion within the signifying limits of identity. The process of self-alteration is deadly to the process of identity. It presupposes—it enables and performs—an *identicide*: the self-dissolution of the self, or in another idiom, the production of nonidentity as self-transformative force.

## Notes

1. To conform to the length requirements of this publication I have to omit here a section, equal to the length I devote to Irigaray, where I discuss Judith Butler's notion of subjectification as subjection and Cornelius Castoriadis's notion of self-alteration, especially in the way the he connects it (politically) to the project of autonomy and (psychoanalytically) to the process of sublimation. Castoriadis elaborates on his own theory of sublimation at great length in his signature work *The Imaginary Institution of Society* (Cambridge: MIT Press, 1987), but for a concise depiction of his psychoanalytic theory in general (in which sublimation and self-alteration play a central role), see also the psychoanalytic section in the collection of essays *World in Fragments* (Stanford: Stanford University

Press, 1997), 125–212. In regard to Butler, see her argument in *The Psychic Life of Power* (Stanford: Stanford University Press, 1997).

2. See "On the Catachresis of Otherness," in *Dream Nation* (Stanford: Stanford University Press, 1996), 267–82.

3. This doesn't altogether mean she avoids lapsing into a certain heterological transcendentalism on occasion. See, for example, the recent essays "Approaching the Other as Other," in *Between East and West* (New York: Columbia University Press, 2002), 121–30 and "La transcendance de l'autre," in *Autour de l'idolâtrie*, ed. Bernard Van Meenen (Bruxelles: Publications des Facultés universitaires Saint-Louis, 2003), 43–54. But at least, Irigaray is careful to refrain from those positions that declare otherness epistemologically off-limits, those who bristle at the suggestion that one can speak from the position of an other. While I understand suspicion against imperializing discourses that preside over monopolies of representation by proxy, the fight is to be conducted strictly on political grounds. It can never be an ontological argument. In presuming to put oneself in the position of an other, one does not strive to *be* the other—the very law of performativity forbids it. In fact, it makes it impossible. One of the most articulate, radical, and moving examples of how one can indeed speak from the position of the other in full cognizance of the impossibility of *being the other* is, to my mind, Jean Genet's last work, *Un captif amoureux* (1986).

4. Luce Irigaray, "The Universal as Mediation" (1986), in *Sexes and Genealogies*, trans. Gillian C. Gill (New York: Columbia University Press, 1993), 133. Henceforth cited in the text as SG, followed by page number. I cannot resist pointing out that this is precisely what Benjamin and Adorno also perceived as a problem in Hegel and attempted to resolve first by "the idea of natural history" and later by "dialectics at a standstill" and "negative dialectics" respectively. The notion of history as second nature (nature's second nature) is a concept that Adorno never abandoned. Neither, of course, addressed this differential relation as a matter of sexual difference, despite various insinuations.

5. Consider that one of the key figures in Hegel's theorization of *Sittlichkeit* is Antigone, whom Hegel never even entertains as being herself possibly an embodiment of *hubris* insofar as she too stages, from her own standpoint (legitimate though it is), a politics of *monos phronein*—the dogmatic singularity of excepting oneself from the polis. I have reviewed this issue at length in "Philosophy's Need for Antigone," in *Does Literature Think?* (Stanford: Stanford University Press 2003), 116–57.

6. It's essential to note here that, while many have criticized Irigaray's later work as a kind of softening of position, the point is not to restrict ourselves to a mode of evaluation that presumes the polemical to be superior to the evocative. No doubt, in her later work, Irigaray wrestles with the articulation of an emancipatory humanism, a humanism that proceeds through its own sublation and the sublation of the terms of so-called '60s-'70s French theory in which she was an unquestionable protagonist. One of the elemental meanings of sublation, let us not forget, is the preservation (albeit in an altered relation) of the sublated terms—in this case, the critique of traditional humanism. (Hegelian *Aufhebung*—as method, not as means to an end—is an exemplary figure of self-alteration.) I would argue

that Irigaray's wrestling with the project of an emancipatory humanism lends a much greater and sharper gravity to her feminism, and specifically to her pursuit of sexual difference as an epistemological condition that explodes at the core of the history of thought. And I would add that the discomfort with her late humanism is analogous to what is expressed against the late writings of Edward Said, though obviously their domains of discussion are different.

Chapter 11

# Hospitality and Sexual Difference

## Remembering Homer with Luce Irigaray

Judith Still

### Introduction

It could be argued that the expression "Homeric hospitality" is merely a rhetorical wave of the hand; here I shall claim, however, that our understanding of our hospitality today is helped by a close analysis of *The Odyssey*.[1] I shall focus on the text we read today as literary critics often do (for aesthetic purposes) without paying the attention to its origins, which a classical scholar might find necessary. Yet it is the representation, and implicit theorization, of social and economic relations in the text that interest me.[2] *The Odyssey* is the classical text of hospitality par excellence; it could be argued that hospitality is the major articulation of this text, and that the key form of relationship in *The Odyssey* is the one between guest and host. Hospitality is a prime motor of the text: hosts detain Odysseus and hold him back from returning home as he would wish, while scandalous guests (the suitors) create the narrative interest on the home front. Furthermore, the social and moral code of hospitality is the chief means of distinguishing between men in ethical terms. Virtuous and wise men follow the code of hospitality, most particularly as hosts but also as guests, whatever their social status.

The issue on which I want to focus is that of hospitality and sexual difference. While some of the key theoretical texts currently influencing the debate on hospitality (notably those by Jacques Derrida)[3] assert the importance of sexual difference in its structure, it is racial, ethnic, or cultural difference that has captured the imagination of most interlocutors. It is perhaps obvious, then, that, while Luce Irigaray's comments on hospitality have been little studied, her work is critical to the reinsertion of the question of sexual difference more forcefully into the debate. It is unsurprising, particularly in the current macrocosmic political situation, that we are concerned by issues of ethnicity and migration. However, Luce Irigaray alerts us to the danger that patriarchy subsumes an apparent plurality of "races" into a kind of uniformity; she argues that only attention to micro- and macrocosmic sexual difference can prevent the slide into sameness that is characteristic of our monoculture.[4] Paying due care to the real difference that is closest to us and attempting to build what she terms a culture of two subjects, will, she argues, improve other kind of relations in difference, including cultural difference.

> Certain historical factors might seem more important to us than treating the difference of the sexes: those tied to the migrations of our age, for example. Now these migrations risk carrying us off toward an increasingly disturbing neutralization and phantomization of the environment and of the individual, accompanied by an authoritarian guardianship that surrounds or integrates the multiple and the foreigner. The recent paternalist era claims to be plural, but it is a plural often remaining inside the closure of the patriarchal world.[5]

While Luce Irigaray has not written at length on Homer, she insists on the crucial importance of Greek mythology to our understanding of sexual difference; we need to return to Greek culture in an attempt to find the crossroads where we took the wrong path. Margaret Whitford writes with reference to *Le Temps de la différence, Je, tu, nous* and *Sexes and Genealogies*:

> Irigaray sees the Greek myths as figurations of a struggle between matriarchy and patriarchy in which patriarchy finally won. There is some suggestion that she sees the struggles as being in some sense still with us. . . . Only now instead of a struggle for dominance she sees it more as a struggle for the maternal principle to return to the light of day.[6]

## Hospitality as an Ethical Structure and Sexual Difference

Hospitality is an ethical structure, a structured social relationship between self and other, that wards off the fantasy of the maternal at the same time as it appeals to that fantasy. It involves bringing the other into the territory of the self for a period of time, and thus can be seen as dangerously invasive of the domain of the self. At the same time, from the perspective of the guest, hospitality is again both desirable and perilous. Different societies have different codes laying down sometimes quite specific rights and obligations on the part of both host and guest—warding off the violence that underlies relationships. But typically a reasoned knowledge of the detailed duties of a host in a technical sense is not the point; hospitality is an art fueled by emotion and sensitivity. In Homer, the prominence of Zeus as the god responsible for hospitality suggests its critical importance—the key relationship between men outside war (and war is the background to the *Odyssey*, of course). But women are always already the intimate ground of hospitality even as they are expelled from primary social relations of hospitality. As Luce Irigaray points out, women are the first home, and represent home for men:

> Western culture is above all masculine, and doubtless we should understand the gesture that appropriates the world for oneself as man's attempt to resolve his problems in relating to his origin. It is not easy for man to have been born of someone other to him, to have lived within her for nine months, to have depended on her for his chance of life or death, to have received from her his first dwelling, his first warmth, his first nourishment, his first sounds or human words, his first emotions and movements.[7]

Luce Irigaray argues that mothers, and women in general, should not be assimilated to the natural element in humanity; motherhood is not a passive condition, but (I would say) a kind of hospitality:

> Rather it [motherhood] is a question of accepting freely to share your life, your flesh, your breath—and thus in a way your soul—with the child to whom you give birth. And not only for a few minutes but for long months, even for long years. That does not mean we should idolize maternity as such, but we should recognize that the woman who engenders the child plays a part on both the human and divine level. We should recognize woman as a fully human subject but different from man, with other tasks to accomplish, particularly on the spiritual plane. Producing the other as a child within yourself, receiving the other in love within yourself, nourishing it with your own flesh, your own breath—these tasks do not demand the same spiritual attitude as engendering outside oneself, making love outside oneself, nourishing by one's work. (TA, 47)

Hospitality is "set up" as a relation between men yet it is suffused with fantasies of sexual difference. Following the code of hospitality is not a simple matter since it prescribes not obedience to a letter, but rather a spirit of generosity that might be understood as simultaneously natural to a good man and cultivated by a virtuous man, but has a fantasmatic relationship to femininity. The imagined superabundance, the excessive hospitality of the womb-home, as we figure it, lies beneath the threat of hospitality that contains and retains the guest even as he is lavishly nourished. Although there are many ways in which hospitality can prove devastating, including the murderer-guest (and the suitors do try to kill Telemachus in Book XV), it is *smothering* hospitality that is critical for father and son in *The Odyssey*. The rational social code of hospitality should prevent excessive hospitality between men—and Menelaus explains to Telemachus how the laws of hospitality dictate moderation,[8] although he seems unable to follow his own dictates. The letter of the laws is never enough—the unbounded spirit is both necessary and dangerous. Menelaus, of all the men in *The Odyssey*, is the closest to the dangerous feminine principle as it is encapsulated in his wife Helen.

If all hospitality harks back to the fear and desire of our first home, what about the position of real women as hosts? I make a distinction, awkward though it is to the ear, between hostesses and female hosts. If not commercial, the hostess implies hospitality offered by the master of the house, the true host, *by means of* his woman, the hostess. Her authority is thus only a delegated one, and she is an intermediary, her body (and mental and emotional faculties) a means for two or more men to communicate and bond. Luce Irigaray insists that women need a space of their own (both in an internal and an external sense) as a first condition of true hospitality. In *The Odyssey*, female *hosts*, by which I mean relatively autonomous hosts who are also female, are characteristically amorous and thus liable to hold our hero back—the two examples par excellence are the nymphs Circe and Calypso. None of the human women who engage in hospitality have this degree of autonomy (instead, they are hostesses), and the majority of them (Helen, Nausicaa (and her mother Arete), Penelope) are perhaps presented as wiser and more generous than the nymphs—less threatening. At any rate, they have less power to detain a guest even if they wish to do so. Nevertheless, in all three cases in three completely different ways, amorous passion and deception are significant elements inflecting hospitable relations.[9]

## Homeric Examples

In *The Odyssey* the hospitality narrative can be divided up into three major strands: Odysseus as guest, Telemachus as guest (and host), and the suitors as guests and hosts.[10] Odysseus as guest is of course the major interest—it is his hosts' desire to detain him that in an important sense provides the rationale for the story of his prolonged homecoming. The "hosts" he encounters run the gamut from Polyphemus who eats his "guests" in Book IX and the Sirens whose entertainment means destruction (XII) to, say, Alcinous and his family who provide clothes, bath, food, shelter, music, gifts, and finally a ship to take him back to Ithaca (VII, VIII, XIII). In between the two poles there are those nymphs who tend him lovingly and provide for all his sensual needs *but* will not willingly release him to continue his journey as he wishes. It would, however, be oversimplistic to suggest either that the hosts can easily be evaluated according to whether they meet the standards of hospitality—many readers have judged Alcinous and his fellow Phaeacians as distinctly lacking in hospitality in spite of the facts briefly summarised above—or that Odysseus and his men always play the part of good guests (see Reece, chapter 5).

The "Telemachy" subplot is considered by Reece to be particularly powerful in the way in which it establishes practical and emotional parallels between father and son. In this respect, I would say, it is homosocial hospitality par excellence. The son has grown up without a father—the story takes place as he reaches manhood and begins to attempt in a rather muddled way to establish some authority over his beleaguered mother. His journey from home to attempt to find (news of) his father reinforces his belief in his paternity; hosts comment on his resemblance to Odysseus and he hears tales of his father's prowess. At the same time he undergoes, in a minor key, experiences that will help him to mature and to understand his father's story: he learns of the ambiguity as well as the value of hospitality, and what it is to be a guest detained. Both Nestor and his family and Menelaus and Helen are very helpful, but not *straightforwardly* helpful, to Telemachus. This helps to bond him to his father.

The Suitors' subplot is more obviously integral to the main narrative, creating the tension that makes a difference exactly when Odysseus returns home, and it makes his homecoming excitingly dangerous in a way that spectacularly reveals both his trademark cleverness and his physical strength. What is of particular concern to me is the fact that the unfolding of this subplot is entirely bound up with the transgression of hospitality. The suitors' wickedness is established (and this is necessary for listeners to rejoice at their destruction) chiefly by showing them to be overbearing and exploitative guests, and dreadful hosts, rather than by the mere fact that they are courting the unwilling Penelope. Social and economic relations *between men* are thus foregrounded, and even the wise Penelope may simply be sent away by her son.

A great deal can be, and has been, said about all this without particular reference to sexual difference. I shall now try briefly to elaborate on some of the ways in which attention to sexual difference opens up the text. The first, perhaps obvious, point to note is that women do not travel in *The Odyssey*—women are not guests.[11] When the goddess Athena, the Father-god's virgin daughter, plays the role of a guest she disguises herself as a man. Women are at home, and must be at home. But if we turn to women as hosts or hostesses, then we might note that while, as Irigaray shows, men are not at home with themselves in terms of their inner economy, in many cases women are not "at home." That expression implies a sense of comfort, of feeling at ease in your own environment; it also implies being willing to receive guests. Women might be in someone else's household (their father's or their husband's or even their brother's or son's) and thus their power to act as hostess would be delegated and secondary. While women outside the home are particularly vulnerable to rape, inside is not completely safe either. Susan Brownmiller would argue that patriarchy plays on that vulnerability to keep women in their place and feeling in need of patriarchal protection.[12] Should the master of the house ever be absent (like Odysseus), what might women do to protect themselves from unexpected guests? Freud picks up in a strangely perverse way on the cultural association between women and weaving—he sees this as a technology that protects their modesty, hiding what they do not have.[13] Women can weave clothes, cloth acting as a shield between men and women. Penelope's weaving, and unweaving, is only the most famous example of the very act of weaving being used for apotropaic effect.[14] The apotropaic shield par excellence, the Medusa's head (borne by Athena) that petrifies men, reminds us how patriarchy plays on women's vulnerability in part because, as patriarchal mythology shows us, women are not only desired but feared for their sexual power. This imagined power is lethal: the power to be unfaithful to a husband threatens the father's immortality through his descendants who might not be his after all; sexual power is also a power to lure men to their deaths as the Sirens do, transform them into beasts as the nymph Circe does, entangle and destroy them like Clytemnestra and her lover. I shall now look briefly at four categorizations of women in *The Odyssey*: the siren, the prize wife, the servant, the father's virgin daughter.

Sirens and nymphs suggest to the listener women as sexually entrapping to a greater or lesser extent—bringing men to their doom or simply imprisoning them. This is how women are—in men's dreams. On the human plane this is played out in a vestigial sense with Nausicaa who immediately looks upon Odysseus as a potential husband (VI). More complicated still is the older generation—in particular the figure of the beautiful Helen. On the one hand she is presented, and *presents herself*, as wise, caring, sensitive, helpful beyond her husband Menelaus (IV). On the other hand, we are reminded of the number of men who lost their lives because of her enchantment by the guest Paris, or by Aphrodite, . . . or was it Helen who was the enchantress? The poet reminds us too of

Clytemnaestra—a tale of feminine adultery, deception, and murder—Agamemnon killed in the bath, the bath that is a key element in so many hospitality scenes. Helen tells Telemachus (and us) a tale of her help to her guest Odysseus, disguised as a beggar, in Troy reconnoitering prior to the building of the horse. Without directly contradicting this story Menelaus counters it with his own story of how Helen accompanied by her *second* Trojan husband (as if one were not bad enough) sought to make the Greeks hidden in the horse betray themselves by calling to them in the voices of their wives. This tale embodies the layers of deception associated with Helen and the perils of containment or enclosure. One of the ways in which Helen entertains Telemachus and his companion is by giving them an Egyptian drug, which makes them forget their sorrows—to the point that they could hear songs of the destruction of members of their families and not weep. It helps them sleep well and could be seen as entirely benign—even if magical like the sleep that overcomes Penelope thanks to Athena (for example, Book XVIII). But it also evokes other episodes such as the visit to the dangerously beguiling land of the Lotus eaters, and Helen's powers, like those of the nymphs who entertain Odysseus, may not be entirely benign.

The prize wife—to be won in myths by the strongest or cleverest as her nearest male kinsman dictates—returns via Penelope (and perhaps lurks underneath the story of Nausicaa and the Phaeacian games).[15] Penelope, usually remembered for her wisdom in keeping her suitors at bay by weaving and unpicking a shroud for Laertes, is treated less favorably in the detail of the text. While a prize for the suitors, she is *already* a wife and mother. Athena and Telemachus seek to keep her in a woman's place, apart from men. When Athena/Mentes appears to Telemachus, s/he tells him:

> [A]s for your mother, if she is set on marrying, let her go back to her father's house. He is a man of consequence, and the family will provide a marriage feast, and see that she has a generous dowry, as is only right for a daughter they value. . . . You are no longer a child: you must put childish thoughts away. Have you not heard what a name Prince Orestes made for himself in the world when he killed the traitor Aegisthus for murdering his noble father? You, my friend—and what a tall and splendid fellow you have grown!—must be as brave as Orestes. Then future generations will sing your praises. (28–29)

Matricide is buried in this speech; Orestes' only crime, here in fact an *exploit*, is killing Aegisthus—his mother is not even mentioned. Similarly, the killing of the daughter (Iphigenia) by her father is often "forgotten" as a motive for Clytemnestra's crime. We modern readers might remember from the *Oresteia* that Orestes (only temporarily mad unlike his sister and co-conspirator Electra who *remains* mad) is redeemed for his matricide by the motherless and chaste Athena and by Apollo, the lover of men.[16] Here Telemachus is urged to renounce his mother too in order to become the man he already is. This is the paradoxical structure of masculinity. Reaching physical manhood with respect to age or biology he is a man naturally (and it is important to cling to this conviction), but also must become a man culturally (striving or struggle is necessary to manhood). Luce Irigaray points how frequently women are assimilated to nature, and sexual difference treated as analogous to the nature/culture opposition; for her it is urgent that both sexes cultivate both their nature and their cultural becoming. She argues that masculine subjectivity has a particular problem with differentiation from the maternal world, and this leads to clumsy attempts to emerge as a separate universal or neutral "one"; relational becoming is particularly difficult for masculine subjects. While Telemachus will refuse to send Penelope away from "his" house, shortly afterward he acts out the expulsion in a lesser form, saying to his surprised mother: "[G]o to your quarters and attend to your own work, the loom and the spindle, and tell the servants to get on with theirs. Talking must be men's concern, and mine in particular; for I am master in this house" (31). Penelope's situation (position and location) is an ambiguous one while her lord and master is away. She is disempowered as hostess in the absence of Odysseus not only vis-à-vis the suitors' wolfish rapacity but also in relation to the series of beggars who exploit her desire to hear news of her husband. Her ways of keeping things going are always suspect; she is imagined at fault and made guilty by the men around her. When Telemachus complains in the public Assembly about the unwelcome guests who are eating him out of house and home, the suitor Antinous replies: "It is your own mother, that incomparable schemer who is the culprit."[17]

The female servants in the master's house often play a key and intimate role in hospitality—for example, bathing the guest. (Nestor's hospitality is marked as particularly warm and informal by the fact that his daughter, rather than a servant, bathes Telemachus.) While Odysseus is away from his house the position of the female servants is difficult, and many of them have sexual relations with the suitors. This is named rape. Odysseus says to the suitors: "You ate me out of house and home; you raped my maids; you wooed my wife on the sly though I was alive" (339).[18] However, the women are also deemed unfaithful and disloyal: in Book XXII they are given a deliberately degrading death and hanged for their crime.[19]

The final category I shall briefly evoke is that of the motherless Athena who sprang fully formed from Zeus's head, as we know from other sources.[20] Luce Irigaray comments briefly on her appearance in the *Oresteia* in "The Bodily Encounter with the Mother"; and argues that this mythology underlying patriarchy has not changed: "Here and there, regulation Athenas whose one begetter is the head of the Father-King still burst forth. Completely in his pay, in the pay of the men in power, they bury beneath their sanctuary women in struggle so that they will no longer disturb the new order of the home, the order of the polis, now the only order" (37).

It could be argued that *The Odyssey* as we know it tells two stories about women. It presents to us Penelope who is wise, strong, and loyal; it also gives us Penelope who is sent to her rooms by Telemachus and ordered not to speak, Penelope about whom Athena warns her son, for example at the beginning of Book XV. It introduces Nausicaa as an interesting and clever princess who is a key factor in the hospitality offered to Odysseus by the Phaeacians, and then drops her from the narrative of Odysseus's stay with the Phaeacians altogether. The Nausicaa episode is also the only instance of a (*brief glimpse* of a) happy mother-daughter relationship. Most striking to the contemporary reader is the representation of Helen. As she plays hostess to Telemachus in a generous and sensitive way she tells him of one of her memories of Odysseus—a memory of her cleverly outwitting the master of disguise in order to play host to him in Troy. But this is set against reminders of Helen's overarching role in the Trojan War—cause of the loss of so many lives thanks to her rape by the ungrateful and deceitful guest, Paris. Menelaus's tale perhaps shows her lethal Siren deceitfulness, her infidelity, *and* her being outwitted by Odysseus. These are two contrasting interpretations of the past (the husband's and the wife's), and the text we have inherited simply allows both to stand. On the other hand, no doubt is cast over the setting in the present. It reveals a particular sexual inequality when it comes to vertical relations, to descendants. When Telemachus arrives Helen and Menelaus are "celebrating" a double wedding—we might note that the son who is marrying is the son of one of Menelaus's mistresses—Helen is now barren we are told. Helen's only child, a daughter, is being married to Achilles' son, the result of a battlefield bargain between the fathers. While sons bring their wives home, the daughter's marriage means her exile to a distant and unknown land. There are echoes here—distantly the echo of Demeter and Persephone, more closely that of Iphigenia, lured to her death with the promise of marriage to Achilles, and Clytemnestra who kills Agamemnon in revenge.

I shall quickly sum up some of the points in these episodes. The first concerns horizontal inequality: sexual infidelity, even if involuntary, of women should by rights be punished (it is a kind of magic that makes Menelaus forgive Helen, the serving women get their just deserts). This magic may cover an issue of land ownership or Menelaus's right to his kingdom, which originally came to him through his marriage to Helen. It is normal for chieftains (Agamemnon, Menelaus, and even Odysseus) to have concubines. The second point concerns vertical inequality: the pleasure of a good relationship between mother and daughter and the pain of losing a daughter for a mother is present but elided. Men bond through the father's gift of a daughter to her husband. Fathers pass on material and cultural inheritance to their sons. And the father should be able to sacrifice the mother's daughter unpunished; Athena, the daughter who is not born of a mother, but of a father, serves the patriarchal cause. Of course, points one and two are linked since the policing of women's sexual infidelity relates to reproduction and genealogy. The third point is the structure of enclosure: women are dangerous and should be contained (nymphs on their islands, wives and mothers in their quarters with their beds and their weaving) or even expelled from the text—although the repressed of course returns.

## Conclusions

For men, hospitality functions as a test of proper virtuous manliness—some are shown to be good, some bad. Zeus is the god who presides over hospitality while some inhuman male hosts (notably Polyphemos) are the antithesis of hospitality. Hospitality as a test of masculine virtue is a difficult one and while many perform well they could do better; it is hard to find exactly the right ground between falling short (being insufficiently welcoming) and going beyond (being excessively officious), between the laws and the Law. We might ask whether it is a mythical feminine hysteral economy of abundance that haunts good old Nestor and Menelaus in their retention of guests. Women meanwhile do not have a place of their own. Nymphs and sirens show listeners what can happen when females do have their own place: they enslave their male guests to their senses. It is not that women are shown as stupid, passive, purely sensual or emotional creatures in Homer as they will be shown in so many later texts. On the contrary, they are wise, active, and rational as well as sensual beings. The problem lies in their interaction with men, their effect on men being often revealed as a lethal one—bringing men to oblivion, if not to death, singly or indeed in multitudes. Luce Irigaray's point that men project fears and phantasms (in particular castration anxiety) onto women as other of the same—deceivers—is here writ large. The effect of female hosts is sticky—leading to stasis, entropy, the forgetting of the project. That could indeed be (we listeners might feel) the effect of hostesses such as Helen or Nausicaa or even Penelope were they not more or less successfully disempowered. Women must be contained in the home to be no more than hostesses as handmaidens to the master of the house. Luce Irigaray, on the other hand, as well as critiquing the patriarchal mythology, suggests a cultivation of sexuate difference (and *not* women as the other of the same). She puts forward hospitality *not* as a fantasized hysteral economy, containing and suffocating as it provides everything in abundance for the other/guest, and not even as a real "placental" economy if we take that either literally or metaphorically. If we take it literally it might seem to suggest a return to the natural pre-Oedipal relation of generation, a purely vertical relation. If we turn it into a metaphor then the material is once again sacrificed to the spiritual. For Luce Irigaray each sexuate subject should be an *hôte* in his or her own place with her or his own natural and cultural identity and both should be involved in creating a third place, a threshold, in-between. This would create a horizontal transcendental between *I* and *you*; you the other (*heteros*) would come within while remaining outside and strange.[21] There would be no exclusion yet also no pressure to integrate. And *I* would be a *you* for *you*.

## Notes

I am in the middle of a study of theories and representations of hospitality in eighteenth-century France and the contemporary period funded by the Leverhulme Trust. See my: "Acceptable Hospitality: from Rousseau's Levite to the Strangers in Our Midst Today," *Journal of Romance Studies* 3, no. 2 (2003); "Language as Hospitality: Revisiting Intertextuality via *Monolingualism of the Other*," *Paragraph* 27, no.1 (2004); "The Stranger Within: The Figure of *l'hôte* in Rousseau's *Confessions*," in *From Goethe to Gide*, ed. Mary Orr and Lesley Sharpe (Exeter: Exeter University Press, 2005); "Derrida: Guest and Host," *Paragraph* 28, no. 3 (2005).

1. I shall refer to book numbers (in Roman numerals) for ease of comparison between editions. For quotations I refer to E. V. Rieu (Harmondsworth: Penguin, 1946).

2. Up until the middle of the last century, the Homeric text, probably "composed" at the end of the seventh or beginning of the eighth century BC, was usually considered to represent the Mycenaean civilization (which collapsed around the end of the thirteenth century BC); this is the period during which the Trojan War is imagined to have taken place. It was the work of Moses Finley, alongside new archaeological discoveries such as Linear B, that convinced the contemporary academic community that the situation was more complex. While many details such as place names or the enumeration of treasures do relate to the "Mycenaean world," Finley argued on the basis of comparative anthropology and the "coherence criterion" that the culture and institutions represented by Homer relate to the (early) Dark Ages that followed. He draws on the work of Marcel Mauss to analyze the complex system of total gift exchange that creates personal bonds in societies less bureaucratic, centralized, and fixed in their hierarchies than those that either preceded or succeeded the Greek Dark Ages. This story of the forgetting, and remembering, of archaic gift practices is highly pertinent to my analysis of the representation and theorization of hospitality. See for example,

Finley, *The World of Odysseus* (London: Chatto and Windus, 1964). See Evelyne Scheid-Tissinier, "L'éthique du don, fondement de la société homérique?" *Europe* 79, no. 865 (2001) for a résumé of recent arguments.

3. See, e.g., *Of Hospitality. Anne Dufourmantelle Invites Jacques Derrida to Respond*, trans. Rachel Bowlby (Stanford: Stanford University Press, 2000).

4. When asked about "diversity" in an interview with Andrea Wheeler (*Journal of Romance Studies* 4, no. 2 [2004], Luce Irigaray replies: "To promote only diversity, as is often the case in our times, runs the risk of remaining in an unchanged horizon with regard to the relations with the other(s). We then entrust this problem to customs, moral rules or religious feeling without questioning our culture about its capability of meeting with the other as such. Furthermore we are unable to open ourselves all the time to others different from us. We need to return to ourselves, to keep and save our totality or integrity, and this is possible only in sexuate difference. Why? Because it is the most basic difference, this one which secures for each bridge(s) both between nature and culture and between us. It is starting from this difference that the other sorts of otherness have been elaborated. And if someone would raise here the problem of races or generations, it could be answered that races and generations do not prevent sexual attraction and that the behaviours with respect to them result from an elaboration, or non-elaboration, of sexual attraction. This attraction is stronger than the difference between the bodies. And it is more spiritual in a way. It also arises firstly between the two. It is more initial and fundamental than diversity and can explain it, while the contrary is not true. Diversity is a means today to escape the question of sexuate difference and to reduce or merge women's liberation in a past world in which woman had not yet discovered and affirmed her own cultural values" (93).

5. *Between East and West: From Singularity to Community* (hereafter BEW), trans. Stephen Pluháˇcek (New York: Columbia University Press, 2002), 16–17.

6. "Irigaray, Utopia, and the Death Drive," in *Engaging with Irigaray*, ed. Carolyn Burke, Naomi Schor, and Margaret Whitford (New York: Columbia University Press, 1994), 388.

7. "La Transcendance de l'autre" (hereafter TA), in *Autour de l'idolâtrie: Figures actuelles de pouvoir et de domination*, ed. Bernard van Meenen (Brussels: Publications des Facultés universitaires Saint Louis, 2003), 46; my translation.

8. "I condemn any host who is either too kind or not kind enough. There should be moderation in all things, and it is equally offensive to speed a guest who would like to stay and to detain one who is anxious to leave" (XV, 238–39).

9. See Luce Irigaray, *Marine Lover. Of Friedrich Nietzsche*, trans. Gillian C. Gill (New York: Columbia University Press, 1991), e.g., the section "Veiled Lips" for a number of pertinent remarks on the representation of woman as foreign to truth.

10. See Steve Reece, *The Stranger's Welcome. Oral Theory and the Aesthetics of the Homeric Hospitality Scene* (Ann Arbor: University of Michigan Press, 1993), a book devoted to the analysis of hospitality scenes in Homer—although without focusing on questions of sexual difference. I refer to this for a number of thorny issues such as the establishment of the text; "conventional" or "type" scenes are likely to have had elements or phrases interpolated. Hospitality scenes are normally composites of smaller type-scenes (for instance, arrival, reception,

seating, bathing, feasting, gift giving) all composed in formulaic diction and in a relatively fixed order. Scribes who left us the many different manuscripts of *The Odyssey* may have been particularly likely to make concordance additions in scenes where convention dictates certain components (such as Circe's feast preparation). For my purposes, issues of attestation are less vital than for those concerned with Homer the poet and the internal consistency or otherwise of his text. Historical *expectations* of hospitality scenes, and versions of Homer that have been read by and have influenced later generations, are of at least equivalent interest to me.

11. "Nomads conquer their territory against the familiarity of the first site, against the sedentary, against the more maternal, more feminine values. They create a culture of between-men, who are enemies or accomplices, for which the divinity is instead patriarchal, God-the-Father" (*BEW*, 13).

12. *Against Our Will: Men, Women and Rape* (London: Secker and Warburg, 1975).

13. See his *New Introductory Lectures on Psychoanalysis*, no. 33, "Femininity."

14. There are many analyses of this—I shall just cite one salient one: Peggy Kamuf, *Signature Pieces on the Institution of Authorship* (Ithaca and London: Cornell University Press, 1988), chapter 6, "Penelope at Work," especially 145–47. Kamuf starts by pointing out that Telemachus twice sends his mother away to weave and spin—leaving men's work such as "discussion" to him. At the same time metaphorically weaving and spinning is seen as crucial to men's poetic language. Women's work and the domestic interior is veiled to men—imagining Penelope in bed at night when in fact she is undoing her weaving.

15. See Reece, 110ff.

16. I am using shorthand here as Irigaray does in her discussions of Athena and Apollo; see "The Bodily Encounter with the Mother," in *The Irigaray Reader*, ed. Margaret Whitford (Oxford: Basil Blackwell, 1991). Athena is not quite motherless—although she is born motherless. According to myth, her father, Zeus, swallowed her pregnant mother the Titaness Metis for fear that she would eventually give birth to a son who would kill him as he killed his own father (Cronus) who had killed his grandfather (Uranus).

17. At the assembly of Ithaca's leaders, Antinous replies to Telemachus's charge that they are frittering away his wealth by explaining how Penelope deceived them for nearly four years by pretending to be weaving a shroud for Laertes, and advises Telemachus: "Send your mother away and make her marry the man whom her father chooses and whom she prefers. She must beware of trying our young men's patience much further and counting too much on the matchless gifts that she owes to Athena, her skill in fine handiwork, her excellent brain, and that genius she has for getting her way. In that respect, I grant she has no equal, not even in story. . . . Yet in the present case Penelope has used these wits amiss. For I assure you that so long as she maintains this attitude that she has been misguided enough to adopt, the Suitors will continue to eat you out of house and home. She may be winning a great name for cleverness, but at what expense to you!" (36–37). Telemachus replies: "It is quite impossible for me to cast out the mother who bore me and who brought me up, with my father somewhere at the world's end and, as likely as not, still alive. Think, first, what I should have to pay Icarius if I took it

into my head to send my mother back to him. Again, when that father of hers had done his worst to me, the gods would step in and let loose on me the avenging Furies that my mother's curses would call up as she was driven from home. And finally my fellow-men would cry shame upon me. . . . If a feeling of shame has any place in your own hearts, then quit my palace and feast yourselves elsewhere, eating your own provisions in each other's houses. But if you think it a sounder scheme to destroy one man's estate and go scot-free yourselves, then eat your fill, while I prey to the immortal gods for a day of reckoning, when *I* can go scot-free, though I destroy you in that house of mine" (37–38).

18. An alternative translation in the Loeb Classical Library is: "You wasted my house, and lay with the maidservants by force, and while I was still alive covertly courted my wife" (trans. A. T. Murray, revised George E. Dimock [Cambridge: Harvard University Press, 1998], 347).

19. Odysseus orders that they should be killed by the sword but Telemachus does not want them to have such a clean death.

20. Joanna Hodge points out how "the motherless Athena and her brother, Apollo, triumph over the chthonic gods and the relation between mother and daughter—between Clytemnestra and Iphigenia—is erased" in her comments on matricide. See "Irigaray Reading Heidegger," in *Engaging with Irigaray*, 192–93.

21. See *EOO*, "Sapprocher de l'autre en tant qu'autre," 162.

## Works Cited


Brownmiller, Susan. *Against Our Will: Men, Women, and Rape*. London: Secker and Warburg, 1975.

Derrida, Jacques. *Of Hospitality. Anne Dufourmantelle Invites Jacques Derrida to Respond*. Trans. Rachel Bowlby. Stanford: Stanford University Press, 2000.

Finley, Moses I. *The World of Odysseus*. London: Chatto and Windus, 1964.

Hodge, Joanna. "Irigaray Reading Heidegger." In *Engaging with Irigaray*, ed. Carolyn Burke, Naomi Schor, and Margaret Whitford, 191–209. New York: Columbia University Press, 1994.

Homer. *Odyssey*. Trans. E. V. Rieu. Harmondsworth: Penguin, 1946.

Irigaray, Luce. *Between East and West: From Singularity to Community*. Trans. Stephen Pluhá ̌cek. New York: Columbia University Press, 2002.

———. "The Bodily Encounter with the Mother." In *The Irigaray Reader*, ed. Margaret Whitford, 34–46. Oxford: Basil Blackwell, 1991.

———. Interview with Andrea Wheeler. *Journal of Romance Studies* 4, no. 2: 91–107, 2004.

———. *Marine Lover. Of Friedrich Nietzsche*. Trans. Gillian C. Gill. New York: Columbia University Press, 1991.

———. "La Transcendance de l'autre." In *Autour de l'idolâtrie: Figures actuelles de pouvoir et de domination*, ed. Bernard van Meenen, 43–55. Brussels: Publications des Facultés universitaires Saint Louis, 2003.

Kamuf, Peggy. *Signature Pieces on the Institution of Authorship*. Ithaca and London: Cornell University Press, 1988.

Reece, Steve. *The Stranger's Welcome. Oral Theory and the Aesthetics of the Homeric Hospitality Scene*. Ann Arbor: University of Michigan Press, 1993.

Scheid-Tissinier, Evelyne. "L'éthique du don, fondement de la société homérique?" *Europe* 79, no. 865 (2001): 193–206.

Still, Judith. "Acceptable Hospitality: from Rousseau's Levite to the Strangers in Our Midst Today. *Journal of Romance Studies* 3, no. 2 (2003): 1–14.

———. "Derrida: Guest and Host." 2005. *Paragraph* 28, no. 3: in press.

———. "Language as Hospitality: Revisiting Intertextuality via *Monolingualism of the Other*. *Paragraph* 27, no.1 (2004): 113–27.

———. "The Stranger Within: The Figure of *l'hôte* in Rousseau's *Confessions*." In *From Goethe to Gide: Feminism aesthetics and the literary canon in France and Germany 1770–1930*, ed. Mary Orr and Lesley Sharpe, 22–33. Exeter: Exeter University Press, 2005.

Whitford, Margaret. "Irigaray, Utopia, and the Death Drive." In *Engaging with Irigaray*, ed. Carolyn Burke, Naomi Schor, and Margaret Whitford, 379–400. New York: Columbia University Press, 1994.

# Chapter 12

# "Raising Love up to the Word"

## Rewriting God as "Other" through Irigarayan Style

Laine M. Harrington

> The air is sweet. Its flowering is in harmony with presence: it is as tender as a caress. I raise love up to the word. I call upon fidelity to make a sign, or at the very least, a sound. I search for a voice inspired by you or which I want you to hear. I await the music of my heart, attentive all the while to yours.
>
> —Luce Irigaray, *To Be Two*

### Prelude

Luce Irigaray's words from *To Be Two* allude to "dialogue" as a rewriting of the dialectic of gender—that is, a style of speaking, writing, listening, hearing, living that includes an "other word," a feminine word as partner to the masculine.[1] Such a conversation, however, implies nuances best articulated through a discussion of sexual difference and Irigarayan style in the context of ancient Greek philosophy. In other words, an Irigarayan sense of dialogue requires an understanding of several critical issues, including the role that style as difference initially plays in allowing for feminine subjectivity and, secondly, in then creating a space for now "two" subjectivities.

Well known for her critique of the vertically based *logos* upon which ancient Greek philosophies are founded, Luce Irigaray challenges the Platonic (and Stoic) notions of dialectic as she moves toward the horizontal nature of authentic dialogue. Doing so, she simultaneously collapses and uplifts the word, rewriting it not only for the feminine, but for its own integrity. If we are honest with ourselves, such integrity will lead us into the heart of things where an awareness of the "other" exists. It is often at this place where we find a sense of spirit, which some will call "god" and others will call "essence."

## *Logos* and the Early Greeks

Exposing the underpinnings of the ancient Greek philosophical term *logos*, Luce Irigaray's work reveals women's exclusion from Western culture—specifically, women's exclusion from Western discourse. As is well known, in her groundbreaking *Speculum of the Other Woman*, Irigaray uses the metaphor of mirror ("speculation/speculum") to traverse backward through Western philosophy's negation of women, beginning with Freud, and ending (or as she says, "at the beginning") with Plato.[2] Hence, much of Irigaray's work with *logos* focuses on the mirroring that Western masculinized discourse requires, thus leading to the exclusion of feminine subjectivity.

By now, we must know that the root of *logos* (λεγ-/λέγω) means "to gather together," or, more precisely, "to pick out things which from some standpoint are alike."[3] Implied in this gathering together of "like things" is the notion of order, for when things of like nature are gathered together, not only do they find their intrinsic order, but an outward sense of order also prevails. It is no mistake that the Greek *kosmos* translates as both order and universe. In this sense, one kind of order mirrors another. Not stopping there, we find a similar attitude reflected in the nature of narrative. That is, when making an account of something—or when gathering together words, which from some standpoint are alike—the proper placement of one word in front of another also reflects a proper ordering of the universe.

Within this sense of order, notions of equal fluctuations, unity, and monism prevail. As such, order suggests a kind of logic, a certain reason. We could say that an account, a narrative, lacking reason falls out of order and becomes chaotic. But, a reasoned format rests with proper measure and proportion, which in turn provides for balance and a kind of "equivalency." Certainly, in their well-tuned universe, the early Greeks believed that such equivalency often arrived as two things responding to each other, most likely, as opposites. From this notion of two things in opposition to each other, though, also came a notion of their connectedness, their "oneness." And, in every case we must consider what *singular* thing connected the two as one. What like values "gathered" them together? Furthermore, we must consider Edward Schiappa's premise that most oppositional pairings also included a notion where a kind of implicit hierarchy existed in that, generally, "one of the two things in opposition was considered in some way preferable to the other."[4]

Similar notions appear throughout a reading of ancient Greek philosophies and *logos* theory. We find them early on in the work of Heraclitus. Certainly we know of the "impossibility of stepping twice into the same river,"[5] words that allude to his theory of fluctuation, the notion that "changes between fire, sea and earth balance each other" and are driven according to the rationality of the universe.[6] Although the notion of opposition in early Greece is well documented and although others (e.g., Hesiod) framed things in opposition to each other, Heraclitus was the earliest person to write to such an extent regarding opposition as reflected in the following pairs: day and night, earth and sea, warm and cool, dry and wet, summer and winter, hunger and satiety, rest and weariness, good and bad, just and unjust, peace and war, immortal and mortal, young and old, up and down, straight and crooked, divine and human.[7] Although the oppositions of male and female are not mentioned, they exist by implication. Allow me to explain.

Early Greek language and culture is so replete with pairings that many rely on the term *bipolar opposition* to explain this phenomenon.[8] Following this, a number of the Presocratic philosophers (both pre- and post-Heraclitus) implicate male and female as one of these oppositional pairings. Ann Bergren writes, "Parmenides claimed the sex of the child depended upon the position of the womb (right for males, left for females), Empedocles, upon the temperature of the womb at conception (hotter for men, colder for women), and Anaximander, the side from which the father's seed came (right for males, left for females)" (201). At this point, it would be helpful to remember not only the sense of "oneness" that holds each opposition together, but also Schiappa's earlier remark that one of the two becomes preferable to the other. Let us also return to Luce Irigaray's work with *logos* to further explicate these matters.

As earlier mentioned, in the first phase of her work, Luce Irigaray recounts the exclusionary "oneness" that Western patriarchal culture and discourse displays toward women. Referring to the auto-mono-centrism of Western culture, Irigaray addresses the logocentrism of implied dualistic hierarchies that exclude the feminine by centering on the philosophical *logos* as "word." Such a logocentric perspective argues that most discourse operates according to binary patterns based on constructed opposites that suggest unity. Implying order, these binary oppositions find their link to *logos* with its regard for "putting together things of like value." But, as we have found, the notion of opposition often misleads. Indeed, the constructive capacity of any two things in opposition must be understood. Vincent Colapietro explains that, in actuality, "It is by means of oppositions that the very identities of some things are formed."[9]

As Irigaray has so carefully shown us, here we may consider the formation of "woman," believed to be opposite to "man." But, as we have also seen, most binary oppositions form according to notions of hierarchy where one term (e.g., "masculine") is privileged over the other (e.g., "feminine"). From a deconstructive point of view, "the notion of binary opposition is unsatisfactory because it represents a nostalgia for 'self-presence' or 'centring.'"[10] Hence, binary structures exclude or relegate to the margins those not located in primary positions in masculinized cultures. Here, again, we can locate Irigaray's work that argues the inexistence of a feminine subjectivity that has been set in opposition to, and defined by, the masculine.

## *Logos* as the "Word of God"

At this point, I would like to extend these notions, which *exclude* the feminine, to *include* theological discourses that define themselves according to a God as *Logos*. It is not such a stretch when we understand that *logos* has found its way from meanings associated with "word," "speech," "thought," and "discourse," to the "Word of God." Whereas many assume that *Logos* innocently suggests the "Word" of an all-embracing, universal God, what is less apparent is the lineage that *logos* travels to arrive at such a notion. Whether borrowed from Heraclitus, Plato, the Stoics, or other sources, most Christian definitions of *logos* imply a "gathering together of like things" that favor the masculine. As such, this "Word," this *Logos* arrives finally at the doorstep of early Christianity, not as an empty word, but as one with its baggage fully packed and centuries of associations with order, proportional equivalence, the unity of opposites, and hierarchy.

To these qualities, we can add Irigaray's work in which she elucidates the logic of the Same that any *logos*-centered discourse brings forth: that in order to carry on a logic of the Same (certainly desired by Western masculinized discourse), the "more preferred" in a binary set will define the "less preferred," thus requiring imitation and mirroring by the "lesser" of the "more." Under such a rule of Sameness, or as we might say, within such a "gathering together of like things," theological discourse, again founded on the *logos*, would seem to disregard any type of asymmetrical "otherness." It also seems that this evokes questions concerning access to the spirit. Certainly, implications for a masculinization of power are immense when the vehicle, *logos*, becomes simultaneously male *and* the Word of God.

As such, the early Christian appropriation of *logos* lays the foundation for a religion that not only bases itself on proclamation (thus, its easy associations with "word"). This appropriation also potentially constructs a God that continues to reproduce itself (as the Same) through moves that extend from Justin Martyr backward to Heraclitus. Certainly, the exclusion of women from Western culture is nothing new. But, where matters of God are concerned, exclusion becomes a different issue. Here, it occurs in a religion founded upon a "Word," which *supposedly* speaks to all.

Consider briefly the following signposts of early Christian appropriations of *logos* that have occurred in both linear and tautological fashion. I have already mentioned Heraclitus's theories of fluctuation, the unity of opposites, and monism. In turn, these influence Plato's preference for the *eidos* (i.e., the ideal world over the real as reflected in their polarities). This, in turn, influences Stoic notions of order, coherence, *mimesis*, and oneness, which influences Philo Judaeus's *dualistic* interpretations of absoluteness in abstraction and order in imitation, which influences Johannine views initiating an imitative, hierarchical reading of Jesus as the divine reflection of a masculine God, which influences Justin Martyr's *true* philosophy (i.e., Christianity) with its beliefs in *orthos logos* ("right reason") passed on according to *logos spermatikos* (or, "lineage").[11]

Thankfully for the work of Luce Irigaray, women, in particular, will begin to understand the implications of a masculine *logos* as God, as we also will better understand the implications of saying that it was the Son of a Father—a God from the beginning (thus, forever will it be)—who arrives in the flesh to save us. Similarly, we can better understand the difficulties that associate any God with a majuscule "Word." As we will see, such a *logos*, such a God, such a Word thrives *only* upon the regeneration of itself to itself (masculine to masculine), leaving no room for feminine subjectivity.

And, if this is so, if the Christian appropriation of an ancient Greek *logos* has constructed a religion that can *only* reproduce itself, that leaves no room for feminine subjectivity, for a feminine "word," for an "other," then I would ask: How *is* it a godly discourse? As I observe many appropriating for themselves this Word of God, it appears instead that this is a discourse that destroys the potential for love in favor of the Same, that devours compassion for the earth with the passion of a warlord. This is a discourse that raises injustice rather than justice to the Word of God, that commands bodies in like manner that he takes territories for himself. This is a discourse that favors the majuscule, that makes triumphant. That imperializes. No, such a world, such a God, such a Word, based upon order that leads eventually to propriety and ownership, does not belong to me. It is not of me.

Is this not the *logos* you expected from me? Are we not prodded, again and again to imitate your Word: told to reflect it, to mirror? If it is awkward, perhaps it is because this is not my word. Rather, it is a *logos* in which I have no part. But, let us be reminded of another way, for as Luce Irigaray offers, we have "a house to build, a love to invent, a spirit to cultivate" (2001, 4).

And, I, taking off on my own to do these things, leaving at the same moment you wish me gone, even so, each of us must arrive. Hopefully, you will welcome this, will desire to become an "other"; will stop imitating, will stop expecting imitation in return. Certainly, having only that which is of yourself around you must be tiring, though I have tried to make it otherwise.

O majuscule, *O Logos*, I do not mean to forsake you. Can you not tell this, by the "reason" of these words? Nor do I mean to forsake your word, even as I write my own. You must trust this, must believe in the depth from which these words arise, where I cannot decide which I will miss more: your Word, or my absence from it. All those years: centuries foretelling our absence from geographies to which we had become accustomed. But I can no longer draw them, draw from them, for they are not of me. Later, I will hope that upon our arrival, upon having drawn our own geographies, we will know how to cross, when to visit, where to meet. Yes, you and I, we must each find our own words, our own ways, our own gods. Which is to say that you can no longer be mine. . .

## Toward an "Other Word"

Deadstillness over droughtlands.
Parched, the heart of the matter.
Panic among smaller animals
used to licking water from cool stones.
Over the great farms, a burning-glass
one-eyed and wild as a jack,
the corn snatched in a single afternoon
of the one-eyed jack's impassive stare.

And in that other country
of choices made by others
that country I never chose
that country of terrible leavings and returnings
in that country whose map I carry on my palm
the forests are on fire: history is on fire.

My foot drags in the foothills of two lands;
At the turn the spirit pauses
and faces the high passes:
bloodred granite, sandstone steeped in blood.
At the turn the spirit turns,
looks back—if any follow—
squints ahead—if any lead—
What would you bring along on a trek like this?
What is bringing you along?[12]

Critical to understanding the importance of Luce Irigaray's work with discourse is her use of the French *la parole*, which generally translates as "speech" or "word(s)." Within *la parole*, however, there also exists a reference to an "assumption of subjectivity in language."[13] Hence, Margaret Whitford writes, "*La parole des femmes* [is] not so much women's language as women speaking on their own behalf" (18). Not uncoincidentally, in one of the Johannine texts in *The New Testament*, it is the French *la parole* that sometimes stands in for the more often translated French *Verbe* ("Word" in English; *Logos* in Greek).[14] Since *Logos* (or, here *la parole*) would be the term that generally develops the doctrine of Incarnation, linking divinity and humanity via "word," it is notable that Irigaray also tends toward a translation that favors *la parole*.[15] In light of our earlier work with the *logos*, and specifically with *Logos* as the Word of God, what becomes apparent as we proceed on this path toward subjectivity and discourse is the necessity for a new language. And, might this not also be a way to a new god, a new spirit?

Laying body over word, and word over body, Irigaray's works lend themselves well to theology with its focus on the Word. Graham Ward argues that her work is "potentially a rich resource for feminist Christology. . . because as one of the most profound contemporary feminist philosophers she recognizes the importance of an incarnational theology."[16] Certainly, the notion of incarnation suggests not only bodily form and substance but also the sense of irreducibility, indefinability, and unfixedness that signifies feminine subjectivity *and* discourse. Indeed, she yearns for a different language, an "other word," a new god. She writes:

> The end of a culture would correspond also to the death of God. Which God? He who forms the transcendental keystone of a discourse used by a single gender, of a monosexed truth. And this would allow the return of the divine, of the god who preaches neither truth nor morality but would seek to live with us and allow us to live here. The cries and words of the last philosophers, of Nietzsche and Heidegger, about the "death of God" are a summons for the divine to return as festival, grace, love, thought. Contrary to the usual interpretation made of them, these philosophers are not talking about the disappearance of the gods but about the approach or the annunciation of another parousia of the divine. Which involves the remolding of the world, of discourse: another morning, a new era in history, in the universe.[17]

Such a discourse would certainly lead us into the unknown, which many will argue holds the mystery of spirit. Similarly, such a move, which would invite the transcendence of many categories, would uphold a different sense of god: possibly in the Tillichian sense of an "ultimate concern," as a "more than" we have been created by the God of traditional Western religion. It is in this sense that we may find both god and ourselves "other than" as defined by the *logos.*

We know that Irigaray has critiqued "masculine discourse," pointing to its codification according to masculine law, that she has linked both man and language to the property of religion where Man becomes God as Word, then Word made flesh. Going beyond these masculinizations, she turns to feminine subversiveness and interiority. It is in this way that style becomes critical to her work, as is apparent in the expansiveness of her own writing: "a cosmic, creative fermentation that is always and forever free" (*Ethics*, 115). To reach such a place, we must turn to our own selves. She writes, "What this implies is that the female body is not to remain the object of men's discourse or their various arts but that it become the object of a female subjectivity experiencing and identifying itself."[18]

The process of extricating oneself from definitions created by another is not an easy task. Initially expressing women's lack via the openness of an "other" discourse, she asks, "How could I cry out that I was living inside you? That I spoke through your mouth?"[19] Seeking to become anew by simultaneously returning to herself and not yet arriving, she writes, "Your blood has become their meaning. They can speak to each other, and about us. But what about us? Come out of their language. Try to go back through the names they've given you. I'll wait for you, I'm waiting for myself. Come back. It's not so hard."[20] Finally, she turns to the imperative, "Let me go where I have not yet arrived" (1992, 25).

A feminine discourse that relies on feminine style gained from a female body cannot be renounced for it would reclaim lack, breathe according to difference, live subversively, seek fluidity—a kind of speaking/writing in which "every break . . . is disrupted, nothing . . . ever . . . posited that is not also reversed" (*This Sex*, 79). Such a discourse would rely on a "style or writing of women which tends to put the torch to fetish words, proper terms, well-constructed forms . . . a style which does not privilege sight but takes each figure back to its own source" (*This Sex*, 79). Such a language would disallow linear readings, evade any sense of right or wrong . . . "resist and explode every firmly established form, figure, idea or concept. Which does not mean that it lacks style, as we might be led to believe by a discursivity that cannot conceive of it. But its 'style' cannot be held as a thesis, cannot be the object of a position" (*This Sex*, 79).

Luce Irigaray's style, her "other," then, begins the process of rebuilding. But, the rebuilding, the architecture of this building—*this* home—belies the boundaries enforced by masculine discursivities. Here, discourse of the feminine is not an object to be claimed, appropriated, made property, proper. She is not to be fenced in, cannot be set aside, gathered, and sorted according to things of like value. She will not imitate that which she is expected to imitate. Neither does she involve herself in the appropriation of herself, nor in the appropriation of another *for* herself. Which is to say, neither will there exist hierarchy or Sameness within her words. Indeed, such a discourse *would* "raise love up to the word" (in French, *j'élève l'amour jusqu'à la parole*)—words, you will note, with which I began. But, "raising love up to the word" might also be understood in a different way. And it is in this sense that Luce Irigaray offers these notions to us: not to be lifted up according to any hierarchical system. But, to be lifted far enough to reach the word, in the hope of becoming, finally, able to meet.

## After Word

"Being faithful." What does it mean to be faithful? And, what is the relationship between "being faithful" and "having faith"? I ask these questions because I have chosen to be faithful, which may suggest that I *have* faith—or, even more, that I will find a faithful place. But, having faith and being faithful hold different meanings, and thus have different relationships to faith's sister, "trust."

We find a kind of steadfast trust in such resemblances to faith as "assurance" and "certainty." Even notions like "belief," "confidence," and "hope," which may be slightly less certain of their relationship, hold heartfelt elements and suggest a kind of reliant symmetry. Often we find these in the best sense of religion when such notions are extended to their farther parameters. Here, having faith in a God—or in an ultimate other—usually expresses a wholeheartedness that is not present at other times. However, too often when we turn to the world of religion we find a kind of faith that disinherits its trusted lineage. Then, the religious conversation includes talk of faith as a kind of "persuasion," as in "of what persuasion are you?" Or, can I persuade you to be something other than you are?

Similarly, "faithfulness" includes notions of trust present in certain ideas of "dedication" and "loyalty" due to some form of "attachment." We find ourselves dedicated and loyal, for example, because we have found ourselves attached in some way or another. However, just as "faith" can include a persuasive quality, so "faithfulness" also can include the idea of "precision." Just how precisely must I be faithful (hence, dedicated, loyal, attached) to you, and according to whose master plan? Must I lay your idea of myself over my idea of myself and become an exact replica of your thought, a perfect reflection? And, along with such a notion of "precision," do you not also expect "persuasion" to be part of our faithfulness to one another?

I wonder if these elements of persuasion and precision have not found their way into both faith and faithfulness bringing with them the problem of discipleship. When practicing discipleship, whose word, whose doctrine, whose master plan, are we to spread? If it is yours (for you have desired disciples), then it is you, rather than I, who have undone the conversation, for I will never be persuasive, nor precise, enough. And, if I cannot be a disciple who persuasively, precisely reflects, have I lost faith and fallen out of faithfulness?

As I have said, I ask these questions because I have chosen to be faithful. I have not chosen to be faithful in a traditionally religious sense—although this sense, the sense that I would remain full of both faith and faithfulness, hence wholehearted—has found its way into a new language, an "other word." Do you suppose this somehow suggests a nearing to love, the possibility of two discourses at hand? And, will this word ever extend itself far enough to reach *her* word?

I would like to believe that the spirit continually presents itself in a leaving of sorts. Whether or not we know it, we find ourselves continuously articulating (and disarticulating) matters of faith, faithfulness, discipleship. And, whether or not you have faith in me and in my words, as a way of gratitude I will attempt to do it, to write a religion, to write a spirit, certain words at its foundation. It is the least I can do: to "leave. . . a sign to mark the false trail, the way [I] didn't go," to "be like the fox who makes more tracks that necessary, some in the wrong direction," to "practice resurrection."[21]

Yet, this resurrection will be of a different sort. It will be my interpretation, not yours, nor theirs, not his, nor hers. Not entirely an interpretation of the birth of woman, nor theirs of her re-birth. In the same way, not his of God, nor hers of goddess. No, these are *my* words; they are of me. It is the only way I know of saving myself, of gathering myself together again. And, in so gathering, of beginning a dialogue anew.

## Notes

1. Luce Irigaray, *To Be Two* (New York: Routledge, 2001), 6–7.

2. Luce Irigaray, *Speculum of the Other Woman* (Ithaca: Cornell University Press, 1985).

3. E. Hoffmann "Die Sprache u. d. archaische Logik," *Heidelberger Abh. Z. Philosophie u. ihrer Geschichte, III* (1925). In Gerhard Kittel, ed., *Theological Dictionary of the New Testament* (Grand Rapids: Eerdmans, 1967), 77.

4. Edward Schiappa, *Protagoras and Logos: A Study in Greek Philosophy and Rhetoric* (Columbia: University of South Carolina Press, 1991), 92.

5. See Heraclitus's Fragment 91, in *Heraclitus: The Cosmic Fragments*, ed. G. S. Kirk (Cambridge: Cambridge University Press, 1954).

6. G. S Kirk, J. E. Raven, and M. Schofield, *The Presocratic Philosophers: A Critical History with a Selection of Texts* (Cambridge: Cambridge University Press, 1983), 197.

7. Robin Osborne, "The Polis and Its Culture," In *Routledge History of Philosophy, Vol. I: From the Beginning to Plato* (London: Routledge, 1997), 96, 102; and Schiappa, 94.

8. Ann L. T. Bergren, "Helen's Good 'Drug'. Odyssey iv. 1–305," in *Contemporary Literary Hermeneutics and Interpretation of Classical Texts* (Ottawa: University of Ottawa Press, 1981), 201; and G. E. R. Lloyd, *Polarity and Analogy: Two Types of Argumentation in Early Greek Thought* (Cambridge: Cambridge University Press, 1966).

9. Vincent Colapietro, *Glossary of Semiotics* (New York: Paragon House, 1993), 52.

10. J. A. Cuddon, *The Penguin Dictionary of Literary Terms and Literary Theory* (New York: Penguin, 1991), 89.

11. Laine M. Harrington, "Rhetorical Homecoming and the Engenderization of *Logos*: Toward an 'Other Word' with Luce Irigaray." Ph.D. diss. Graduate Theological Union, 2002.

12. Adrienne Rich, "Turning," in *Time's Power: Poems 1985–1988.* (New York: W. W. Norton, 1989), 51.

13. Margaret Whitford, ed., *The Irigaray Reader* (Oxford: Blackwell, 1996), 18.

14. See John 1:14: "And the Word became flesh and lived among us, and we have seen his glory, the glory as of a father's only son, full of grace and truth." In Bruce Metzger and Roland E. Murphy, eds., *The New Oxford Annotated Bible with the Apocryphal/Deuterocanonical Books: New Revised Standard Version* (New York: Oxford University Press, 1991), 125.

15. See Luce Irigaray, "La rédemption des femmes," in *Le souffle des femmes: Luce Irigaray présente des credos au feminine* (Paris: Luce Irigaray and L'Action Catholique Générale Féminine, 1996).

16. Graham Ward, "Divinity and Sexuality: Luce Irigaray and Christology," *Modern Theology* 12, no. 2 (April 1996): 221–37.

17. Luce Irigaray, *An Ethics of Sexual Difference.* (Ithaca: Cornell University Press, 1993), 140.

18. Luce Irigaray, *Je, tu, nous: Toward a Culture of Difference.* (London and New York: Routledge, 1993), 59.

19. Luce Irigaray, *Elemental Passions* (New York: Routledge, 1992), 26.

20. Luce Irigaray, *This Sex Which Is Not One* (Ithaca: Cornell University Press, 1985), 205–206.

21. Wendell Berry, "Manifesto: The Mad Farmer Liberation Front," in *The Collected Poems: 1957–1982* (New York: North Point Press, 1984).

## Chapter 13

# Dynamic Potentiality

## The Body that Stands Alone

Claire Colebrook

Why read the Greeks today? Why would, or should, a feminist attend to the ancient Greek legacy? And why is feminist *reading* a viable approach to such a body of texts? A relatively simple answer to this complex of questions relies upon the project of destructive genealogy that runs from Friedrich Nietzsche, through Martin Heidegger, to Hannah Arendt, Luce Irigaray, and Giorgio Agamben. To look *back* at the Greek world is to open the closure of the present. If certain decisions, divisions, and occlusions were effected in the Greek past then our entire metaphysical vocabulary will determine the structure of our present thinking. And this determination and orientation in thinking will not only dominate metaphysics in the narrow sense, as a quite specific branch of academic philosophy; it will also orient our everyday relations to the world. Philosophy as early as Aristotle has insisted that the condition for living in this world is the possession of *a sense of being*. We do not just have immediate relations with the present but perceive the beings of this world as having this or that form which remains the same through time (Aristotle 694 [434a7–10]). Thus, for Aristotle, human life—as opposed to merely nutritive or perceptive life—is possessed of a rational capacity to intuit the first principles of being (Aristotle 1554 [982b5–10]). It is this capacity, to live in accord with what one takes to be properly or fully human, that gives life meaning: through philosophical enquiry and discussion human beings can discern that which makes each being *what it is* (Irwin 1988). Aristotle's concept of *proper potentiality*—which is different from the accidental potentials of what something might or might not be—does not only allow human beings to discern what gives each being its definition—it also defines an ethical human life (Aristotle 1653 [1047a4–7]). Human beings have the potential to reason, and have this potential even when they are not reasoning. We can say that a man is being *irrational* when he is failing to actualize his reason, but we would not call an object or an animal irrational even though they lack reason. The potential to reason defines what we ought to become in order to actualize our being; and this potential to reason means that we only live our lives fully when we move beyond mere nutritive and perceptive movements, and order our lives as a whole (Aristotle 1804 [1142b31–33]). For Aristotle, one lives as a human being only with a sense of the whole of life, with a subjection of present pleasures to the being that I will be in the future. In Aristotle, what it means to be human is to live a life *of meaning*; a happy life—or a movement of the soul in accordance with virtue—is one in which the self forms itself as a coherent and ongoing narrative whole.

What I wish to argue in this chapter is that the idea of proper potential—of a being that strives to actualize itself—is not an idea that might simply be read in the ancient Greek texts of the past. A certain norm of life—as actualization, coming to presence, self-realization—governs the way in which we read the past, and also dominates the way in which that past has seemingly been criticized. It is this "opening to infinity" or the establishment of philosophy as the thought of being *for any subject whatever* that occurs in the Ancient Greek passage from political/social norms to philosophical ideas (Derrida 1989; Arendt 1998). When Heidegger wished to retrieve the question of being from the Greek heritage he argued that it was precisely because a sense was given to being, precisely because some beings were said to *properly be,* that we can recognize ourselves as those who have the potential to question being, even if this potential is covered over, forgotten, or misunderstood. Only a being who *can* ask the question of being can interpret his being inauthentically by taking himself to be a "man" or thing within the world (Heidegger 1996, 10).

For Heidegger, if it is the case that there is something like "life" which strives to actualize and disclose itself—a Being that brings itself to presence—then this potential for disclosure is lost or abandoned as soon as *Dasein* takes himself to be a thing, a mere body in the world. *Dasein* can only grasp its ownmost potential in recognizing its potential for inauthenticity, its tendency to forget its power of disclosure, truth, and thinking. For Heidegger, *truth* is not some content or fact that we might discover but is just this capacity to relate to the world as that which reveals itself. Heidegger therefore establishes the *question* of being as the proper potential of *Dasein*. Heidegger, like Irigaray, also reads Plato's cave allegory as the establishment of a norm or logic outside the sensible (Heidegger 1988, 166). But Heidegger is critical not of the establishment of the question of truth, but of the fact that we have forgotten to think about *how* the soul turns from shadows and appearances to face the originating light of the sun. For Heidegger, a return to this Greek moment when Plato recognized that truth needed to be wrested from the hidden will allow us to question today's unthinking humanism, where we mistakenly believe that there is a proper logic or method that dictates human development. What we need to retrieve, according to Heidegger, is a sense of truth as *aletheia*. If it is possible for us to be in error, to see the world as so much fully present matter, then this is evidence both that we can forget our proper relation to the true, and that truth has a tendency to hide itself or withdraw. Only if we recall the revealing or unveiling of being—the coming into truth of the true—will we once again live authentically.

It is this norm of life as unfolding, of disclosure, of unveiling and revelation that is challenged by Irigaray. Not only does she challenge the idea of an originary light from which life and relations unfold, she also questions a mode of reading that would find such a light of truth *in* a textual scene. For it is through the production of divisions and distinctions that Plato's text marks out the appearing shadows from their originating idea. It is this quite specific form of textualism that marks Irigaray's true value for a radical feminist historicism; she does not merely argue for a rereading of the past in order to open the present, for she also challenges the notion of a body of texts that might reveal or disclose the proper relation of our being. It is Plato's *text*, she argues, that produces borders and divisions between the proper and the improper, between the image and its right sense, and between a scene as allegory and the supposed true sense that gives life to that scene. What Irigaray questions is both an image of proper order and relations that we find *in* Plato's text *and* the idea that there is a truth of life that governs our relations to texts—placing the text as image or metaphor through which we know the world. Irigaray's work is therefore more pertinent than ever, for not only has there been an increased interest in life and vitalism—whereby the human organism determines the relations it establishes to its own world—there has also been a renovation of the Aristotelian ideal of life whereby human living is defined by a capacity to open out a world, with human potentiality being realized in communication and social relations. The most sophisticated renewal of the question of life and potentiality in its ancient Greek sense has come from Giorgio Agamben whose work both interrogates the simple acceptance of a properly human potential and maintains the propriety of rethinking that potential through Aristotle. What I hope to prove in this essay is that Agamben's mode of retrieval and questioning remains with the norm of the life of *man*. By raising the question of sexual difference, Irigaray opens the possibility of a life whose relations have no proper potential, a life dispossessed of truth and presence, a life whose relations will have to be effected and achieved.

Agamben clearly follows Heidegger in his commitment to a notion that being is disclosed *historically*. Whereas being was, originally, disclosed through discussion and dynamic social relations—speaking about *what is*—we become increasingly focused on a truth of method and logic. Thus, whereas the Greeks thought of truth as *unveiling* or a coming into presence, truth has now become what is already fully present: facts and self-evidence. What we forget, then, is the revealing or coming to presence—*the work*—of truth. For both Agamben and Heidegger we can read this forgetting of the question or opening of the world in the work of art (Agamben 1999, 101). For Heidegger, the work of art discloses the difference between earth and world, between what merely is, and the way that being is lived as one's own (Heidegger 1971, 34). For Agamben, however, art has fallen into mere technology, the production of objects for enjoyment and spectatorship, and this is because what was once unified in ancient Greece—all acts of making (*techne*)—split into those forms of making that had a repeatable function (*techne* in the now narrow sense) and those that were fully realized in themselves (art). There was a time, in the ancient Greek world, prior to the diremption between the created work of art and other human productions, when all making was a "pro-duction into presence" (Agamben 1999, 60). Art and the artist were included within a more general political arena of world disclosure. However, in the passage toward modernity certain crucial decisions separate the work of art from content, from expressing or disclosing the world; the work of art is now nothing other than pure form, no longer saying or expressing anything other than itself. What we see or admire in the work of art is not what it *says*, but merely its pure act as art. Art is neither world production nor world disclosure; it no longer bears a relation to what is not itself. Art becomes subjective and self-referential (Agamben 1999, 64).

For Agamben this trajectory of the work of art is tied closely to a political trajectory. Originally all polities are founded on a "state of exception," the inauguration of a border between the institution of the law and the execution of the law (Agamben 1998, 37). The establishment or opening of law cannot itself be governed by any law; a decision and distinction has to be drawn between mere life and political life. This border is evidenced in the curious function of *homo sacer*: a body that is not a political citizen, not within the law, but a body that also may not be killed (Agamben 1998, 83). This anomalous border figure discloses the state of exception, where there is no determined system of laws within which life is negotiated. Bare life is that condition where a body is no longer a citizen with the law, but is nothing more than an object of a power that decides between life and death. If the ancient figure of *homo sacer* exposed the state of exception at the limits of the polity—the point at which law takes its hold over life before there are determined laws—the contemporary conditions of the death camp and modern biopolitics evidence an increasing loss of that border between *bios* and *zoe*, between mere life and the life of this formed, determined, and bounded polity. In the death camp the body is allowed to remain alive; in modern politics the law functions in the face of terror only to secure the maintenance of life. As in the modern work of art what is lost is the question of the relation between life and world: "Whenever a work of art is pro-duced and exhibited today, its *energetic* aspect, that is, the being-at-work of the work, is erased to make room for its character as stimulant of the aesthetic sentiment, as mere support of aesthetic enjoyment" (Agamben 1999, 66). Life is managed, organized, maintained, and mastered, but there is no longer an attempt to think the disclosure, opening, or determination of that life (Agamben 1999, 67). Such a question does, however, present itself today precisely because biopolitics and the state of exception are threatening to operate without opposition or limit. For Agamben it is now possible, once again, to return to the Greek opening to the world precisely because the originating distinction has now reached a point of exhaustion: "Yet it is also starting from this self-suppression of the privileged status of 'artistic work,' which now gathers the two sides of the halved apple of human production in their irreconcilable opposition, that it will be possible to exit the swamp of aesthetics and technics and restore the poetic status of man on earth in its original dimension" (Agamben 1999, 67).

We would once again be able to ask the question of the world. We would no longer assume that "man's" potentiality to have his own world would unfold necessarily and essentially, for as modernity demonstrates, it is possible for man to be reduced to mere life, devoid of world, speech, and disclosure. It is precisely the *loss* of all that was once taken to be human—expression through art, lawful communicative existence—that such potentials might be opened once again in new forms. Agamben's authentic return to the Greek past is enabled by the exhaustion of the present, and only in this exhaustion—he insists—might we once again ask the question of life. Far from assuming that man is a political, rational, articulate, and lawful being, we would have to ask how it is that life can both give itself a world of law, speech, and decision *and* be reduced to mere existence.

Irigaray's work might at first appear to be similar to Agamben's Heideggerian project. Both Agamben and Irigaray maintain the importance of the question or the problem of life. For Agamben this problem was once partly open to view. Like Heidegger, Agamben draws on the ancient Greek text and vocabulary in order to look back to a time when present distinctions or divisions were *not yet drawn*. Once there was a clear sense of the difference between a natural life that unfolds from itself and technologies that created according to a clear and predetermined model, but now all life has become technological—managed according to simple formula of maximization and efficiency. Today we need both to *regain* the unity that has separated poetic production from technical production, and *retrieve* the distinction between the life that gives itself its own world and the life that is mere force without decision, form, or act.

Irigaray's approach to life appears equally urgent and critical. She too argues that if we are to live we need to rethink the very relation to the world, and she sees the dominant modern paradigm of subjectivism—a self that is nothing other than the representation and mastery of objective life—as grounded in the Western metaphysical heritage. However, Irigaray does not read the Greeks to retrieve and regain some authentic opening to the world or life that has now been lost in a world of technological subjectivism. Not only is she critical of the very idea of a proper, authentic, or original relation to life, she is also critical of the very model of reading and retrieval that is presented both in the Greek text and its interpretive heritage. Irigaray reads the Greeks, not to return us to some original question, but to criticize the ways in which questions of life have been dominated by images of reading. The concept of *aletheia,* which both Heidegger and Agamben wish to retrieve from the Ancient Greeks, is read by Irigaray as a symptom of a history of philosophy that has oriented bodies toward a transcendent truth that is the condition for the sensible but which itself cannot be sensed. The idea that there was an original Greek relation toward the visible—that one could bring into speech what was illuminated by the light of truth—means that one can always "cash in," complete, reward, and fulfill relations of difference:

> The *a-letheia* in the very negation/denial that it speaks, may be interpreted as the affirmation of a possibility of reviewing what has been forgotten within an economy of representation that prescribes its neglect. The *a-letheia* would theoretically function henceforth as *the bond offered as security for what has been forgotten* in the Socratic dialectic from the dawn of Western photological semantics, as the representation of representation which keeps the sun from the place(s) of its tropical beat(s). Forcing the sun in some manner to spin around, to turn eternally in its own orbit, forever to return to the same point in the circle where it would always already have been placed in order to keep every system in order, including, paradoxically, its own. The sun is fixed, frozen, the keystone supporting the whole—phallic—edifice of representation that it dominates, illumines, warms, makes fertile, and regulates by scattering its beams everywhere. (Irigaray 1985, 267)

For Irigaray *aletheia* has functioned to create a future or orientation of experience whereby all that is given is merely a path toward some proper realization. That proper realization or full presence can never be finally given but always remains out of sight, elsewhere—thereby presenting relations among bodies as determined by some "higher" or transcendent Idea: "*Aletheia* will come into play when denomination occurs but in fact, silently, it has determined the whole functioning of the language, its terminology, its syntax, its dramatization" (Irigaray 1985, 262). Not only is the figure of unveiling presented in the Greek text, where Plato presents bodies turning away from the shadows to the source of light; the cave allegory also presents itself *as metaphor*, as not the truth itself but as a figure or double for a truth that can never be given in itself. We are thereby precluded from thinking the *exorbitant* power, or the power that has produced relations of before and after, true and false, origin and copy: "Yet this exorbitant power is hidden in the fact that it is *also* used as a metaphor and evoked and recalled. Not without the assistance of a (de)negation: the word is *a-letheia*" (262). *Un*veiling for Irigaray—wresting the truth away from the merely given or sensible—is both an idea given *in* Greek thought, and orients our relation to the Greeks. Only by rereading our heritage will we discover the truth of who we are, and in that primal scene truth will be given by negation, as *not* what is immediately apparent.

Irigaray's work strives to criticize the assumption of life's *proper* potentiality. The question of sexual difference is central to this critique precisely because the image of *a* life that gives form to itself and goes through time in order to disclose and actualize itself has both been traditionally associated with the masculine, and also—essentially—precludes sexual difference (Fielding 2003). As long as truth is understood as an idea that governs relations, or as that which orients the perception of bodies in advance, there can be no genuine difference. Where Irigaray's critique is most pertinent today, I would argue, is in her criticism of an image of life that unfolds from itself and goes through time only to realize its proper form; such time is a "dead time" (252). And such a living or moving is never a genuine becoming but is only an unfolding or revealing of what was there to be unveiled; life is not allowed to be *affective* but must be oriented toward the representable: "A ban on pulsations, rhythmic intervals that are unlike and yet the same again" (252). Plato's cave is therefore also a figure of a mode of vision that is fixed, frozen, purely receptive; the truth is there to be viewed as the same for any body: "A motionless retina, a reticulum without nerves, a mere concave surface, reflecting light and shadows" (254). Greek metaphysics determines all that is seen *as* some determined form; we must therefore relate to the visible according to some idea or schema. Accordingly, that which is immediately viewed—"the hystera protera that has been inverted and turned backward by Plato"—is seen as only potentially real, as having its true being in the idea or truth that gives it form. There is a reversal whereby the sensible is regarded as having its full being or actuality elsewhere. Something can only be said to *be* insofar as it *is* some determined being; that which is viewed thereby receives its being from the Idea that gives it form, that allows one to say that it *is*: "confusion of the hystera and sun in an ecstasy of the copula" (254).

When Irigaray argues, in *Speculum,* that *any* theory of the subject has always been appropriated by the masculine (133), she does not only target the modern subject, where the self who views is also the ground or foundation of all that is viewed. And she does not only target the Platonic and Aristotelian problem of intuiting that which truly *is*, or remains the same through time, as the subject or ground of accidents and predications. She also criticizes the orientation or turn whereby all perception, experience, relations, time, or transcendence are governed by notions of fulfillment, realization, production, maximization, fruition, and the arrival of potentiality to its proper form. This is an economy where matter is taken up and brought to fullness by form. Against a reading and perceiving in which the self will be maintained and strengthened, she describes relations where the self *cannot* master relations, where differences do not produce more of the selfsame. Whereas the bodies in Plato's cave must be turned around to recognize the logic and author of their own being, a relation of sexual *difference* would be oriented to what exists *without relation*, so that perception, experience, and reading would not be a re-finding or a return: "The feminine, the maternal are instantly *frozen* by the 'like,' the 'as if' of that masculine representation dominated by truth, light, resemblance, identity. By some dream of symmetry that itself is never unveiled" (265).

Irigaray is thus critical of a certain style of reading, and a certain image of the work as that which discloses the hidden secret of being. The cave metaphor in Plato is not only a thesis about being that splits the idea from the copy; the text itself produces a scene of reading where the gaze will be directed by and oriented to some proper form, an origin that will determine all becoming. Time is therefore nothing more than the return to the beginning, and experience is nothing more than the re-finding of what will have been. Reading will be the discovery of our origin. Against the idea that life unfolds from itself in order to arrive at what properly is, Irigaray gives a *positive* sense to that which does not disclose, reveal, surpass, or unveil itself; in her understanding of the sexual relation, the two terms are not governed by some higher logic or norm of production. Sexual *difference* could only occur outside a sexual *relation*, where the masculine is not the proper form that brings matter into presence, and where the feminine is not potential awaiting spirit and actuality. In this sense, she challenges the ethic and image of life that is often appealed to nostalgically in Platonic and Aristotelian philosophy. Whereas Heidegger had argued that Plato's cave allegory marks a transition from a notion of truth as engaged disclosure of the world, to truth as some logic that is present and that governs being, Irigaray intensifies and surpasses Heidegger's critique of the forgetting of the passage from the hidden to the disclosed. For Irigaray, what remains unveiled and unexaminable is the textual construction of a scene that divides the sensible from the intelligible, the merely potential from the full light of day. Irigaray's sense of "sexual scenography" challenges both the drive to interpretation and the image of full presence at work in the text. Plato's cave allegory marks out a scene, presenting the wall of the cave as a screen upon which images are projected; his text therefore creates a surface across which differences are distributed. Against this, Irigaray argues that the scene can never be comprehended; for any scene is only possible through a distribution or division. Against a single source of light and life that opens out into a textual scene, and against taking the text as an allegory that would double some underlying truth of life, Irigaray insists on the positivity of difference. If man or the subject has always stood for a life that recognizes and gives form to itself, and that can turn back and master its own origin, then sexual difference can open the possibility of a distribution that does not come to full presence, that remains distanced and dispersed.

A normative image of life governs both Plato's allegory of the cave *and* our way of reading that allegory. All allegory presents a semblance, sign, or image that covers over or veils what *properly is.* It is the task of reading, living, and perceiving to reveal, disclose, or arrive at the true vision that subtends difference. Irigaray's work can therefore be set against projects that attempt to restore life through a return to proper origins *and* more recent attempts to present all life as a process of self-maximization. The bodies in Plato's cave are constrained only to look forward, and must be turned around to recognize the true source and condition of their being. This allegory thus places truth at an origin that might be re-found simply by turning the body around *on itself*: "This is how the system and the transactions of the recognition of truth operate. And, let us note, its justification is to sanction, organize, regulate, and arbitrate the relationships between men, particularly by means of theorization. And this is so in the *polis* as well as the cave" (265). Sexual difference, by contrast, would be oriented not to a re-finding of some grounding condition, but to the creation of further differences. It is precisely because the relation between female and male has been *the* figure through which the passage from potential to actuality is represented that there has been no sexual difference. Female matter is the potentiality that requires masculine form in order to be what it properly is. Sexual *difference*, by contrast, would be deprived of any logic or norm for the relation between bodies. We could therefore contrast Irigaray's work with those projects that would posit a logic of life that gives an orientation and direction to the proper actualization of bodies. Woman, no longer figured as the matter that must receive intelligible form to achieve actuality, might now be thought of not as different *from* man, but as a new mode of difference. If potentiality does not have its becoming or relations determined in advance, and if bodies are not already governed by some proper relation, then woman might stand for a style of becoming or potentiality that is not oriented to comprehension, full presence, and self-maintenance. If "man" is the image of one who differs from himself only to re-find himself, woman is the figure of that which stands alone, without self-recognition: "She knows nothing (of herself). And remembers nothing. Providing the basis for the wise man's auto-logical speculations, she lives in darkness" (345). Irigaray is not only, therefore, critical of a project of textual retrieval in which we would re-find ourselves in the origin we ourselves produced, she is also critical of any *subjectivism*, any notion of a life in general that unfolds and discloses itself through the sexual relation. Sexual *difference* would be a relation of *proximity*—not two bodies who reveal themselves through each other—but bodies that allow the other to stand apart.

We can now return to the ways in which Irigaray's reading of the Greeks might be contrasted with other projects of revelation and of actualization. While recognizing the importance of reading the texts that have produced a sexual imaginary—where potentiality is always that passive, feminized matter awaiting active spiritual form—she also criticizes a sexual imaginary of reading. As well as dividing the sensible from the intelligible, Plato's cave allegory is also a production of the relation of allegory and metaphor. Just as the light of the sun produces the shadows that only seem to have being but which should lead the perception to the true source of being, so perception and reading should pass from figures, mimes, shadows, and images to the originating source, "a photological systematics" or "heliotropism" (267). The very idea that a text is a sign or surface that veils some fully present sense that might be revealed and recovered and that resists plurality, reflection, diffusion, and division is itself part of Plato's sexual scenography and phallic time, where all difference and becoming will be in the service of revelation. It is in her emphasis on the positivity of dispersal that Irigaray differs most from the Heideggerian style of the history of philosophy. Against the idea that there was an original difference or disclosure that might be regained through rereading—against the image of a subject that differs from himself in order to return to himself—the figure of sexual difference is one of dispersal and distance, without some underlying ground or preceding origin.

By contrast, despite its manifest critique of the fall of art and life into a single manageable domain of life, Giorgio Agamben's appeal to the difference between poiesis and praxis remains enthralled to the myth of a single originating life whose differentiation we might once again retrieve. Agamben's retrieval of the Greek legacy is pertinent today for a number of reasons. First, it brings to the fore the curious urgency of the rereading of the history of metaphysics. Agamben is quite clear that reopening the original divisions and decisions of Greek thought is not only a metaphysical, ethical, and aesthetic issue; it also concerns immediate questions of politics and policy. Because life was originally distinguished as properly human only in its status as *bios*, or as different from the mere life that might simply be managed or maintained, then the increasing focus today on an administration of life is what allows the constant state of emergency—the suspension of all questions regarding what "man" might be if he has potentiality beyond mere existence. Second, as well as directly bringing the question of the human and of life to the fore, Agamben does so—tellingly—through an appeal to the potentially redemptive status of the work of art. The Greeks distinguished between two types of *poiesis*—two ways of bringing something into being: both the work of art and all crafts were different from the natural object in that they had to be made and did not have their source of movement in themselves. Today, this unity is lost and we distinguish between technology that can be endlessly produced, repeated, circulated, and distributed without any meaningful relation to its origin, and the work of art that is now so distinct and so fully self-realizing that it can have no content, no reflection *of* anything other than its own actualization. Where this all ends, for Agamben, is in the reduction of art to mere potential, something that can be viewed, circulated, enjoyed, liberated from any content or relation to presence. The work of art has become both increasingly subjective—nothing other than the mere act, without content, of the artist—and increasingly governed by spectatorship; we view the work, not with any sense of engagement or world-disclosure, but merely as one more example of that which can be enjoyed in pure detachment from its origin. What Agamben hopes to retrieve, by rethinking the distinctions between *bios* and *zoe*, and *poeisis* and *praxis*, is the more profound concept of potentiality: If life can be both mere life and political life, how can we think about the creation of the human from the inhuman? If art can be both the thoughtful disclosure of the world—a full bringing to presence—and a merely circulated object always available for potential enjoyment, how can we move beyond art's exhaustion? In his reading of the opening distinction between bare life and political life, between the actualizing artwork and mere enjoyment, Agamben elevates the Greek text to the status of the author and origin of the enigmas "man" faces today: "Whether and when art will again have the task of taking the original measure of man on earth is not, therefore, a subject on which one can make predictions; neither can we say whether *poiesis* will recover its proper status beyond the interminable twilight that covers the *terra aesthetica*. The only thing we can say is that art will not simply be able to leap beyond its shadow to climb over its destiny" (Agamben 1999, 102–103).

By contrast, Irigaray challenges this principle of reading as re-finding, and also challenges the concomitant image of potentiality. Plato's cave allegory depicts a reversal whereby the sensible becomes the screen or matter upon which and through which form can come to presence, granting materiality full being. The text presents itself as an image or allegory through which the reader must find his proper relation to truth, his intelligible relation to his own sense. And when we reread our literary heritage today, when we look again at the work of the text, we have two paths before us. The first is to see the literary heritage as a collection of fragments that might be restored to sense, brought to full presence in order to disclose our own proper potentiality. The second, as demonstrated both in Irigaray's own style of reading, is to refuse the text's proper relations, to multiply its enigmas, lacunae, gaps, and points of unreadability. This would give us a quite different sense of the work, not as a bringing to presence or fulfilment, but as a creation of dissonance.

Why such an argument is important for feminism, and for thinking about the type of problems proposed by Irigaray's work, becomes clear if we think through some initially counterintuitive observations. It is no accident, I would argue, that Agamben's talk about human potentiality concerns "man," and no accident either that man is both deprived of, and completed in, his potentiality through the work of art. It might seem at first that Agamben's critique of subjectivism, his emphasis on rethinking a time when creation was not yet reduced to mere production but was located in social relations, and his appeal to a work of art that is neither a mere technical thing nor an isolated fetishized art object would be in accord with Irigaray's work. She, too, is critical of the subject whose relations to the world are determined, in advance, by some already given logic—precluding any genuine difference. She also suggests that a certain moment in Greek metaphysics marks a loss of a relation toward that which cannot be calculated, manipulated, or circulated as endless potential for the production of the same, self-recognizing man. Irigaray herself says far less about the work of art, but insofar as her later ethics privileges relations, sensibility, and the creation of some form, we might imagine an appropriate feminist aesthetics that affirmed the dynamic revelation of the world, rather than an artwork that was mere enjoyment or isolated act. However, this seeming congruence misses what is most original, challenging, and worthy in Irigaray's approach. Far from simply privileging relationality, connectedness, and the thought of proper potentiality that must go through time to become what it properly is (to reveal itself), Irigaray's thought of sexual difference is the thought of the nonrelational.

For Agamben the problem with the modern work of art, and its distance from the Greek origin, is that it remains mere potentiality—available for spectatorship and enjoyment but possessing no revelation or content. The proper artwork, by contrast, bears a full actuality and genuinely brings a presence into being that the viewer must not merely enjoy but must *actually* engage. The fallen artwork of today appears to be nothing more than an object of market forces, of viewing whims, of enjoyment and commodification. The modern art object is caught up in relations not its own; a genuine artwork produces relations from itself, opens up its own world. It is not mere stuff or matter that might be used now this way, now that, but bears its proper actualization within itself. Far from merely viewing the artwork as thing, we should be drawn into a presence not already given. Similarly, while the man of global capitalism seems to be fully caught up in the space of the world, as long as he remains as mere life to be managed, mastered, and allowed to live, his relations are extrinsic. What needs to be thought is how human life opens up its world, and this can only be thought when the work of art is not the production of man's will, but a genuine bringing to presence of the world: "[W]hat the Greeks meant with the distinction between poiesis and praxis was precisely that the essence of poiesis has nothing to do with the expression of a will (with respect to which are is in no way necessary): this essence is found instead in the production of truth and in the subsequent opening of a world for man's existence and action" (Agamben 1999, 72). Agamben wants to rethink potentiality, not as something that merely discloses itself, but that is productive of relations not determined in advance. However, what he wishes to retrieve from the Greeks is a genuine *birth* in art, not a mere remaining within-itself of modern subjectivism (Agamben 1999, 73). What we have lost is art as *divine*, as taking the human beyond itself to what might be disclosed: "Gone is the time when the artist was bound, in immediate identity, to faith and to conceptions of his world; no longer is the work of art founded in the unity of the artist's subjectivity with the work's content in such a way that the spectator may immediately find in it the highest truth of his consciousness, that is, the divine" (Agamben 1999, 47).

Irigaray's rereading of the tradition targets this complex of associations. Significantly, her emphasis on some form of *feminine* divine would open the possibility of a theology that was not that of a God as pure *act* who brings all potential being to presence. The moment that sexual *difference* is introduced there could no longer be a pure act that has no determination other than itself. Irigaray is highly critical of all forms of subjectivism, all arguments that would argue for a proper or grounding being that would be the origin of all relations. Instead, I would argue, her ethics and her theology begin from a radical disengagement of potentiality from relations. It has always been the case that the sexual relation has been figured as one of potentiality arriving at proper actuality: mythically the two sexes or principles are required for being to come to presence—female matter and male form.

Irigaray's work is not an inclusion of both sexes within the possibility of coming to full realization, for she is critical of the privileging of actuality over potentiality. And it is here that her work engages *both* with Plato's text and its drawing of a border between the sensible and the intelligible, the origin and the copy, *and* with those contemporary retrievals of the Greek origin of thought's proper potential that has now been lost in the reduction of life and art. Her own relation to the text is one of disclaiming proper relations; the text cannot master its own scene, cannot command what it wants to say. On the one hand, one needs to reread the primal sexual scene that places the sensible within a network of proper relations. On the other hand, this moment of reading cannot be a restoration or return. The response to a text that produces a scene of mastery, of comprehension and propriety, is the affirmation of a dispersion and difference that does not arrive at itself. Irigaray therefore displaces the relation of commentary, with the production of difference, replaces *aletheia* or faithful doubling and mimesis with distortion, dissimulation, difference, and non-relation.

## Works Cited

Agamben. Giorgio. 1998. *Homo Sacer: Sovereign power and bare life.* Trans. Daniel Heller-Roazen. Stanford: Stanford University Press.

———. 1999. *The man without content.* Trans. Georgia Albert. Stanford: Stanford University Press.

Arendt, Hannah. 1998. *The human condition.* 2nd ed. Chicago: University of Chicago Press.

Aristotle. 1984. *The complete works of Aristotle.* Ed. Jonathan Barnes. 2 vols. Princeton: Princeton University Press.

Derrida, Jacques. 1989. *Edmund Husserl's* Origin of geometry*: An introduction by Jacques Derrida*, trans., John P. Leavey. Lincoln: University of Nebraska Press.

Fielding, Helen. 2003. Questioning nature: Irigaray, Heidegger, and the potentiality of matter. *Continental Philosophy Review* 36: 1–26.

Heidegger, Martin. 1971. *Poetry, language, thought.* Trans. Albert Hofstadter. New York: Harper and Row.

———. 1988. *Pathmarks.* Ed. William McNeill, Cambridge: Cambridge University Press.

———. 1996. *Being and time.* Trans. Joan Stambaugh. Albany: State University of New York Press.

Irigaray, Luce. 1985. *Speculum of the other woman.* Trans. Gillian C. Gill. Ithaca: Cornell University Press.

Irwin, T. H. 1988. *Aristotle's first principles.* Oxford: Clarendon.

# Chapter 14

# Sameness, Alterity, Flesh

## Luce Irigaray and the Place of Sexual Undecidability

Gayle Salamon

Luce Irigaray raises a number of questions in "Place, Interval" about place, sexual difference, and the body as it is given through relation.[1] I want to ask whether a nonheteronormative reading of body and relation is possible within the logic of this piece, and, if so, what room might be made for sexual relationships that fall outside the scope of the strictly heterosexual, or bodily and identificatory configurations that cannot be understood as strictly male or female. I want to follow Irigaray in insisting on the importance of a theory of place and relation to such questions, and want to depart from her by moving toward a number of points at which such an intervention might begin, a queer reading of Irigaray in which bodies, boundaries, and relations of sexual difference need not exclude the sexually different, or the differently sexed.

Irigaray's reading of Aristotle in "Place, Interval," like her readings of other philosophers, is primarily concerned with relation, with self and other, where "self" is figured as the masculine subject of philosophy, and "other" as its elided feminine. Central to her reading of Aristotle is an inquiry into the place of that relation between self and other. Woman, Irigaray will argue, is allied with place in the same way that she is allied with matter against the masculinity of form, and place resembles form in several crucial ways, but is not reducible to it. This is at first a surprising strategy, a reversal of the ways in which matter has been historically allied with the feminine, and form with the masculine. Irigaray proceeds quite differently here, and her reading of form and boundedness, rather than matter, as feminine nevertheless relies on its anchor in the sexual specificity of the body. Irigaray's reading hinges on the fact that matter in Aristotle's account is both density *and indeterminacy*, and the view of matter which we are given in *Physics IV* understands it to be fundamentally without form or shape. In "Place, Interval," Irigaray reads form in Aristotle as a description of the feminine, as a description of place. As we shall see, there is an impossibility of place for the feminine: place is what the feminine is for the masculine, but what the masculine can never be for the feminine, or indeed, what the feminine can never quite be for herself. Irigaray helpfully reverses this, and reads the feminine as the container, that which houses the masculine, and functions as the fixed external boundary for his moving center. The problematic, as Irigaray poses it, is for the feminine to find or to become a place for herself and thus find herself in place, and this is accomplished in order that she might become place for the masculine. The means through which she accomplishes this, a reclaiming of the skin, reads at first as a strategy that might be deployed as successfully by the masculine as by the feminine, a means of finding body and place, but there are important ways in which a "corporeal surveying" of the outermost layer of the body, the skin—or indeed, of the body *as* that which is bounded by its skin—might even confound the familiar divisions between masculine and feminine as they are articulated here.

In my reading of Irigaray's reading of Aristotle, I want to make two claims about place, the first, following Irigaray, having to do with the place of self, and the second, departing from her, having to do with the place of relation. Thinking seriously about the external contours of the bodily boundary, as Irigaray suggests that we do with "skin," can help us understand how a body—especially a female body—might find its own place, and thus be able to move from its own place toward relation with others. The second claim I want to make is about that relation to others. Irigaray has offered sexual difference as "the major philosophical issue of our age,"[2] and turns to Aristotle to theorize relations across sexual difference, asking how bodily and sexual relations might bridge the interval of sexual difference.[3] I want to suggest that even with Irigaray's often dazzling conceptual reversals, the interventions by which her own text comes to be folded around Aristotle's like a skin, the question of sexual difference ends at an impasse in "Place, Interval." This impasse stems from a fundamentally *hylomorphic* understanding of sexual difference: a conviction that male and female, like matter and form, must always be ontologically conjoined.

Is it possible that Irigaray's notion of sexual difference and her insights into the ways in which sexual difference is crucially generative might be of use in an account of sexual difference that aims to challenge heteronormativity? What would it look like if the divide of sexual difference were not fixed in place, marked as the boundary between "male" and "female"? Were that boundary not mapped onto the body in strictly determinative ways, we might be able to theorize sexual difference between women, between men, or between bodies and psyches who do not find easy home or place in either of these categories. A queer reading of the place of sexual difference, then, might be able to answer the second question by way of the first.

Midway through the *Physics*, Aristotle turns to the question of place, explaining that the physicist must have a thorough understanding of place if he is to understand both existence and motion, "both because all suppose that things which exist are *somewhere* (the non-existent is nowhere—where is the goat-stag or the sphinx?), and because 'motion' in its most general and primary sense is a change of place."[4] Contrary to the hope that place will be able to give things a solid anchor in existence, we find that place is reckoned only through relation. The place of things, and thus the "thing" of place, is only found through other things. According to Aristotle,

> [T]he existence of place is held to be obvious from the fact of mutual replacement. Where water now is, there, in turn, when the water has gone out as from a vessel, air is present. When therefore another body occupies this same place, the place is thought to be different from all the bodies which come to be in it and replace one another. (208b, l.1)

When Aristotle first introduces us to place in the above quotation from the beginning of *Physics* IV, he does so indirectly. We are led to infer place not from any direct experience with or of it, but because of the loss of a body or object, its displacement (or destruction) by another object. "The existence of place is held to be obvious from the fact of mutual replacement." Place is the nonmaterial residue of two different, separate bodies. The question of place is from the outset already a question of relation, of mobility, of replacement, of bodies. Place reveals itself through a succession of different bodies, one supplanting the other in the same space—water, then air—and the relation of these different bodies is mutual only to the extent that it is mutually exclusive: place stands as a testament to the fact that the two bodies cannot share the same space. Place is the marker of the bounded and separate identity of the two bodies, and only by virtue of this does space become transmogrified into place. Place is the space where two bodies can never coexist, the space that they cannot ever share.

Place then is testament to a lack of relation, of the progression from water to air, where neither leaves the trace of itself, leaves no mark that it was housed or held there. Place is place to the extent that it is different from either of these, water or air, and neither leaves any trace. Place persists emptily, and is established through a network of relations of mutual exclusivity. Place exists to the extent that it is demarcated and separate from the things which inhabit it, and it persists to the extent that the things that inhabit it, in this first instance, at least, are different from one another, and pass through it leaving no part of themselves in it.

Aristotle at first seems to be offering place as a relation, or non-relation, of mutual exclusivity. Place develops as the text continues, however, becoming the location where relation happens and eventually becoming that very relation. Place is eventually established as *only* relation, only established by the proximity of the two bodies who share it, neither of which is quite place. "Place," writes Aristotle, "is the boundary of the containing body at which it is in contact with the contained body." We are still presented with two separate substances, neither partaking of the other, but are now offered a place which is entirely comprised of the touch between them. Aristotle eventually concludes that "*the innermost motionless boundary of what contains is place*" (212a l.20). That is, an object, a body, moves within the context of a fixed and bounded something which does not move. And that fixed and bounded something is not merely a space of contact, but is itself another body, a body that is necessary for the establishment of place but is not reducible to it, is not the same as place itself: "If then a body has another body outside it and containing it, it is in place, and if not, not" (212a l.32). Place would then be the plane of contact between the body that encapsulates and the body that is held.

Here we may note the problematic which Aristotle touches briefly upon, and Irigaray dwells upon at some length: if place is the *innermost* boundary of the body containing, this leaves the external layer of that body without its own place, outside of place. In order to see if the outermost surface of the containing body, the feminine body, might become housed in itself, or cast a place around itself, Irigaray suggests that we read this external boundary as skin.

> But each of us (male or female) has a place—this place that envelops only his or her body, the first envelope of our bodies, the corporeal identity, the boundary, that which delineates us from other bodies. Form and configuration also determine one's size and all that makes one body unsubstitutable by another. Could this be called a corporeal *surveying*?[5]

We will return below to this question of corporeal surveying: What exactly is it? Is it a scopic activity? A tactile one? What are the proper, and improper, objects for such a survey?[6] Here we will note Irigaray's claim that to become place for the man, woman must be place for herself. Like Aristotle, she introduces us to place by showing us the existence of place prior to relation, a radical boundedness into which the other does not—cannot—move. We have the place of the self established as the place of the body, and the place of the body understood as its outermost boundary, its envelope, its skin. In the Aristotelian model, however, place does not yet encompass the outermost boundary of this body. The task as Irigaray describes it is to transform the skin into something that also contains, to feel the skin as its own bounding envelope so that the body might house itself. The body must perform that bounding function for itself before it can properly house the masculine. The first step toward relation between feminine and masculine, Irigaray suggests, is for woman to find and claim her body as a discrete and separate entity.

I will return in a moment to the collapse of feminine and woman here, and see if it might not be possible to coax those two categories apart, in order to give them a relation to one another that is not only a relation of sameness. It is important to understand this relational bind that Irigaray describes, which lies in the fact that woman's own emergence as a discrete entity cannot come before her encounter with the other, but rather only emerges in relation to this other who is proximate to her, installed inside of her, away from whom she needs to retract to the outermost extensions of her body and being in order that she might return with something like place to offer him. In order to find the place that each of us, male and female alike, *is*, the feminine retracts into the particularity of herself, but finds the same problematic enacted at the level of her own individual body: If our skin is what "delineates us from other bodies," the other body is already installed at the exact moment and precise place at which I find myself; this other who is not me delineates my own boundary. The body belongs to the self to the extent that it "delineates us from other bodies," and thus the feminine finds her place as inescapably bordered by and bound to the place of the masculine, with the result that she cannot even extend into her own skin without feeling the press of the masculine on the other side of it.

But even though male and female are perfectly and inescapably joined, or perhaps *because* they are inescapably joined, Irigaray makes clear that we must not then understand them to be collapsible or substitutable. The shared border between male and female becomes the occasion of the shoring up of the boundary between them. And this boundary, this determinant of categorization, turns out to be bodily form, since "[f]orm and configuration also determine one's size and all that makes one body unsubstitutable by another." Irigaray, like Aristotle, reckons the body here as something more precise and distinct than merely the mass of matter of which it is comprised. Mapping my own body means feeling not only its weight, but its form and shape, and these latter are only perceptible as I feel the press of myself out toward the world, where another body, another self, is located. We see again in Irigaray's text another surprising reversal: whereas what secures place in Aristotle is the substitutability of one kind of body for another, Irigaray points here toward the limits of that substitutability, and suggests that the form and shape of the body secure for it an identity (but not a sameness) that allows and enables proximity.

If one kind of thing is unsubstitutable for another, then two bodies might share the same space, inhabit the same place, with no fear of engulfing or annihilating each other. Though they are determined and constituted in relation to one another, their differences of form and configuration, their distinct *morphology* secures and solidifies their distinct identities. This last is crucial, for if one thing, in the act of replacing in space, takes over or overcomes another kind of thing, it is not only the thing that is vanquished, but place itself.

What does it mean to suggest that one body is unsubstitutable for another? And how can this help us make sense of sexual difference? I am most interested here in the ways that the singularity or unsubstitutability said to characterize bodies across sexual difference is secured by ascribing an interchangeability to bodies *within* sexual difference. The logic by which the male body is unsubstitutable for the female body is the same logic that comes to constitute every male body as able to stand in for any other, or viewing women, in some sense, as interchangeable parts of Woman. What is unsubstitutable about these bodies is not just any singular quality, not even the vicissitudes of size and shape, but their morphology as "masculine" or "feminine." Irigaray writes: "For the masculine has to constitute itself as a vessel to receive and welcome. And the masculine's morphology, existence, and essence do not really fit for such an architecture of place" (39). Understood in this way, it is not a difficulty of relation or a failure of imagination which makes the masculine unable to receive and welcome, it is rather the poor "fit" of the morphology of the masculine that Irigaray deems determinative.

But what if we were to understand masculinity as something different from the male body, femininity as not reducible to the vessel of the womb? What if sexual difference were not parsed between the registers of morphology so neatly, so that masculinity might be less simply a matter of morphology and also a mode of relation? Must sexual difference be legible at the surface of the body? And is sexual difference the same thing as "natural" sex? There are, of course, a number of ways to pose the question of sexual difference that would not reduce it to the category male or female, determined by bodily or genital morphology. One could, for example, formulate sexual difference in such a way that would not require the identificatory possibilities it extended to relate mimetically to the dimorphic tendencies of genital morphology assumed to be the material markers of that (bodily) difference. That is, if one thinks sexual difference in other than binary terms, the category can become unyoked from determinative bodily materiality in a way that makes it easier to resist the temptation to posit genital morphology as essentially determinative not only of sexual difference, but also of the self. If sexual difference is categorically and functionally indistinguishable from *genital* difference, which is itself understood to manifest (as) a binary, then sexual difference is genital difference is genital dimorphism.

Like the goat-stag or the sphinx, Aristotle and Irigaray would seem to agree that the sexually undecidable does not exist, and is located nowhere ("The non-existent is nowhere—where is the goat-stag or the sphinx?"). The goat-stag and the sphinx, which are themselves ambivalently located and fundamentally undecidable in terms of sexual difference, appear in the first sentence of Book IV in order to proclaim that they are located nowhere. Aristotle seems at first to be offering this monstrous couple to demonstrate that everything that exists must have its proper place. The passage as it stands, however, appears to be making this claim from the other direction: what secures the ontological primacy of place is precisely the fact that anything that is categorically undecidable cannot be located in any proper place. What renders a thing or being impossible is literally that it *has no place*. It is not quite that an understanding of place might be discerned by a thorough examination of existence, but rather that a proper orientation toward place can help us determine what things exist. We look around, in no place do we find a goat-stag or a sphinx, this absence is evidence for our conclusion that such things do not exist.

We look around, we notice that the beings we encounter are male or female, and we make a swift and sure conclusion about the place of gender and of sexual difference. The feminine is the female is the one with a womb is woman, the masculine is male, and this of "morphology, existence, and essence." It remains to be determined, however, by what measure, what method of corporeal surveying the masculine or the feminine might be decided. I am thinking here of transgendered bodies or other bodies that challenge the familiar divides by which we are accustomed to parsing sexual difference. Irigaray suggests that coexistence in place, the establishment of a place where masculine and feminine could reside together, is the ultimate goal of relation and can only be established once the distance between masculine and feminine is closed, "if the split between them were bridged" (37), and she suggests a "corporeal surveying" as the method by which the establishment of this new place might become possible. The corporeal surveying Irigaray suggests would then close up the interval between the two bodies, span the gap between them, and allow masculine and feminine to coincide in sameness, in place. And yet, even granting that this interval exists (though Aristotle is quite deliberate in demonstrating that that this interval is an illusion, a trick of form, in 211b 1.15–20), it is unclear that the most productive response to this split, this gap, this embodied difference it is to close it up. Indeed, we might think "corporeal surveying" as a method of apprehending not only the difference of the other as Irigaray suggests, but also as a way of taking measure of the difference that inheres in my own flesh. Irigaray is insisting that we attend to the difference that is always already installed at the level of not merely the blunt materiality of my body, but also the labile boundary with the other that finally comprises my form. In this way, place becomes not the shared and self-identical space of sameness, but more generatively, and more radically, the place where I confront the otherness of the other without annihilating or canceling that difference, or replicating the other in my own image.

What, then, are the effects of this "corporeal surveying"? It is attempted in order to close up the gap between the male and female, but I will suggest that this is only an incidental effect of the survey. Its aim is to find the outermost boundary of woman, which must be located and inhabited for woman to be able to establish place for herself. Locating this boundary is crucial for woman in particular because she is, for Irigaray, perpetually open, never closed off or sealed up. But the unbounded body can never be whole, whether that body is a mundane material object or the human form. Woman relies for her coherence on the boundary of difference that demarcates her singularity, the external edge of the masculine. What this "corporeal surveying" seems to show us is a condition of bodily being in which the masculine acts as place to house the feminine—an exact reversal of Irigaray's most familiar figuration of sexual difference—to define her borders and guarantee her existence. As place is coincident with the thing and boundaries are coincident with the bounded, so too is masculine necessarily always coincident with feminine, and male always coincident with female. Whereas we are accustomed in Irigaray's work to understanding the feminine and the female as the condition of possibility for the masculine and the male, within this scene the masculine becomes the constitutive outside of the feminine, her condition of being.

Although Irigaray would seem to offer us the concept of the interval as a way of circumventing the logic of masculine form giving shape to the otherwise formless unboundedness of the feminine, we must stray far from the Aristotelian model in order to consider this possibility, as it requires an impossible extension between bodies. As these bodies are shown to be always in necessary continuity with another, we then have man and woman inescapably conjoined, as a result of Irigaray's insistence that these bodies are male and female.

Thus is magically guaranteed an indissoluble nearness between two categories that are at first posited as entirely separate. The insistence on the radical boundedness of each kind of being across the divide of sexual difference secures for each not only a coherent and concrete identity, but also an eternally proximate point of contact and place of meeting. This suggestion that the relation between members of different categories will be nearer and more vital than members of the same category is a particularly Aristotelian formulation, encapsulated in his observation that "bodies which are united do not affect each other, while those which are in contact interact on each other" (212b, 130). It is the same logic that underlies Irigaray's proclamation that "man and woman are the most mysterious and creative of couples."

Striking as the consequences of this position are for theorizing relations across sexual difference, they turn out to be even more stark when we consider relations among people who are nominally "of" the same sexual category. That is: relation within sexual difference turns out to be no relation at all. Woman's position relative to another woman can only be one of sexual indifference. There has been much contention on this point, and her work on ethical relations and sexual difference has been located at various points on the spectrum between heteronormative and homophobic. Irigaray has responded to charges of this kind by affirming the primacy of sexual difference, suggesting homosexuality is a question of sexual *choice* rather than sexual *difference*, and that the problem of sexual difference is as primary for homosexuals as it is for heterosexuals. Their homosexuality, in Irigaray's eyes, is merely a flight from this problem, not a renegotiation of its terms.

This is absurd for a number of reasons: its insistence that sexual choice and sexual difference are strictly separate and separable realms, its figuration of "choice" as the proper rubric for understanding homosexuality, further emphasizing her view of both homosexuality and proper gendering as inevitable, if not compulsory. Perhaps most alarming is the assertion that homosexuality is a flight from difference, is merely love of the same which has no relationship of difference at work within it. In order to achieve an ethical relationship, Irigaray has said that it is necessary for a couple *to be two*; as she understands things, this is not something that a gay or lesbian couple—or some other, queerer pairing—can ever quite manage.

And yet, even as she appears to be dismissing homosexuality as a flat and frictionless non-relation, her own theory of relation offers the tools for describing its possibilities otherwise. What is presented as an insurmountable dilemma becomes immediately more potent and promising if we reconfigure the location of the sexuate border that Irigaray proposes, if we shift its *place*. For if we do not restrict our scope to the categories of male and female as they are most strictly conceived, and extend our consideration to the myriad ways in which gender is performed even within the category of, for example, femaleness, we can begin to discern differences, perhaps even difference itself. These are differences which are emphatically bodily, undeniably material, even as they are also psychic, emotional and relational differences.

What seems useful—crucial, even—within Irigaray's schema is its insistence on locating difference at the heart of relation, on insisting on the importance and generative power of the border between self and other. This boundary between male and female is characterized by Irigaray at times as a vaporous gulf, an immaterial divide or chasm that cannot be spanned, and at other times as a tactile boundary, as palpable and dense as flesh. But in insisting on the importance of the divide of sexual difference, what or who is served in drawing that divide only and always between male and female? If we take the example of a butch and a femme couple and note that they exemplify different and contrasting modes of comportment, styles of embodiment, methods of bodily inhabitation, and affective tendencies, what investments demand the withholding of the term "sexual difference" as a descriptor of these oppositions? In a relationship between a transman and a straight woman, is it not clear that the difference between them is decidedly bodily, and resolutely "sexuate"? Acknowledging the sexual difference between a couple consisting of a transman and a gay man in relation allows us to resist the easy collapse of all masculinities into one undifferentiated category of male, while at the same time recognizing that each member of that couple is indeed a man. These pairings can help us conceive of sexual difference without requiring that one sex be quarantined away from another. The trans body can also help us understand the traversal of sexual boundaries not as an unrepresentable breach but as a negotiation of difference. Recognizing that movement is possible across the borders of male and female means that the bodily envelope cannot only be understood as the symbolic marker of the absolute otherness of sexual difference. Indeed, transition can be understood as a means of "reclaiming the skin," the project Irigaray enjoins women to undertake.

Irigaray's corporeal survey of sexual difference concerns itself with the primacy and place of difference, and can show us that that even inhabiting one's own body necessitates an encounter with sexual difference. But it misunderstands the place of sexual difference, locating it always *over there*, in that other who is a perpetual mystery to me and never reachable or knowable. This impossibility of any true encounter with sexual difference, the assertion that it may be proximate to me but can never be known or understood, renders my sexual being closed and isolated away from difference, even as I endeavor to engage with it. When each sex is given its own proper domain which the other can never traverse, the place of sexual difference is always beyond the scope of understanding, just out of grasp. The effect is finally an inoculation against sexual difference in the guise of an engagement with it.

It may in fact be true that there is a certain ineffable power, some nearly magical catalyzing force, in sexual difference. But it seems important to remember, as Penelope Deutscher reminds us, that the concept of sexual difference—particularly as the ground for an ethics or politics—is animated by the tension between its possibility and its impossibility.[7]

It is imperative to consider the ways in which this difference does not reside only in the contrast between male and female, where these are both understood as immutable designations. If we are to give difference its due as a vital force, as Irigaray invites us to, we must also acknowledge that femininity is compossible with the category of male, that the masculinity expressed within some iterations of femaleness is as ontologically robust as any other kind of masculinity. To exclude these pairings from the realm of ethical, productive, generative relation is to understand both sex and difference in the most reductive and biologistic of terms. Genders that find no easy home within the binary system are still animated by difference. Sexual undecidability does not condemn the subject to placelessness, but rather locates difference at the heart of both subjectivity and relation.

## Notes

1. Luce Irigaray, "Place, Interval: A Reading of Aristotle, *Physics IV*," in *An Ethics of Sexual Difference*, trans. Carolyn Burke and Gillian C. Gill (Ithaca: Cornell University Press, 1984), 34–55.

2. Ibid., 5.

3. Tina Chanter opens her book *Ethics of Eros, Irigaray's Rewriting of the Philosophers* by reformulating this statement to point to feminist contestations of the concept of sexual difference: "One of the most powerful categories of analysis that has served the needs of feminism in recent years is that of gender." Tina Chanter, *Ethics of Eros, Irigaray's Rewriting of the Philosophers* (New York and London: Routledge, 1995).

4. Aristotle, *Physics* Books I–IV, trans. R. P. Hardie and R. K. Gaye (Oxford: Oxford University Press, 1930), 208a, l.30.

5. Irigaray, "Place, Interval," 36–37.

6. On bodily boundedness, unboundedness, and corporeal surveying in Irigaray, see Elizabeth Grosz, *Volatile Bodies* (Bloomington: Indiana University Press, 1994).

7. Penelope Deutscher, *A Politics of Impossible Difference: The Later Work of Luce Irigaray* (Ithaca and London: Cornell University Press, 2002). This is particularly apparent in her emphasis on the uncertain temporality of sexual difference: "Sexual difference could only be that which is to come. Difference does not lie between two identities, the male and the female. That should not be sexual difference" (121).

# Chapter 15

# "Women on the Market"

## On Sex, Race, and Commodification

Ewa Plonowska Ziarek

Is it not ironic that Irigaray, a theorist most frequently accused of essentialism,[1] might in fact allow us to diagnose the shortcomings of the essentialism/antiessentialism debate in the '80s and '90s, and to reinterpret this debate as an unacknowledged symptom of commodification? Unlike the essentialism/social construction binary, the logic of commodification produces triple effects: first of all, it abstracts social relations from all the vestiges of materiality, concrete labor, and the temporality of becoming; second, it conceals this abstract character of social mediation behind the appearances of immediacy; and finally, it disavows the traumatic limits of signification constituted by the "disappropriating" character of sexual difference and racial traumas. What commodification reveals is the schism between the abstraction of the commodity form, which determines the value of the object in total separation from its materiality, and the concomitant devaluation of the non-sublated remnants of materiality to mere waste or markers of social death. This schism between the abstraction of social values and the nonsymbolizable material refuse is itself a source of injustice, inscribed in the modern conceptions of racial and sexual differences. Feminist criticism has addressed very well the problem of immediacy, by reconstructing again and again the obfuscated process of mediation and by demonstrating that what is posited as an intrinsic signification of the body, gender, or race, is in fact an effect of its social constitution.[2] Yet, what has not been contested enough is the specific mode of social mediation characteristic of commodity fetishism, namely, the abstraction of social form and the disavowal of the traumatic limits of signification.[3]

In order to rethink the impact of commodification on the contemporary feminist theories of race and gender, I intertwine Luce Irigaray's reading of Marx's and Aristotle's theories of value with Hortense Spiller's reading of American "grammar" of slavery. Although such an engagement with black feminism constitutes a detour from Irigaray's relation to "the Greeks," it is nonetheless necessary to reconstruct the obfuscated role of race and slavery in Irigaray's and Marx's theories of commodity and in their reading of Aristotle. Referring to Marx's reading of Aristotle's *Nicomachean Ethics* in the "Commodity" chapter in the first volume of *Capital*,[4] Irigaray defends her analogy between the female bodies and commodities, between the sexual and economic exchanges, by arguing that it was in fact Aristotle who conceptualized the relation between matter and form, so crucial to Marx's thinking of the commodity, on the basis of the sexual relation between the masculine and the feminine (*This Sex*, 174). Her reading of Marx aims, therefore, to expose this obfuscated reference to sexual difference and to analyze the consequences of the commodity form for the conceptualization of female embodiment. However, Irigaray misses the issue of slavery, which Marx evokes to set up the distinction between Aristotle's and his own theory of value. Marx claims that Aristotle failed to see the equality of labor in the equalization of products for the precise historical reason that "Greek society was founded on the labor of the slaves, hence had as its natural basis the inequality of men to their labor power" (*C*, 152). Nonetheless, by confining slavery to antiquity and by equating modernity with equality which is yet to be realized in social life, Marx and Irigaray can disregard modern forms of slavery, racism, and white supremacy in their account of the commodity form. Consequently, the references to Aristotle's ethics in Marx's and Irigaray's texts do more rhetorical/political work than these authors ostensibly acknowledge: they testify to the attempts to subordinate the mutually constitutive network of relations among commodification, femininity, slavery, and racism to one dominant term, such as labor or gender, by confining slavery to ancient history and disregarding its impact on the formation of modern ideas of commodity, freedom, and embodiment.

As Irigaray's reading of Marx implies, the dichotomy of essentialism and social construction arises out of a double and antithetical form of the commodity manifesting itself as exchange value and use value, together with all the oppositions underlying this structure: materiality and form, the natural and the social, the passivity of matter and the activity of production/construction.[5] Irigaray argues that "the commodity, like the sign, suffers from metaphysical dichotomies. . . . A commodity—a woman—is divided into two irreconcilable 'bodies': her 'natural' body and her socially valued, exchangeable body."[6] Consistently associated with the "physical body" (*C*, 126), substance, and coarse materiality, "natural" form constitutes the use value of the object, whereas value form, characterized by "total" separation from diverse physical qualities of the product, expresses a homogenous social substance: undifferentiated social labor. For

Marx, "there is nothing mysterious" (*C*, 163) about the "natural form" of use value (*C*, 138), even though this form is already an effect of the social negation of nature by concrete labor. The mystery of the commodity, like the enigma of femininity, resides in its social form expressing the value of social labor. This contradiction in the double value of the commodified bodies points to the total dissociation of social form from the sensuous body, which, as a result of this separation, is reduced to passive, coarse matter. Marx's concept of the commodity diagnoses, therefore, the indifference of social form to the "coarsely sensuous objectivity" of matter and concrete labor under the capitalist conditions of exchange. On the basis of this schism, Irigaray claims that when women are exchanged, their bodies are split into "two things at once: utilitarian objects and bearers of value," into "matter-body" and the ungraspable mysterious "envelope" of value (*TS*, 175).

Although it might not be immediately apparent, Irigaray's brilliant rereading of the commodity form in the context of female embodiment depends on a synthesis of Marx's and Aristotle's theories of value. Ostensibly, Irigaray points to Aristotle's deployment of sexual difference in his discussion of form/matter relation. Yet far more crucial for her interpretation of commodification of femininity is the Aristotelian analysis of the source of value in the needs/desires (*chreia*) of producers. According to Aristotle, "this measure [of value] is need (*chreia*). . . . And so, though things so different cannot become commensurate in reality, they can become commensurate enough in relation to our needs."[7] Exceeding biological needs, the diverse connotations of *chreia* range from lack, want, obligations, to debts, business affairs, maxims, or intercourse. It is these economical, sexual, and rhetorical associations of the Aristotelian *chreia* that allow Irigaray not only to equate the phallus with gold but also to claim that female bodies "mirror the need/desire for exchanges among men" (*TS*, 181). By contrast, Marx ignores Aristotle's discussion of needs as the basis of exchange in order to argue that for Aristotle exchange is "something foreign to the true nature of things," and thus does not yet represent a truly modern concept of value (*C*, 151). To support his claim, he quotes a rather misleadingly truncated excerpt from *Nicomachean Ethics*: "[I]t is . . . in reality impossible that such unlike things can be commensurable" (*C*, 151). In so doing he excludes Aristotle's claim that "*needs*" (*chreia*) make things "commensurate enough" for the purpose of exchange. Consequently, Marx's distinction between the modern concept of value and the Greek theories of exchange is based on the double exclusion: of needs/desires, on the one hand, and of slavery, on the other.

In order to analyze the value form of women's bodies Irigaray negotiates between Aristotle's notion of lack/needs/desires and Marx's notion of abstract labor. At stake in this negotiation is not only the relation between needs/desires and labor, but also the contrast between the remainder of the nonidentity in Aristotle's interpretation of exchange and Marx's diagnosis of the "total" abstraction of the modern form of value. Indeed, it is the abstraction of commodity form that is at stake in Irigaray's critique of commodification. As she points out, "money as a means of mediation represents . . . a universal abstracted from the natural without a suitable spiritualization of this natural."[8] In contrast to the concreteness of use value, the social form of the commodity is characterized by a triple abstraction. First of all, labor (construction) as the source of the commodity's value is abstracted from concrete, diverse social activities and reduced to the pure expenditure of homogenous labor power. This leveling of diverse kinds of social work into a homogenous abstract labor is itself an effect of capitalist exchange, which cannot manifest the equality of labor otherwise than through abstract economic equivalence. Second, time becomes abstracted from discontinuous and unpredictable becoming by being reduced to the mathematical units of measurement.[9] Finally, the social form is abstracted from all the material particularity of the object. That is why Irigaray argues that commodified women's bodies become abstractions without any intrinsic value: *"[W]oman has value on the market by virtue of one single quality: that of being a product of man's 'labor'"* (*TS*, 175). Thus, commodity form performs an erasure of all particularity pertaining to the object, temporalization, and concrete labor, and substitutes for it "the phantom-like objectivity" of abstract, homogenous social labor (*C*, 128). Furthermore, the language of Marx's analysis suggests that the obverse side of abstraction is an infliction of bodily injury: by "extinguishing" all sensuous characteristics (*C* 128) the value form mortifies and wipes out the physical body without a trace.

These three kinds of abstraction performed by the commodity form—the abstraction from concrete labor, temporality, and the particularity of the object—are mutually interdependent. As Adorno argues, what is at stake in separation of the abstract labor from physical work is the denial of the necessary dependence of concrete labor on materiality, and the remainder of nonidentity, which cannot be appropriated by the laboring social spirit.[10] According to Adorno,

> [T]here is nothing in the world that shall not manifest itself to human beings solely through social labor . . . But the step by which *labor sets itself up as the metaphysical principle pure and simple* is none other than *the consistent elimination of the "material"* to which all labor feels itself tied, the material that defines its boundary for it . . . and relativizes its sovereignty. (*H*, 26, emphasis added)

Again we see here a crucial difference between the Aristotelian and the modern form of value. Based on the "needs/desires" of producers, Aristotle's notion of value is only approximate, it still preserves the remnant of nonidentity and otherness of objects in exchange: "[T]hough things so different cannot become commensurate in reality, they become commensurate enough in relation to our needs."[11] It is this emphasis on the persistence of nonidentical in exchange that prompted Marx to argue that Aristotle did not yet discover the true basis of equivalence in abstract labor. By contrast, the abstraction of modern form of value eliminates all the "ties" to the material and nonidentical, and in so doing, denies that there is any "outside" to the principle of capitalist exchange. Consequently, abstraction turns labor into an ideology, which is coextensive with the appropriation of the labor of others and the domination of their bodies. Working in the service of equivalence and domination, this ideology of abstract, sovereign labor dissolves not only every qualitative difference but also every trace of the nonidentical and the incommensurate. We may wonder at this point whether feminist theories of social construction are not vulnerable to a similar critique of the ideology of labor, which sets up production as "absolute." Insofar as these theories consider any "outside" to the abstract mediation of bodies as the remnant of essentialism, they turn social construction into a "metaphysical principle pure and simple," to use Adorno's term—that is, into a metaphysics of autonomous production that knows no limits.

This transformation of social labor into a metaphysics of production is nowhere more evident than in the spiritualization of bodies. Both Irigaray and Marx associate the abstraction of socioeconomic form with the spiritualization of the body. By endowing the object/body with "a soul" (*C*, 143), commodification bestows social significance upon bodies, while at the same time transforming them, in Irigaray's words, into "value invested idealities" (*TS*, 181). As the culmination of metaphysics, the commodity form discloses the historical truth of the Hegelian spiritualization of matter—that is, the complete transformation of matter into a mere reflection of social spirit. Extending Marx's analysis, Irigaray points to the analogous imaginary function of femininity: "*[C]ommodities, women, are a mirror of value of and for man.* In order to serve as such [mirrors], they give up their bodies to men as the supporting material of specularization, or speculation" (*TS*, 177).

What is paradoxical about this process of specularization, which turns bodies into a reflection of abstract social labor, is that it erases its movement of mediation, through which the commodity acquires its social value, and presents its speculative result as if it were an inherent property of the object "endowed by nature itself'" (*C*, 149). As Marx puts it,

"The movement through which this process has been mediated vanishes in its own result, leaving no trace behind" (*C*, 187). It is this vanishing process of mediation that can be most readily associated with essentialism insofar as the most mediated ideality—the abstract soul of the commodity—appears as the concrete immediacy of the body. Let us notice here in particular a parallel between the speculative "soul" of the commodity produced through the reiteration of market exchanges and the speculative character of sex constituted by the reiteration of gender norms, analyzed by Judith Butler. According to Butler, "'[S]ex' is a regulatory ideal whose materialization is compelled, and this materialization takes place . . . through certain highly regulated practices."[12] Yet to expose the illusory immediacy of sex as the most speculative result of social mediation is merely the first step of the critique of the commodification of bodies. The second necessary move is to contest the abstraction of social mediation/social construction as an equally illusory autonomy from every residue of materiality and nonidentity. As Adorno's and Hegel's critiques of abstraction show, the abstraction of social form "can never be made absolutely autonomous vis-à-vis what it is abstracted from . . . the quality of what it is abstracted from is always, in a certain sense, preserved in it at the same time" (*H*, 15). To assert the absolute autonomy of social construction, to deny its dependence on the residue of the material and nonidentical, would, paradoxically, lead to another form of free-floating idealism. In the context of Adorno's work we could say that feminist critiques of essentialism and social construction binary have to "acknowledge the insolubility of an empirical, nonidentical moment" *within* social mediation, "a moment that doctrines of the absolute subject, idealist systems of identity, are not permitted to acknowledge as indissoluble" (*H*, 17).

Ultimately, the reinterpretation of the essentialism/social construction binary in the context of use/exchange value relativizes and contests the fixity of this opposition. First of all, both of these terms emerge from and to a large extent reproduce the historical process of the commodification of bodies. Furthermore, it is only through the mutual negation of their untruth that these opposites can demonstrate their partial insight. Thus, the falsity of antiessentialism lies in the "absolutization" of the autonomy of construction, in the denial of the persistence of the material and nonidentical even in the most abstract social form of mediation. Nonetheless, it reveals the truth of the historical fact that in capitalism there is nothing, including bodies themselves, that is not mediated by social production and economic exchange. On the other hand, the obvious untruth of essentialism lies in its confusion of the limits of mediation with immediacy, as if it were possible to transcend production and exchange and find a positive value in bodies themselves. Yet, through this falsity, the recurrent suspicions of essentialism inadvertently bear witness to the remainder of damaged materiality, exteriority, and otherness, which, although reduced to social waste, nonetheless constitute nonsublatable limits of construction/social labor. By misreading this remainder as essentialism and by disregarding the damaging abstraction of social form, the social construction argument remains in complicity with the metaphysics of production, which asserts its "absolute" autonomy and "tolerates nothing outside itself" (*H*, 26).

It is only through this double critique of essentialism and social construction—that is, through the negation of both immediacy and the abstract autonomy of production—that we can diagnose those forms of domination that the essentialism/antiessentialism binary fails to acknowledge, namely, the injury of racialized, sexed bodies inflicted by the process of commodification. For Luce Irigaray the damage of commodification manifests itself primarily in the objectification of female bodies and the destruction of any possibility of a culture of sexual difference. As she argues, Marx's definition of commodity fetishism as the abstract social relation among men reveals the fact that the economic regulation of gender is predicated on sexual indifference—an indifference that constitutes a paradoxical compromise between patriarchy and the dissolving power of capital. Such an erasure of sexual difference[13] in the economic regulation of gender produces a homosocial order of exchange in which women mediate misrecognized, sublimated relations among men, in which homosexuality is prohibited, and in which the hegemony of monosexual white heterosexuality is predicated on the erasure of difference and incommensurability.

If Irigaray claims that the damage of commodification produces the erasure of sexual difference, her own analysis reproduces not only Marx's exclusion of slavery from the modern forms of exchange but also the racial indifference characteristic of so many foundational texts of white feminism. A symptom of a widespread historical and textual blindness, Irigaray's failure to take race into account ignores the fact that the economic equation of blackness with property under the regime of slavery constitutes the most horrific paradigm of the commodification of human bodies.[14] One could argue, for instance, that the commodification of black female sexuality in modernity in terms of exoticism and primitivism represents a most characteristic moment of the production of the "phantom" immediacy of unrestrained sexuality through highly mediated, abstract systems of cultural and economic exchange. Furthermore, Irigaray's reading of Marx betrays not only a historical but also a textual blindness. Irigaray fails to contest Marx's simultaneous disavowal and reference to slavery in order to account for the limits of Aristotle's theory of value. And although she is an extremely attentive reader of the persistent rhetorical references to the body in Marx's *Capital*, she ignores the explicit racialized meaning of these references ranging from "tribal religions" to the appropriation of the crucial term *fetishism*. Originating in sixteenth-century European trade with West Africa, the term *fetishism*, as William Pietz has documented, was intertwined in the eighteenth and nineteenth centuries with the colonial, racist representation of the "primitive" mentality of Africans, based on religious superstitions, irrational fear, and institutionalized social delusion.[15] Thus, Hegel for instance concludes, that the African "*Fetich*" is but one manifestation of the Africans' lack of any awareness of universality and their "*contempt* for humanity which . . . is the fundamental characteristic of the race."[16] It is precisely by evoking and disavowing these racist connotations of fetishism that Marx can extend this term to describe the "*contempt* for humanity" and the irrationality of commodity exchange in capitalist societies.

Yet, what is at stake in the critique of Irigaray's white solipsism is not only a necessary contestation of the exclusion of black femininity from the foundational texts of white feminism. What is also crucial in this critique is the analysis of the damage inflicted on the captive black bodies, which at once exemplify the process of commodification as such and, at the same time, constitute an exception to the commodified gender regulation. As Hortense J. Spillers's influential essay, "Mama's Baby, Papa's Maybe: An American Grammar Book," suggests, the commodification of gender relations cannot take fully into account the traumatic reality of the black flesh stripped from values and reduced to social illegitimacy.[17] Spillers's argument that the traumatic legacy of the enslavement of black bodies still threatens to disarticulate the very conception of gender and kinship makes a crucial intervention both to feminist psychoanalysis and Marxist criticism alike.[18] As her analysis of the 1965 Moynihan "Report," which blames black mothers for the destruction of the black family, shows, the grammar of racialized bodies remains "grounded in the originating metaphors of captivity and mutilation so that it is as if neither time nor history, nor historiography . . . shows movement" ("MBPM," 68). One of the deadly contradictions of the "grammar" of slavery is that the commodification of the captive body was in fact synonymous with the destruction of the social significance of gender. Enslaved African persons, Spillers writes, "were culturally unmade . . . Under these conditions one is neither female nor male, as both subjects are taken into 'account' as *quantities*" ("MBPM," 72). In the juridical codes of slavery, "slave appears in the same context with beasts of burden, *all* and *any* animal(s) . . . and a virtually endless profusion of domestic contents from the culinary item to the book" ("MBPM," 79). Ultimately, the commodification of black enslaved bodies leads to gender undifferentiation and the destruction of kinship structures—all these social distinctions collapse into what Spillers calls a "lacerated" black flesh as the traumatic zero degree of social mediation.

In order to analyze bodily crimes inflicted by enslavement (injuries illegible within essentialism/social construction distinction), Spillers's analysis of the economics of slavery adds a new category of flesh, which functions as the traumatic, invisible double of the socially valued body:

> Before the "body" there is the "flesh," that zero degree of social conceptualization that does not escape concealment under the brush of discourse. . . . Even though the European hegemonies stole bodies—some of them female—out of West African communities. . .we regard this human and social irreparability as high crimes against the *flesh*, as the person of African females and African males registered the wounding. If we think of the "flesh" as a primary narrative, then we mean its seared, divided, ripped-apartness. ("MBPM," 67).

The "ungendered" flesh of the slave suffers a double damage: not only traumatic physical violations but also traumatic symbolic destruction of the social significations of kinship, gender, and name. Thus, Spillers's notion of lacerated flesh allows us to detect quite a different meaning of Marx's analysis of "the total mortification" of the body by economic exchange—in this case, total mortification reveals a replacement of the erased symbolic and social values by bodily wounds. As Orlando Patterson suggests, this destruction of the value of the enslaved body is in fact synonymous with the "social death" of the enslaved person.[19] Emerging in the aftermath of the destruction of the social and symbolic signification of the body, the "hieroglyphics" of wounded flesh ("MBPM," 67) mark the traumatic effects of the violent stripping of the black body from all social values. It is precisely these unbearable "hieroglyphics" of violated black flesh that are excluded, Spillers argues, from both a "cultural seeing" obsessed with the visibility of color and from the feminist analysis of "'the Female Body in Western Culture'" ("MBPM," 67).

In the "grammar" of slavery, the "re-gendering" of black flesh occurs only retrospectively through the conjunction of enforced biological reproduction and the social reproduction of slavery as "social death." In contrast to white femininity, the economic value of the enslaved female flesh reduced to compulsory maternity and yet robbed of all parental function does not reflect white homosocial relations but reproduces the social non-value of slavery. Thus, contrary to Irigaray's claim, enslaved female bodies are not divided into the natural substratum and the "bearers of value," but rather they are seen as the bearers of non-value. Through the juxtaposition of Irigaray and Spillers we can see more precisely the racist division of labor and the damage suffered by white and black female bodies: whereas white bodies erase their materiality in the reflection of social values, enslaved bodies reproduce the failure of spiritualization of matter, which is associated with the destruction of social values. In so doing, they become the bearers of social death, illegitimacy, and invisibility. This racist attribution of the failure to specularize matter to black enslaved bodies consolidates the monopoly of whiteness on production of social value. Consequently, the difference between the commodified white female body and the enslaved black female body is that the economic value of the latter depends on its inability to spiritualize/specularize matter. In Hegel's philosophy of history, the racist attribution of the "failure of spiritualization" to enslaved bodies is extended to Africa itself and used to justify the enslavement and the exclusion of the entire black race from the historical progress of freedom: "What we properly understand by Africa, is the Unhistorical, Undeveloped Spirit, still involved in the condition of mere nature, and which had to be presented here only as on the threshold of the World's History."[20] By displacing the remnant of materiality that the racist metaphysics of production cannot spiritualize away onto black bodies, white supremacy associates these bodies with the enslaving nature and in so doing excludes them from the realm of the social spirit, that is, from the historical realization of freedom.

Despite their different diagnoses of the commodification of black and white female bodies, both Spillers and Irigaray pose a crucial question whether it is possible to elaborate and institute a different model of mediation of bodies, beyond the opposition between the sacrificial spiritualization of matter culminating in the abstraction of commodity exchange and an even more destructive "despiritualization" of enslaved bodies culminating in social illegitimacy. For Spillers the possibility of such alternative mediation for black women lies not in claiming the commodified white female gender, but in "*claiming* the monstrosity (of a female with the potential to name) which her culture imposes in blindness" ("MBPM," 80). This provocative reappropriation and redefinition of monstrosity as an alternative means of black women's resistance implies a double strategy. First of all, the monstrous power to name, which racist ideology has always associated with the destructive power of the black mother, jams the reproduction of social illegitimacy and rewrites the function of the maternal body: rather than reproducing social non-value, it contests the white/paternal monopoly on value and the autonomy of social production. As Spillers argues elsewhere, such a usurpation of the symbolic power is intertwined with the radicalization of the negative, which "'overreaches' the given discursive conditions," rather than producing identifications with existing racial and gender norms.[21] In the context of Adorno's work, this monstrous radicalization of the negative implies a certain spiritualization of black bodies since the movement of social spirit, understood as the struggle for freedom, depends on the contestation of oppression and the negation of social injustice. By repositioning black female bodies as the bearers of embodied freedom rather than social illegitimacy, such monstrous spiritualization does not erase all the remnants of materiality and nonidentity but, on the contrary, reclaims what the commodified gender and racist systems of exchange disavow: sexual and racial differences, traumatized stolen flesh, the damaged remnants of materiality. By negating these disavowals, spiritual monstrosity transforms the failure of specularization, associated in racism with social death and refuse, into a vital source of resistance to the "total mortification" of bodies by the economic values of racist homosociality. Consequently, Spillers's reappropriation of monstrosity also implies a different model of social mediation. Through the negation of the autonomy of production and the abstraction of social values, such mediation preserves the "hieroglyphics" of wounded flesh as a source of resistance and thus as a necessary moment of the materialization of the "spirit" of freedom.

If Spillers contests the exclusion of the black bodies from the social spirit as the mark of social death, Irigaray opposes the work of death and the mortification of sexual bodies as the basis of social spirit. What is at stake for her is to make the disappropriating "difference between the sexes the motor of the dialectic's becoming" so that we are "able to renounce death as sovereign master" (*ILTY*, 82). Although she emphatically rejects any regression to "natural immediacy" (*ILTY*, 107), at the same time she insists that mediation does consist in "renouncing the sensible, . . . sacrificing it to the universal" but rather in the sublimation of the sensible "to the point when it becomes spiritual energy" (*ILTY*, 24). Irigaray's "sensible transcendental" (a neologism invented to contest the opposition between immanence associated with sensibility/matter and transcendence ascribed to productive spirit) implies a nonabstract mediation, in which damaged materials play an active role of resistance to the metaphysics of production. Thus, in contrast to the subjugating abstraction of commodity form, such mediation establishes a dynamic and reversible relation between the excluded particulars and the universal, between the sensuous and the spiritual. On the one hand, this dynamic exchange between flesh and spirit exposes the damage of abstraction and gives new significance to the remnants of materiality reduced to social waste. On the other hand, it particularizes and materializes the abstraction of social spirit up to the point where its autonomy breaks down and reveals both its dependence and struggle with the disavowed others: flesh, sexuality, remnants of matter. In so doing, art breaks "the taboo" on the affective, the impure, and the hybrid. In so doing, it foregrounds not only the materiality of social exchanges but also their indeterminacy and openness to what is yet to come. Even though this model of mediation is most explicitly elaborated in *I Love to You*, Irigaray give numerous figures of such mediation already in her earlier work: the chiasmus of the two sets of lips, the work of female sublimation, production of the sensible transcendental, and so forth.

Yet, we may wonder in the context of Spillers's work whether "making the difference between the sexes the motor of the dialectic's becoming" (*ILTY*, 82) is in fact sufficient to elaborate such a model of mediation. Does the inclusion of the disappropriating character of sexual difference necessarily negate the white monopoly of value? Can it contest the lingering historical legacy of the exclusion of black bodies? Should we not contest not only the abstract specularization/mortification of matter in the constitution of social value of whiteness but also the despiritualization of some bodies as the basis of their exclusion from the realm of signification and freedom? Needless to say, such a violent despiritualization is different from both immediacy and essentialism; in fact, it takes us much closer to the realm of abjection analyzed in different ways by Julia Kristeva, Judith Butler, and Tina Chanter.

By reading Irigaray's engagements with Marx, Aristotle, and Adorno, I located the genealogy of essentialism/social construction binary in commodity fetishism; by reading Irigaray with Spillers I ended up recasting this initial binary. It seems to me that if we are to continue to work on the Irigarayan project of a new symbolic and Spillers's project of a new grammar of race and gender, we have to begin with a contestation of much more complex opposition between the abstract specularization of matter reflecting white monopoly on value and the violent despiritualization of bodies reproducing social non-value and invisibility of blackness. To contest this opposition, and to diagnose the damages it inflicts on female bodies, I have reclaimed for feminist purposes the category of mediation Spillers associates with monstrosity, and Irigaray—with sensible transcendental. Although it approaches damaged bodies as always already regulated by social mechanisms and economic exchange, such a monstrous mediation also preserves remnants of non-sublatable materiality as a source of resistance to the absolute autonomy and sovereignty of production. In so doing it materializes social spirit up to the point where the hold of abstract equivalence breaks down and reverses into a liberation of divergence, where the semblance of the reconciliation between the universal and the particular, the abstract and the sensible, turns into a conflicting and contested relation between them.

## Notes

For my earlier discussion of commodification in the context of aesthetics see Ewa Plonowska Ziarek, "The Abstract Soul of the Commodity and the

Monstrous Body of the Sphinx: Commodification, Aesthetics, and the Impasses of Social Construction," *differences* 16, no. 2 (2005): 88–115.

1. For my extensive analysis of the debates on essentialism in the context of Irigaray's writing, see Ziarek, "The Abstract Soul of the Commodity and the Monstrous Body of the Sphinx," 88–90 and Ewa Plonowska Ziarek, *An Ethics of Dissensus: Postmodernity, Feminism, and the Politics of Radical Democracy* (Stanford: Stanford University Press, 2001), 160–61. See also Naomi Schor, "This Essentialism Which Is Not One," in *Engaging with Irigaray*, ed. Carolyn Burke, Naomi Schor, and Margaret Whitford (New York: Columbia University Press, 1994), 57–78 and Tina Chanter, *Ethics of Eros: Irigaray's Rewriting of the Philosophers* (New York: Routledge, 1995), 21–44.

2. Gayatri Spivak writes that value form is "the possibility of mediation as it were, which establishes exchange, its appropriation and extraction as surplus and so on. This way of understanding of Marx's project would not underestimate the importance of class, but would not see it as trafficking in ineluctable essences" (365). Although I agree with Spivak about the way the theory of value establishes a nonessentialist notion of class, I do want to stress that the split between use/exchange value coupled with the abstract character of value form is precisely what produces the impasses of essentialism/antiessentialism. Gayatri Spivak with Ellen Rooney, "'In a Word': Interview," in *The Second Wave: A Reader in Feminist Theory*, ed. Linda Nicholson (New York: Routledge, 1997), 356–78.

3. For a critique of the "linguistic monism" of constructivism and the impasse between determinism/voluntarism see Judith Butler, *Bodies that Matter: On the Discursive Limits of Sex* (New York: Routledge, 1993), 4–12.

4. Karl Marx, *Capital*, vol.1, trans. Ben Fowkes (London: Penguin, 1990), 151–52. Subsequent references to this edition will be marked parenthetically as *C*.

5. I agree here with Ellen Rooney that one of the reasons the problem of essentialism does not "go away" is because it has not been historicized (Rooney and Spivak, 361).

6. Luce Irigaray, *This Sex Which Is Not One*, trans. Catherine Porter (Ithaca: Cornell University Press1985), 179–80. Subsequent references to this edition will be marked parenthetically as *TS*.

7. Aristotle, *Nicomachean Ethics*, Book 5, chapter 5, 113a27; 1133b, 19–20.

8. Luce Irigaray, *I Love to You: Sketch of a Possible Felicity in History*, trans. Alison Martin (New York and London: Routledge, 1996), 31. Subsequent references to this edition will be marked parenthetically as *ILTY*.

9. As Derrida briefly points out, this abstraction and ideality of time is a condition of "any ideologization and any fetishization." Jacques Derrida, *Specters of Marx*, trans. Peggy Kamuf (New York: Routledge, 1994), 154–55.

10. W. Theodor Adorno, *Hegel: Three Studies*, trans. Shierry Weber Nicholsen (Cambridge: The MIT Press, 1993), 23. Subsequent references to this edition will be marked parenthetically as *H*.

11. Aristotle, *Nicomachean Ethics*, Book 5, chapter 5, 113a27; 1133b 19–20.

12. Judith Butler, *Bodies that Matter: On the Discursive Limits of Sex* (New York: Routledge, 1993), 1.

13. For further discussion of Irigaray's concept of sexual difference, see Ziarek, *An Ethics of Dissensus*, 151–82. In her *A Politics of Impossible Difference*, Penelope Deutscher has brilliantly analyzed this impossible status of sexual difference as both the historically excluded possibility—as the pair of empty brackets—and as a mark of the futurity of sexual difference, as that which is yet to come. Penelope Deutscher, *A Politics of Impossible Difference: The Later Work of Luce Irigaray* (Ithaca: Cornell University Press, 2002), 28–49, 107–22.

14. Indeed, as Gilroy argues, the enslavement of the body represents a "deeper experience of reification than anything that can be mapped through the concept of the fetishism of commodities." Paul Gilroy, *The Black Atlantic: Modernity and Double Consciousness* (Cambridge: Harvard University Press, 1993), 124.

15. Williams Pietz, "The Problem of Fetish, IIIa. Bosman's Guinea and the Enlightenment Theory of Fetishism," *Res* 16 (1988): 87–88.

16. G. W. F. Hegel, *The Philosophy of History*, trans. J. Sibree (New York: Dover, 1956), 95.

17. Hortense J. Spillers, "Mama's Baby, Papa's Maybe: An American Grammar Book," *Diacritics* 19 (1987): 65–81. Subsequent references to this edition will be marked parenthetically as "MBPM."

18. Paradoxically, gender and blackness might not belong to the same order of difference. This is a reversal of the typical psychoanalytical claim that sexual difference, marking, as Lacan claims, the failure of meaning, does not belong to the same order as the social differences of gender, race, and class. For an eloquent articulation of such a claim see Joan Copjec, *Read My Desire: Lacan against Historicists* (Cambridge: The MIT Press, 1994), 202–204. Yet, Spillers's analysis of black flesh shows the instance where blackness, ejected from the realm of signification, does not belong to the same order as gender either.

19. Orlando Paterson, *Slavery and Social Death. A Comparative Study* (Cambridge: Harvard University Press, 1982), 4–14, 38–46.

20. G. W. F. Hegel, *The Philosophy of History*, 99.

21. Hortense J. Spillers, "'All the Things You Could Be by Now if Sigmund Freud's Wife Was Your Mother': Psychoanalysis and Race," *Critical Inquiry* 22 (1996): 710–34, 725.

## Chapter 16

# Irigaray's Challenge to the Fetishistic Hegemony of the Platonic One and Many

Tina Chanter

Ironically, it is precisely where Irigaray has been found to be most wanting—with some justification—that I think she might have something to offer that has so far been largely ignored. I have in mind here her illegitimate privileging of sexual difference over other salient social differences, not the least of which is race, but let's not forget class, transgender or differently abled persons, and a host of other differences that are routinely used as grounds for discrimination. I am thinking, for example, of an observation that Judith Butler made in *Bodies that Matter*. She described the nature of Irigaray's intervention as "hyperbolic." Butler says,

> The largeness and speculative character of Irigaray's claims have always put me a bit on edge, and I confess in advance that although I can think of no feminist who has read and reread the history of philosophy with the kind of detailed and critical attention that she has, her terms tend to mime the grandiosity of the philosophical errors that she underscores. This miming is, of course, tactical, and her reenactment of philosophical error requires that we learn how to read her for the difference that her reading performs.[1]

Butler adds, "Sometimes a hyperbolic rejoinder is necessary when a given injury has remained unspoken for too long" (1993, 37). Butler's suggestion that Irigaray's miming is tactical, and that we must learn to read her for the "difference that her reading performs" is crucial, as is the idea that a hyperbolic rejoinder might carry with it a certain necessity, given the gravity of the injury that has not only been suffered but has also been without expression for so long. I want to stay with this impossibility of having been unable to express the injury of marginalization suffered for so long.

To put this in Jean-François Lyotard's language, at stake in the differend is precisely the inability of a marginalized identity to be heard, to find a voice, or to be recognized by the dominant discourse. As we have learned from Gayatri Spivak and others, in the subaltern position, we encounter a double bind. To be heard is precisely to cease, in some significant sense, one's occupation of an alternate position, so that one must have evacuated that position, however momentarily, in order to have been heard. In terms of Emmanuel Levinas's saying, which subsides into a said, what is at stake is the impossibility of remaining true to the ethical impulse that gets converted into a static, congealed position or statement. Psychoanalytic discourse can insist all it wants on the fact that the phallus guarantees the law, but this somehow misses the point. The point is how to elaborate what in a more Derridean register we might call the law of the law. If instrinsic to the operation and elaboration of the symbolic is not only the necessity of abject positions, together with the impossibility of their articulation within the systems they maintain, but also the production of new abjects, it might be wise to pay attention to the logic of this operation, rather than merely resting on its authority.

Since the legitimacy of the symbolic is so far bound up with paternal authority in psychoanalytic scenarios, and since the possibilities of identification are so intimately tied to the same authority, the question of the priority of sexual difference (vis-à-vis race, for example) cannot be adequately raised without raising it as a question of the very possibility of language, representation, intelligibility as such. The very identity of the subject understood psychoanalytically, along with the sanctioning of its possible identifications, is enmeshed in a sexually marked distribution of the imaginary to the feminine register, and the symbolic to the paternal. The possibility of language—the possibility of a subject designating, thematizing, desiring an object, is bound up with foundational fantasies, the effective transmission of which are themselves bound up with what constitute the possibilities of reification. Until those foundational fantasies are challenged, there will be no genuinely new possibilities for the symbolic. This is why Irigaray's challenge to the phallogocentric economy is so important. For her, until there is a possibility of the couple, of a relationship between two that is not always already overdetermined by the one—a relation in which one member of the couple is implicitly an inferior copy of the other, who occupies the position of the law—there is no possibility of genuine multiplicity or difference. While there is no question that in her formulation of sexuate rights, Irigaray falls prey to racism, and to a perpetuation of the invisibility of whiteness, she also issues a challenge to both psychoanalytic theory and philosophy that has yet to find an adequate response. That challenge concerns the possibility of formulating a new symbolic that does not submit to monological, totalizing discourse—phallic or otherwise—a challenge which itself depends on mobilizing a social imaginary that traverses the fantasy of the one. This fantasy is heavily dependent—whether in the phallic, psychoanalytic myth or that of social contract theory—on an imaginary body image that is masculine, white, privileged, and enabled.

The phallic logic of the symbolic order appeals to a monological meaning that suppresses differences. Even the logic of hegemony tends to replicate this monologism insofar as it posits a unilateralism inherent in dominant discourse that doesn't sufficiently recognize the different logics spawned by hegemonic processes, which create genuine paths of resistance. These paths of resistance create new versions of the master/slave dynamic in their attempt to establish themselves as legitimate, so that even progressive politics of democracy, far from being immune from divisive relations, is replete with them. By refusing to allow particulars to stand merely for the many in relation to the one, Irigaray sees herself not only as subverting the Platonic model, which assumes the priority of the one over the many, but also what she construes as an inversion of that model—the priority of the multiplicity over the one.[2] Thus, Irigaray implicitly targets a politics of multiculturalism for merely overturning the Platonic model, emphasizing the many over the one without challenging the mimetic relation that remains between them. Politically, her error is to fail to apply the logic she so assiduously applies to the constitutive exclusion of the feminine to raced others—or to other others. Yet one cannot sustain a plausible argument to this effect without taking on board Irigaray's challenge to a politics of multiculturalism that remains immersed in a mere reversal of the Platonic tradition.

Irigaray's claim that sexual difference needs to be thought for the first time as a relationship between two, in which one is irreducible to the other, does indeed provide an accurate analysis of a problem confronting feminist theory and practice, which remains largely driven by the institutionalization of feminism as white, middle-class, and heterosexist. It reflects the dominant values of patriarchy, merely requiring that they be extended to a select, privileged group of women, rather than demanding fundamental social change. In this way, the success of feminism consists in its mimicking, rather than challenging, the order it calls into question. In this sense Irigaray is right to call for the need to think sexual difference for the first time, rather than merely replicating the already extant privileges of race, class, and sexuality by extending them to women. The question remains, What authorizes the privilege of sexual difference as Irigaray's starting point? Is it anything other than the historical accident of having been born a white European woman, anything other than the dogmatism of a European feminism that necessitates the central role Irigaray accords to this difference over other differences?

I suggest that the fault lies on the one hand in her acquiescence to the Hegelian legacy of marking civil society as masculine and designating nature as akin to women, an association that she accepts even as she tries to undermine it. Irigaray is far from alone among Western feminists in having inherited from Hegel political categories in a way that presents the public/private distinction as if it were solely a matter of sexual difference, as if its strategic mapping were not also always a matter of class and race. On the other hand, the fault lies in Irigaray's unquestioned allegiance to the psychoanalytic dictum that language acquisition is structurally bound up with sexual difference. However much she distances herself from Lacan, she accepts that the very conditions of intelligibility are bound up with sexual difference, and that is why sexual difference remains for Irigaray the foundational site of transformation, the site of excavation at which we must begin, in order to explore the possibility of introducing a new symbolic. Yet what if sexual difference itself were constituted on the basis of a repressed discourse of racial difference, what if psychoanalytic discourse itself is formulated on the basis of the repression of class difference? What if our very notions of male and female have come to be concepts only on the basis of a violent repression of racialized, classed, and transgendered others? What, in other words, if the very terms in which sexual difference has become legible as the dominant psychoanalytic category of meaning are terms constructed on the basis of a culturally specific Oedipalized family that privileges sexual difference over other differences, by repressing other differences that are therefore not permitted to be as salient? Sexual difference would have come to stand for a host of other differences, including race and class.[3] There are numerous passages about "primitives" to be found in Freud, which for the most part psychoanalytic critics gloss over.[4]

Is there a sense in which Irigaray's hyperbolic rejoinder to Freud and Lacan mirrors back writ large the question of sexual difference only by continuing to repress class and race difference? I suggest there is, and that when Irigaray insists on the foundational character of sexual difference, she recognizes something important—not the foundational character of sexual difference, but the formal problematic of thinking difference without relapsing into another version of the same. That is, Irigaray's hyperbolic strategy exposes the immense difficulty of thinking the relation to the other as a relation to the genuinely new, different, other—thinking duality or multiplicity without reverting to the same. That she locates this effort in the privileging of sexual difference is problematic inasmuch as it mirrors the Eurocentric privileging of sexual difference by psychoanalytic theory—which is itself only possible due to the repression of the extent to which colonial expansion has facilitated the flourishing of Western capitalism, and produced the rest of the world as Europe's other. That Irigaray succeeds in dramatizing the problem is crucial: she exposes the rhetoric of the West *as* a formal problem.

It is a formal problematic with which Irigaray's analysis of the philosophical relationship between the one and the many, which so preoccupied Plato, is also concerned. Irigaray's critique of "Western philosophy" for assuming "a singular subject" comes into its own in *Democracy Begins between Two*. With a nod to Michel Foucault's work, Irigaray acknowledges that there was some attempt on the part of the still imperialist subject—who might have been "a little less imperialistic"—to admit the existence of "identities different from his own," that is, "children, for example, or mad people, savages and workers" (2001, 121). This acknowledgment is reminiscent of an observation Irigaray had already made in *This Sex Which Is Not One*, where she says,

> If the unconscious consists, at present and in part, of the repressed/censured feminine element of history, the repressed/censured component of the logic of consciousness, is this unconscious not still, finally a *property of discourse*? Whatever blows Freud may have struck against discursive logic, does not the unconscious still belong to the system of this logic? And does not this logic, which is beginning in a certain way to exhaust itself, find *reserves* for itself in the unconscious as in any form of "otherness": savages, children, the insane, women?[5]

The question of the unconscious of psychoanalysis, and its othering, is also a question about its history:

> The problem is that psychoanalysis does not question, or questions far too little, its own historical determinants. . . . So long as psychoanalysis does not interpret its entrapment within a certain type of regime of property, within a certain type of discourse (to simplify, let us say that of metaphysics), within a certain type of religious mythology, it cannot raise the question of female sexuality. (125)

What then would it mean for psychoanalysis—which itself is embedded in a series of discursive, ultimately metaphysical assumptions—to become answerable for its historical determinants? Irigaray takes the question of sexual difference to be fundamental by reading it as the site at which there is a negotiation between nature and culture, one that has resulted in a systematic privileging of culture over nature, and one that has operated in favor of masculinity to the detriment of femininity. Claiming for itself one side of this divide—that of culture—patriarchy has relegated femininity to nature. It has done so on the basis of identifying itself with the productive sphere, and requiring the feminine to occupy the reproductive sphere. Irigaray's response is to take up the organizing opposition "state of nature" versus "civil state," and to contest the way in which the first term has been used as a way of containing women to the sphere of reproduction, while the second term has been construed as the exclusive preserve of men. Her solution is to argue in favor of a series of rights that would specify the female subject as a subject who partakes in the civil sphere in her own terms. Irigaray's earlier work shows her to be fully aware of the difficulties inherent in such a project, insofar as it requires the normative stipulation of feminine subjectivity. In *This Sex*, for example, Irigaray is circumspect about the dangers of defining the feminine as a concept. She says: "To claim that the feminine can be expressed in the form of a concept is to allow oneself to be caught up again in a system of 'masculine' representations, in which women are trapped in a system of meaning which serves the auto-affection of the (masculine) subject. If it is really a matter of calling 'femininity' into question, there is still no need to elaborate another 'concept'—unless a woman is renouncing her sex and wants to speak like men" (1985, 122–23). What, then, has changed, such that Irigaray is impelled to offer precisely the kind of conceptual delineation for women against which she had earlier warned? I think the answer lies in Irigaray's call for the development of new symbolics, the danger of which is that these new symbolics become in their turn hegemonic.

In contesting the way in which femininity has been required to occupy the sphere of nature or the private sphere, while masculinity has stood for culture, or the public/political sphere, Irigaray is following the lead of Hegel. Yet the predominance of the public/private divide in feminist theory itself occludes the racial and class dynamics that have been both constitutive of, and rendered invisible by, the claims of white feminist theory to legitimate itself by appealing to the public/private distinction as crucial.[6] Let me follow through this problematic with reference to Irigaray's discussion of, and dependence on, Marx, who also of course inherits Hegel's problematic foundational distinctions, even as he infuses them with new meaning. The movement that Marx follows through in his discussion of commodity fetishism operates as a model for Irigaray's analysis of the role played by women in psychoanalysis. In commodity fetishism, commodities take on a life of their own, becoming the master of men (instead of vice versa).

The aspect of Marx's commodity fetishism that I want to emphasize is its thoroughly historical nature. Commodity production, Marx tells us, is a "mode of social production" that is "historically determined."[7] It is a mode of production in which the "personal relations" characteristic of the relation between serf and lord in medieval Europe become "disguised." It is no longer the case that "every serf knows that what he expends in the service of his lord is a specific quantity of his own personal labour-power" (170). Rather, the "money form" of the world of commodities "conceals the social character of private labour and the social relations between the individual workers, by making those relations appear as relations between material objects, instead of revealing them plainly" (168–69). What determines the proportions in which products can be exchanged is merely a matter of custom, and as soon as "these proportions have attained a certain customary stability, they appear to result from the nature of the products, so that, for instance, one ton of iron and two ounces of gold appear to be equal in value" (167). Is the value that Freud attaches to the penis susceptible to such a reading? Could it be that Freud has made the mistake of naturalizing the phallus by taking it to provide the gold standard by which all pleasure is to be measured, such that he even finds confirmation in biology and science?

Values thus take on the appearance of being fixed, given, or unchangeable. "The forms which stamp products as commodities and which are therefore the preliminary requirements for the circulation of commodities, already possess the fixed quality of natural forms of social life before man seeks to give an account, not of their historical character, for in his eyes they are immutable, but of their content and meaning" (168). In fact, however, one only has to compare the form of commodity production to other social forms of labor organization, and the mystical quality whereby values appear to be fixed, and whereby men appear to be governed by commodities that seem to be endowed with transcendent powers, vanishes. "The whole mystery of commodities, all the magic and necromancy that surrounds the products of labour on the basis of commodity production, vanishes therefore as soon as we come to other forms of production" (169). Similarly, I suggest, until and unless other forms of production—those created by feminist imaginaries, for example—create new symbolics, which not only circulate but also gain a certain legitimacy, the mystery of the phallus, and the natural status it confers on its particular version of the symbolic, will not be exposed in its particularity. The problem is that the process of gaining legitimacy tends to proceed by way of spawning new abjects, so that the very practices through which new symbolics are generated and sustained as meaningful are liable to operate to the detriment and invisibility of those not specifically articulated as subject in need of legitimation. Hence, the production of feminist symbolics, unless they proceed with the specific intent of correcting racial biases, will reproduce them, in much the same way that Freud's theory of fetishism rests upon an abjection of homosexuality.

To return, however briefly, to the notion of commodity fetishism, and in particular, the *historical* character of this mode of production, helps to illuminate the sense in which psychoanalysis protects itself from the kind of encounter with alterity that Marxist theory appeals to. For Marx, it is when commodity fetishism, as the mode of production that characterizes capitalism, is confronted with another mode of production, that its particularity comes to fore. In this confrontation, the mythical and enigmatic quality of the commodity, the way in which it appears to stand for something natural, is made to account for itself. Here then lies the possibility of rendering the possibility of change, and here too lies the insight into the historical character of social forms of organization that is covered over by commodity fetishism, which presents itself as if it were natural, and therefore universal and impossible to change.[8] What would it take for psychoanalytic theory to be capable of a similar confrontation? Commodity fetishism, in particular the way in which Marx returns to Aristotle in his discussion of the phenomenon, provides a way of raising a crucial question concerning the priority of sexual difference over racial classifications with regard to philosophy. With these comments in mind, I turn to Irigaray's essay, "The Poverty of Psychoanalysis."

Recall that Marx wrote an essay under the title of "The Poverty of Philosophy" (*Misère de la philosophie: réponse à la philosophie de la misère de M. Proudhon*), first published in French in 1847. A familiarity with Marx's essay reveals clearly that it serves Irigaray as a model for her critique of the poverty of psychoanalysis. She transposes many of Marx's concerns into her polemic against Lacan. Irigaray specifies that language is understood by the Lacanian psychoanalysts she is addressing to be governed by the masculine, that the "subject always speaks the same gender," since the Phallus is "the emblem, the signifier and the *product* of a single sex," and proceeds to challenge her gentlemen addressees.[9] She provides a commentary on the title of her essay, which she develops throughout the essay, in which she bets that its significance will be lost on many, who will not be able to "understand this title, what it evokes, what it refers to, what memory gives it meaning, in which history it is inscribed, in which discourses it has already had a place, what desires it speaks or counterfeits" (79).

Irigaray predicts the reactions of her imagined Lacanian readers, suggesting that they will be prevented from understanding the reference in her title by "at least two systems of screens. Of censorship or of repression" (79). The first reaction will be a psychic "repudiation" that will protest "in no way does psychoanalysis suffer from poverty [*la misère*]." She reads this reaction as "resistance" (79).

> You refuse to admit that the unconscious—your concept of the unconscious—did not spring fully armed from Freud's head,

> that it was not produced *ex nihilo* at the end of the nineteenth century, emerging suddenly to reimpose its truth on the whole of history—world history, at that—past, present and future. The unconscious is revealed as such, heard as such, spoken as such and interpreted as such within a tradition. It has a place within, by and through a culture. (1991, 80)

Marx wrote, in an observation that signals the importance of his essay, "This book contains in embryo what after a labor of twenty years became the theory that was developed in *Capital*."[10] The essay, which begins with a discussion of the distinction between use value and exchange value that was to become so central to Marx's conception of commodity fetishism, is a polemic against Proudhon and other economists such as Ricardo. One of the major points Marx is concerned to make is that Proudhon misunderstands Hegel, merely reproducing surface contradictions as if it were dialectical thought (see Marx 1976, 162–63; 167–68). Irigaray adopts Marx's model in her essay, shows how their Lacanian works reproduce a system that claims to be universal, immutable, and applicable to both sexes, when in fact it represses, and misrecognizes the desire of one sex, much as bourgeois categories of thought at the hands of the economists are taken to be fixed, when in fact they only apply to the capitalist class. The reality for those who produce the wealth, namely the proletariat, is very different (see Marx 1976, 176).

Does Irigaray short-circuit her interrogation of the "cultural capital and general economy" underlying psychoanalysis by limiting her analysis to an "analogical" interpretation of Marx's categories? Irigaray anticipates this objection in a footnote. In "Women on the Market," Irigaray draws a parallel between the enigma that constitutes commodities for Marx and the enigma of women according to Freud. Women are objects of exchange in patriarchal societies. Just as commodities are only valued in relation to one another under the commodity form of production, in which the capitalist economy ensures that the exchange of products creates profit, so women are only valued insofar as they can be circulated in a symbolic economy whose terms are dictated by men and for men. Irigaray draws out the (male) homosexual character of the laws of circulation, in which women only figure as commodities that confirm the value and importance of men.

In the footnote Irigaray says, "Will it be objected that this interpretation is analogical by nature? I accept this question, on condition that it be addressed also, and in the first place, to Marx's analysis of commodities. Did not Aristotle, a 'great thinker' according to Marx, determine the relation of form to matter by analogy with the relation between masculine and feminine? Returning to the question of the difference between the sexes would amount instead, then, to going back through analogism" (1985, 174, n. 3). This argument suggests that, because the fundamental categories of Western metaphysics, such as form and matter, were associated with the masculine and the feminine respectively, this association has had a determining effect on our ways of thinking, an implication that is undoubtedly true. Yet, one could equally go back to Aristotle's *Politics* to find arguments that emphasize the capacity of slaves for bodily labor, comparing their utility to that of tame animals and suggesting that slaves differ from masters to the same extent that bodies differ from souls and beasts from men. Aristotle also, of course, denies slaves the capacity to deliberate (see 1252a33–1260a12). If this is not quite the racist thinking of the modern state, certainly Aristotle's classifications are concerned with different, ostensibly natural types. While some men in the polis have the luxury to stop and think what they are doing, as Arendt would put it, others, whose lives are governed by necessity, do not. Where then does this necessity come from, who imposes it, and how does it come not only to permit the luxury of thought to others, but also to shape that thought in racist, sexist, or classist ways that then become indistinguishable from apparently reflective thought itself? That is, what are the maneuvers by which theoretical reflection protects itself, by immunizing itself from the capacity to be self-critical about that which might endanger its hegemonic purchase? Designating certain individuals as incapable of deliberation, and then importing this justification into a metaphysics of the state, as if that state were not always already constructed according to political imperatives, seems to involve a sleight of hand worthy of interrogation.

Marx makes the following observation in his discussion of value, when he is trying to explain why Aristotle did not go as far as he might have in understanding exchange value. According to Marx Aristotle lacked "a concept of value" as determined by human labor because he lived in a society in which labor power could not be seen as equally applicable to all:

> Towards the bed, the house represents something equal, in so far as it represents what is really equal, both in the bed and the house. And that is—human labor.
>
> Aristotle himself was unable to extract this fact, that in the form of commodity-values, all labour is expressed as equal human labour and therefore as labour of equal quality, by inspection from the form of value, because Greek society was founded on the labor of slaves, hence had as its natural basis the inequality of men and of their labour-powers. (1976, 152)

The historical limitation that Marx identifies in Aristotle's social imaginary is that the commodity-form does not present itself as universal, but remains particular. For Irigaray the Western model of the subject is fundamentally masculine. What determines, then, Irigaray's decision to see Aristotle's remarks about form and matter as decisive in relation to sexual difference, but not to see his remarks about slavery as crucial? In order to take genuine account of difference, is it not necessary to keep in play at one and the same time race, class, sexual, and gender difference? Rather than taking one as foundational, and deriving the others from it, what is called for is that we think through how feminist theory continues to privilege whiteness so long as it does not systematically confront this privileging. Where Irigaray's analysis remains powerful, even indispensable, is in its identification of the immense difficulty we have, as theorists and practitioners, in resisting the monological impulse that reduces all difference to the same. Witness the facility with which the discourse of fetishism has replicated itself across cultural theory, including feminist theory, race theory, and film theory. Freud and Lacan are contested by theorists who then go on to recycle their fetishistic theories without contesting the masculinist, heterosexist imaginary that informs them. Within the field of postcolonial theory, Frantz Fanon and Homi Bhabha are representative of this tendency.[11] In the apparently infinitely adaptable trope of fetishism we can identify a lasting truth that Irigaray's work helps us see: the phallus is uncannily malleable and in its capacity to reinvent itself, to prove so abundantly flexible, it assures its authority. The anxiety of castration retains a privileged place, forestalling or repudiating any other source of anxiety as authentic. Following Fanon, Bhabha can appropriate the discourse of fetishism for postcolonial theory, but this appropriation precisely leaves in place, rather than contesting, the interpretation of women's genitalia as horrific, traumatizing, and in need of disguise—in need, that is, of a fetish. Race is thereby theorized as a fetish that covers over the originary wound of sexual difference, without confronting the myth of the same, the economy of *hommo-sexualité* that legitimates and informs it. This is not to deny that, within the limitations of this discourse, Fanon and Bhabha have illuminated the dynamic of race oppression with impressive facility. Rather, it is to point out that in doing so their analyses repeat the occlusion of women as a sex in our own right, the blind spot of an old asymmetry that Irigaray so eloquently elaborated in Freud's texts.

Marx can analyze effectively the alienation of class relations through the spectrum of commodity fetishism, but only through a sustained neglect of sexual difference. What this suggests is not the foundational—even if provisional—character of sexual difference, but the difficulty, or well nigh impossibility of thinking through more than one difference at a time, without reducing them to one ostensibly foundational model. The theoretical question this prompts is this: What is it about the nature of social oppression and its intellectual analyses that lends itself so repeatedly to a failure to sustain a serious interrogation on multiple fronts? Is there simply too much anxiety in thinking or taking on more than one difference at a time? Is it characteristic of the form of intellectual thought itself, and philosophy in particular, to be incapable of confronting genuine diversity, difference, or complexity, without reducing it to an overall scheme that proceeds according to a foundational priority of one type of difference over others? Does such a formal problematic find itself reproduced in politics?

Given the frequency with which attempts at political enfranchisement resort to tactics that, whether consciously or unconsciously, malign or abject other minority groups, one might conclude that there is indeed an ineluctable tendency for even apparently radical politics not only to blind themselves to the claims of other minority groups, but even to enforce the minority status of such groups all the more stringently in the effort to secure a viable political platform. The value of Irigaray's analysis lies in her trenchant critique of the facility with which the alterity of others is reducible to an ideological mirror-reflection of oneself.

## Notes

1. Judith Butler, *Bodies that Matter. On the Discursive Limits of "Sex"* (New York: Routledge, 1993), 36.

2. See Luce Irigaray, *Democracy Begins between Two*, trans. Kirsteen Anderson (New York: Routledge, 2001), 128–29.

3. Sander Gilman has established the importance of Freud's Jewishness for a theoretical reading of his work, and Anne McClintock has shown how a repressed narrative about class subtends Freud's overt narrative about maternity and femininity. See *The Case of Sigmund Freud: Medicine and Identity at the Fin de Siècle* (Baltimore: Johns Hopkins University Press, 1993).

4. While it is not my purpose here, elsewhere I have started to track the insistent references to the primitive that accompanies Freud's discourse about femininity, particularly in relation to fetishism.

5. Luce Irigaray, *This Sex Which Is Not One*, trans. Catherine Porter with Carolyn Burke (Ithaca: Cornell University Press, 1985), 124.

6. Anannya Bhattacharjee, "The Public/Private Mirage: Mapping Homes and Undomesticating Violence Work in the South Asian Immigrant Community," in *Feminist Genealogies, Colonial Legacies, Democratic Futures*, ed. M. Jacqui Alexander and Chandra Talpade Mohanty (New York: Routledge, 1997).

7. Karl Marx, *Capital: A Critique of Political Economy*, vol. 1, trans. Ben Fowkes (New York: Vintage Books, 1977), 169.

8. See Donovan Miyasaki, "The Confusion of Marxian and Freudian Fetishism in Adorno and Benjamin," *Philosophy Today* 46 (2002): 429–43.

9. Irigaray, "The Poverty of Psychoanalysis," in *The Irigaray Reader*, ed. Margaret Whitford (Cambridge, MA: Basil Blackwell, 1991), 79.

10. Karl Marx, "The Poverty of Philosophy," in *Karl Marx, Frederick Engels, Collected Works*, Vol. 6. (New York: International Publishers, 1976), xviii.

11. Frantz Fanon, *Black Skin, White Masks*, trans. Charles Lam Markmann (New York: Grove Press, 1967); Homi Bhabha "DissemiNation: Time, Narrative, and the Margins of the Modern Nation," in *Nation and Narration*, ed. Homi K. Bhabha (New York: Routledge, 1990).

# Chapter 17

# Who Cares about the Greeks?

## Uses and Misuses of Tradition in the Articulation of Difference and Plurality

Eleni Varikas

> And no way to find what happened then—
> None at all—unless, of course, you improvise
>
> —Eavan Bowland

> *A quelques ajouts ou réductions près, notre imaginaire fonctionne toujours selon le schéma qui se mat en place à travers les mythologies et les tragédies grecques*
>
> —Luce Irigaray

It is hard to repress a feeling of uneasiness each time ancient Greece appears as the universal matrix of the modern psyche, each time that its mythologies and tragedies are assumed to provide the scheme according to which our imaginary always functions. This is not a matter of undue reverence to "white dead men." It is rather a reflex acquired by many people of my generation in Greece, a sort of automatic response to universalizing assumptions which bring back compulsively and with Proustian precision a taste of origins, declamations on ancestry, or, worse, repudiation of any nonconventional approach to tradition as "un-Greek" or "un-national beliefs." *Whose* "imaginary"? one is tempted to ask, thinking of the way in which we were schooled in understanding mythology as mere description of the past. A past in which the labors of Hercules had the same cognitive status as the Peloponnesian War or, for that matter, the nineteenth-century national revolution, set as they were in a continuous narrative—origins of a mythical grandeur that "we" had to, were destined to, recover. No wonder that in the Greece of the 1950s and 1960s, love of the classics had to be hidden as a sign of conformism if not outright conservatism.

Yet the entrances into mythologies and tragedies are at least as manifold and inscrutable as the ways of the almighty. Mine were opened by my grandmother, a refugee schoolteacher from Cappadocia; brought up, herself, with stories from the *Odyssey* narrated in Turkish, she had been sent to a college in Smyrna with a scholarship to study Greek, then came back to initiate her Turkish-speaking community to what, in the irredentist discourse of the time, was called the "long-forgotten idiom of our ancestors." Historical events interrupted so commendable a mission; but she eventually managed to introduce her granddaughter to the classics and to lastingly associate their "mythologies and tragedies" with her unique blend of Enlightenment devotion to the distinction between mythology and history and fascination for the never-ending interpretive potential, the complexity and openness of myth.

This is to say that the question I am asking here is not who *cares* about "the Greeks" but rather *who* cares, that is, what are the political uses and the strategies of legitimization underlying this interest, the explicit and implicit ways in which our readings and interpretations mediate between the needs of the moment and the authority of the past.[1] From this angle, I propose to question some major problems with the ways in which genealogies and interpretations of myth are used in the writings of Luce Irigaray to shape female imaginaries but also actual political strategies. I shall argue that both her theoretical and methodological approach and her actual interpretations of "tragedies and mythologies" point to an instrumental and conventional use of tradition; that they support a perception of "sexual difference" that reduces all other modes of difference to the heterosexual relation, thus restricting the utopian horizon of future possibilities of change in gender relations and other configurations of power. Rather than the radical de-authorization of tradition promised by the philosopher's earlier writings, and which some commentators still seem to discern in her thought,[2] in the writings of the late 1980s and the 1990s, it is rather the authoritativeness of tradition that is summoned to plead for the privileged, all-encompassing but also clear-cut character of sexual difference set up, *ni plus ni moins*, as "the most appropriate content for the universal."[3]

> Sexual differetnce is an immediate natural given and it is a real and irreducible component of the universal. The whole of humankind is composed of women and men *and of nothing else*. The problem of race is, in fact, a secondary problem—except from a geographical point of view [*sic*] . . . and the same goes for other cultural diversities—religious, economic, and political ones. Sexual difference probably represents the most universal question we can address. Our era is faced with the task of dealing with this issue.[4]

It is this utterance "*of nothing else*" and its theoretical and political implications that interest me here. It calls attention to the relation between the rigid, closed character of the theoretical posture and a (literally) conservative appeal to tradition for univocal and unifying "either/or" answers. Both descriptive and prescriptive, as in the good old gender order, "sexual difference" and the division into two sexes is that which is assumed as a natural given and which has nevertheless to be realized in the double sense of "conceiving vividly as real" and of accomplishing. "Sexual difference" is a "positive fact" and, at the same time, that which needs to be established *beyond any contestation*. This could account for the otherwise puzzling retreat of the author of *Speculum*, to the "objective" discourse of science as "the ultimate source of legitimization";[5] the declaratory, axiomatic "neutrality" of sentences such as "Nature . . . is at least *two*: masculine and feminine," "Air and sexual difference are perhaps the two indispensable dimensions of/to life"[6]—which would have been dismissed as commonplaces coming from any other pen—aim to "establish" the *truth* of the world's two-ness. In Irigaray's more didactic texts of the last decades, "truth" and "error" are indeed central categories for the treatment of theoretical disagreement, almost always eschewed or explained away as "errors of translation," erroneous interpretations, ignorance, or incapacity to understand.[7] I don't contend that Irigaray is easy to understand or translate. What I am saying is that any posture, experience, or desire that tends to contest the "reality" of the sacrosanct two-ness of the world or risk to unsettle the ordered clarity of the division, is ethically devalued as the irresponsible whim of the privileged, in a vein that could be envied by the most authoritarian and dogmatic traditions.

> Some of our prosperous or naive contemporaries, women and men, would like to wipe out this difference by resorting to monosexuality, to the unisex and to what is called identification: even if I am bodily a man or woman, I can identify with, and so be, the other sex. This new *opium of the people* annihilates the other in the *illusion* of a reduction to identity, equality and sameness, especially between man and woman, the ultimate anchorage of *real* alterity. The dream of dissolving material, corporeal or social identity leads to a whole set of *delusions*, to endless and unresolvable conflicts, to a war of images or reflections and to powers being accredited to somebody or other more for imaginary or narcissistic reasons *than for their actual abilities*.[8]

Here, the dismissal of the aspiration to self-definition is not based uniquely on political considerations, which, after all, may always be questioned and reconsidered; it has a strong scientistic component delegitimizing in advance any attempt to disidentification with "really existing" gender norms. Besides being politically dangerous, the "dream of dissolving material, corporeal or social identity," in other words, of going beyond the prison-house of gender, is also a "delusion": a false belief maintaining—despite indisputable evidence to the contrary (i.e., our "actual abilities")—that we have the power to defy anatomy in order to reconfigure *who* we are or *who* we may become through the sheer force of desire and imagination.

It has been argued that, apart from "the minimal natural determination that sex is two," sexual identity is paradoxically without content[9] because it is also formed by the spiritual work that occurs through one's *respect for* the other sex and the collective nurturing of cultural values that are "faithful to one's own sex." According to Irigaray, Simone de Beauvoir notwithstanding, I *am* born a woman, and yet *I must still become this woman that I am by nature.*[10] But why do I *have to* become this woman? And if what I have to become is "contentless" *how do I know that I am not unfaithful to my sex?* Pheng Cheah and Elizabeth Grosz argue that *respect for* the other sex, and *fidelity to* one's own, are not necessarily incompatible with *desire* for the same sex. Yet, the strong, aggressively (hetero) normative discourse of the last decades leaves hardly any space for such liberalities as it calls back to order any "capricious" desire or "immature" temptation to pre-oedipal sexuality "exercised to the detriment of becoming human as a genus, as two genders."[11] Here we have come a long way from that Sex which was not one. Indeed, as Irigaray points out, "Lack of definition of the alterity of the other has paralysed thought in an idealist dream, appropriate to the male subject alone." In this context, "the neuter of the lack or of the loss of identity" exists not only "in unfaithfulness to one's gender,"[12] but also in infidelity to political autonomy. But whose political autonomy? If, for the philosopher, a really autonomous *we* implies *always* "being two," the recognition of two differences, man and woman, the restitution of such a *we* is a specifically female ethical task because "women are more destined [*sic*] to the relation to the other. Because of this *quality* of their subjectivity," it is for them to open up the horizon of the one, of the same, even the multiple. The recognition of otherness is therefore first and foremost *their* recognition of "man's" otherness. Such a move, we are told, is a "necessary stage in the affirmation of their [i.e., women's] autonomy," allowing the transition "from a natural identity to a cultural and civil identity without disavowing the/ir nature (*la/leur nature*)."[13]

What is at stake here is not whether Irigaray's theory is essentialist, whether the fully sexuate culture she advocates is utopian or dystopian or even its naïve soteriology, but the authoritarian element in it. If, as we are reminded, loyalty to one's gender, implies "one way to love and to engender, one way of desiring and thinking," then it is not only our prosperous and naïve contemporaries who may shudder at the idea of a world's two-ness restoring the *one* among women, but all the other *others* who are thus expelled not only from the right to self-definition, but also from the very concept of an autonomously defined *we*. For this conception of sexual difference reiterates the privileging of the heterosexual couple, thus imposing a heterosexual prism of, and primacy over, gender, sexual, racial, and class politics.[14] Furthermore, Irigaray's perspective is not deployed as one out of many possible visions of radical change within the perspective of a dialogical process of self-definition among women. Such a reading disregards not only the heavily injunctive quality of its enunciation, but also the very historicity of the categories it mobilizes, the institutional and political contexts which "both accrue a certain ontological weight and meaning and force and inherit it."[15]

It is a source of wonder, in this instance, that many commentaries on Irigaray's work across the ocean take so little notice of the ways in which her writings in the last twenty years have developed within, and become a part of, a discourse of "experts" aiming to explain to the profane the *limits of democracy and self-institution,* as they are paradigmatically illustrated by the possibilities and impossibilities of change in gender destinies within the political community. Indeed, the gradual abandonment of negativity in Irigaray's critique of patriarchy, the shift from a contentless perception of sexual difference into a heavily positive definition of "woman" take shape in a period marked by the growing visibility of gender and sexuality in European mainstreaming policies. In France, this period has also been marked by a legitimization crisis of the so-called *universalisme à la française* and its politics of representation and with a coextensive crisis of national identity. The mobilizations aiming at the recognition of the colonial and racist crimes of the past, the struggles against xenophobic immigration policies and racist discrimination against citizens of colonial origin, the campaigns for equal representation of men and women in elected assemblies, the adoption of the PACS (the civil solidarity pact recognizing partnerships between individuals independent of sex) and the outburst of homophobia it gave way to,[16] and finally, the heated debate over equal rights to adoption and lineage (*filiation*) for same-sex couples, have situated gender at the heart of what Henri Meschonnic so accurately refers to as "the market of decline" today.[17]

The market of decline has, of course, always prospered with gender anxieties, but the rhetoric out of which it used to grow has traditionally been conservative rather than liberal or radical. The new "French" language of sexual order as it has flourished in the last decades under the pens of liberal intellectuals and a number of well-known feminist scholars, has everything to disenchant the last believers in the long-standing fantasy of French sexual permissiveness. Speaking with the authority of prestigious academic institutions and, sometimes, of their known feminist convictions, anthropologists, psychoanalysts, philosophers, social scientists, and historians from different political horizons have been joining in public praise of the political, psychic, and civilizational merits of sexual difference and the complementariness of the sexes it implies. Deployed as the national trademark of French political exceptionalism, "*la-différence-des-sexes*" has become a language on the peculiarities of the French, opposing to the "Anglo-Saxon" mores of gender strife the harmonious commerce (or reconciliation) of the sexes, historically favored by the unique blend of a woman-friendly "political culture" going back to court society and leading through the French Revolution to the Third Republic. At the same time, "*la-différence-des-sexes,*" as it manifests itself in dominant family arrangements, the system of kinship, heterosexual love, and motherhood are universalized, deployed as anthropological givens that any political understanding should conform to.[18] Exorcising the internal division of the *République*, as paradigmatically incarnated in gender antagonism, the specter of sexual un-differentiation brandished, once more, against any attempt of trespassing gender or sexual boundaries and territories, exorcises at the same time the racial, class, and other forms of social unrest. Illustrating the limits of democracy and self-institution, the division into *two sexes* has joined the rest of primordial and unmediated truths such as race, ethnicity, culture, religion providing not only an insuperable limit to political action but also a universal key into the interpretation of past and present.

The power and efficiency of this ideological configuration was first revealed in the terms in which the campaign in favor of *parity* was launched, fought, and eventually adopted, at least formally, by the French parliament as a law requiring equal numbers of men and women candidates. Unlike most other countries where mobilizations for women's presence in elected assemblies were fought—often with clearly better results[19]—as a plain issue of affirmative action, the campaign in France systematically refrained from establishing any connection between women's exclusion from politics and that of other oppressed groups. Avoiding a frontal contest against the doctrine of *one and indivisible* body politic on its general, exclusive dynamics, the dominant argument stressed, instead, the constitutive two-ness of this body—*e duibus unum*—women, it was argued, are not *a category* as are, say, immigrants, gays, ex-colonial subjects; they are not a *minority*, but half of humankind and, *consequently*, half of the body politic. Therefore, in integrating women *qua women* the indivisibility of the Republic did not have to be challenged. Gradually abandoning the ground of social justice and democratic rights, the parity campaign opted for the more consensual themes of modernization and women's specific qualities, promising to miraculously regenerate national and international politics.

Predictably, the first miracle of the constitutionally consecrated Consubstantial and Indivisible *Binity* was not gender equality in politics, but the lasting establishment in the political arena of the new experts who, after having enthusiastically backed parity on the grounds of humankind's duality, now used the same line of argument to stress the vital necessity—for the survival of civilization—to preserve sexual difference and the symbolic division it entails against the demand for gay rights to adoption and *filiation*. Shutting out the voices and expectations of other oppressed groups from what could have been a legal "precedent" for affirmative action and recognition of the constitutive plurality of the Republic, the institutionalization of political duality—represented as two legs of a single body and yet not interchangeable[20]—enthroned the heterosexual couple and family, as *the* acceptable and recognized form of family but also the unique source of an ethical stance "necessary for the existence of civilization."[21]

It is within this institutional, political, and ideological configuration, in which Luce Irigaray has been, herself, both an active participant (on the national and European level) and a theoretical reference, that her evolution in the last decades should be revisited and evaluated. Seen from the perspective of the institutionalization of sexual duality and the modes of legitimization it made possible, Irigaray's ontologization of sexual difference[22] and the exhortative, alarmist style in which it is phrased, operate as an injunction to live up to the responsibilities and obligations imposed on us by nature, whether the latter is presented as the cosmos, human nature, or the nature of things. Before being psychological, biological, sociological, or epistemological," sexual difference is, for her, ontological.[23] Even if, on a purely "empirical" level, difference can be established between women (or between men), the radical incommensurability whose recognition makes us able to rethink (and respect) plurality emerges *only* in a relation between a man and a woman. Why this is so? Irigaray concedes that it is difficult to answer the question, seeking refuge in the all too "feminine" mode of the inexpressible and the intuitive ("It is not the same thing," "I don't know if this is easy to understand"). "There is an irreducible mystery between man and woman, which participates in the order of being"[24] —a mystery that, we are told, Simone de Beauvoir and contemporary movements for gay rights were unable to understand! Yet, she adds, it's "because I am able to situate *there* the difference and the negative which I will never surmount . . . that I'm able to respect the differences everywhere: differences between the other races, differences between the generations, and so on." Here, to say the least, some serious doubts are permitted given the hierarchic scale of importance in which she places different power relations, as in the case of homophobia, which she reduces to a mere question of "sexual choice" deemed "secondary" in comparison to a *fundamental parameter of the sociocultural order* such as "sexual difference."[25]

Delivered in the middle of the demands of gays and immigrants for recognition and equality, the old (Maoist) distinction "*contradiction principale et secondaire*" (which has long ago dismissed the centrality of women's struggles) operates as a dismissal of the struggles of minorities and their legitimacy and allows for a discourse that, in the context it is uttered, comes dangerously close to the ordinary antigay rhetoric: "In France since 1980, homosexuals have rights and women no longer have them. That is, they are classified as men [*hommes*] with regard to their rights. They have rights only as a share of men's rights. As women they have no genuine rights. In France at present more attention is paid to minorities [*sic*] than to that half of the world called women. In my opinion that's because with the other minorities the patriarchy can remain that which condescends generously toward minorities, whereas in the horizontal man-woman relation there is no more patriarchy."[26] As is the case with the invocation of the "insurmountable" limits of sexual difference invoked by anthropologist Françoise Héritier against the PACS[27] or the casting of the division into two sexes as a prerequisite for culture and civilization by sociologist Irène Théry, Irigaray's ontologization of sexual difference participates in the new forms of naturalization of the social that appeal to the cultural and anthropological "evidence" rather than to straightforward biologically grounded arguments; it can thus be more easily appropriated and used in rehabilitating the authority of the given. The peculiar mixture of the commonsensical and the scientific; the appeal to the unreflected, everyday, and binding existence of social forms and their authoritative sanction by "high" theory; the irruption of anthropological and psychoanalytical jargon in the parliamentary debates—and, inversely, of everyday *clichés* in otherwise sophisticated theoretical argument—in short, the all too familiar *odor of scientism* that always accompanies the irruption of "experts" in the public space constituted a setting in which the growingly didactic, pamphlet-like style of Irigaray's writings have found their place and acquired new kinds of intelligibility.

Irigaray's approach to mythologies and genealogies and her revisiting "the Greeks" participate in this peculiar mixture of the commonplace and the scientific whereby interpretations are forced upon readers as simple, universal, all-encompassing truths. The tension between the loose, poetic, interrogative mode of enunciation and the affirmative, univocal delivery that marked her earlier writings has growingly attenuated as the project of "filling the blank" of woman's identity has growingly overpowered the negativity of her critique of patriarchy. Reference to tradition is primarily reduced to a legitimizing function. In this sense her mythologies and genealogies are . . . genealogical only in the conventional sense of a quest for origins, for the first and primordial. Operating a (deliberately?) caricature-like reappropriation of dominant narratives, a reappropriation whose theoretical status is almost never spelled out but rather left to commentators for speculation, Irigaray replays the official stories by highlighting, within them, "hidden" or "repressed"[28] genealogies of the feminine operating both as references or models of female identification and as "evidence" of a bisexuated natural and political order of things. Not that "the Greeks" are the sole sufferers of this approach. *Between East and West* provides a more recent example where the nostalgic idealization of a pre-Aryan gender paradise lost is offered as a blueprint for a redefinition of singularity and community premised on the assertion that a sexually differentiated order is the *conditio sine qua non* for the respect of all other differences.[29] Reminiscent of colonial British Indology and the stereotypical oppositions and homogenizing prism of Orientalism, this approach offers a case study of the ways in which the privileging of gender over all other differences marginalizes other power configurations such as those inherited from slavery, colonization, and imperialism, which are euphemistically referred to as a "factor related to the migrations of our time" and deemed *secondary to*, of lesser importance than, and *derivative of*, sexual difference.[30]

Irigaray's "Greeks" do not provide a terrain for exploring the variety of instances in which sexual difference appears and takes shape in Ancient thought, nor a field where new possible configurations of gender can be imagined and worked out.[31] Hers is an apodeictic approach where mythologies and tragedies are put on the Procrustean bed of a predefined and fixed conception of sexual difference they are called to validate. Closely attaching the authority of her political project of the moment to the veracity of the "facts" or "events," her interpretation of female and linguistic genealogies, the modes of legitimizing to which she resorts reactivate some of the more questionable themes (*origins*, *decline*, *restitution*), assumptions, and rhetoric tropes of nineteenth-century German historicist Hellenism. Mythical narratives "illustrate the major lines of development of a given period."[32] Ancient mythology "proves" that a gynocratic society existed before patriarchy.[33] It testifies to an initial pre-oedipal mother-daughter relationship. In case the language of "proof" and "truth" does not suffice to convince those of us who keep thinking there is a difference in the epistemological registers of myth and history, a series of exhortations appeals to our feminine loyalty and esprit de corps: "If we are not to be accomplices in the murder of the mother, we also need to assert that there is a genealogy of women."[34]

Myth is the field of the demonstrably true (or false), even though the successive interpretations following the inflections in Irigaray's theory of sexual difference could have us think otherwise. However, whether

Antigone is the sister who will strangle herself in order to save at least the mother's son,[35] "the anti-woman" who "is still a production of a culture that has been written by men alone,"[36] the desexualized representative of the other of the same,[37] or the paragon of sexuate civil rights whose "faith" in and "fidelity" to maternal genealogies was punished by death, the discourse of authority in which she comes always wrapped orients our attention to *the* definition of sexual difference that has to be drawn in the "light of Antigone's truth,"[38] shutting out invitations to look at her in other unauthorized perspectives.

What is cruelly missing from Irigaray's genealogies is, then, an openness to such unsought for, unauthorized meanings susceptible to popping up univited in the master narrative (or in "oppositional" rereadings imbued with the "givenness" of the existing sexual order) to destabilize gender (and other) certainties. What is missing is the obstinate "work in the interstices" of authorized systems of representation, the "interstitial knowledge" claimed (and produced) by Nicole Loraux in *La Grèce au feminin*.[39] Loraux is of great interest here, not the least because she is an eminent member of the "Paris School" whose sharp break with German historicism in the postwar period tremendously widened the perspective of classical studies by introducing into the epics of its narrative the dissonant figures of social oppression (slaves, women, metics, barbarians). Loraux is more than skeptical as to the possibility of rewriting women into history without reducing them to the representations of the "feminine." To trace singular women's experiences and lives through the "ocean of discourses,"[40] which are exclusively male discourses, constitutes an "impossible task" (*αδυνατον*). Impossible tasks, however, are the more "intellectually exciting."[41] This is why, at the very moment she enumerates (under the auspices of Virginia Woolf) the various facets of this "impossibility," this pathbreaking Hellenist deploys a panoply of epistemological detours aiming to neutralize the obstacles, and this simultaneity constitutes one of her most precious legacies.

Is it possible to go beyond the "composite being" that "pervades poetry from cover to cover" but "is all but absent from history"?[42] The question haunts Loraux's work on women and gender but also her general outlook on the treatment of tradition. If, as Margaret Whitford has suggested, the simplistic style of Irigaray's genealogies is part of a deliberate attempt to compensate for the lack of "any 'linguistic, social, semiotic, iconic, mythical' representations,"[43] it would be interesting to compare the different ways in which the two thinkers deal with this question. Preoccupied with the creation of a female positive tradition, Irigaray superbly ignores the very pertinence of the question. Eliding the operations of the unrelenting writing and rewriting of myth in Greek literature and philosophy, she elides, by the same token, the polysemy of myth's interpretive potential. As if myth existed by itself, a brute archival material in which female genealogies could be picked up, as if the first and the originary were not already *mediated* and reshaped by poetic imagination.

While insisting on the distinction between *women's historical experiences* and the *representation of sexual difference*, as well as on the different epistemological registers this distinction implies, Loraux admits the impossibility of retrieving what is lost or erased forever. Unless, of course, we improvise![44] Unless we accept the "queerness" of the "composite being" the Greeks have handed down to us and, abandoning the fantasy of an alternative narrative, we track down the procedures of generation of this "odd monster," "making use of all the liberties and the licenses of a novelist."[45] On one condition: "never to dissimulate the constructed nature of the (any) narrative but on the contrary *always name the accomplished operations*."[46] The creative, learned, and imaginative improvisation to which Nicole Loraux, and her fellow authors invite the reader of *la Grèce au feminin* has no doubt the uncertainty of archeological findings whose discontinuities and blanks are not filled up, but integrated in the historical narrative through a patient "interstitial work," allowing—in the different possible versions patiently sought out and enunciated—to be set free meanings that had been "imprisoned" within the continuous readings of the past. That these stories do not say what "really happened," that "behind Aspasia crowd the Diotima of the *Banquet*, the Artemisia of Herodotus or the Ionian Thargelia" and many other more or less historical figures, matters little as long as, from the bits and fragments, the "half-discourses" and the careful teasing of the words put together may emerge some solid knowledge gained "in the interstices."[47]

What is at stake in confronting the imaginary of sexual difference, at work in the myth, with concrete situations of women in history (let's say of Melissa, "a tyrant's wife, who has also been *that* particular woman")[48] is not just to show that the constructions of the masculine and the feminine (the matriarcate,[49] the Amazons) do not correspond to "real facts." It is also to track down the presence of myth at the heart of history, in the very terms in which the polis constructs its self-representation.[50] To ignore the myth, to accept at their face value the discourses neatly assigning every one to her place in the sexual order of the polis is a perilous enterprise. As Loraux has brilliantly shown in the *Experiences of Tiresias*,[51] the feminine does not always refer to women, and neither is the "feminine man" necessarily a "third term" in the world of Greek gender; it may appear as a position on a gender continuum, thereby suggesting that gender, for men as for women, was a spectrum of possibilities, extending between the two poles of masculinity and femininity.[52] Destabilizing the projection of current gender norms onto "the Greeks," her analysis reveals "an entire range of Greek thought focused on sexual differences" in no way reducible to "the endless verification of man's active role in the opposition between passive and active."[53] An analysis confirmed by Froma Zeitlin who shows in her studies of "women" on the tragic stage that femininity, even when adopted by real women, is always a disguise of sorts, and so subject to suspicion."[54]

It is in that which blurs sex boundaries, in the inconsistencies, the tensions, and the silences casting a doubt on the existence of a clear-cut sexual difference corresponding to the social division, that the "reality" of gender appears, even if momentarily, in all its complexity: as simultaneously a structure and a meta-discourse of power whose repression as an *instituted order* is also the repression of *plurality* and *conflict* which, even if denied, constitutes any political community.[55] If it is highly problematic to search in mythologies, in other words in literary fictions, the truth regarding an originary order of things, literary fictions are in no way anodyne. Situated at the heart of the political—and what is excluded from it as a dangerous excess—sexual difference and division haunt the unrelenting processes through which the unity and stability of the polis is affirmed and legitimized. Moving from the thematic of women's exclusion from democracy to the variety of exclusions through which this legitimacy becomes possible, the obsessive revisiting of autochthony, as a discourse of exclusion, reveals the unending interpretive potential of myth when it is confronted with and understood against the historical investigation of political and institutional stakes. But such a move also reveals the highly polemical if not explosive nature of this discourse and of its political appropriations for the present and the dangers of using tradition unselfconsciously, without making explicit the *deliberately* anachronic strategies through which our present communicates with the past that counts, with the past in which we feel concerned.

Breaking with the harmonious, linear narratives focusing on tragic heroes, ethical positions, and political origins, the dissonant, contrapuntal stories of the Paris school, which curiously had little or no impact at all on the rethinking of the Greeks by theorists such as Irigaray, opened up readings that make Greek tradition less smooth and in many ways more familiar to us than the readings of our Hegelian legacy. The disquieting presence of slaves or of the danger of enslavement of free persons, the attention to mourning and civic strife, the repressing of political violence, the complexity and ambiguity of dramatic art as it is worked by what is banned from the official discourse[56] are precious materials for a new self-conscious reflection on the relation of past and present.

In Irigaray's rehearsal of the Hegelian master narrative there is no place for this kind of complexity. There is no place for the particular histories of *other* others to emerge and be woven together in a narrative on the polis and its discontents.[57] No place for that which is *neither one nor the other*, the *ουδέτερον,* this troubling gender which, though banished from Irigaray's grammatical genealogies, can be traced in the passionate discussions on the sophists and those taking place in Greek comedy. There is no place for the whole range of possibilities which the imaginary of Greek tragedy allows to rewrite, no place for the Socratic oxymoron designating Aspasia as *ἡ διδάσκαλος* (the *she* master), for that which unsettles or casts a doubt on the clear-cut distinctions between the masculine and the feminine, or even for the total erasure of the feminine. No place for the plurality of representations of difference: for the foreign, the ecstatic, the enslaved, and the colonized which are always there, haunting the imaginary of the tragics and our own.

## Notes

1. See Nicole Loraux, *Myth and Politics in Athens* (Ithaca: Cornell University Press, 2000).

2. See Pheng Cheah and Elizabeth Grosz, "The Future of Sexual Difference: An Interview with Judith Butler and Drucilla Cornell," *Diacritics* 28, no. 1 (1998): 23.

3. Luce Irigaray, *I Love to You: Sketch of a Possible Felicity in History*, trans. Alison Martin (London: Routledge, 1996), 47.

4. Ibid; my emphasis.

5. Naomi Schor, "This Essentialism Which Is Not One: Coming to Grips with Irigaray," in *Engaging with Irigaray,* ed. Carolyn Burke, Naomi Schor, and Margaret Whitford (New York: Columbia University Press, 1994), 70.

6. Irigaray, *I Love to You,* 69.

7. See Elizabeth Hirsh and Gary A. Olson, "'Je—Luce Irigaray': A Meeting with Luce Irigaray," trans. Elizabeth Hirsh and Gaëtan Brulotte, *JAC* 16, no. 3 (1996).

8. Irigaray, *I Love to You,* 61–62; my emphasis.

9. See Pheng Cheah and Elizabeth Grosz, "Of Being Two: Introduction," *Diacritics* 28, no. 1 (1998): 12. More recently, and in a different vein, Joan W. Scott has also taken up this argument to justify the argumentative strategies in favor of "parity" in France. See *Parité: Sexual Difference and the Crisis of French Universalism* (Chicago: University of Chicago Press, 2005). Published in French as *Parité ! L'universel et la différence des sexes* (Paris: Albin Michel, 2005).

10. Ibid., 109.

11. Irigaray, *I Love to You,* 27.

12. Ibid., 144–45.

13. Luce Irigaray, "La question de l'autre," *labrys, études féministes* 1–2 (2002); my emphasis.

14. See Pheng Cheah and Elizabeth Grosz, "The Future of Sexual Difference: An Interview with Judith Butler and Drucilla Cornell," *Diacritics* 28, no. 1 (1998).

15. Ibid.

16. See Daniel Borrillo, Eric Fassin, Marcela Iacub, eds., *Au delà du PACS. L'expertise familiale à l'épreuve de l'homosexualité* (Paris: PUF, 1999); "'Différence des sexes' et 'ordre symbolique,'" *Les Temps Modernes* 55 (2000).

17. Henri Meschonnic, *Modernité Modernité* (Paris: Folio essais, 1988), 243.

18. See Irène Théry, "L'homme désaffilié," in "Malaise dans la filiation," ed. Irène Théry, *Esprit* 12 (1996): 51.

19. Suffice it to say that, as recently as 2005, France occupied one of the last positions in the European parliament, with 13.9 percent of the representatives in the European Parliament, as compared to countries such as Sweden (45.3), Austria (32.2), and Spain (30.5), which did not have recourse to a constitutional sanctioning of the two-ness of the body politic. See *Pourcentage de femmes siégeant dans les parlements européens* Source: Rapport mondial sur le développement humain http://ecjs.stlouis.stemarie.chez-alice.fr/femme-politique.htm.

20. For examples of this kind of neo-organic image of the political community see Claude Servan-Schreiber, "Pourquoi la parité est nécessaire et légitime," *Après-demain* 380–81 (Jan.-Feb. 1996) and Eliane Vogel-Polsky, "Les impasses de l'égalité, ou pourquoi les outils juridiques visant à l'égalité des femmes et des hommes doivent être repensés en termes de parité," *Parité-Info* (mai 1994). For a critique of these perceptions see my "Elementi del dibattito europeo: parità versus uguaglianza," in *Genere e Democrazia*, ed. F. Bimbi and A. del Re (Paris: Rosemberg and Sellier, 1997).

21. Irène Théry, "Le contrat d'union sociale en question," *Esprit* 10 (1997): 178.

22. "Femmes et hommes, une identité relationnelle différente," *La place des femmes, Les enjeux de l'identité et de l'égalité au regard des sciences sociales*, ed. Ephesia (Paris: La Découverte, 1995); "La famille commence à deux," *Panoramiques*, ed. G. Neyrand (Arlea-Corlet, 1996); "What Other Are We Talking About?" *Legacy of Levinas*, special issue of *Yale French Studies* 104 (2003); Interview by Alice Jardine and Anne Menke, "The Politics of Tradition: Placing Women in French Literature," ed. Joan DeJean and Nancy K. Miller, *Yale French Studies* 75 (1988).

23. "'Je—Luce Irigaray': A Meeting with Luce Irigaray."

24. Ibid.

25. Ibid.

26. Ibid.

27. See Françoise Héritier, *Masculin/Féminin: La pensée de la différence* (Paris: Odile Jacob, 1996). The argument deployed in the book is also exposed in an interview on the issue of applied to same-sex "filiation": Françoise Héritier, "Aucune société n'admet de parenté homosexuelle," interview by Marianne Gomez, *La Croix*, 9 November 1998, 16.

28. I do not address here the otherwise interesting issue of "causes" attributed to such a repression by the French philosopher, sometimes pointing to a conscious misogynist order while at other times, mainly in her recent work stressing reconciliation of the sexes, pointing to ignorance and forgetting.

29. Luce Irigaray, *Between East and West* (New York: Columbia University Press, 2002), 15.

30. Cf. Malini Johar Schueller, "Analogy and (White) Feminist Theory: Thinking Race and the Color of the Cyborg Body," *Signs* 31, no.1 (Autumn 2005): 63. See also P. Deutscher, "*Between East and West* and the Politics of 'Cultural Ingénuité': Irigaray on Cultural Difference," *Theory, Culture & Society,* special section on Irigaray, 20, no. 3 (2003): 65–75.

31. See Judith Butler, *Antigone's Claim. Kinship between Life and Death* (New York: Columbia University Press, 2000).

32. Cf. Luce lrigaray, *Le Temps de la différence, Pour une révolution pacifique* (Paris: Livre de poche, 1989), 112; translated by Karin Montin as *Thinking the Difference: For a Peaceful Revolution* (London and New York: Continuum-Routledge, 1993).

33. Ibid., 113.

34. Irigaray, *Sexes et parentés*, 24.

35. Luce Irigaray, *Speculum* (Paris: Editions de Minuit, 1974), 219.

36. Luce lrigaray, *An Ethics of Sexual Difference* (Ithaca/New York/London: Cornell University Press-Continuum, 1993), 119.

37. Luce Irigaray, *Sexes and Genealogies*, trans. Gillian C. Gill (New York: Columbia University Press, 1993), 111.

38. This last interpretation was delivered in a speech on sexuate civil rights, before a huge audience of men and women at the Festival of *Unità*, the Italian Communist Newspaper, who were encouraged to rethink civil rights "in the light of Antigone's truth." See Irigaray, *Le Temps de la différence*, 84–85.

39. Cf. *La Grèce au féminin*, sous la dir. de Nicole Loraux (Paris: Les Belles Lettres, 2003), XI.

40. Nicole Loraux, "Notes sur un impossible sujet d'histoire," *Les Cahiers du GRIF,* special issue *Le Genre de l'Histoire* 37–38 (1988) sous la dir. de M. Riot-Sarcey, Ch. Planté, E. Varikas, 113.

41. *La Grèce au féminin*, XI.

42. Virginia Woolf, *A Room of One's Own,* (London: Panther Books, 1977), 43.

43. See Margaret Whitford, *Luce Irigaray: Philosophy in the Feminine* (London: Routledge, 1991), 76.

44. Cf. As we are invited to by Eavan Boland in the poem opening her *Outside History.* Quoted by Thomas O'Grady, "Irish Women Poets," *Verse* 14, no. 3 (1998): 147.

45. *La Grèce au féminin.*, 6.

46. Ibid., XVIII–XIX; emphasis by the author.

47. Ibid., XIX.

48. Nicole Loraux, "Mélissa, épouse et fille de tyran," in *La Grèce au féminin*, 33.

49. "Matriarcat—Gynécocratie: situation, dont il n'existe pas d'exemples attestés, où l'autorité est exercée exclusivement ou principalement, par les femmes," in "Glossaire de la parenté," établi par Laurent S. Barry, Pierre Bonte, Nicolas Govoroff, Jean-Luc Jamard, Nicole-Claude Mathieu, Enric Porqueres i Gené, Salvatore D'Onofrio, Jérôme Wilgaux, András Zempléni, Françoise Zonabend, *L'Homme, la revue française d'anthropologie* (avril-sept 2000); Cf. aussi Stella Georgoudi, "Le matriarcat n'a jamais existé," *L'Histoire* 160 (1992).

50. Cf. Nicole Loraux, *Children of Athena: Athenian Ideas about Citizenship and the Division Between the Sexes* (Princeton: Princeton University Press, 1991) and *Born of the Earth Myth and Politics in Athens* (Ithaca: Cornell University Press, 2000).

51. Nicole Loraux, *The Experience of Tiresias*, trans. P. Wissing (Princeton: Princeton University Press, 1995).

52. Ibid., 8.

53. Ibid., 16–17.

54. See Froma Zeitlin, "Travesties of Gender and Genre in Aristophanes' *Thesmophoriazouae*," in *Reflections of Women in Antiquity*, ed. Helene Foley (Philadelphia and Berlin: Gordon and Breach Science Publishers, 1981), 181. Also "Playing the Other. Theater, Theatricality, and the Feminine in Greek Drama," *Representations* 11 (1985): 63–94.

55. Cf. Eleni Varikas, "Inscrire les expériences des femmes dans le passé," *Les voies traversières de Nicole Loraux ?Une helléniste à la croisée des sciences sociales*, Espaces Temps Les Cahiers/Clio. Histoire, Femmes et Sociétés (2005), 115.

56. See Page du Bois, "Toppling the Hero: Polyphony in the Tragic City," *New Literary History* 35, no. 1 (2004): 63–81.

57. See Charles Maier, "Doing History, Doing Justice," in *Truth v. Justice: The Morality of Truth Commissions*, ed. Robert I. Rotberg and Dennis Thompson (Princeton: Princeton University Press, 2000), 274–75.

## Chapter 18

# Conditionalities, Exclusions, Occlusions

Penelope Deutscher

### Exclusions

Does Irigaray appropriate the general space of exclusion, domesticating it for a reflection on sexual difference in particular? If so, what might be the appropriate critical response? As Judith Butler observes, "[S]laves are characterized as those who do not speak [Plato's] language, and who, in not speaking his language, are considered diminished in their capacity for reason." To some extent, even Irigaray acknowledges "xenophobic exclusion" and the multiple forms of exclusion of what is considered less than rational.

> This domain of the less than rational human bounds the figure of human reason, producing that "man" as one who is without a childhood; is not a primate and so is relieved of the necessity of eating, defecating, living and dying; one who is not a slave but always a property holder; one whose language remains originary and untranslatable.[1]

In a sense, there is no reason for Irigaray to avoid an exploration of all those figures rendered "other" to the rational citizen, nor to avoid exploring the relations between those figures. Yet she does not, and this may be considered an exclusion in her own work, perhaps a constitutive oversight? Is the condition of her foregrounding of women's exclusion the occlusion of other forms of alterity?

Irigaray has rejected criticism that she neglects race and cultural difference. She analyzes the feminine as the "elsewhere," rather than asking, simultaneously, what we may further render "elsewhere" by focusing on the feminine as elsewhere. Questions directed at her by Butler have included: Does the elsewhere of the feminine have its own elsewhere? What differences are submerged or occluded by the focused account of femininity as the elsewhere?[2] In contrast with her statements, Irigaray's own work opens up such methodological questions. In other words, how thoroughly can an analysis of exclusion, as embodied in a feminist philosophy, negotiate with its own possible exclusions?

The fact that her own project reinterprets the breaks, exclusions, openings, and conditions of other philosophers makes it more, not less, appropriate that her work be similarly reinterpreted. As her project coalesces, it must include problematic conditions and occlusions, although this may have been the scenario Irigaray has least wanted to envisage with respect to her own work.

Yet, the question provoked here, particularly given the nature of Irigaray's project, concerns the most appropriate methodology for the exploration of those conditions. Constitutive exclusions, when they are attributed to Irigaray's work, have sometimes provoked the mode of criticism from her critics: perhaps the least innovative approach to take to her work. At its most interesting, her project amplifies and displaces exclusions in the work of other philosophers. This would be the apposite response to bring to the exclusions in her own work. Perhaps gestures of mimesis are called for, the location of her own blind spots, of her conditionality, her excluded hypotheses? Just as appropriate is the enfolded, "looping" criticism through which the critic, all the while as she or he locates the exclusions in Irigaray's work, is in turn opening up her or his own response for a similar reading in kind.

In other words, the form of Irigaray's projects could lead to interest in new forms of criticism that suit the nature of those projects better. One possibility, in the exploration of occlusions in her work, would be a concurrent reflection on inevitable occlusions arising from the location of occlusion.

Describing Irigaray's work as "rude and provocative," Butler mirrors the wording to offer her own self-described "rude and provocative" reading of Irigaray. She suggests of Plato's *Dialogues* that "Plato's scenography of intelligibility depends on the exclusion of women, slaves, children, and animals," but that "Irigaray does not always help matters here, for she fails to follow through the metonymic link between women and these other Others, idealizing and appropriating the 'elsewhere' as the feminine."[3]

Butler appropriately identifies founding exclusion and strategic oversight in Irigaray's work.[4] And while reflection on occlusion is importantly directed at Irigaray's work, the scope for application of such a methodology loops back to envelop her interlocutors. The very question directed at Irigaray draws the reader's attention, in turn, to Butler's indirect grouping together of those "other Others" ("slaves, children and animals") under the sign of a possible *non*-appropriated alterity.

Irigaray appropriates alterity, but under what conditions could alterity not be appropriated? One could redirect the interrogation leveled by Butler at Irigaray back at the form of Butler's interrogation. The interrogation is entirely to the point, and also beckons to a further interrogation of the complexity involved in articulating the exclusions effected by Irigaray's work on exclusion. For once the alterity occluded by Irigaray is associated with "slaves, children and animals," we presume that the problem repeats. Is not such alterity, excluded by Irigaray, further excluding alterity once it is so identified? The list is finite, and of necessity, occluding.

What nonexcluding depiction of alterity could Irigaray accomplish?

This is a good, if abyssal, question to direct at Irigaray, and it might also be that the occlusions located by Butler in Irigaray's work also hold further potential for a fruitful disruption of the terms of Butler's own response. One could widen out the conceptual space opened up here. Accordingly, Butler's work would invite the questions she asks of Irigaray. To the extent that there is a naming of "excluded alterity" or any constitutive outside, has there been a domestication of alterity? Alternatively, one could further interrogate the possibility that in the Butlerian imaginary lurks, indirectly, a vision of a nonappropriated alterity? Again, the point is certainly not that Butler directly figures a possible, nonappropriated alterity. But, as she raises the concern about an appropriation of alterity, a pathway is opened for further reflection on the indirect expression of an alternative. This would be the impossible thought of a nonappropriated alterity, or, a philosophy of alterity that did not take the route of effecting exclusions. Thus, the amplification of what is deemed occluded in Irigaray's work can in turn provoke a more extended engagement with the conditionality of the question. Reflecting on the opening up of such pathways might be one of the better prospects for good encounters between Irigaray and her readers. With what methodology should we approach the blind spots of Irigaray's work? Perhaps we've done just about everything with Irigaray except read her like Irigaray.

## Sexual Difference as *Arrivant*

It has sometimes seemed that the word *arrivant,* though not used by her, is a good term for sexual difference as it is conceptualized by Irigaray.[5] In a sense, since the term *sexual difference* stands in for the anticipation of a reformulated sexual difference, it is not even its own name. Intermittently in her work, Irigaray necessarily gives sexual difference the widest possible definition. It is the rethinking of space, time, the interval, generation, culture, religion, race, love, nature, law, language, sex. Although Irigaray often emphasizes relations between men and women, her project requires the simultaneous insistence that sexual difference is not "itself" and envelops a field much broader than "itself."

Sexual difference therefore gets intermittently diffused as a concept in Irigaray's work, and, it can be argued that this is an imperative of her work. Her work imagines the thorough transformation of sexual difference. According to Irigaray, "[W]e have to take a step forward in human becoming." We've "entered a new era in History for which the existing institutions are no longer adequate." "We must now change the context in which we live and, more radically, the framework of our identity. This entails a revolution as wide, if not far more wide ranging, than the Copernican one."[6]

This "revolution" counters and displaces historical formulations of sexual difference that have been nourished by their inevitable excesses, their enfolded exclusions. At the extreme, a rethinking of the spatiality of envelopment is certainly an ethics of sexual difference, but thought at that extreme, it can also be unrecognizable as such. Irigaray also anticipates that unrecognizability with her reference to wide-ranging revolution, and her stress that rethinking the framework of identity includes rethinking "political, cultural and religious families. . . co-existence between genders, between races, between generations, but also between religions, cultures, political parties or regimes."[7]

Those interested in the thematics of *arrivant*, and in its possible application to the problematics of conceiving the total transformation of sexual difference, will note that the term serves as a helpful reminder of the latter's open content. Does Irigaray assume that the transformed version would replicate the space currently held by men and women? No—the largeness of her vision of transformation suggests that we can't have confidence that the reformulated identities of "men" and "women" would replicate in that fashion. Remember Irigaray's emphasis that the new culture she has in mind would involve a rethinking of identity, time, and space. Paradoxically, that makes an ethics of sexual difference a clay-footed version of the very philosophy—an ethics of sexual difference—opened up by her work.

As a result, a maximal version of an ethics of sexual difference would think it very widely indeed. Thus, Irigaray flings out a conceptual loop very widely ("we have to rethink the model of subjectivity"). Irigaray needs to fling that loop out wide, but it will hardly have escaped her readers that she goes on stressing sexual difference: "[T]he subject is at least two, man and woman, a two in relations that are not biunivocal."[8]

The snap back of that far-flung elasticity—retraced back to "a man and a woman" —is peculiarly Irigarayan. This looping, or snap, back, has troubled many of her readers. For we're not sufficiently in the mode of sufficient transformation if we're positing transformed relations between "a man" and "a woman." Yet the project also collapses if Irigaray does not propose that particular transformation.

It is ironic, and indicative of the nature of Irigaray's work, that the sexual difference so consistently stressed by the philosopher, must also be "lost" in a way that her work both requires, but that it also resists. A place is given in this overall swinging movement for "a man and a woman" but these terms are also undermined by the radically broad conceptual scope that sexual difference eventually encompasses. As a conceptual emphasis, "a man and a woman" gain rhetorical strength or provisional sedimentation in Irigaray's work, and as they do, the infinitely open scope of "sexual difference" is temporarily sacrificed. To adopt the position that "there is" and "there is not" sexual difference does not quite capture the intertwined relationship between the "there is" and the "there is not." Each position immediately sacrifices, and beckons to the other, as its excess and exclusion.

This provokes the question of how best to occupy these simultaneous positions? Irigaray could endeavor to bear witness to that sacrifice textually. Instead, her texts also have a tendency to emphasize either the one direction or the other. While it is certainly not the only reason, it may have added to concerns that alterity is hijacked in Irigaray's work and tethered to sexual difference.[9]

For example, consider the passage in which Alice Jardine asks Irigaray whether she is as convinced "as [she] was when *Speculum* was published, 'that the introduction of the female body into the male corpus is an essential strategy,'" to which Irigaray answers:

> It makes me wonder how *Speculum* could have been translated in America for me to hear such misunderstandings of this book. Of course, it is a difficult book. . . also extremely difficult to translate. . . . But. . . I think there are other reasons for these misunderstandings. . . the reduction of fact to rumor or opinion. . . . Thus *Speculum* cannot suggest getting the "female body" to enter the male corpus, as the female body has always figured in the male corpus.[10]

There is a more complex answer that could be given. The female body has traditionally been figured as receptacle for progeny, as the property of father or husband, a resource for male reproduction, a resource for the birthrate or the future of a people, a cultural resource for childrearing. In this sense, female embodiment has been included in culture, but simultaneously excluded. While it is recognized as "cultural resource," female embodiment is denied insofar as it irreducible to that role. Female embodiment has been simultaneously included and excluded. These positions are premised on each other, and cannot be separated. Irigaray's work operates from the concurrent insistence on the traditional *and* the "excessive" (excluded) feminine.

Speaking to her work, however, Irigaray sometimes settles—or locks the conceptual field—into one or the other possibility, such as the "historical" in favor of its "excess," even though her work also makes a case for the counterweighting necessity. Reacting against interpretations she considers poor, in her dialogue with Jardine, for example, she does not emphasize the figuring of the female body as "impossible," but as possible.

What seems to be needed here is the acknowledgment of a provisional sacrifice. Possibility needs to be stressed as impossibility from the moment that the reverse is stressed. Conflicting positions are required by Irigaray's work, and articulated in it. When the one position is taken, so would its counterpart be required (infinity *and* the finite; that sexual difference is and is not the concern of a man and a woman). While it would be impossible to name sexual difference, one names it in saying so. A similar problem is arising in Irigaray's stress of the relations between men and women. Rather than asking whether Irigaray domesticates alterity, one might ask how well she negotiates what should be the pendulum-like swinging theoretical motions between the naming, and the impossibility of naming, sexual difference.

## Conditionality

Thinking about the conditionality of Irigarayan feminism, Ewa Ziarek has argued that a robust negotiation with violence is missing from Irigaray's feminism. If so, the latter is premised on an exclusion of antagonism between women: "[I]t becomes clear that what is missing in Irigaray's concept of sexual difference is the analysis of the way the impossible actualization of subjective identities reveals multiple and conflicting identifications along the lines of gender, race and class."[11] Again, this is an important interrogation to direct at Irigaray's work. One can also say that in attaching an interrogation of "the antagonistic relations among women" to "the differences of race,"[12] Ziarek takes up less directly the myriad forms of antagonism between and within women. Intergenerational relations between women[13] and child-mother relations are also areas of Irigarayan occlusion.

Consider how, in her figuring of birth and hospitality, the possibility of violence is missing from Irigaray's depiction of the placenta as a means of thinking the relationship between mother and fetus. The connotations of this relationship, as Irigaray manipulates the figure, are only harmonious. The placental emblem does not allow for Irigaray's negotiation of aggressive affect, encroachment, or violent intent in the mother-fetal relationship, nor in relations between mothers and children, and women and others more generally, for which the placenta provides Irigaray an emblem.

Irigaray has demonstrated that phallocentric relations between men, in domestic contexts, in the public sphere, and in the familial transmission between father and son are premised on an appropriated maternal body. But that appropriated maternal body may also be appropriating, inhospitable, conditional. On Irigaray's reading, a mother's appropriative, hostile, or violent relation to her child is symptomatic of the dysfunctional workings of patriarchy. It may indicate a woman's envy, jealousy, or desire to be made complete, or it may indicate despair. Insofar as it indicates an aberrant maternity, a phallocentric culture is blamed for the aberration. In other words, it is the impoverished situation created by that culture for women which leads, in Irigaray's view, to women's most negative and aggressive impulses toward others. Similarly, the possibility of aggressive impulses toward the mother from the child are again symptomatic of the plight of both women and children in an impoverishing phallocentric context. As a result, both the feminine body and the maternal body are, in Irigaray's work, figured as originally nonappropriative except in the aberrant case. The interest in the metaphorized placenta as emblem of the mother-child relation is symptomatic of this Irigarayan mother-child imaginary.

Because the hostile mother is taken as aberrant, it seems that a default mother is imagined as receptive and sympathetic, although Irigaray does not idealize the maternal in such terms. Yet it is the more problematic forms of maternity that call for explanation and diagnosis.

The amplification of this unsaid possibility in Irigaray's own work might amount to a further reflection on women in terms of an impossible anticipation of a monstrous possibility by which they are enveloped. Irigaray suggests that children may turn away from their mothers toward their fathers because the women are abandoned to a culture of sexual "in-difference," needy and suffocating, looking for compensation.[14] The suggestion is that different social and subjective conditions could permit a better relationship with its mother. But what of unpredictability in the mother-child relation as a necessary, and not just an aberrant, inhabitation, an unpredictability that must include the possibility of the worst?

Accordingly, one could think about figures occluded in Irigaray's reflections on the Oedipus-Creon-Antigone nexus?[15] What of Jocasta, not figured in Irigaray's reflections on Greek tragedy? She has the potential to slightly displace the figuring of the mother in Irigaray's work. Jocasta could be thought of as incarnating the uncertainty and openness to a radical unknown involved in the relationship Irigaray herself metaphorizes as corporeal hospitality to a child. Integral to the unpredictability of that relationship is that, just as the parent might prove the source of risk to the child, the child might also return as the unrecognizable adult, the foreign or dangerous quantity, might break up the house. This unavoidable unpredictability is a familial permutation of Greek tragedy not considered by Irigaray. Irigaray's work recognizes the possibility of the child's murderous rage toward the mother, just as it recognizes the possibility that feminism coincides with "the emergence of some useful Athenas who spring whole from the brain of the Father-King, dedicated solely to his service and that of the men in power."[16] But these eventualities are explicable as maternity and feminism and gone wrong. They are not figured as integral to the body of women and their aspiration; a kind of unpredictable outcome women and feminism might hope most to avert, but whose potential they incorporate, and as such, to some extent must affirm as integral, interrupting, dividing, constitutive.

The child might be dangerous for the parent and the parent for the child—and not just because of an aberrant version of kinship provoked by social inequity, but as a risk built into intergenerational relationship.

## Irigaray's *Arrivant*

Following a discussion of Ancient Greek tragedy in *Sexes and Genealogies,* Irigaray uses the image of housing and home to discuss the first bond between fetus and mother. Discussing "our first sojourn in utero," she refers to "that primary home and that first nurse" and to what "the child received in its mother's womb: life, home, both the home of its own body and of the mother's body that it inhabits, food, air, warmth, movement, etc."[17]

And yet, provisionally exploring this metaphor of housing Irigaray's material seems to indicate—although she does not put the point in this form—that the fetus has been provided a home with potentially monstrous results. Irigaray's references to tragedy include the murder of Clytemnestra by her son, Orestes, with the help of her daughter, Electra. Irigaray deems the story "topical." Today, she reflects, it is just as important that we "not be accomplices in the murder of the mother."[18] For "everything described in the Oresteia is still taking place."[19] Through the examples, a reminder is offered that—as Derrida has also suggested—insofar as we welcome the other, we enter into the possibility that the other might come and destroy the home. Here the prospect can be more specifically explored in relation to the mother and her relationship with her progeny. But it is, in Irigaray's work, a prospect to be lamented, a symptom of aberration.

Given their mutual reference to the risk as well as the possibility posed by the child, Derrida and Irigaray could be considered at this point, insofar as they enter into a virtual discussion about how best to conceptualize hospitality with respect to the child that comes.

Writing about the prospect of a potential violent and destructive *arrivant*, Derrida points out that while an unconditional hospitality might not be possible—indeed, a thoroughly unconditional hospitality would be impossible—we are in engagement with that impossibility insofar as we negotiate with conditional hospitality. If ever we say, "come"—to the other, to the future, to democracy, or to an unconditional hospitality—it is only insofar as it is also impossible to thoroughly do so. In this sense, hospitality is always conditional, and alterity domesticated. This does not mean that *any* domestication of alterity is to be affirmed. But the concern about domestication requires the concurrent acknowledgment of its inevitability, at the same time as it amounts to a tracing by the impossibility, and alterity, of unconditional hospitality. That is not to be lamented.

With the metaphorics of accommodation, Irigaray's work also raises the question of how one should best imagine the risks, possibilities, and impossibility of the child that comes. How should hospitality best be conceptualized, if so? What are the conditions of that conceptualization in Irigaray's work? How does one negotiate with impossible unconditionality, and to what extent does Irigaray raise that question in the context of reproductive genealogy? And what is the relationship between two figures of the *arrivant* that could be said to emerge from Irigaray's work, the anticipation of the child, and the anticipation of a refigured sexual difference? To what extent are these figured as unpredictable and, in their unpredictability, as necessarily encompassing undesired possibility?

## Derrida's *Arrivant*

Irigaray has not often engaged with the work of Jacques Derrida. Still, her work facilitates a critical attention to the metaphorics concerning the child, sexual difference, and hospitality in his late work.

In material that includes discussions of ancient Greek hospitality, Derrida underlines that women have often been the conduit for hospitality offered and received between men.[20] When the wandering Oedipus, expelled from Thebes, offers himself up to the hospitality of the Athenians, he is accompanied and helped by his daughter, and encouraged by her to speak. Ismene goes on Oedipus's behalf to perform rites to appease the gods on whose ground Oedipus has trespassed, so that he may be received on Athenian land. Antigone negotiates on his behalf, begging the Athenians to have pity on him. Yet she is described by Theseus as helpless at Oedipus's side—women are rarely thematized either as the subject or the object of hospitality. As daughter or wife, women might accompany the stranger, or facilitate the extension of hospitality by the head of the household. In biblical stories, women are notoriously—as are Lot's daughters and those of the pilgrim's host on Mount Ephraim—sacrificed to the hospitality extended by men to men.[21] But, since men are traditionally household heads, and the strange, wandering traveler is likely to be male, Derrida is not confronted with a multitude of narratives about hospitality between women to analyze, nor of instances in which the woman is the host, the stranger male, nor the contrary. Since Derrida is not thematizing hospitality from, to, or between women, the theme of monstrosity between women similarly does not arise in his work, let alone an always possible monstrosity that would have to be affirmed between and by women in an unconditional hospitality.

Women are not specially figured in Derrida's work as the unpredictable *arrivant.* Nor are they figured particularly in a relation to anticipation of the unpredictable *arrivant.* Yet, at one point in *Echographies*, Derrida does propose the child as an instance of the unpredictable *arrivant* whose prospect one might—impossibly—welcome.[22] Reproduction (and also immigration) are associated with the unpredictability for the *arrivant*, which can be associated with the child. This engagement with the prospect of the uncertain arrival is attributed both to a nation-state or community, and also to a "family" who, we are told, does (but because this is an unknown quantity, cannot) "amortize" (*amortit*) a child's arrival. But, attributed in a sex-neutral way to the state, community, or family, this engagement with the prospect of the uncertain arrival is not attributed by Derrida to the mother in particular—not even when the *arrivant* is the child.

Hospitality (with or without the particular inflections given to the intersections between conditional and unconditional hospitality) may not be the most appropriate terminology for conceiving relations between mother and child, still less between mother and fetus. But it is Derrida who, in thematizing hospitality, thematizes the inability to "amortize" the child. From this point on, the maternal relationship must be counted in the context of his work in terms of the problematics of the *arrivant's* unpredictability. Instead, the mother is an unmentioned figure in this configuration. The child is unpredictable in general, or more specifically for a people, a state, or a family, but this is not a problematic Derrida associates with women in particular. As a result, it could be said that women and maternity are occluded from the *arrivant's* critical interest for Derrida. So too are they excluded from his engagement with the thematics of monstrosity.

Irigaray's work heightens our attention to the occlusion of women's corporeal hospitality, and of hospitality between women, in Derrida's work. When it comes to figuring the *arrivant*, women—and maternity—are figured only conditionally, as when the child is the figure of the *arrivant*, without a concurrent exploration of the mother's relation to the *arrivant*.[23]

And, just as Irigaray's work can bring an important interrogation of Derridean conditionality, the latter's reflections on hospitality, associating the *arrivant's* unpredictability with the child, prompts another reading of Irigaray as occluding an affirmation of constitutive unpredictability in her own considerations of intergenerationality and anticipation. Enveloping Irigaray's actual and virtual criticisms of his conditional depictions of women and reproduction, Derrida's analysis of the intertwining of conditional and unconditional hospitality also loop out to draw our attention to the conditionality of Irigaray's conceptualization of a corporeal hospitality between women and progeny.

This accords with the loop flung by Irigaray's work: at its best, Irigaray offers a methodology that can allow for a critical redoubling her project, one that allows us to read it from the perspective of its own conditionality, and what it "does not want to say." Accordingly Irigaray's placenta metaphorics would reemerge as occlusion point through the lens of her conditional remarks on Greek tragedy. From this perspective could arise the proposal, not directly explored in an Irigarayan thematics, that an unpredictable, potential monstrosity is integral, not aberrant, to the maternal relationship.

## Notes

1. Judith Butler, *Bodies that Matter: On the Discursive Limits of "Sex"* (New York: Routledge, 1993), 48.

2. Ibid., 49.

3. Ibid., 36, 49, also citing Luce Irigaray, *This Sex Which Is Not One* (New York: Routledge, 1993), 27.

4. Consider also Butler's comments on Irigaray in *Antigone's Claim*. When Irigaray aligns Antigone with the claims of kinship against those of the state, one can again ask what the reading overlooks. Antigone troubles kinship as much as she stands for its claims. Moreoever, she mimics or iterates some aspects of authoritarianism as much as she resists Creon's authority. Where Irigaray suggests that the claims of the mother have been taken over by the claims of the father, Butler notes that we can interrogate the conditions of possibility of the mother's claims. What institutes these? We could also remember the other dead members of Antigone's family whose possible mourning by Antigone seems occluded in her vigorous concern for the dead Polynices' claims. Judith Butler, *Antigone's Claim: Kinship between Life and Death* (New York: Columbia University Press, 2000), 6, 10, 23.

5. A possible dialogue between Irigarayan divinity and Derridean messianicity is briefly explored in John Caputo, *More Radical Hermeneutics* (Bloomington and Indianapolis: Indiana University Press, 2000).

6. Luce Irigaray, *Democracy Begins between Two*, trans. Kirsteen Anderson (London: Athlone Press, 2000), 4, 5, 6.

7. Ibid., 5.

8. Ibid., 6.

9. Butler, *Bodies that Matter*, 48.

10. Luce Irigaray, *Je, tu, nous: Toward a Culture of Difference*, trans. Alison Martin (New York: Routledge, 1993), 59.

11. Ewa Ziarek, *An Ethics of Dissensus: Postmodernity, Feminism, and the Politics of Radical Democracy* (Stanford: Stanford University Press, 2001), 180.

12. Ibid., 152.

13. Toni Morrison's *Beloved*, discussed by Ziarek separately from her discussion of Irigaray, stresses the interconnection of race, gender and intergenerational violence, as do other works mentioned by Ziarek, such as *The Bluest Eye*.

14. Luce Irigaray, "And the One Does Not Stir Without the Other," *Signs: Journal of Women in Culture and Society* 7, no. 11 (1981): 60–67.

15. This question is asked extensively in Butler's *Antigone's Claim*, though Butler does not turn to a discussion of Jocasta.

16. Luce Irigaray, *Sexes and Genealogies*, trans. Gillian C. Gill (New York: Columbia University Press, 1993), 12.

17. Ibid.

18. Ibid., 12, 19.

19. Ibid., 12. Mothers, on Irigaray's argument, have been murdered in the sense that historically and culturally they have been desubjectivized and othered. Some women take up positions of subjectivity by aligning themselves or identifying with male power. Others who fight are in some way or other "buried."

20. Jacques Derrida, *Of Hospitality: Anne Dufourmantelle invites Jacques Derrida to respond*, trans. Rachel Bowlby (Stanford: Stanford University Press, 2000), 85.

21. Ibid., 71, 153.

22. Jacques Derrida and Bernard Stiegler, *Echographies of Television: Filmed Interviews*, trans. Jennifer Bajorek (Cambridge, UK: Polity Press, 2002), 12.

23. This form of conditionality with respect to the depiction of women in Derrida's work on autoimmunity is further explored in "'Women, and So On': Derrida's *Rogues* and the Auto Immunity of Feminism," *Symposium: Canadian Journal of Continental Philosophy* 11, no. 1 (2007): 101–19; and also in "Derrida's Impossible Genealogies," *Theory and Event* 8, no. 1 (2005) (at http://musedev.jhu.edu/journals/theory_and_event/v008/8.1deutscher.html). Derrida's association between autoimmunity and women's rights (in addition to children's and worker's rights) is notable given that an occlusion of women can be said to occur in that context, as it arguably also does in his reflections on women's role in facilitating hospitality.

# Chapter 19

# The Return

Luce Irigaray

Why does Western culture have to start with Greece? Why mark such a cut with earlier traditions? With other cultures? What is it to begin with the Greeks? Would it be an emergence of man as such, which also signifies an exile, a wandering, a growing away from home? Does the same go for all cultures? Does knowing necessarily mean an estrangement from oneself? Or does such a knowledge represent only a required historical passage? A kind of journey to come back home. A sort of sojourn abroad in order to appreciate returning to one's own country, one's own land—as Heidegger commented on some of Hölderlin's poems.

But the country, the land, and even the house do not yet correspond to the self. Nevertheless, Western tradition keeps alive such a confusion, probably because its culture is mediatized by exteriority without a cultivation of the interiority of the self. And it is also a culture of uprooting from natural origin and belonging. Western culture corresponds to a culture of the outside, not of the inside. We make plans outside us in order to construct, to love, to know, and then we become, in some way, merely the consequence of the events that take place outside us. We are not that which gives measure to our culture, except indirectly as a result of a going outside ourselves, and of marks that we make or leave there.

About ourselves, we know almost nothing. And even when we imagine ourselves as constructing the world, it is as much this world which constructs us. Our projects with regard to the world are mostly a projection, and an evasion of ourselves, an escape from ourselves. Without a possible turning back to ourselves, in ourselves. In fact, a great part of history amounts to a succession of episodes of our rushing forward to build a world, including a world of knowledge, which little by little substitutes itself for us. A world in which historians will be in search of some traces, some "skins," as testimonies of humanity's passage on earth.

Parallel to the estrangement from home, from oneself, we find, in Western culture, the theme of the return. It is not a pure coincidence that the text given as a reference to the earliest Greek culture tells us about both the departure of the hero who is going to war and his eventful journey in turning back home. This double epic gives us an overall picture of our tradition, as do the motive put forward for waging war and the diverse episodes that prevent the hero from returning home. The first part of this prophetic account corresponds to the supposedly positive aspect of our culture, and the second part to its negative or reverse side. The first part talks about the emergence of a world of men among men, and the second part about the loneliness of the man who tries to return home. He finally succeeds because of his cunning character, but not without undergoing great trials that perhaps correspond to the stages of a passage from one era of the story to another.

The hero goes back home, but does he return to his self? I am not sure. Perhaps he comes back to the order of the hearth, of marriage, but not to the order of his self, to intimacy with his self. And if we hear many things about his relations with feminine figures outside the home, it is not the case with respect to his wife. We hear of him defeating his wife's suitors through his ruse and his skill with projectiles, which cause people to remember him. But the suitors seem to want the possession of the goods of the hero rather than love as such. In other cultures, we know a lot about amorous rituals, about the comparison of lovers to divine figures, and about the impact of love itself on the cosmic order. With this first epic of Greek culture, love is already becoming an institution bound to the *πολις*, what we would call the State. And lovers already obey external public rules as much as, if not more than, their own affects. They are moving away from nature, from the body, from the economy of affects, and are becoming subjected to external laws.

Nevertheless, the hero still bears witness to self-affection. Ulysses is moved, he weeps, he worries. . . and these affects are expressed in Greek language by the middle-passive or middle voice, a morphologic form that expresses that he is affected in himself, with himself, outside of the economy of the pair of opposites: active-passive. This often happens with a certain loneliness, secretly and without an other sharing the affect. The journey of man is not yet deprived of self-affection, but this seems not to provide him with happiness and is lacking in reciprocity.

## For What Does Western Man Feel Nostalgic?

The journey of Ulysses, his return home, happens before the construction of Western metaphysics, and announces it. After the end or accomplishment of metaphysics, the theme of the return is insistently anew.

I could cite Hölderlin and Nietzsche, for example, and comment on their feeling of nostalgia for an impossible return. Both of them have been removed from their own self by Western culture—by a Western culture firstly embodied in an other thinker—and they cannot turn back to this self. As you know, their journey will end in a kind of madness, even though they are searching for a going back home in a different way. For Hölderlin, the matter is rather one of again finding familiarity or intimacy with a country, a landscape, a house, and also with friends or beloved. For Nietzsche, the matter is one of overcoming metaphysics through assuming an eternal return of the same, by bringing it together in a circle. The two are in search of an access to a beyond of metaphysics, but if they announce the necessity of exceeding metaphysics, they do not succeed in such a surpassing of their path, of their story, of their self. The inability to do that in part comes from the lack of a woman who could help them, above all in their self-affecting through love. They thus have both an intuition of the fact that the solution to their ill-being, to their failure in making their way, cannot be found in their cultural background or surroundings as they are, and that something or someone else has to arrive in order to go beyond such a horizon.

Some thinkers thus seek other values, shrouded or forgotten in our culture. But often their plan is one of integrating these values into our culture in order to improve it, without changing themselves. Once more, the question would be of going abroad in order to stay better at home—in one's own country, one's own culture, one's own home. Some also imagine that the solution to the nostalgia for a return might be a perpetual nomadism—an estrangement from home until one forgets what staying at home could be. In the era of globalization that is ours, we can observe two trends: that of the stay-at-homes who try to preserve at all costs their home, country, or culture as they are, and that of the nomadic people who denigrate any home. Both of them disregard the relation with the other, which requires an ability to dwell with the possibility of opening oneself to the other, of leaving home to meet with the other but remaining able to return home, to oneself, within oneself in order to keep the two, the one and the other.

Such a going there and back to home, to the self, within the self, is lacking in our tradition, notably because man has searched for himself outside the self and not by making his way in his own self. And also because he searched for his becoming in objects, things, and their representations or mental reduplications. Man has searched for himself outside the self while intending to appropriate this outside, notably through representations. And this does not correspond to a cultivation of interiority, but to an exile in an external world that he intends to appropriate by means of a technique that reduplicates the real, of a logic through which he makes the world his own, the *logos*.

Why such a wish? And why has man imagined that the key to the happiness that has been lost, to the unaccomplished blossoming, could be found in his culture, his country, his home or language, and not in a maturity that is still to be reached? Why, above all, has man chosen a culture of performance, of know-how, of mastery, including through language, and not a culture of being-with, of speaking-with; that is, a culture of being in relation with the other? Why has man sacrificed a great part of himself to such a cultural orientation? Why has man immolated affectivity, desire, and even life itself to a mental mastery? Why has man compared the evolution of Western consciousness to an inescapable Calvary—as Hegel wrote in his *Phenomenology of Spirit*? Probably because man has wanted to give himself a proper identity without caring enough about differentiating himself from the relation with the first human with whom he shared life: his mother. He has intended to master the world before becoming conscious of the first world that he formed with her. They originally lived in the same horizon, without a clear separation between two worlds. It is by dwelling in the same world as she that he was born, has grown, has reached the surrounding environment, the external universe. Western man did not interpret such a sharing with and lack of differentiation from the mother. And neither the *logos*—a sort of generalized mental bobbin with respect to the world, to speak as Freud—nor the law of a natural, political, or spiritual father might allow a passage from the first sensible immediacy of the relation with the mother to a level of consciousness that can transform it without abolishing it.

Western man has remained in some way confused with the maternal world, stuck to it, and no strategy of Western culture has been able to cultivate this first situation or experience. It stays, one could say, absolute and blind. Thus, a sort of maternal incest is generalized in Western culture—as is masculine homosexuality. And the taboos surrounding one and the other are all the more virulent since they are not found in the place where the question arises.

Thus, what does it mean, the insistence on the theme of the return? In particular, what does the present turning back to Greek culture mean? And to what Greek culture are we turning? Are we in search of a completeness that we have lost? Or are we urged on by a want of something of which our cultural path has deprived us?

With regard to Greek culture, both are at stake, in my opinion. I think that we are trying to find the crossroads at which we have taken the wrong path. I will attempt to give some indications on this point, starting with the notable disappearance of some morphological forms or meanings that still exist in the first Greek culture. As examples, I will take the term ετερος, the verbal form called middle-passive or middle voice, and the evolution of the meaning of the word γενος, but also of the value of female or feminine genealogy, all these being accompanied by a loss of a sensible transcendental, in the relations with nature and the other, especially the different other.

In the early stages of Greek culture, the word *ετερος* expresses first of all a relation only between two, two who are different and cannot be confused in a one, as is the case in the relation with the mother and also with God. While the word *αλλος* signifies the other in a group or a series, the word *ετερος* means the other of two; for example, the other hand, the other eye, and also the other sex or gender. In Greek language, we find "*ετερο*" as a prefix in many terms. There remain only a few of such terms in our language; for example, heterodox, heterogeneous, heterosexual. And, in some of these words, the meaning of "hetero" has already lost its reference to the number two, and now refers to several, many, not two.

It is fitting to add that the term *ετερος* is not the only allusion to the number two. We also find the nominal and verbal dual form. For example, we could say in English: "You two are beautiful and you will make it in the cinema"; "We two are nice and we will leave Paris to help people in difficulty." In these sentences, the dual form could be used for the verb, and also for the subject and the predicative adjective. It could also be used when there is reciprocity: "We two love one another." The dual form does not exist in all cases nor all tenses and it is employed above all in Attica; in other areas of Greece, the plural is used as well as, and even more than, the dual form.

With regard to the term *γενος*, I could note that originally this word refers as much to gender or sex as it does to generation, as well as having other meanings. What I would like to emphasize is the fact that the meaning "generation" or "genealogy" has gradually supplanted the meaning of "gender" or "sex" for which the dual form can be used. I will try to suggest an explanation for this as well as for the disappearance of the morphological verbal form: the middle-passive or middle voice.

The middle-passive or middle voice does not have the meaning of our reflexive, which presupposes a split of the subject, but marks a certain return of the action upon the subject. Thus, it can be partially reflexive—"I wash my hands"—or reflexive in an indirect way: that is, the subject acts in its own interest—to itself, for itself, from itself. For example, to obtain something for oneself, to remove a danger from oneself. "To marry" can be expressed by the middle voice (above all for a woman). To return in oneself to draw energy, inspiration, wisdom is also expressed by the middle voice. Sometimes this form can be used when the action's return is on the whole subject, but only if the body alone is concerned, or if it is a question of habits ("I take a swim"; "To dress oneself"). The middle voice is also used to express reciprocity: "They love each other."

I would like to stress the fact that the middle-passive or middle voice is a form that conveys both activity and passivity, and requires an involvement that is not only mental. It can thus express a process of self-affection, and even of reciprocity, that neither simple active nor passive forms could convey. Now, in later cultures, the pair of opposites active-passive, and also the reflexive, will become substitutes for the middle voice. But, if they presuppose a split of subjectivity, which is the norm in our tradition, they do not permit self-affection, nor reciprocity.

I will also question the simultaneous disappearance of these terms, meanings, and morphological forms, and that of the original representation of the feminine lips, of the female or feminine genealogy, and of a transcendental feeling that could be linked to such an evolution.

## Self-affection in the Masculine

The modalities of self-affection are not the same for man and woman, and neither are their lack or perversion.

For man, self-affecting is linked more with oneness, with the constitution of a world of his own, with the cultivation of this world until its idealization. As I am not a male subject, it is difficult for me to define what self-affection could be for a man. It would amount to substituting myself for him. I can only question a culture in the masculine. I note, then, that masculine subjectivity did not become differentiated enough from the maternal world. Thus, the total relation that the male child has with his mother—the first other for him—has not been cultivated as such and, one could add, has not been submitted to a dialectic process. This has brought about several outcomes:

1. It is through a division into body and mind, nature and culture, sensible and intelligible that masculine subjectivity has tried to emerge from an undifferentiated link with the first other.
2. More generally, it is through a logic of pairs of opposites that masculine subjectivity seemingly separated off from its natural and affective origin, but such couplings became substitutes for difference between subjects belonging to the two sexes and, firstly, between the mother and the male child.
3. Such a logic is thus ordered by genealogy, in particular in relation to certain of the couplings that are decisive for relational life: activity/passivity, love/hatred, nearness/distance, but also male/female and even I/other(s); and these couplings wil have an influence on self-affection and the possible reciprocity between people, especially between two people.

4. This lack of differentiation from the maternal world prevents the definition of masculine subjectivity as a singular and, above all, a sexuate subjectivity.
5. Hence the fact that the relations between subjects in our culture are reduced to relations among "ones" or "somebodies" who are suppressed and can be substituted the one for the other,
6. And the fact that affect is imposed on the subject from the outside and that it is more a source of imbalance than of harmony, or of enriching becoming; it has thus to be reduced by a turning back to homeostasis.
7. From this results the necessity of a closed mental world in order to protect oneself from affects,
8. And the absence of subjective difference, first of all of subjective sexuate difference; this has not been recognized and cultivated as such with regard to the mother, and, thus, difference has become in some way only quantitative and, for example, referred to God as the absolute other, the absolutely higher other.
9. The lack of cultivation of sensible immediacy as an important dimension for the relational becoming of humanity.

The Western masculine subject has maintained an adhesion to the maternal world, which he never submitted to a dialectical process. Beyond the fact that this has paralyzed his total becoming, notably his sensible and affective growth, it has perverted his perception of truth. The separation of intelligibility from sensibility does not solve the problem; rather, it denies or represses it. This repression results in a veiling of the perception of truth, which acts in every entering into presence. It is through a certain sleep or dream that man approaches the world. Pretending to unveil truth through his *logos*, by fabricating truth or the world itself by himself, he increases illusion instead of clarifying it. The world that man constructs in this way is a dream world, and such a dream sometimes takes a dramatic turn, as is the case today.

Furthermore, the world that man has built to supplant the adhesion to the maternal world, to assert himself against the mother, against the participation in her world, has become a screen, even a weapon, which intervenes between the masculine subject and himself, and prevents any man from turning back to himself, in himself. Man has fallen into his own cultural trap. He is not only sheltered but also enclosed by his *logos*, becoming a prisoner of his own productions. Even in his attempts to return, or turn around or reverse, he is trapped by substitutes of his unconscious beginnings to which he remains blind. Going back home is perhaps possible after many efforts, after suffering great hardships. Turning back to the self is no longer possible. Without freeing himself from his adhesion to the other, the first other, man cannot return to his self. Because of the lack of cultivating the sensible relation with his mother, that is, of his first affects, man has cut himself off from experiencing his own self-affection.

The masculine culture as it is prevents man from turning back to himself. And even in his tradition, his country, his house, man is not "at home." The familiarity or intimacy that he feels is a web of habits or customs, and not a real nearness. Wanting to master the alternation between near and remote through his *logos*, notably by transforming spatial distance into temporality, man has lost the possibility of approaching—the things, the other(s), in particular the other of a different sex or gender. Familiarity has become made for him from mastery, repetition, and even from confusion in worlds—unless it is mediatized by the other, in particular the feminine other. It does not result from a sharing of intimacy, not even with oneself. Self-affection becomes confused with a dependence on the surrounding world, through which man believes he touches himself again. But the world that surrounds him is, in part, a substitute for a relation with the mother—a kind of placenta or of construction for mastering the maternal beginning of his life, employing an energy and a world common to the two. Culture, which intends to separate man from the maternal world, uses for its elaboration the relation with the mother herself.

In fact, the autonomy that man has gained is only apparent. Hence, the necessity for him of being and acting violently in order to enter into relations with the other: he tries to break the screen that divides him from everything and everyone. He attempts to demonstrate his competence, his know-how, while, or because, he is lacking in affective education, and even affective feeling, except at the quantitative level. What he feels is more or less intense but seems to be without nuances and singularities.

Not having worked out the first relation to the mother as an intersubjective relation, man merges with her in an energetic sharing, and merges with other men in a world made up of impersonal "someones." All men are supposed to share the same culture, the same values, and it is through such a uniformity that they should be affected from an outside—material or spiritual—without each being capable of affecting oneself according to one's own interiority. But without such an inner economy, affects have an immediate impact on energy; this increases and needs a release, or it spreads and gets lost because of fear, dread, and lack of concentration. That which provokes affects is often something that bursts into the closed horizon that man considers his world. That which affects him, in an immediate way, is strange to the man's world, at least to his supposedly own world. And the masculine subject is all the more immediately affected since he has not elaborated in himself a cultivation of self-affection. Thus, any affect troubles his usual economy—his homeostasis, as Freud wrote. And this explains why any disturbance to his habits, all that which perturbs what is familiar to him—for example, the attraction or desire for the other or the coexistence with a foreigner—must end in a release, must become canceled in one way or another. The surplus of energy produced by the relation with the other as different cannot be stored and cultivated through the internalization of self-affection. It must be dissipated or invested in things or actions that are part of the surrounding world.

Western man has at his disposal very few markers, very little information to make his way along in relation with the other. Freud himself did not allude to a possible becoming in relation to sexual maturity, the so-called genitality. He spoke only about procreation, and about its necessity for the happiness of a marriage, the wife becoming able, in this way, to be a mother for her husband, and to give back to him his first lost relational world. Freud did not ask man to renounce his first relation with the mother or to sublimate it. On the contrary, he suggested that the wife has to substitute herself for the mother and become a mediation for the satisfaction of immediate male affects. The family will thus repeat on a small scale the cultural world based on the lack of differentiation between the subject and the maternal world. In any case, this constitutes the surroundings, including as other, that affect man without real self-affection internalized on his part.

In contrast to our culture, the relation with the mother has not been kept in the dark in all cultures, and it seems that the more it is eclipsed as natural origin and first sensible relation, the more it has influence on culture. This repressed dimension of our tradition has ultimately led to an overshadowing of another decisive natural dimension, that of sex or gender. The denial of the importance of the link with the mother has resulted in an emphasis on genealogy to the detriment of gender as sexuate identity. So the Greek word *γενος* increasingly came to express the vertical, and in some way hierarchical, genealogical dimension, and less and less the horizontal dimension of gender.

But emphasizing genealogy amounts to emphasizing natural reproduction and relations—a stress that is accompanied by many taboos in relation to nature—more than a relational cultivation of desire and love. A cultivation that asks us not to separate spirit from body, mind from affect. A cultivation that also requires each gender to care about its own self-affection, and to respect that of the other. Woman thus has not to substitute herself for the mother of man, but has to cultivate her self-affection as a means of turning back to herself, and helping man in the discovery of his own self-affection—outside or beyond any sensible immediacy in their relations, be it intensely close or possessive.

## Self-affection in the Feminine

In contrast to man, woman is familiar with being two. A girl does not form a "dyad" with the mother but a real duality. The similarity of their bodies and their psyches in their relational dimensions, among others with respect to generation, protects them from merging into a unique entity. The two of the mother-daughter couple nevertheless does not suffice in securing an autonomous self-affection. Of course, the two of the mother-daughter couple—which does not amount to the mother-son dyad—can protect the girl from projecting all she has, all she is, onto a masculine subject. But the two of the mother-daughter relation run the risk of perpetuating an original given situation, which is not yet cultivated as a possibility of a return to one's own self. The adhesion to the maternal world is different to that of the boy, but it can exist as a continuation or a repetition of an original situation, including a situation of dependence with respect to the mother and a given context.

Thus, to reassert the value of female or feminine genealogy is certainly useful, above all in allowing woman to relinquish her dependence on masculine genealogy. But going no farther than genealogy could be a trap, an obstacle to the becoming of the subject. If dependence on masculine genealogy forces the girl or woman out of her own subjective becoming, going no farther than female or feminine genealogy, in particular only in its natural dimension, as is too often the case today, generally amounts to an adhesion to a first relation, which prevents girls and women from becoming wholly autonomous and accomplishing their subjectivity.

The self-affection of feminine subjectivity cannot stop with the mother-daughter couple. But it has more to do with duality than the self-affection of masculine subjectivity. I suggested that the morphology of the two lips could be a privileged place for woman entering into a process of self-affection. Such a suggestion is supported by personal experience but also by a piece of cultural information. For example, in the archaeological gallery of Syracuse in Sicily, there are many statues of the goddess Kore. Of course, I have listened to the guide emphasizing the statues of gods, and presenting all of these Kore as "simple women," perhaps only "maid servants." He did not know of the existence of the goddess Kore, even though her name was inscribed on the work. But the most interesting aspect was that these Kore do not have the same lips according to the century in which they were sculpted. The most ancient of them have closed lips, which touch one another and could be a good illustration of self-affection in the feminine. In later sculptures the mouth is open and the lips no longer touch one another. And, finally, the mouth remains open and the lips are also deformed.

You know, I imagine, the story of Kore taken from her mother, the great goddess Demeter, by the god of the underworld. He raped her and kept her in the underworld—even changing her name—until her mother provoked a great famine on earth so that her daughter would be restored to her. You could understand, in this way, that the evolution of Kore's lips is linked to a change in self-affection, which leads her to become dependent on an external instrument, or an other as instrument, for self-affecting, as a boy or man is. You could also perceive here what I try to mean when I talk about the virginity of woman as a condition for autonomy. I allude to an ability to affect oneself through the lips touching one another without any external intervention or tool. It suffices that woman cares about gathering with herself, and remains concentrated on the affect that results from this touching, outside any other intervention or activity. It is interesting to experience what then happens, is felt, notably with respect to the two—that is, the other and oneself—in a relationship. Such a gesture allows woman to come back to the self, within the self, and to respect the other, preserving a free space between the two.

How could we save this privileged place of self-affection in order to be able to return within ourselves, to be faithful to our self, and to cultivate our own becoming—a necessary condition for entering into a dual relation with the other that does not amount to a repetition of the first link with the mother? How can we reach a relation in two that does not reduce itself to a "dyad" or a pair of opposites? This requires another culture to be elaborated. The cultivation of masculine subjectivity does not correspond to the same necessities, thus to the same values, as those of feminine subjectivity. Also, in the case of feminine subjectivity, a process of dialectization of sensible immediacy is necessary but in a different way from that which is needed by masculine subjectivity.

The feminine world is, by birth, more relational than the world of the boy, notably because of the privileged situation of the girl with respect to the mother, a same as the girl. This permits a duality of people from the very beginning, in particular through a relation to engendering different from that of the boy, of the man. The girl knows what it means to beget, it is a familiar experience for her already, through intuition or feeling. Turning back to birth, or beyond, does not seem a dangerous abyss to cover, to veil, as is the case for a masculine subject. The problem for feminine subjectivity is how to escape from what is only a natural state, both at the level of birth but also at the level of relations with the other(s)—be they the mother, the lover, or the child, for example. What she has to do is to maintain an irreducible difference between the other and herself, while preserving her natural origins or roots. This can happen by arranging and keeping a transcendental dimension between the other and herself, particularly the other who belongs to a different origin—the masculine other. The matter, for a woman, is one of interposing between the other and herself a negative that cannot be overcome. Thus, the transcendental would not be immediately deferred to the absolute "you" of a God—who, in fact, then substitutes himself for the mother, the first other—as is too often the case for man in our culture. The transcendental must unceasingly intervene between the other and myself—the "you" and the "I"—turning the sensible immediacy of the relation into a cultivation of affect that can save the irreducibility between the other and myself, the insuperable difference between the two—the "you" and the "I."

## Self-affection Needs to Be Two

A cultivation of self-affection by each one is what allows for the preservation and the becoming of attraction and desire between the two, by saving the difference between the two. It also permits an individual becoming, thanks to a process of going back and forth between the self and the outside with regard to the self—an other subject, object, or world.

A cultivation of self-affection seems to be lacking for us Westerners, in particular for man. Perhaps some mystics and artists tried to approach it? But, even if they felt a nostalgia for self-affection, most often they did not succeed in enjoying it. What could allow us to reach such a culture—beyond a cultivation of our own life, for example through a practice of breathing—is a cultivation of the relationship between two subjects, a two different from the dyad formed by the mother and the male child. A cultivation of desire and love between the two sexes and genders is needed, not, firstly, as a sexual relation, but as a relation between two differently sexuate identities, whose self-affections are different and needed as such. This "two" can help man to leave a horizon built without a real differing from the mother's world—except through the neutralization of a "someone," a so-called neuter or neutral subject. It can also help him to escape the prison of loneliness and the dependence on other or external objects for self-affecting. Desire, in fact, affects an energy internal to the subject and appeals to another subject, to reciprocity with another subject. At least it should be so. Otherwise, it is not a question of desire, rather of instinct or drives. But only desire is really human.

Thus, the relation between two is that which can help man and also woman to gain access to an autonomous and internalized self-affection. At the grammatical level, one could say: to return to the middle-passive or middle voice as a way of internalizing the middle-passive and not the opposition between active and passive: to affect/to be affected, which is perhaps fitting to the parents-children relationship. This pair of opposites, which we have inherited from the first relation with the mother, has often been transferred between man and woman, with a reversal at the level of polarity: man becoming generally active with respect to woman, except, for example, in masochistic behavior. But if the opposition active/passive becomes a substitute for the middle voice, replaces it, such an opposition prevents us from cultivating our affects toward their internalization and cultural becoming, among others through reciprocity.

An anonymous world formed by "someones" also leads us to the passivity of each one in relation to affects coming from the outside, and does not allow the economy of the middle voice, which requires us to pass from the outside to the inside of the self. A passage that only a relation between two permits, a relation that our tradition has deferred onto a unique God, whom humans would meet in another world.

Self-affection, expressed by the middle-passive or middle voice—and not an alternation between active and passive—is dependent on a relation in two; two who are different, even if they can form a whole, and who are not united by genealogy or hierarchy.

## To Conclude

In Greek culture, we still find the existence of the middle-passive or the middle voice, of the verbal and nominal dual form, and of a pronoun—*ετερος*—that expresses the relation in two or between two, two who are different, a difference that will later take on the value of subjection or opposition. The prounoun *ετερος* does not have the same meaning as *αλλος*, which is closer to our word: other. This *αλλος*—or other—in fact refers to any other and not to this other with whom I am in relation as two. The word *other* is suitable for a world of "someones" but does not favor the relation with an other as different. It refers to a neuter or neutral, or better a neutralized, other, a kind of abstract individual about whom we can speak, but whom we would meet only with difficulty as a concrete and living other. It seems that we could communicate between "someones," but we exchange only through a supposedly common world; and this does not yet reach a communication between subjectivities.

Our nostalgia for a return, among others to Greek culture, could arise from a want of a return to our own self, within our own self, through self-affection. Cultivation of self-affection by woman as such seems to be the path that could allow man to leave the maternal world to reach his own self-affection.

Self-affection is not secondary nor unnecessary. Self-affection—which once more does not amount to a simple autoeroticism—is as much necessary for being human as is bread. Self-affection is the basis and the first condition of human dignity. There is no culture, no democracy, without the preservation of self-affection for each one.

Self-affection today needs a return to our own body, our own breath, a care for our life for us not to become subjected to technologies, to money, to power, to neutralization in a universal "someone," to assimilation into an anonymous world, to the solitude of individualism.

Self-affection needs faithfulness to oneself, respect for the other in their singularity, reciprocity in desire and love—more generally, in humanity. We have to rediscover and cultivate self-affection starting, at each time and in every situation, from two, two who respect their difference, in order to preserve the survival and the becoming of humanity, for each one and for all of us.

# Contributors

**Athena Athanasiou** is assistant professor of Social Anthropology at Panteion University of Social and Political Sciences, in Athens, Greece. She has been a postdoctoral fellow at the Pembroke Center for Teaching and Research on Women, Brown University (2001–02). She has published articles on biopolitics, gender theory, sexual politics, technologies of the body, nationalism, cosmopolitics, postcoloniality, affect, and psychoanalytic theory. She is the author of *Life at the Limit: Essays on the Body, Gender, and Biopolitics* (Ekkremes, 2007) (in Greek) and the editor of *Feminist Theory and Cultural Critique* (Nissos, 2006) (in Greek). She is currently working on a book on the aporetic politics of mourning, memory, and amnesia/amnesty (*Unthinkable Mourning: Affect, Performativity, and the Political in "Women in Black"*).

**Anne-Emmanuelle Berger** is professor of French Literature at Cornell University and professsor of Comparative Literature and Gender Studies at the University of Paris 8, France, where she heads the Centre d' Etudes Féminines et d' Etudes de Genre. She has written on poetry, the French Enlightenment, the cultural politics of French and Anglo-American gender and postcolonial studies, the politics of language in the Maghreb, and the work of Jacques Derrida. Her most recent publications include *Algeria in Others' Languages* (Cornell University Press, 2002) and *Scènes d'aumône: Misère et Poésie au XIXe siècle* (Champion, 2004) (in French). She is currently preparing a collection of essays on the animal after Derrida with Marta Segarra.

**Tina Chanter** is professor of Philosophy at DePaul University, Chicago. She is author of *Ethics of Eros: Irigaray's Re-writing of the Philosophers* (Routledge, 1995), *Time, Death, and the Feminine: Levinas with Heidegger* (Stanford University Press, 2001), *Gender* (Continuum Press, 2006), *The Picture of Abjection: Film Fetish and the Nature of Difference* (Indiana University Press, 2007). She is editor of *Feminist Interpretations of Emmanuel Levinas* (Penn State University Press, 2001), co-editor of *Revolt, Affect, Collectivity: The Unstable Boundaries of Kristeva's Polis* (State University of New York Press, 2005), and co-editor of *Sarah Kofman's Corpus* (State University of New York Press, 2008). Her current book project is *Antigone's Affect: Political Legacies.*

**Dianne Chisholm** is professor of English at the University of Alberta. She is author of *H. D.'s Freudian Poetics: Psychoanalysis in Translation* (Cornell University Press, 1992) and *Queer Constellations: Subcultural Space in the Wake of the City* (University of Minnesota Press, 2004). She is the editor of "Deleuze and Guattari's Ecophilosophy," a special issue of *Rhizomes: Cultural Studies in Emerging Knowledge* 15 (2007). Recent publications include: "Climbing like a Girl: An Exemplary Adventure in Feminist Phenomenology," *Hypatia* 23, no. 1 (2008), and "Benjamin's Gender, Sex, and Eros," in *A Companion to the Works of Walter Benjamin*, ed. Rolf Goebel (in press). She is currently researching two new book projects: *Landscapes for a New Earth: Trajectories and Becomings in the Landscape Compositions of Literary Ecology*, and *Home, Home on the Deranged: A Field Guide to the Colliding Landscapes of Alberta's Front Ranges.*

**Claire Colebrook** is professor of English at Penn State University. She has published articles on contemporary European philosophy, feminist theory, literary theory, contemporary music, dance, visual culture, and political theory. She is the author of *New Literary Histories* (Manchester University Press, 1997), *Ethics and Representation* (Edinburgh University Press, 1999), *Gilles Deleuze* (Routledge, 2002), *Understanding Deleuze* (Allen and Unwin, 2003), *Irony in the Work of Philosophy* (Nebraska University Press, 2002), *Irony: The New Critical Idiom* (Routledge, 2003), *Gender* (Palgrave, 2004), *Deleuze: A Guide for the Perplexed* (Continuum, 2007), and *Milton, Evil and Literary History* (Continuum, 2008). She is currently completing two book-length studies, one on vitalism and another on William Blake and aesthetics.

**Penelope Deutscher** is professor of Philosophy at Northwestern University. She is the author of *Yielding Gender: Feminism, Deconstruction, and the History of Philosophy* (Routledge, 1997), *A Politics of Impossible Difference: The Later Work of Luce Irigaray* (Cornell University Press, 2002), *How to Read Derrida* (W. W. Norton, 2005), and *The Philosophy of Simone de Beauvoir: Ambiguity, Conversion, Resistance* (Cambridge University Press, 2008), and co-editor (with Kelly Oliver) of *Enigmas: Essays on Sarah Kofman* (Cornell University Press, 1999) and (with Françoise Collin) of *Repenser le politique: L'apport du féminisme* (Campagne Première 2004) (in French).

**Stathis Gourgouris** is professor of Comparative Literature at the Institute of Comparative Literature and Society and the Department of Classics at Columbia University. He is the author of *Dream Nation: Enlightenment, Colonization, and the Institution of Modern Greek* (Stanford University Press, 1996) and *Does Literature Think? Literature as Theory for an*

*Antimythical Era* (Stanford University Press, 2003), and editor of *Freud and Fundamentalism* (Fordham University Press, forthcoming). He has published articles on Ancient Greek philosophy, modern poetics, film, contemporary music, Enlightenment law, psychoanalysis. He is currently completing work on two books of secular criticism: *The Perils of the One* and *Nothing Sacred.*

**Laine M. Harrington** is a postdoctoral fellow and visiting scholar with the Beatrice M. Bain Research Group on Women and Gender at the University of California at Berkeley. She has written on the work of Luce Irigaray, poetics, rhetoric, and the philosophy of religion. She has collaborated with Luce Irigaray on the book *Luce Irigaray: Key Writings* (Continuum, 2004).

**Lynne Huffer** is professor and chair of Women's Studies at Emory University. She is the author of *Maternal Pasts, Feminist Futures: Nostalgia and the Question of Difference* (Stanford University Press, 1998), *Another Colette: The Question of Gendered Writing* (University of Michigan Press, 1992), and numerous articles on feminist theory, queer theory, and French literature. She is also the editor of a special issue of *Yale French Studies: Another Look, Another Woman: Retranslations of French Feminisms* (1995). She has just completed a book called *Mad for Foucault: Rethinking the Foundations of Queer Theory*, and is nearing completion of another book project on the problem of ethics in feminist and queer theories.

**Luce Irigaray** is director of research at the Centre National de la Recherche Scientifique (CNRS, Philosophy Commission) in Paris, and she has held teaching positions in Paris and internationally, including positions at the University of Rotterdam, the University of Toronto, and the University of Nottingham. She has been a grassroots activist and a practicing psychoanalyst. She has written on continental philosophy, psychoanalysis, linguistics, feminist theory, cultural analysis, and literature. Her published books include: *Speculum of the Other Woman* (trans. Gillian C. Gill, Cornell University Press, 1985), *This Sex Which Is Not One* (trans. Catherine Porter and Carolyn Burke, Cornell University Press, 1985), *Marine Lover* (trans. Gillian G. Gill, Columbia University Press, 1991), *Elemental Passions* (trans. Joanne Collie and Judith Still, Routledge, 1992), *Je, Tu, Nous: Toward a Culture of Difference* (trans. Alison Martin, Routledge, 1992), *An Ethics of Sexual Difference* (trans. Carolyn Burke and Gillian G. Gill, Cornell University Press, 1993), *Thinking the Difference* (trans. Karin Montin, Routledge, 1994), *I Love to You* (trans. Alison Martin, Routledge, 1996), *The Forgetting of Air in Martin Heidegger* (trans. Mary Beth Mader, University of Texas Press, 1999), *To Be Two* (Routledge, 2001), *Between*

*East and West* (trans. Stephen Pluhacek, Columbia University Press, 2002), *The Way of Love* (trans. Heidi Bostic and Stephen Pluhacek, Continuum, 2004), *Luce Irigaray: Key Writings* (Continuum, 2004).

**Mary Beth Mader** is associate professor of Philosophy at the University of Memphis. She is the author of *Sleights of Reason: Norm, Bisexuality, Development* (State University of New York Press, forthcoming), and articles on the work of Luce Irigaray, Michel Foucault, and Sarah Kofman. She is the translator of Luce Irigaray's *The Forgetting of Air in Martin Heidegger* (University of Texas Press, 1999).

**Dorothea Olkowski** is professor and chair of Philosophy at the University of Colorado at Colorado Springs. She is the author of *Gilles Deleuze and the Ruin of Representation* (University of California Press, 1999), and *The Universal (In the Realm of the Sensible)* (Edinburgh University Press and Columbia University Press 2007). She has edited *Resistance, Flight, Creation, Feminist Enactments of French Philosophy* (Cornell University Press, 2000) and co-edited *Gilles Deleuze and the Theater of Philosophy* (with Constantin V. Boundas, Routledge, 1994), *Merleau-Ponty, Interiority and Exteriority, Psychic Life and the World* (with James Morley, State University of New York Press, 1999), *Re-Reading Merleau-Ponty, Essays Beyond the Continental-Analytic Divide* (with Lawrence Hass, Humanity Books, 2000), *Feminist Interpretations of Maurice Merleau-Ponty* (with Gail Weiss, Penn State University Press, 2006), and *The Other—Feminist Reflections in Ethics* (with Helen Fielding, Gabrielle Hiltman, and Anne Reichold, Palgrave Publishers, 2007). She is currently working on a book entitled *From Nature to Love.*

**Gayle Salamon** is assistant professor of English at Princeton University. Her areas of specialization are phenomenology, psychoanalysis, gender theory, and queer theory and she has recently completed a manuscript on embodiment and trans-subjectivity. Recent articles include "Transfeminism and the future of gender," *Women's Studies on the Edge*, ed. Joan Scott (Duke University Press, 2008) and "'Boys of the Lex': Transgenderism and rhetorics of materiality," *GLQ: A Journal of Lesbian and Gay Studies* (2006).

**Gail Schwab** is associate dean of the College of Liberal Arts and Sciences at Hofstra University, and professor of French in the Department of Romance Languages and Literatures. She is the translator of Luce Irigaray's *Parler n'est jamais neutre*, as well as of several pieces appearing in the new anthology of Irigaray's work, *Key Writings* (Continuum, 2004), and co-translator with Katherine Stephenson of *Sexes et genres à* *travers les langues.* She has published many articles on Irigaray's work, and is currently working on a book on Luce Irigaray and language. Her latest publication is "Reading Irigaray (and Her Readers) in the Twenty-First Century," in *Returning to Irigaray* (Maria Cimitile and Elaine Miller, eds., State University of New York Press, 2007).

**Gayatri Chakravorty Spivak** is university professor and the director of the Institute for Comparative Literature and Society at Columbia University. She has published on feminism, Marxism, deconstruction, and globalization. Among her books are: *Myself Must I Remake: The Life and Poetry of W. B. Yeats* (1974), *Of Grammatology* (translation with critical introduction of Jacques Derrida, *De la Grammatologie*, 1976), *In Other Worlds: Essays in Cultural Politics* (1987), *Selected Subaltern Studies* (ed. 1988), *The Post-Colonial Critic: Interviews, Strategies, Dialogues* (1990), *Thinking Academic Freedom in Gendered Post-Coloniality* (1993), *Outside in the Teaching Machine* (1993), *Imaginary Maps* (translation with critical introduction of three stories by Mahasweta Devi, 1994), *The Spivak Reader* (1995), *Breast Stories* (translation with critical introduction of three stories by Mahasweta Devi, 1997), *Old Women* (translation with critical introduction of two stories by Mahasweta Devi, 1999), *A Critique of Postcolonial Reason: Towards a History of the Vanishing Present* (1999), *Song for Kali: A Cycle of Images and Songs* (translation with introduction of poems by Ram Proshad, 2000), *Chotti Munda and His Arrow* (translation with critical introduction of a novel by Mahasweta Devi, 2002), *Death of a Discipline* (2003), *Other Asias* (2005), *Red Thread* (forthcoming).

**Judith Still** is professor of French and Critical Theory at the University of Nottingham. She is the author of *Justice and Difference in the Work of Rousseau* (Cambridge University Press, 1993), *Feminine Economies: Thinking against the Market in the Enlightenment and the Late Twentieth Century* (Manchester University Press, 1997), and editor of *Men's Bodies* (Edinburgh University Press, 2003). She is also co-editor (with M. Worton) of *Intertextuality* (Manchester University Press, 1990) and *Textuality and Sexuality* (Manchester University Press, 1993), co-editor (with D. Knight) of *Women and Representation* (WIF Publications, 1995) and co-editor (with S. Ribeiro) of *Brazilian Feminisms* (CTCS Publications, 1999).

**Elena Tzelepis** is lecturer at the Department of Classics at Columbia University. She writes on continental philosophy, theories of genealogy and representation, contemporary readings of Ancient Greek philosophy, the politics of difference, the intersections of the political and the psychic, and the workings of critique. She is the editor of the collective volume *Antigone's Antinomies: Critical Readings of the Political* (Ekkremes, forthcoming) (in Greek). She is currently working on a book manuscript on mimesis, eventuality, and the feminine, and a collection of essays on borders and representations of strangeness and alterity in contemporary Europe based on the writings of Jacques Derrida.

**Eleni Varikas** is professor of Political Science and Gender Studies at the University of Paris 8. She has published on the history of feminism, gender in political theory, citizenship and the construction of otherness in modern universalistic systems, and the theoretical status of experience and subjectivity in social and political analysis. Among her books are: *Les rebuts du monde: Figures du paria* (Stock, 2007) (in French), *Penser le sexe et le genre* (Universitaires de France, 2006) (in French), *Theodor Adorno, Critique de la domination: Une lecture féministe* (Tumultes, 2004) (in French), *With a Different Face: Gender, Difference, Universality*, (Katarti, 2000) (in Greek), *Les Femmes de Platon à Derrida: Anthologie Critique*, with F. Collin and E. Pisier (Plon, 2000) (in French).

**Elizabeth Weed** is director of the Pembroke Center for Research and Teaching on Women at Brown University, of which she was founding associate director in 1981. She is also the founding co-editor with Naomi Schor of *differences: A Journal of Feminist Cultural Studies*, published by Indiana University Press, 1989–2002, and currently by Duke University Press. She publishes in feminist theory, psychoanalytic theory, and critical studies, and teaches at Brown in Modern Culture and Media and in Gender Studies. She is currently working on a book entitled *Reading for Consolation: Psychoanalysis, Feminism and the Waning of Critique.*

**Ewa Plonowska Ziarek** is Julian Park professor of Comparative Literature and the founding director of Humanities Institute at the State University of New York at Buffalo. She has published articles on Kristeva, Irigaray, Derrida, Foucault, Levinas, Fanon, feminist theory, and literary modernism. She is the author of *The Rhetoric of Failure: Deconstruction of Skepticism, Reinvention of Modernism* (State Univeristy of New York Press, 1995), *An Ethics of Dissensus: Feminism, Postmodernity, and the Politics of Radical Democracy* (Stanford University Press, 2001), the editor of *Gombrowicz's Grimaces: Modernism, Gender, Nationality* (State University of New York Press, 1998), and the co-editor (with Tina Chanter) of *Revolt, Affect, Collectivity: The Unstable Boundaries of Kristeva's Polis* (State University of New York Press, 2005) and *Intermedialities: Philosophy, Art, Politics* (forthcoming). She is currently working on a book project on feminist aesthetics.

# Index